ASSESSING THE VIETNAM WAR

ASSESSING THE VIETNAM WAR

A Collection from the Journal of the U.S. Army War College

Edited by

Lloyd J. Matthews

and

Dale E. Brown

Introduction by

General Bruce Palmer, Jr., U.S. Army (Ret.)

Published under the auspices
of the U.S. Army War College Foundation, Inc.

PERGAMON-BRASSEY'S
INTERNATIONAL DEFENSE PUBLISHERS
(a member of the Pergamon Group)

WASHINGTON · NEW YORK · LONDON · OXFORD
BEIJING · FRANKFURT · SÃO PAULO · SYDNEY · TOKYO · TORONTO

U.S.A. (Editorial)	Pergamon-Brassey's International Defense Publishers, 8000 Westpark Drive, Fourth Floor, McLean, Virginia 22102, U.S.A.
(Orders)	Pergamon Press, Maxwell House, Fairview Park, Elmsford, New York 10523, U.S.A.
U.K. (Editorial)	Brassey's Defence Publishers, 24 Gray's Inn Road, London WC1X 8HR
(Orders)	Brassey's Defence Publishers, Headington Hill Hall, Oxford OX3 0BW, England
PEOPLE'S REPUBLIC OF CHINA	Pergamon Press, Room 4037, Qianmen Hotel, Beijing, People's Republic of China
FEDERAL REPUBLIC OF GERMANY	Pergamon Press, Hammerweg 6, D-6242 Kronberg, Federal Republic of Germany
BRAZIL	Pergamon Editora, Rua Eca de Queiros, 346, CEP 04011, Paraiso, São Paulo, Brazil
AUSTRALIA	Pergamon-Brassey's Defence Publishers, P.O. Box 544, Potts Point, N.S.W. 2011, Australia
JAPAN	Pergamon Press, 8th Floor, Matsuoak Central Building, 1-7-1 Nishishinjuku, Shinjuku-ku, Tokyo 160, Japan
CANADA	Pergamon Press Canada, Suite No. 271, 253 College Street, Toronto, Ontario, Canada M5T 1R5

First edition 1987

Library of Congress Cataloging in Publication Data

Assessing the Vietnam War

Essays originally published in the U.S. Army War College's journal Parameters.
1. Vietnamese Conflict, 1961–1975. I. Matthews, Lloyd J. II. Brown, Dale E. III. Parameters.
DS557.7.A87 1987   959.704′3   87-14243

British Library Cataloging in Publication Data

Assessing the Vietnam War : A Collection from the Journal of the U.S. Army War College.
1. Vietnamese Conflict, 1961–1975
I. Matthews, Lloyd J. II. Brown, Dale E.
III. U.S. Army War College Foundation
IV. Parameters, ISSN 0031–1723
959.704′3   DS557.7

ISBN 0-08-035182-4 (Hardcover)
ISBN 0-08-035181-6 (Flexicover)

Printed and bound in Great Britain by
Hazell Watson & Viney Limited,
Member of the BPCC Group,
Aylesbury, Bucks

Contents

IV.   The Lessons of the War

V.   The Aftermath of the War

Acknowledgements

The most enjoyable task in assembling any book comes with the opportunity finally to thank those whose inspiration and labors made the book a reality. Since the present volume is the product of many hands, the task, as well as the enjoyment, becomes correspondingly greater.

Our prime debt of gratitude is of course to the authors themselves. In summoning the time and effort from arduous workdays to contribute articles to *Parameters*, they have provided a rich synthesis of ideas from which defense policy improvements can ultimately emerge.

We recall too Lieutenant General DeWitt C. Smith, Jr., US Army War College Commandant during the periods 1974–77 and 1978–80, whose determination to hasten the War College's march toward becoming a leading center of contemporary military thought found principal expression through the College journal, *Parameters*. General Smith's support and encouragement were major elements in establishing *Parameters* as a respected national forum for the treatment of defense issues. Thanks go as well to Major General James E. Thompson, the War College Commandant today, whose historical vision permitted the present publishing effort to go forward. Another substantial debt is owed to the Army War College Foundation, Inc., which kindly agreed to sponsor this work. The Foundation's Executive Director, Colonel LeRoy Strong, US Army Ret., has been an instant source of assistance and cooperation.

Not to be forgotten are the successive *Parameters* editors, whose work touched the present articles in silent but always indispensable ways – Colonel Roland R. Sullivan, US Army Ret., and Colonel William R. Calhoun, Jr. Finally, we acknowledge two of the most important contributors of all – Mr. Gregory N. Todd, the Assistant Editor of *Parameters*, the influence of whose expert editorial hand inheres in every line of the present volume; and Mrs. Lisa A. Ney, the *Parameters* Editorial Assistant, without whose shining competence and indefatigable labors the voices herein would never have emerged in the printed word.

The Editors

Introduction

This collection of essays from the US Army War College's widely acclaimed journal, *Parameters*, comes at a time when our national fascination with the Vietnam War continues to build all across the land. One manifestation is the current outpouring of books, of practically every description, that continues unabated. American interest in Vietnam, moreover, does not seem narrowly based or sharply focused, but reflects a rather genuine desire on the part of a broad diversity of citizens to learn more about America's 30-year involvement in Southeast Asia commencing at the close of World War II.

Although many good books have been written about the war and most of the readily apparent aspects have already been researched, studied, and debated, I suspect that some important areas yet remain unexplored. Moreover, access to private papers and still-classified documents concerning the period may not be granted for years to come. One area that needs more thorough examination concerns high-level civil-military relations during the war, especially during the Kennedy-Johnson-Nixon years. Here I have in mind the triangular relationships between the president as commander in chief, the secretary of defense, and the JCS. The role of the JCS under current statutes continues to be ambiguous with respect to the chain of command, a question that may not matter much in peacetime, but could be a cause of grave concern in time of war. Other areas deserving further study, for example, concern:

•The inordinate length of time (over a decade) that elapsed before the United States finally devised an effective way to organize the numerous US agencies involved in the so-called pacification effort under one head in South Vietnam.

•The absence of effective US military advice during the last phase of the war, from the January 1973 ceasefire to Saigon's collapse in April 1975. (Surely we could have helped the South Vietnamese develop a better strategy and concept of operations to meet the vastly changed situation that would exist after all US and other foreign forces had been withdrawn.)

Our national failure to achieve our objectives in Vietnam has provided probably the main impetus to a revival of interest in military history in both civilian and military components of our society. Basic and blunt questions are being asked, for example: After 20 years of American training, advice, and support, and billions of US dollars in military and economic aid, why did the South Vietnamese government and armed forces collapse so suddenly under the final North Vietnamese onslaught in the spring of 1975?

In addressing such questions, one major focus has been on the high-level military aspects of our failure, starting with the absence of an effective strategy to guide the employment of *all* allied forces – US as well as South Vietnamese and foreign forces that were committed to the defense of South Vietnam. The US "strategy" had two main components: the air offensive against North Vietnam, only remotely related to the decisive component, the ground war in the South (the United States made it clear to Hanoi that it would not invade North Vietnam or otherwise try to overthrow its government). The US air offensive was undertaken in early 1965 primarily to raise morale in South Vietnam and encourage its government to continue to fight the war. Only secondary was the motive of inflicting heavy damage on North Vietnam in the hope of persuading Hanoi to cease its efforts to subjugate the South. Thus, instead of a sustained all-out air offensive, President Johnson allowed only a graduated, piecemeal escalation. Consequently, Hanoi had time to condition its people against air attack and, with Soviet aid, to build a formidable air defense that thereafter exacted its toll on our attacking air forces.

In the ground war, the United States elected to fight a war of attrition, deliberately limited to the defense of South Vietnam proper. But without an overall scheme of employing American, South Vietnamese, and other available forces in a rationally integrated manner with specific objectives in mind, attrition was no strategy at all. It devolved simply to a design for killing or otherwise eliminating as many enemy soldiers as possible. In the kind of war we chose to wage, Hanoi had the initiative and decided where and when its forces would fight, thus in a very real sense enabling it to regulate its own and Viet Cong casualties. Hanoi had the manpower to fight a war of this nature indefinitely and was not vulnerable with respect to its wartime material needs. Virtually all of its arms and other war-making necessities came from the Soviets, or the Chinese, whose support seemed to be assured. These basic facts of life, incidentally, soon became evident to US combat forces in the field in South Vietnam. American units would engage enemy units and inflict heavy casualties, only to have the remnants disappear into border sanctuaries in Cambodia, Laos, or North Vietnam itself, and reappear a few months later in the same area of South Vietnam refilled with newly trained replacements, fully armed and equipped, and ready to fight again. Frustration caused by such circumstances was one of the main reasons why many American career officers and noncommissioned officers prematurely left the service.

The absence of a true US strategy, as well as the lack of an encompassing operational plan to link strategy and the tactics employed, resulted in the piecemeal, almost aimless deployment of American troops all over South Vietnam. It also implied an open-ended, unlimited commitment of US resources with no clear idea of where this would lead and its ultimate consequences. This lack of sound US strategic thinking during the Vietnam War has helped to revitalize the study of strategy and the art of operational, or campaign, planning in our armed forces, especially in the US Army's higher-level schools.

The renaissance of interest in military history within our armed forces has probably been helped, too, by the fact that for some years, the United States has not been engaged in major hostilities, although it is true that we still have large forces deployed overseas and at sea, and that there are plenty of potential hot spots involving American interests throughout the world. Nevertheless, many of our military personnel on active duty should now be able to enjoy the rewards of thinking long and hard about Vietnam and earlier hostilities as well. These circumstances also provide our armed forces the opportunity to learn all they can from those active and retired members who have fought in past wars.

The present *Parameters* collection, consisting of 18 articles by both civilian and military authors and published during the period 1979–1986, provides an extraordinarily fine survey of the diverse aspects of the Vietnam War.

The first part, dealing with the literature of Vietnam, leads off with a book review essay by Harry G. Summers, Jr., a well-known military affairs commentator who made his reputation while serving on the faculty of the US Army War College. Summers treats in his lucid, vivid style a Vietnam War history by Stanley Karnow and one by the present writer, plus a book by Stuart A. Herrington recounting the final tragic days of Saigon. In addition, he skillfully weaves into his essay a historical perspective and insights that should expand our understanding of this difficult period in our history.

Richard A. Hunt, in the second article of this section, reviews two recent books on the nature of the Vietnam War, both focusing on the relatively unheralded American-South Vietnamese counterinsurgency efforts called "pacification," the struggle for control of the people. Hunt's fine short piece is balanced and to the point, capturing the essence of Robert W. Komer's *Bureaucracy at War* and Thomas Thayer's *War Without Fronts*. Hunt shows how these two studies complement each other in developing new analytical approaches to understanding some of the fundamental problems that plagued us during the war.

The last article in this segment is an excellent historiographical survey by Joe P. Dunn that discusses Vietnam War literature from the beginnings to the year 1979. Dunn traces the earlier domination of Vietnam literature by anti-war radicals as well as liberal, more moderate critics, during the 1960s, followed by a "mild revisionism" in the 1970s that produced more mature and less subjective literature about the war. Dunn stresses the elusiveness of "the true lessons" and properly predicts that the "search for knowledge, meaning, and lessons of Vietnam will continue."

The second segment of the collection concerns the strategy and nature of the war. Harry G. Summers, Jr., again leads off with a cogent essay titled "A Strategic Perception of the Vietnam War." In it, he stresses the fatal weaknesses of the US strategy pursued in South Vietnam using as a framework Clausewitz's theory of war. Summers' article is essentially a distillation of his landmark work, *On Strategy: A Critical Analysis of the Vietnam War*, published in 1981.

In the next essay, "Vietnam: The Debate Goes On," John M. Gates quietly but convincingly disputes Summers' thesis that the conflict was not a revolutionary war, but rather a classic conventional one. My own views parallel those of Gates; that is, the so-called "big-unit war" (which involved Viet Cong as well as North Vietnamese Army main force units) and the revolutionary war (involving "pacification") were both essential elements of Hanoi's strategy. In the Northern view, there were never two such separate wars; rather, they were each indispensable, carefully orchestrated components of the same war. Gates, moreover, is right in pointing out that the Summers thesis, while popular in many circles, unfortunately tends to let the military off the hook, absolving them of all responsibility for our national failure and placing the blame elsewhere.

The third article in this section, by János Radványi, a former Hungarian diplomat and now an American citizen, is one of the most fascinating essays in the entire collection. Radványi does not dwell long on events in Southeast Asia, but moves directly to the arena of the Great Powers – the United States, the Soviet Union, and China. From his insider's vantage, he brings out the roles and views of the communist East European nations and the clever way that Hanoi dealt with its several benefactors without antagonizing any of them. His brief but cogent portrait of Ho Chi Minh is one of the more accurate ones to be found. His exposé of the interplay between the USSR and China is particularly informative, showing us, for example, why Henry Kissinger could not play the "China card" to achieve US aims in Southeast Asia.

The final piece in this section, by Jeffrey Clarke, is titled "On Strategy and the Vietnam War." Clarke makes some excellent points and asks some good questions, but leaves room for argument. For example, he questions the logistic feasibility of conducting "more ambitious" military operations from South Vietnam into Laos but gives no explanation for this view. If there was one aspect of the war, however, where we were eminently successful, it was logistics. One can fault us for being extravagant and wasteful, but the fact remains that our logisticians and the support troops rarely, if ever, failed our combat forces. Our overall logistic capability in Vietnam, involving all services and several large American and Korean contractors, was enormous. We built huge new ports and associated bases such as the Newport-Long Binh complex and the Cam Ranh Bay base; international-class jet airfields; scores of helicopter pads, fire bases, special forces bases, and C-130 capable airstrips; an extensive backbone communications system throughout South Vietnam; a first-class medical support system; hundreds of miles of all-weather roads; and over 25 major US unit base camps; and we enlarged and improved numerous

South Vietnamese ports and bases throughout the country. With a different strategy and concomitant troop deployment that positioned the bulk of US and other foreign forces in the north – where they could deny the demilitarized zone as an approach route into South Vietnam and threaten if not block the Ho Chi Minh Trail through the Laotian panhandle – there is not the slightest doubt in my mind that our logisticians would have solved the difficult logistic problems incurred. Moreover, this would not have required major additional logistic resources because some bases we did build (Cam Ranh Bay, for example) were not necessary after the war moved away from the area. Further, a northerly deployment of US and other foreign forces would have greatly reduced the logistic facilities needed in other parts of South Vietnam.

The third segment of the collection, concerning the conduct of the war, begins with a provocative essay by Alexander S. Cochran, Jr. Titled "American Planning for Ground Combat in Vietnam: 1952–1965," it covers the period of the First Indochina War between the French and Ho Chi Minh's Viet Minh, and the subsequent period of US involvement up to July 1965, when President Johnson committed major US ground forces in South Vietnam. Cochran argues that American military planning was neither hasty nor reactive in nature, but evolved naturally over the years as US planners grappled with shifting perceptions of the threat and the proper role of American troops in a counterinsurgency environment. Cochran gives the impression that our planners did their job well and that those who "are still obsessed with the 'whys' of a lost war must look elsewhere." But what Cochran calls "planning" constituted only US Pacific Command's deployment plans, which stipulated the entry points in Vietnam for those US forces available at the time and their area of initial employment. Pacific Command's overall war planning was focused on general war, which was primarily concerned with employment of American air and naval power against strategic targets, and only tangentially concerned ground combat.

Pacific Command's contingency plans, on the other hand, did involve the employment of US ground forces. The contingency plans for Vietnam, however, had no broad strategic concept and no operational plan for the employment of American and South Vietnamese troops that could be the basis for projecting the total US resources and the probable time required to achieve US objectives. Only a starting point, these "plans" were far from complete and essentially left the heart and guts of the plan to be developed by a yet-to-be-designated commander with no existing staff. The same could be said for intelligence. Pacific Command had excellent intelligence on strategic targets to be attacked by air or naval forces, but enemy ground order of battle was practically nonexistent. Thus when, in early 1962, the US Military Assistance Command (MACV) was established in Saigon as an operational headquarters superimposed over the US Military Assistance Advisory Group, it was almost starting from scratch. In essence, the JCS and Pacific Command left it up to

MACV to develop the ''strategy'' and operational approach, at least for the ground war in the South. In this instance, it seems that the JCS should have provided a great deal more than just general guidance.

The second essay concerning the conduct of the war, written by Michael W. Davidson, is titled ''Senior Officers and Vietnam Policymaking.'' Initially, Davidson describes the close relations between the military chiefs and the president as commander in chief during the Roosevelt-Truman-Eisenhower years. He then traces the continuing downgrading of military advice following the simultaneous creation of a secretary of defense (and the consequent growth of a large civilian defense bureaucracy) and a toothless JCS – a joint committee with no assured access to the president. Davidson describes how this state of affairs led to faulty decisions on Vietnam by civilian policymakers who never faced up to the eventual high costs of the war. The JCS was unable to get across clearly to the president and his civilian hierarchy the full implications of such decisions.

This organizational situation continues today, even though the Defense Reorganization Act of 1986 designates the Chairman, JCS, as the principal military adviser to the president and the secretary of defense, one of the intents of this legislation apparently being to bring about more timely advice from the JCS system. The basic situation is not changed, however, because a civilian secretary of defense remains placed in a position of command, with no corresponding assumption of the accountability, obligations, and responsibilities that accompany command. One cannot quarrel with granting the secretary all the authority he needs in peacetime to budget for, man, arm, equip, and manage our armed forces, but the secretary of defense should not be responsible for the performance of our forces in battle. The United States can afford only one wartime commander in chief – the president; the operational chain of command in time of war, or grave emergency, should run from the president directly to the JCS and the unified commands. In my opinion, our defense organization is still seriously flawed in this respect, a weakness that could be a recipe for disaster.

For the military professional, at least, the next essay in this section, ''Communist Offensive Strategy and the Defense of South Vietnam,'' is the ''crown jewel'' of the collection. The author, Hung P. Nguyen, is a scholar at the Johns Hopkins University School of Advanced International Studies. Written clearly and concisely, the article is an absorbing exploration of Hanoi's total strategy, as well as of the organizational and operational concepts governing the communist forces. It is not just a theoretical discussion. In illustrating major communist principles, it analyzes briefly several actual enemy offensive campaigns such as the 1951 Viet Minh campaign in the lower Red River delta, the 1962 Viet Cong campaign in the Mekong River delta, the Tet 1968 offensive, the Easter 1972 offensive, the 1973–74 campaign in the Mekong delta, and the final offensive in 1975.

Hung Nguyen's revealing analysis is exceptionally well documented and has the ring of authenticity and truth. His sources include books, monographs, and articles written by senior military leaders from both Vietnamese sides, as well as by American, French, and British authors, both military and civilian. One of his principal North Vietnamese sources is the book *Ending The Thirty Years' War* (1982), written by General Tran Van Tra, the commander of Viet Cong forces in South Vietnam from 1963 to 1965. At that time, the Central Office for South Vietnam (COSVN) was established to enable the communist forces to meet the far different military problem posed by the introduction of U S ground combat troops. (COSVN controlled the war within the area included in the South Vietnamese IV, III, and southern II Corps Tactical Zones, in other words from the tip of the Mekong Delta to just south of Ban Me Thuot.) Tra commanded COSVN from 1967 to the end of the war and is credited as the "guiding hand" behind the communist offensives of Tet 1968, Easter 1972, and the final one in 1975, even though several different views on how to fight the war existed among the senior strategists in Hanoi.

Interestingly, after the American intervention with major troop deployments in 1965, there were those Vietnamese communists who favored a protracted guerrilla war in the lowlands and river deltas to gain control of the population as the key to victory; others who saw the war as having become essentially a conventional one of attrition between two armies; and a third, dominant school (that of Tra and others, both civilian and military), who rejected any compartmentalization of the conflict, but saw the war as remaining one complex whole.

Though Hung Nguyen employs General Tra's remarkable book with telling effect, some have tried to downplay it. They allege that Tra's memoirs were written to help the Viet Cong regain some measure of power in the postwar south, now apparently monopolized by Hanoi and northern Vietnamese. Such assertions simply do not wash. Tra's illuminating analysis of communist strategy is very much borne out by the actual experience in Vietnam of both French and American veterans of the Indochina Wars, as well as by scholars and historians of the era. Tra, a man of brilliant intellect, without a doubt played a major role in Hanoi's ultimate victory and we should heed his words.

Hung Nguyen's essay also analyzes allied counter-strategy efforts and possible alternative strategies, showing their strengths and weaknesses, and concluding that the attempt to secure "every nook and cranny of South Vietnam" was a fatal mistake made by both the Americans and the South Vietnamese. This fundamental error allowed the communists to deploy their forces well forward and dispose them in such a way as to prevent the development of a coherent, consolidated defense line, that is, "a war with fronts," in any part of South Vietnam.

The communists do not share one commonly held American notion that Vietnam was a "double war" of two components – the big-unit war of attrition and the pacification war of population control. They believe that our basic weakness lay in our relative timing and separation of these integral parts of the same war. Hanoi saw the war as one, inseparable, and highly interdependent, coordinated effort. Complex calculations of how the two components were to be harmonized always lay behind determinations of how and when their forces would be engaged. Hanoi, moreover, clearly considered the "revolutionary war" for control of the population in the lowlands as indispensable to the success of the big-unit war in the jungles and mountains, even though the latter at the end of the war was decisive.

Hung Nguyen, however, points out that Hanoi's strategy did have an Achilles heel – a counter-strategy that would permanently disrupt the essential linkage between their local, guerrilla, and main forces. For this reason, Hanoi feared any form of enclave strategy.

Toward the end of the war, South Vietnamese General Cao Van Vien, the Chairman of the Joint General Staff, urged President Thieu to give up the northern coastal plains and the Central Highlands, and defend a truncated South Vietnam in the southern region, protecting at all costs the vital Mekong delta area, the most important "enclave" of all. But Thieu would not listen. To offset the obvious weaknesses of their deployments, with all their major forces committed, inadequate forces in reserve in their four corps tactical zones, and a very small strategic reserve, Vien tried to organize mobile regional commands that could perform both territorial security and mobile combat missions in order to help out their outnumbered and overcommitted army and marine divisions, but the effort began too late. Vien's concept was similar to the French "groupement mobile" scheme, an enclave strategy that defeated the Viet Minh offensive in the Red River delta in 1951 (described in Hung Nguyen's essay). But the French forfeited their success when they decided to take the war to the mountains and thus allowed the Viet Minh to regain control of this vital enclave south of Hanoi.

The account above suggests that we Americans might not have fully understood the communist strategy that forced the French to quit in 1954. The French had nothing like the air and naval power, tactical mobility, and firepower, not to mention the much larger and more powerful ground forces possessed by the United States, yet they came close, apparently unknowingly, to devising a successful counter-strategy. On the other hand, MACV commander General Creighton W. Abrams, Jr., in my opinion, came very close to finding the key to defeating the communist strategy when, during the period 1969–1971, allied forces were clearly winning the pacification campaign while at the same time keeping the enemy big units at bay. But by that time the withdrawal of US ground combat forces was almost completed, and without direct US military support South Vietnamese forces could not possibly maintain these substantial gains – there was simply too much geography to defend.

In any event, Hung Nguyen's article is an enduring contribution to our knowledge of the strategy of wars of national liberation. It must be read more than once to capture its full meaning. Finally, it should be required reading for any course of instruction involving strategy and the operational art.

The last article in this section, authored by John D. Stuckey and Joseph H. Pistorius, concerns the US failure to mobilize during the Vietnam War. Well organized and written, the essay documents in some detail President Johnson's rejection of mobilization and his deliberate concealment of the magnitude of the war and its costs – a record of presidential deceit that has few parallels. (The essay challenges the argument that Johnson did not realize the ultimate costs of prosecuting the war, and shows that he was well aware of them, yet could not bring himself to accept them, primarily for fear of ruining his cherished dream of "The Great Society.") An account of the active Army's poor performance with respect to the small token mobilization in the spring of 1968 is also included in this article. Bitter words, such as "gross ineptitude," "impudently unsuitable," "contemptuous," and "comedy of errors," which appear in the final paragraph, should not be taken lightly because the US Army is now more dependent than ever on its National Guard and Reserve forces for a significant part of its capability to fight a sustained war. A Vietnam-type nonmobilization, or token mobilization, during a major national emergency could happen again.

The Stuckey and Pistorius essay makes no mention of the adverse effects of nonmobilization, coupled with a one-year tour policy in Vietnam, on our total forces, especially the US Army. The proud Seventh Army in Germany became a *de facto* part of the army's replacement base and over time was destroyed as a combat-effective force, while only one division, the 82d Airborne, remained ready in the United States. In fact, the strategic posture of the United States was precariously off balance because our forces in Europe and the Atlantic were singularly unready and we lacked strategic reserves in the United States. In the absence of mobilization, the expansion of US forces during the war, particularly the Army, resulted in spreading available experienced leadership too thinly throughout the ranks. This factor, combined with the policy of a one-year tour in Vietnam, badly hurt unit cohesion and continuity throughout the Army, as well as continuity of experience and knowledge of Vietnam in Vietnam itself. As one observer put it, we fought the same war ten times in Vietnam.

Guenter Lewy and Paul Kattenburg, both eminent political scientists and historians, are the authors of the first two articles, respectively, in the fourth segment concerning the lessons of Vietnam. Both are thoughtful, well-crafted essays. Lewy makes a more comprehensive analysis of both the ground war in South Vietnam and the US air offensive against North Vietnam, the latter in my opinion being the most solid and illuminating examination yet written on the strengths and weaknesses of US strategic air power, not only as employed in Southeast Asia, but also as employed to date. Kattenburg comments on the salient results of the war as he perceives them today, and concludes with a discussion of the Vietnam syndrome. His analysis is perhaps less secure when he attempts to apply the lessons of Vietnam to the Central American-Caribbean region, for truly herculean policy dilemmas confront those of our Latin American friends who are trying to develop enlightened democratic regimes in the face of constant siege by relentless, ruthless enemies with Marxist-Leninist coloration.

The final essay on Vietnam lessons by David Petraeus is an excellent piece. Petraeus concentrates on what he interprets to be current US military thinking on the subject and warns of the pitfalls of carrying the Vietnam analogy too far. But his most important point is that the American military, the Army in particular, must put more emphasis on the dilemmas posed by unconventional warfare and insurgency in the Third World and develop the doctrine and the forces to fight such so-called "small wars."

The fifth and final section concerns the aftermath of the Vietnam War. In the first article, W. W. Rostow (President Johnson's national security adviser during the period 1966–1968) presents a masterful exposition of the strategic importance of Southeast Asia to the United States. He concludes with an upbeat assessment – all has not been lost in Southeast Asia – but we, the American people, must come to a deeper appreciation of the stakes involved in the region. In the next article, Douglas Pike, one of our foremost authorities on Indochina and Vietnamese communists, traces the course of American-Vietnamese relations since the fall of Saigon in the spring of 1975. He examines the issues between the Americans and the present Vietnamese, and explores the feasibility of establishing formal relations at some time beyond the foreseeable future, and how this might come about.

The next essay of this segment concerns Secretary of Defense Weinberger's six criteria for the use of military force. Written by David T. Twining, the essay quotes each criterion and follows it with a short discussion of its rationale. Twining then concludes with a brief discourse on the disadvantages democracies face in limited war, particularly a protracted one. In my view, while the Weinberger "doctrine" constitutes a statement of laudable principles, it does not have much practical value for dealing with the numerous ambiguous situations that will continue to confront the United States worldwide. Twining concludes that, provided "our basic freedoms remain intact," the Weinberger "guidelines will permit thoroughly democratic means to be mobilized properly and appropriately against those seeking anti-democratic ends." These are noble sentiments, but the world, unfortunately, is not that simple and true democracies have a way of being unpredictable.

Finally, Rod Paschall examines low-intensity conflict doctrine as a counter to externally sponsored insurgency in Third World nations. Based on an examination of the Asian experience, he concludes generally that host nations themselves should fight the internal low-intensity war (aided by US advice and training/materiel support) while the United States conducts mid-intensity offensive ground operations against the nations sponsoring the insurgency.

In my opinion, this collection is a timely and valuable contribution both to our knowledge about the Vietnam War and to a deeper understanding of it. It clearly brings out contrasting views, while at the same time clearing up some of the misleading Vietnam mythology that abounds in the United States and abroad. While most Americans have a personal bias on the subject, some of my own having been revealed in the foregoing comments, readers should nevertheless profit from this collection.

We Americans made it through the Great Depression and World War II even though we lost much of our innocence about the world. In the postwar period, we emerged as the leader of the Free World and believed there was nothing we could not accomplish if we put our minds and muscles to it. The Korean and Vietnam wars have been sobering experiences, damaging our confidence and making us realize there are limits to our power. In the Vietnam years, we learned much about ourselves as a people and a nation – both strengths and weaknesses. Memories and impressions of Vietnam will be with us for many years to come and only future generations can come to any final judgments. Meanwhile, there is some evidence to show that plain old American common sense will prevail in the end and that, eventually, we will be able to put Vietnam behind us and emerge a wiser people.

General Bruce Palmer, Jr.
U S Army, Retired

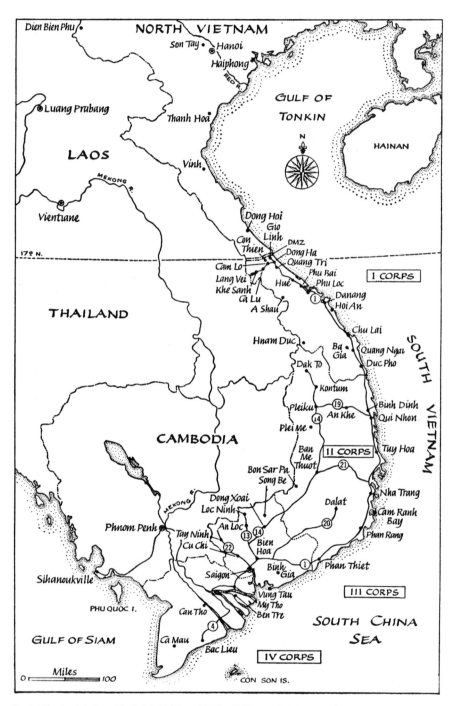

Reprinted by permission from *A Soldier Reports* by General William C. Westmoreland (New York: Doubleday 1976).

I. THE LITERATURE OF VIETNAM

1

Palmer, Karnow, and Herrington: A Review of Recent Vietnam War Histories

by HARRY G. SUMMERS, JR.

Vietnam: A History. By Stanley Karnow. 670 pages. Viking Press, New York, 1983.
Peace with Honor?: An American Reports on Vietnam, 1973–75. By Lieutenant Colonel Stuart A. Herrington. 240 pages. Presidio Press, Novato, Calif., 1983.
The 25-Year War: America's Military Role in Vietnam. By General Bruce Palmer, Jr. 236 pages. The University Press of Kentucky, Lexington, Ky., 1984.

A century and a half ago that master military theorist, Carl von Clausewitz, warned of two impediments to comprehending the true nature of war. One was what he called "the *vividness* of transient impressions" and the other "the tyranny of fashion."[1] Presenting an elective on Vietnam War Strategy at the Army War College for the past four years to classes composed almost entirely of Army, Navy, Air Force, and Marine combat veterans of the war has reaffirmed the validity of that Clausewitzian insight.

Paradoxically, for military officers their own combat experience works against them. Their view of the nature of the war is very much dependent on when and where they served. The "vividness" of the battlefield experiences of officers who served in Vietnam prior to 1965, or officers who served in the Mekong Delta, led them to believe that the war was exclusively a guerrilla war against lightly armed Viet Cong insurgents. The "vividness" of the battlefield experiences of officers who fought the Battle of the Ia Drang in November 1965 or of officers who served along the Demilitarized Zone led them to believe that the war was primarily against well-armed North Vietnamese army regulars. Few American officers witnessed the North Vietnamese tank- and artillery-supported Eastertide Offensive of 1972 and even fewer witnessed the North Vietnamese four-corps, cross-border blitzkrieg in 1975.

3

In academia the "tyranny of fashion" evidently served a similar function. In lecturing at several midwestern universities in the aftermath of the Cambodian incursion in 1970, it was remarkable to discover how rigid and doctrinaire opinions had become (and, as *Commentary* editor Norman Podhoretz found in his examination of attitudes among the intellectual and academic communities during the Vietnam War, this was more than just a local phenomenon[2]). Everyone, students and faculty alike, agreed that the war was patently illegal, immoral, and unjust, and woe betide anyone who had the audacity to challenge this received truth. Recent articles in these pages have illustrated that this mindset lingers on, for there are those who still contend that the struggle in Vietnam was a civil war pure and simple, a war in which the United States – and, for that matter, the "illegitimate" Republic of Vietnam – should never have become involved. They have attempted to lock history into place circa 1970, but unfortunately for their peace of mind, historical truth is and has always been subject to reexamination, revision, and reinterpretation.

Many found their beliefs specious to begin with – a much better case could be made that the Korean War or, closer to home, the attempts by the United States to invade Canada in 1812, were both "civil wars" since both warring factions involved a common ethnic stock, a common language, and common histories and traditions. Much depends on which side you are on. As Clausewitz said, "The aggressor is always peace-loving (as Bonaparte always claimed to be); he would prefer to take over [a] country unopposed. To prevent his doing so, one must be willing to make war."[3] While the North Vietnamese may well have justified their actions as a "civil war," the South Vietnamese – and the majority of the world's nations – saw it as naked aggression. Not only was the sovereignty of the Republic of Vietnam recognized by some 60 of the world's nations, but, as journalist Stanley Karnow reveals in his *Vietnam: A History*, "The Soviet Union even suggested a permanent partition by proposing in early 1957 that both North and South Vietnam be admitted to the United Nations as 'two separate states,'" an initiative rebuffed by the United States.[4] Ironically, however, it has been not American "revisionists" but the Viet Cong themselves who have most decisively challenged the 1970-era misconceptions. Founder of the National Liberation Front (NLF) and former Viet Cong Minister of Justice Truong Nhu Tang ruefully now admits that not only American academics but the Viet Cong themselves were deliberately blinded to the true nature of the war. The Viet Cong leadership, "southerners committed to the idea of a separate policy for South Vietnam," discovered too late that from the very beginning "the North Vietnamese communists had engaged in a deliberate deception to achieve what had been their true goal from the start, the destruction of South Vietnam as a political or social entity in any way separate from the North."[5] This disillusionment was corroborated by Stanley Karnow during his 1981 visit to Vietnam. "I've been a communist all my life," former Viet Cong Deputy Minister of Health Dr. Duong Quynh Hoa told him, "but now, for the first time, I have seen the realities of communism.

It is a failure – mismanagement, corruption, privilege, repression. My ideals are gone." She went on to decry "the northern communists who now ran the south," and such "animosity toward northerners" led Karnow to question the presumption "that the communists were a monolithic force in the country."[6]

Yet another "tyranny of fashion" still lingers on – the notion that the war in Vietnam was a "revolutionary war" and that defeat there was caused by failure to implement properly the doctrines of counterinsurgency. This misperception is the more dangerous of the two since it clouds and confuses the very real problems we confront today in assisting allies faced with an internal insurgency. Emphasis on "counterinsurgency" obscures the fact that (unlike the French in Indochina or the British in Malaya who were in political control) for the United States the war in Vietnam was not a counterinsurgency war but instead a coalition war in support of an ally attempting to combat an insurgency. Failure to make this distinction led to American overinvolvement in the war and subsequent undermining of the confidence, self-sufficiency, and self-reliance of the very ally we were attempting to support.

Such arguments over the nature of the war are not limited to the United States. A recent *Parameters* article perpetuates this guerrilla mythology with a synopsis of the memoirs of Viet Cong General Tran Van Tra.[7] What the article does not say is that these memoirs were an attempt by the Viet Cong to reestablish their claim to power and to challenge the (from my personal experience, correct) version of the North Vietnamese final offensive written by North Vietnamese army General Van Tien Dung.[8] As Stanley Karnow points out, Tra's memoir "was banned almost immediately after its publication [and] he himself disappeared from sight," concluding that "Tra, who was dedicated to the cause of communism in the south, may have been purged for criticizing his northern comrades."[9]

The war in Vietnam did not validate counterinsurgency doctrine. What it did validate was the truth of Clausewitz's dictum that "In war, the will is directed at an animate object that *reacts*."[10] From 1954 to 1959, according to former CORDS [Civil Operations and Revolutionary Development Support] Director Ambassador Robert W. Komer, "MAAG concentrated on . . . preparing ARVN for a conventional delaying action against what it regarded as the most serious threat: a conventional, Korea-style NVA attack across the DMZ . . . [and] little was done . . . to develop an effective counterinsurgency capability."[11] The North Vietnamese reacted to these preparations not by meeting them head-on but instead by launching a Hanoi-directed guerrilla war.

According to public statements on French television in 1983 by North Vietnamese army commanders Vo Nguyen Giap and Vo Bam, the North Vietnamese government set up the NLF in Hanoi in 1959 to "reunite the country." Two years before President Kennedy stepped up American support by sending 685 advisors to South Vietnam, the North Vietnamese army sent 20,000 guerrilla-war cadres along what was to become the Ho Chi Minh Trail and in 1961 committed 30,000 laborers to expand that infiltration route.[12] This tactic almost succeeded, and by 1965 the Hanoi-directed guerrilla war had brought the Republic of Vietnam to the verge of collapse. All this changed, however, with the intervention of American combat forces. From that point until the Tet Offensive of 1968, the war was a mixed bag waged by local Viet Cong guerrillas, organized Viet Cong battalion- and regiment-sized main force units, and North Vietnamese army regular units. As the Viet Cong now admit, however, the guerrilla-war phase was decisively ended in the aftermath of the Tet Offensive of 1968,[13] and for the next seven years the war continued under North Vietnamese control and direction.

With guerrilla war an obvious failure and the shattering of their ideological illusion – a tenet of "revolutionary war" doctrine – that, given the opportunity, the majority of the people would flock to their colors, they again reacted by changing from guerrilla to conventional tactics – i.e., their abortive Eastertide Offensive of 1972 and their successful blitzkrieg in 1975. Among the other great ironies of the war is the fact that the North Vietnamese final victory was won by "a conventional, Korea-style NVA attack across the DMZ." Within two decades, the war had come full circle.

The Public Broadcasting System series "Vietnam: A Television History," advertised as derived from Karnow's *Vietnam: A History*, has given many a false impression of that work. The truth is, as the foregoing quotations illustrate, that Karnow's book is far more objective and evenhanded than the television series. Part of the reason is structural. Karnow could portray all of the facets of a situation – for example, not only the Saigon police chief's execution of a Viet Cong terrorist, but also the depravations of the Viet Cong death squads that led to that incident – but the television program was restricted to the footage available, and no TV camera crews accompanied the Viet Cong death squads.

A former *Time/Life* and *Washington Post* war correspondent, Stanley Karnow drew on 30 years' experience in the field and thus was able to avoid both the "vividness of transient impressions" and the "tyranny of fashion." With one of the most balanced overviews of Vietnam yet written, *Vietnam: A History* begins with the heritage of Vietnam's legendary past, including the French colonial period, the Japanese occupation in World War II, the First Indochina War between France and the Viet Minh, and thereafter provides a detailed account of America's involvement in the Second Indochina War between North Vietnam and South Vietnam. As a result of a 1981 visit to Vietnam, he also gives insights on the aftermath of that war. As he reports, soon after their conquest "the communists proceeded to shunt 400,000 South Vietnamese civil servants and Army officers as well as doctors, lawyers, teachers, journalists, and other intellectuals into 're-education' centers." "Locked in the same 'tiger cages' that the South Vietnamese government employed to incarcerate its dissidents – and which aroused protests in America during the war," these prisoners included "opponents of the Saigon authorities . . . [and] Viet Cong veterans.'' He goes on to discuss the ''nearly a million people [who] have risked their lives to escape from the country.''[14]

Some have complained that Karnow has perpetuated the myth that Ho Chi Minh was the George Washington of Vietnam. But while Karnow may have overemphasized Ho's nationalism, he accurately portrays the excesses of the 1955 land reforms where ''thousands died and thousands were interned in forced labor camps,'' as well as the brutal suppression of the revolt in Ho's own home province where Ho Chi Minh ''sent a division of troops out to quell the disorders, and they killed or deported some 6,000 peasants.''[15] (And just to think, if when General George Washington moved out of Carlisle Barracks to put down the Whiskey Rebellion in 1794, he had killed the rebels instead of putting the revolt down without bloodshed, he could have gone down in history as the ''Ho Chi Minh of America.'') The question of whether Ho was more a nationalist or more a Stalinist functionary is still very much alive, most recently debated in an article in the January 1985 *Atlantic*.[16]

A more telling criticism is that in his 670-page book, Karnow devotes only some 15 pages to the fall of South Vietnam. But this deficiency is more than compensated for in *Peace With Honor?* by Lieutenant Colonel Stuart Herrington. Although a personal bias is involved – Herrington was my Deputy Negotiations Officer with the United States delegation Four Party Joint Military Team in 1974–75 and we worked together on the Saigon evacuation – other sources confirm my belief that he has written the landmark book on the final days of the American presence in Vietnam. Combining the analytical skills of an intelligence officer with the initiative and drive of an operations officer, Colonel Herrington played a key role in the evacuation and – as with his earlier book, *Silence Was a Weapon* – he has given us a remarkable testimony on American actions during the war.

Although Karnow did not dwell on those final days, he does report that ''after the war was over . . . Americans overwhelmingly repudiated the intervention as having been a blunder. But roughly the same proportion of the nation holds in retrospect that, once involved the United States ought to have deployed all its power to succeed. Postwar opinion polls show that Americans blame their political leaders for denying victory to the US Forces in Vietnam.''[17] These public opinion polls – polls corroborated by public response to recent lectures on campuses and in the civilian community on the war in Vietnam – reveal not so much the truth of what went wrong in Vietnam as they do the strange role the military plays in American society.

Thanks to the lasting legacy of Oliver Cromwell, as former MACV Commander and Army Chief of Staff General Fred C. Weyand once put it, ''Americans have a long and proud tradition of irreverence for and distrust of their military.''[18] But from the very beginning of the Republic, the military has provided the foundation for America's security, and ''security'' (as Maslow pointed out in his famous hierarchy of needs) is a basic and fundamental necessity upon which all other societal requirements are built. Thus while Americans may not revere their military, they have always taken it for granted that their military would protect them from harm. When this subliminal belief is threatened – as with America's defeat in Vietnam – primordial passions are aroused. If the American people sense that their military is incompetent and unable to provide for their security, then their basic foundations become unstable. Better, then, to place the blame elsewhere – on the media, for example, or on the anti-war movement, or on (as Karnow found) "their political leaders" – for with such explanations, their feeling of security remains intact. Too many today, especially those come of age after the Vietnam War, have placed the blame for America's failure on such scapegoats.

And those who served in Vietnam – including the senior leadership of the Army today whose combat service was at the platoon, company, and battalion levels – are not immune from such illusions. As Karnow reported, "A survey conducted in 1980 for the Veterans Administration disclosed that 82 percent of former US soldiers involved in heavy combat there believe that the war was lost because they were not allowed to win."[19] Since at the tactical level, as the North Vietnamese themselves admit, America's combat forces won every major engagement on the battlefield, the "vividness of their transient impressions" blinds combat veterans, in and out of the Army, to the military's strategic failures. But the senior leadership of the Army during the war knew better. A most poignant example was provided in a recent letter from a retired brigadier general which told of a 1977 conversation he had with General Harold K. Johnson, the Army's Vietnam-era Deputy Chief of Staff for Operations and later Army Chief of Staff. The retired general asked General Johnson, "If you had your life to live over again, what would you do differently?" General Johnson replied:

I remember the day I was ready to go over to the Oval Office and give my four stars to the President and tell him, "You have refused to tell the country they cannot fight a war without mobilization; you have required me to send men into battle with little hope of their ultimate victory; and you have forced us in the military to violate almost every one of the principles of war in Vietnam. Therefore, I resign and will hold a press conference after I walk out of your door."

According to the general's letter, General Johnson then told him "with a look of anguish on his face" that "I made the typical mistake of believing I could do more for the country and the Army if I stayed in than if I got out. I am now going to my grave with that burden of lapse in moral courage on my back."[20] The story has the ring of truth, for in a visit to the Army War College shortly before he died, General Johnson revealed the terrible despair and deep sense of personal responsibility that continued to haunt him. "For over five years after the war," he said, "I could not even bear to think about it."[21]

Fortunately for the future security of the United States, his former deputy, General Bruce Palmer, Jr., *has* been thinking about it. Army Operations Deputy in the Joint Chiefs of Staff in the early days of the war, Commander of

II Field Force and later of USARV during the war itself, and Army Vice Chief of Staff in the closing days of the war, General Palmer has provided an insider's account unequaled in the literature of the war. His book *The 25-Year War: America's Military Role in Vietnam* is of particular value to the military.

General Palmer's analysis begins at the Army War College. A member of the Class of 1951, he took part in an examination of US policy in Southeast Asia. Among other things, his study group concluded that "the United States had probably made a serious mistake in agreeing with its allies to allow French power to be restored in Indochina." They went on to find that "Indochina was of only secondary strategic importance to the United States" and that "militarily, the region in general and Vietnam in particular would be an extremely difficult operational area."[22] These findings came back to haunt him when in 1963 General Palmer became the assistant to then Lieutenant General Harold K. Johnson, the Army DCSOPS. "During the next twenty months," General Palmer "had a ringside seat at the deliberations of the Joint Chiefs of Staff." Detailing the deliberations that led to the commitment of American ground combat forces to Vietnam, General Palmer admits that "there seems to have been insufficient timely discussion in Washington as to how and to what purpose US forces were to be employed in South Vietnam, that is, the US strategy to be pursued in conducting the crucial ground war in a decisive way."[23] He concludes his account of his 1963–67 experiences on the Joint Chiefs of Staff with the admission, "Not once during the war did the JCS advise the Commander-in-Chief or the Secretary of Defense that the strategy being pursued most probably would fail and that the United States would be unable to achieve its objectives."[24]

Among the more valuable contributions that General Palmer makes is his detailed discussion of alternative strategies. While this drives historians wild, it is, as Clausewitz has emphasized, an essential element in critical analysis. "Critical analysis is not just an evaluation of the means actually employed, but of *all possible means* . . . . One can, after all," Clausewitz wrote, "not condemn a method without being able to suggest a better alternative."[25] While General Palmer does not claim that such alternatives would have been successful, he does point out that they would have played to America's military strengths rather than to its military weaknesses.

The 25-Year War concludes with "the larger lessons." Among these lessons is the need to reexamine our organization for combat. As General Palmer says, the principle of "*Unity of Command . . .* did not exist with respect to US efforts in Southeast Asia."[26] To correct this deficiency General Palmer lays out five proposals to strengthen our chain of command. These are recommendations that cannot be ignored, for as General Palmer states, "The United States cannot afford to put itself again at such enormous strategic disadvantage as we found ourselves in in Vietnam."[27]

As these three volumes indicate, the literature on the war in Vietnam has undergone significant improvement in the past several years. Once dominated by emotional, one-sided, and in some cases deliberately distorted accounts, now at long last evenhanded and objective works are finding their way into publication. Stanley Karnow's *Vietnam: A History* is the best single-volume overview of the war, a book particularly recommended for those who would put our involvement in Vietnam in perspective. Reminding us of the terrible price of our failures, Stuart Herrington's *Peace With Honor?* is likewise the best account of the last days of Vietnam and the evacuation of Saigon. Both of these volumes would be valuable additions to any military library.

But while these two volumes would be nice to have, *The 25-Year War*, by General Bruce Palmer, Jr., is an absolute must for any officer who considers himself a military professional. Moral courage is an all-too-rare commodity and it is especially rare when it is combined with intellectual acumen and practical battlefield experience. By exemplifying these virtues, General Palmer has given us a standard toward which to aspire. As Confucius said a few thousand years ago, ''The way of the superior man is like that of the archer. When he misses the center of the target, he turns and seeks the cause of his failure in himself.'' In Vietnam the Army missed the center of the target, and we owe it to the American people not to blame this failing on others but to seek the causes in our own institutional structure, in our own internal policies, plans, and operations. General Palmer has given us the tools to do just that.

NOTES

1. Carl von Clausewitz, *On War*, ed. and trans. by Michael Howard and Peter Paret, with introductory essays by Peter Paret, Michael Howard, and Bernard Brodie and a commentary by Bernard Brodie (Princeton: Princeton Univ. Press, 1976), pp. 108, 162.
2. Norman Podhoretz, *Why We Were in Vietnam* (New York: Simon & Schuster, 1982), pp. 138-93.
3. Clausewitz, p. 370.
4. Stanley Karnow, *Vietnam: A History* (New York: Viking Press, 1983), p. 224.
5. Truong Tang, ''The Myth of a Liberation,'' *New York Review of Books*, 21 October 1982, pp. 31-36.
6. Karnow, p. 37.
7. Hung P. Nguyen, ''Communist Offensive Strategy and the Defense of South Vietnam,'' *Parameters*, 14 (Winter 1984), 3-19.
8. Van Tien Dung, ''Great Spring Victory,'' *Foreign Broadcast Information Service*, Vol. 1, FBIS-APA-76-110, 7 June 1976; Vol. II, FBIS-APA-76-131, 7 July 1976.
9. Karnow, p. 658.
10. Clausewitz, p. 149.
11. Robert W. Komer, *Bureaucracy Does Its Thing: Institutional Constraints on US-GVN Performance in Vietnam* (Santa Monica: Rand Corporation, August 1972), p. 130.
12. ''Vietnam: We Lied to You,'' *The Economist*, 26 February 1983, p. 56.
13. Tang, ''Myth of a Liberation.''
14. Karnow, pp. 29, 34.
15. Ibid., pp. 225-26.
16. Stephen J. Morris, ''Vietnam's Vietnam,'' *The Atlantic Monthly*, 255 (January 1985), 79-80.
17. Karnow, p. 15.
18. Fred C. Weyand, ''Serving the People: The Need for Military Power,'' *Military Review*, 56 (December 1976), 8.
19. Karnow, p. 15.
20. Personal correspondence.

21. Personal interview.
22. Bruce Palmer, Jr., *The 25-Year War: America's Military Role in Vietnam* (Lexington: Univ. of Kentucky Press, 1984), pp. 2–3.
23. Ibid., p. 44.
24. Ibid., p. 46.
25. Clausewitz, p. 161.
26. Palmer, p. 193.
27. Ibid., p. 210.

This article appeared in the spring 1985 issue of *Parameters*.

2

On Our Conduct of the Vietnam War: A Review Essay of Two New Works

by RICHARD A. HUNT

Bureaucracy at War: U.S. Performance in the Vietnam Conflict. By Robert W. Komer. 174 pages. Westview Press, Boulder, Colo., 1986.
War Without Fronts: The American Experience in Vietnam. By Thomas Thayer. 276 pages. Westview Special Studies, Westview Press, Boulder, Colo., 1985.

Within recent years, General Bruce Palmer and Colonel Harry Summers have written widely discussed analyses of the Vietnam debacle that have become the touchstones of most recent debate.[1] Each seeks to understand why America failed to defeat the communist side and raises questions about the nature of the war and the way the United States fought. Although Palmer and Summers offer individual interpretations, both argue that the United States should have focused its military efforts against North Vietnam, whose invading divisions crushed South Vietnam's army in 1975. According to Summers, "Instead of focusing our attention on the external enemy, North Vietnam – the source of the war – we [the United States] turned our attention to the symptom – the guerrilla war in the south – and limited our attacks on the North to air and sea actions only."[2] Thus, the strategy of counterinsurgency constituted a mistaken response that diverted the United States from taking more effective military action against North Vietnam.[3] In General Palmer's book, he argued for stationing an international military force along the DMZ that would have driven into Laos and cut off the North Vietnamese army's infiltration into South Vietnam.[4] He does not dismiss pacification, or counterinsurgency, as Summers does, but only treats it in passing.

Into this continuing discussion about the American role in Vietnam comes a "revised and updated" monograph, *Bureaucracy at War*, by Robert W. Komer, who played an important role in the pacification program. This work advances the argument he first made in his 1972 study for the Rand Corporation,

"Bureaucracy Does Its Thing." In its new format, his argument deserves as much attention as the books by Palmer and Summers have received. Relying heavily on the so-called *Pentagon Papers*, memoirs of policymakers, the secondary literature of the Kennedy and Johnson years, as well as insights gained as a participant in many of the debates over policy and strategy, Komer compellingly develops a broad and provocative thesis.

Komer's starting point is similar to Summers': why did such a vast expenditure of American military and financial resources yield such meager results? But he soon parts company with the author of *On Strategy*, characterizing American neglect of counterinsurgency, largely called pacification, as one reason for poor performance. Policymakers in Washington seemed to recognize the importance of counterinsurgency but had difficulty in the 1950s and 1960s getting South Vietnamese or American civilian and military agencies to carry out an integrated counterinsurgency strategy and programs. Institutional constraints, the military and the civilian agencies "playing out their institutional repertoires," to use Komer's phrase, led them to carry out the kinds of activities they were trained to accomplish instead of adapting missions, organizations, and programs to counteract the unusual political and military threat of the Vietnamese communists.

Komer peppers his book with examples of bureaucracies doing what came naturally. The American Army trained the South Vietnamese army as a conventional military force. Consequently, training, equipping, and advising the paramilitary forces were neglected until 1967, relatively late in the war. This neglect was also one cause of President Diem's failure to defeat the insurgency.

After American combat units entered the war, the US Army mounted search-and-destroy operations to engage and kill enemy "main forces." The Army relied on attrition because it had superior mobility, firepower, and resources which would allow it to wear down its foe. As Komer puts it, "Armies like to fight other armies." The American military command in Vietnam "tended to focus all the more on the 'big unit' war to the neglect of other facets of the conflict."[5] It was less comfortable carrying out clear-and-hold operations, which would have helped provide a shield for pacification to get underway and which Komer believes were a more suitable response to the insurgency.

Likewise, "the air forces pressed to do what they knew best: to mount massive bombing campaigns both in the South and against the North," reflecting then current doctrine on how to employ air power.[6] Although Komer concedes the bombing was not carried out the way its advocates wished, he argues that the results of the air war were limited largely because North Vietnam, with few industries or other militarily lucrative targets, was not as vulnerable to air attack as our previous military experience tended to suggest.[7] He may be pushing his point too far when he suggests that we conducted a major bombing campaign of interdiction simply because we had the capability to do so, but it is probably true that the Air Force would have carried out the air war differently in the absence of the B-52 bomber.

Komer is seeking to understand American performance, not looking for scapegoats. He attributes much of the American failure to obtain results in Vietnam to the way large civilian and military bureaucracies constrained the thinking and practices of their leadership and rank and file, making it difficult for them to adapt to a unique challenge. Protecting their individual domains, agencies resisted attempts to have them pool their efforts with other offices and reduce duplicated programs. Government bureaucracies also were reluctant to yield authority over programs in the interest of unity of management. The absence of a single manager in Washington or Saigon, short of the President, to oversee the activities of the armed services and a host of civilian agencies was a critical shortcoming of the US conduct of the war.

One example Komer cites of a moderately successful American adaptation to the peculiar needs of the war is the organization he helped establish and then managed, CORDS (Civil Operations and Revolutionary Development Support). This organization, located in South Vietnam and composed of soldiers and civilians from the State Department, AID, and the CIA, provided under Komer's leadership unified management of American support of South Vietnam's pacification program, and it led to a significant expansion of the money, men, and materiel devoted to the ''other war.''

Komer's message on the advantage of organizational change to meet new challenges is clear, but unfortunately he chooses not to document the case for CORDS' success,[8] which is presented almost as a given. In outline, his argument is that CORDS solved serious management and organizational problems of pacification support, and thus the South Vietnamese pacification program enjoyed some success. To detail systematically what CORDS accomplished may have exposed Komer to charges of self-promotion and parochialism, but it would have strengthened his argument considerably. The skeptical reader may find it difficult to accept at face value his assertions about CORDS' success.

Komer's thesis raises questions about the other parties to the war. In his view, the Americans lost partly because of the flawed nature of our ally, South Vietnam. Komer is right to criticize South Vietnam's shortcomings, which seriously impeded American military and civilian efforts, and he implies that perhaps the United States was doomed to fail because of our ally's inadequacies.[9] If that judgment is correct, then solving the organizational and doctrinal problems of American bureaucracies could be interpreted as irrelevant to the outcome of the war.

Although at no time does Komer imply that if we had more effectively tailored our forces and organizations we could have won the war, he does not seem to have taken sufficient cognizance of the enemy's adaptability and dogged retention of the initiative throughout most of the war.

Thayer's book, a unique contribution to Vietnam War studies, makes a convincing case that the US Army did not fight as a counterinsurgent force, and that the enemy was to a great extent able to control the pace of the fighting as well as his losses and thus hold the initiative.[10] He also presents the kind of evidence that Komer could have used to elaborate his case for pacification's success after 1967.

The author served as Director of the Southeast Asia Division in the Defense Department's Office of Systems Analysis from 1967 to 1972. While in that position he helped compile operational data on many aspects of the war. Much of Thayer's analysis originally appeared monthly in a classified Defense Department publication, the *Southeast Asia Analysis Reports*, and was contemporaneous with the events described. That publication did not please everyone. Articles critical of pacification drew Komer's ire, and critiques of the attrition strategy and the air interdiction campaign at times sorely vexed Army and Air Force brass. The appearance of this material, important in its own right, is also significant for presenting in some detail the informed critique of the air war and of attrition that civilian Pentagon officials made in the midst of the war. The publication of this work in the public domain allows it to reach a wider audience.

To Thayer, the war had two salient characteristics. First, unlike World War II and Korea, the Vietnam War was a war without front lines, which made it difficult to understand. Second, to understand the war it was necessary to discern the patterns underlying the fighting, a task requiring the systematic analysis of statistical data.[11]

Thayer's carefully accumulated data on the casualty rates suffered by South Vietnamese and American forces and the kind and number of enemy attacks reveal that most enemy actions were small in scale. Battalion-sized attacks, which were a more serious threat than raids and political harassment, constituted a slim percentage (3.7) of all enemy ground assaults.[12] Even in 1972, a year of unusually heavy conventional fighting during the Easter Offensive, enemy ground assaults and indirect attacks by fire amounted to only 21 percent of all enemy-initiated incidents.[13] The preponderance of the enemy's effort throughout the war, as measured by Thayer's statistics, was weighted toward political coercion, terrorism, sabotage, and indirect attacks by fire.[14] The purpose of this pattern of activity was to wear down the internal security forces of South Vietnam – its police, militia, and territorial forces providing population security. Casualty figures also support the contention that the communists concentrated on weakening Saigon's security forces. With the exception of 1968, the Regional and Popular Forces protecting the villages and districts of South Vietnam had a higher combat death rate than the South Vietnamese army. The combat death rate for the RF/PF was also higher than for American units.[15] Thayer's figures lead inexorably to the conclusion that the insurgency was no sideshow to the main-force war, but an integral part of the communist strategy to defeat the Saigon government. Rather than a wrong-headed obsession as Summers alleges, the American concern with pacification, as limited as it was, was essential to the defeat of the communists.

That the United States neglected to focus its military effort on the source is another Summers assertion that is not borne out by Thayer's data. Most of the money, according to Thayer, went to fund expensive military activities, the air war and the attrition campaigns, which were largely directed against North Vietnamese military units and installations and which proved ineffective. According to data for Fiscal Year 1969, the preponderance of American expenditures went to finance the air war (47 percent), largely an interdiction effort that failed to stem the infiltration of men and supplies from North Vietnam, and the ground forces' war of attrition (30 percent), which, Thayer argues, failed to prevent the other side from exercising considerable control over its own rate of losses, from replacing its losses, or from retaining the strategic initiative inside South Vietnam.[16]

That is not to say that attrition and bombing did not seriously hurt the communists. They certainly did, but these flawed instruments, as used by the United States, were insufficient to defeat North Vietnam's military and were not integral to the key effort to build a strong South Vietnamese government and military that could compete with the communists. Not enough funds or attention were devoted to the pacification program (less than five percent in 1969), even though its goal was central to American policy.[17] Thayer's conclusion from his data underscores Komer's thesis: large American organizations involved in the war "tended to play out their institutional repertoires instead of making major adaptations to meet the situations they faced."[18]

Thayer's statistics should form a logical starting point for discussion of how the war was fought and what was achieved. Although skepticism may be warranted for specific statistics, Thayer's argument rests on the long-term patterns and trends his data disclose, some of which he believes duplicate the experience of the French in their war against the North. Additional research may invalidate or modify some of his conclusions, but to my knowledge no one else has yet even tried to assess systematically our performance in Vietnam. The time has come to understand what really happened in the war and heed the lessons. Thayer's study is a valuable starting place.

NOTES

1. Bruce Palmer, Jr., *The 25-Year War: America's Military Role in Vietnam* (Lexington: Univ. Press of Kentucky, 1984); Harry G. Summers, Jr., *On Strategy: A Critical Analysis of the Vietnam War* (Novato, Calif.: Presidio, 1982).
2. Summers, p. 65.
3. Ibid., p. 56.
4. Palmer, pp. 183-85.
5. Robert W. Komer, *Bureaucracy at War: U.S. Performance in the Vietnam Conflict* (Boulder, Colo.: Westview Press, 1986), p. 49.

6. Ibid., p. 52.
7. Ibid., p. 55.
8. In an article written before the war ended, Komer made the case for the success of the pacification program. See his "Pacification Impact on Insurgency," *Journal of International Affairs*, 25 (No. 1, 1971), 48-68.
9. Komer, *Bureaucracy at War*, p. 22.
10. Thomas Thayer, *War Without Fronts: The American Experience in Vietnam* (Boulder, Colo.: Westview Press, 1985), pp. 92-93.
11. Ibid., p. xxiii.
12. Ibid., p. 46.
13. Ibid., p. 45.
14. Ibid., pp. 45-48.
15. Ibid., pp. 119, 163.
16. Ibid., p. 25.
17. Ibid., pp. 23-24.
18. Ibid., p. 23.

This article appeared in the autumn 1986 issue of *Parameters*.

3

In Search of Lessons: The Development of a Vietnam Historiography

by JOE P. DUNN

No event in American history has inspired so many didactic pages as has the Vietnam War. Contributors include an array of journalists, academics, politicos, participants, moralists, philosophers, and protesters from every part of the political spectrum. From the first, a quest for "the lessons of Vietnam" dominated the literature. Most will agree that time and distance are prerequisites for dispassionate, definitive assessments; but the nation, caught up in one of its most divisive experiences, could not afford to wait 20 or 30 years before confronting the meaning, the lessons, and the implications of the Indochina entanglement. The history and meaning of Vietnam evolved in stages as events unfolded. Looking back, we can define these stages, focus upon the debates and prevailing issues of each period, and trace the evolution of the Vietnam historiography. Vietnam literature suffered from all the ills of "presentism" and "instant history," and much of the work was of marginal or transient value, but a portion will stand the test of time. Today, as we enter an era of serious scholarly reflection on the Vietnam experience, it appears instructive to survey the development of the Vietnam historiography with its emphasis upon meanings and lessons.

Until the early 1960's, few Americans had heard of Vietnam. Only the most politically aware knew of the French Indochina War or of America's increasing involvement with the Diem regime. Dr. Thomas Dooley's *Deliver Us From Evil: The Story of Vietnam's Flight to Freedom* (1956) was a bestseller, but readers related more to the courage and humanity of the young doctor, his emphatic anti-communism, and the plight of the poor and "backward" peoples of the world than to the political dynamics of the area.

English language scholarship on Vietnam was limited. The exhaustive bibliography of Austrian Joseph Buttinger's *The Smaller Dragon* (1958), a survey of Vietnam's history to the 20th century, contained 600 titles, including 490 in French and less than 100 in English. American students of Vietnam were rare.

Few existed other than Ellen B. Hammer and French expatriate Bernard B. Fall, authors of excellent books on the French Indochina War, and Wesley Fishel and Roy Jumper, participants in the Michigan State University team of advisors to the Diem government.

As American involvement in the war increased in the early 60's, the literature grew proportionally. Many of the early books on US participation came from the first generation of American war correspondents in Saigon. Journalists Malcom Browne, David Halberstam, and Robert Shaplen, and former diplomats John Mecklin, Robert Scigliano, and Victor Bator were critical of the Diem regime, internal Vietnamese politics, and American optimism in the face of increasing political turmoil. An Australian journalist of the left, Wilfred G. Burchett, began a series of tracts on American "neocolonialism" in Vietnam which unswervingly echoed the Hanoi line. On the other side of the coin, conservative journalists Marguerite Higgins, Anthony T. Bouscaren, and Australian Denis Warner staunchly supported Diem and advocated greater American commitment.

Bernard Fall emerged as the foremost American scholar on Vietnam. Although he became increasingly disenchanted with American policy, he did not lose his concern for the fighting men in the field. Just as he had gone into combat with the French legionnaires in the early 1950's, Fall often went on operations with American troops. In February 1967, on a mission with the Marines in the Central Highlands, he was killed by a land mine. Fall's death was tragic, for his perspective, reason, and moderation were unfortunately rare. His several books remain the best studies available on Vietnamese society and politics in the 50's and early 60's.

As American participation in the war escalated in 1965, the literature became more polemical. A new generation of "radical revisionist" historians and social scientists, dedicated to the use of scholarship for political purposes, was gaining stature in academia. To these new activist scholars – the New Left, as they came to be called – history should be employed for present purposes. Doyen of the New Left scholars, William Appleman Williams, asserted that history's great value was to help "formulate relevant and reasoned alternatives." Staughton Lynd averred that "the past is ransacked not for its own sake, but as a source of alternative models of what the future might become." Howard Zinn wanted "neither the gibberish of total recall nor the nostalgia of fond memories; we would like the past to speak wisely to our present needs."[1]

More traditional scholars warned of the dangers inherent in this approach. Otis Graham complained that often "a scholar is so influenced by contemporary political pressures . . . that he distorts the past for present purposes," and he reflected that "too many scholars go to the past as a Hanging Judge . . . and flawed history is almost invariably the result." Adam Ulam noted that many who call themselves historians might be moralists or publicists, but because they fail the test of objectivity they are not really historians in the truest sense. Political scientist Hans Morganthau proclaimed, ''I cannot escape the impression that historians tend to read more meaning into history than the historic events will support.''[2]

The New Left read much meaning into history and produced a large volume of literature on Vietnam. Although full of sound and fury, little of this writing will stand the test of time. The radical analysis suffered from hasty conclusions and superficial evidence. Leading New Left spokesmen such as Tom Hayden, Staughton Lynd, Noam Chomsky, Howard Zinn, Mary McCarthy, David Horowitz, and Daniel Berrigan considered American involvement a product of the racist, imperialist, chauvinist tendencies of a capitalist power struggling to suppress leftist ascendancy and maintain global hegemony. While they vilified Johnson, Nixon, and other political leaders, the radicals believed that Vietnam represented far more than the errors and caprices of policymakers: Vietnams were endemic to the American political economy itself. Less extreme views existed on the left as well. Sandy Vogelgesang's *The Long Dark Night of the Soul: The Intellectual Left and the Vietnam War* (1974) categorizes the various groups and portrays the evolution of their protests.

Liberal antiwar critics were as vociferous as the radicals and nearly as caustic. Liberals offered the major challenge to American Vietnam policy. Although there was no consensus among them, liberals tended to view the war simply as a mistake – the product of incorrect premises, wrong decisions, errors, misperceptions, a weak policy process, poor leadership, or bungling. Many originally supported the war. Some, such as Arthur M. Schlesinger, Jr., in *The Bitter Heritage* (1966), argued that the US stumbled into the morass. Others, such as Daniel Ellsberg in *Papers on the War* (1972), found American actions more purposeful and calculated, if erroneous. Early major liberal critiques included Theodore Draper's *Abuse of Power* (1966), William Fulbright's *The Arrogance of Power* (1966), Harrison Salisbury's *Behind the Lines – Hanoi* (1967), Ward Just's *To What End* (1968), Ernest Gruening and Herbert Beaser's *Vietnam Folly* (1968), Henry Brandon's *Anatomy of Error* (1969), Townsend Hoopes' *The Limits of Intervention* (1969), and Robert Shaplen's *The Lost Revolution* (1965) and *The Road From War* (1970).

The first two ''texts'' on the Vietnam War pursued the liberal ''mistake'' thesis. *The United States in Vietnam* (1967) by George M. Kahin and John W. Lewis chronicled the corruption, authoritarianism, and ineptitude of the South Vietnamese government, and the myths, misperceptions, and failures of American policy. Joseph Buttinger's two-volume *Vietnam: A Dragon Embattled* (1967), which brought his Vietnam history forward from *The Smaller Dragon*, did the same. In 1968, Buttinger condensed the three volumes into *Vietnam: A Political History*, a useful 500-page survey.

Studies on the origins of the Vietnamese revolutionary movement and hence the roots of the conflict, by scholars such as Paul Mus, John T. McAlister, Jean Lacouture, Dennis Duncanson, Alexander Woodside, Jean Sainteny, David G. Marr, William J. Duiker, and Robert L. Sansom, cannot be fitted neatly into categories; but they all challenged Johnson's and Nixon's explanations of the war as simplistic, pointing up American misunderstanding of the underlying forces in Vietnam.

Jonathan Schell's *Village of Ben Suc* (1967) and *The Military Half* (1968), Harvey Meyerson's *Vinh Long* (1970), Jeffrey Race's *War Comes to Long An* (1972), and F. J. West's *The Village* (1972) are tales of mistaken policy, failure, and tragic consequences. Susan Sheehan's *Ten Vietnamese* (1967), Don Luce and John Sommer's *Vietnam: The Unheard Voices* (1969), and Daniel Lang's *Casualties of War* (1969) are emotional and often moving accounts of the war's painful impact upon the Vietnamese. Donald Zagoria's *Vietnam Triangle* (1967) explores Hanoi's relations with her Soviet and Chinese allies.

The theme of the war's lessons is also prominent in the more specialized accounts of the era. Joseph C. Goulden's *Truth is the First Casualty: The Gulf of Tonkin Affair – Illusion and Reality* (1969), Gordon Winchey's *Tonkin Gulf* (1971), and Anthony Austin's *The President's War: The Story of the Tonkin Gulf Resolution and How the Nation was Trapped in Vietnam* (1971) raise questions about whether the Tonkin affair was exploited to deepen the American commitment. David Kraslow and Stuart Loory trace the several *sub rosa* peace attempts in *The Secret Search for Peace in Vietnam* (1968); Raphael Littauer and Norman Uphoff in *The Air War in Indochina* (1972) assemble a group of essays challenging the validity of the bombing policy; Don Oberdorfer's *Tet!* (1971) is a first-rate journalistic treatment of the 1968 communist offensive; and Richard Boyle's *The Flower of the Dragon* (1972) is one of the better examples of a large literature on the impairment of the American military in the post-Tet period.

The My Lai massacre, which occurred during Tet 1968, raised more questions, anguish, and debate, thus evoking more lessons of the war, than any other single event. Seymour Hersh's *My Lai Four* (1970) and *Cover-Up* (1971); Richard Hammer's *One Morning in the War* (1970); the *Report of the Department of the Army Review of the Preliminary Investigation into the My Lai Incident* (1970), known as the Peers Report; and *The My Lai Massacre and Cover-Up* (1976) edited by Joseph Goldstein et al., tell the story. Retired Lieutenant General W. R. Peers' *The My Lai Inquiry* (1979) is now the definitive account of that tragic episode. Telford Taylor's *Nuremburg and Vietnam* (1970); *Crimes of War* (1971) edited by Richard A. Falk, Gabriel Kolko, and Robert Jay Lifton; Falk's four-volume *The Vietnam War and International Law* (1967-76); John N. Moore's *Law and the Indo-China War* (1972); and the postwar collection edited by Peter D. Trooboff, *Law and Responsibility in Warfare: The Vietnam Experience* (1975), discuss war crimes in larger context.

Among the hundreds of books of this era, two stand out as Vietnam classics. Each was somewhat premature and each has flaws, but each develops a sophisticated interpretation of America's entanglement and addresses the lessons of the experience. David Halberstam's *The Best and the Brightest* (1972) explains America's descent into the Vietnam quagmire as the legacy of a cold-war mentality shared by a cadre of policy elites who, like the Presidents they served, suffered from idealism, machismo, hubris, and an excessively optimistic "can do" attitude. These intellectual, driving, success-oriented managers, "the best and the brightest" that the nation had to offer, believed unflaggingly that commitment and will would bring success. American policy, according to Halberstem, was neither sinister nor self-seeking; rather it was mechanistic, incremental, and sanguine. The rationale was that of always pursuing "the next logical step." Interwoven among the author's biographical glimpses of policy elites and his fascinating vignettes, which make the book one of the most readable on Vietnam, Halberstam's lessons are clear. The book is an indictment of the cold-war warrior manifestations of postwar liberalism and a petition for a more open, democratic, pragmatic policy process. Concentrating on men and decisions rather than on larger social and economic forces, it is the ultimate liberal manifesto.

While Halberstam focuses upon the American side, Frances Fitzgerald's *Fire in the Lake* (1972), winner of the Pulitzer Prize, the National Book Award, and the Bancroft Prize in History, concentrates on Vietnamese culture and society. Fitzgerald, a journalist with two Vietnam tours to her credit, was steeped in the literature of Chinese and Vietnamese society and deeply influenced by her mentor Paul Mus, the leading student of Vietnamese religion and culture; she contends that America misunderstood the revolutionary process in Vietnam. The National Liberation Front operated in accord with Vietnamese social structure and the Confucian *tao*, while the US and the westernized government of Vietnam destroyed traditionalism and broke the bonds of society. In effect, according to Fitzgerald, the US attempted to transform a traditional Asian society to fit the American mold. Lyndon Johnson could not understand why Asians did not think and respond as Americans would; the results were tragic. Fitzgerald writes with balance and restraint; if her thought-provoking argument is correct, the lessons are numerous. While not the definitive word, *Fire in the Lake* will remain one of the classic studies.

The war also had its defenders, particularly among policymakers and military leaders. Much of Lyndon Johnson's *The Vantage Point* (1971) defended his Vietnam policies. Unfortunately, the bland and superficial book is among the worst Presidential memoirs in print. General William Westmoreland and Admiral U. S. Grant Sharp's *Report of the War in Vietnam* (1969), and the memoirs of Maxwell Taylor, Edward Lansdale, and civilian policymakers Walt Rostow and Robert Komer defended American efforts and proclaimed lessons quite different from those of the war critics. Frank Trager's *Why Vietnam?*, one of the few defenses of the war by an academic, is not a strong work. Chester Cooper's *The Lost Crusade* (1970), one of the best books written on Vietnam during this era, criticized many Vietnam War policies, but the book is primarily a sympathetic chronicle of America's long and frustrating search for a negotiated peace. Foreign Service and CIA officer Douglas Pike's *Viet Cong* (1966), *War, Peace, and The Viet Cong* (1969), and *The Viet Cong Strategy of Terror* (1970) challenged many of the romantic myths about the Vietnamese communists. Howard R. Penniman's *Elections in South Vietnam* (1972) did the same.

Predictably, the end of the war triggered a new round of scholarship. Alexander Kendrick's *The Wound Within* (1974), focussing on the internal impact of the war on America, was the first such survey through the 1973 Paris accords. Weldon A. Brown's *Prelude to Disaster* (1975) and sequel *The Last Chopper* (1976) together complete the story of the Vietnam experience through "the final days." Brown's lessons of the Vietnam experience are presented in themes of feeble and vacillating leadership, lack of national resolve and will, and moral opprobrium for a nation gone soft. Anthony T. Bouscaren's anthology *All Quiet on the Eastern Front* (1976) and Louis A. Fanning's *Betrayal in Vietnam* (1976) are bitterly condemnatory of America's withdrawal. William Corson's work, *The Consequences of Failure* (1974), is an impassioned, critical, but thoughtful examination of the adverse effects of US capitulation.

More useful appraisals include Anthony Lake's collection of post-mortems, *The Legacy of Vietnam* (1976); Allan R. Millett's collected end-of-the-war commentaries in *The Washington Post* in 1973 and 1975, entitled *A Short History of the Vietnam War* (1978); Peter A. Poole's slim text, *Eight Presidents and Indochina* (1978); and George C. Herring's *The United States and Vietnam, 1950-1975* (1980). Dave Richard Palmer admits that his military history, *Summons of the Trumpet: U.S.-Vietnam in Perspective* (1978), is far from definitive, but it is an interesting attempt to address the military lessons of the conflict. Palmer notes that he strove to write as a historian, but the viewpoint of the book is that of a soldier. In the soldier's perspective, the military bore the onus for poor policies and lack of direction from the civilian policy sector.

Cliché has it that no nation can develop its full military potential until it has lost a war. Long before the denouement, the military was preoccupied with the lessons of the Vietnam experience. In the late 1960's, following the precedents of World War II and the Korean War, each service initiated extensive historical programs on all phases of the involvement. A number of volumes were published by the Government Printing Office before the war ended. Topics included the role of field artillery, financial management of the war, medical support, base development, logistics, military intelligence, and riverine operations. Ambitious postwar projects already in print include the first volumes of multi-volume histories published by the Navy, the Marines, and the Coast Guard. The first in the Army's 21-volume series will appear sometime after 1980.

Traditionally, the lessons of war figure prominently in the accounts of its leaders. General William C. Westmoreland's *A Soldier Reports* (1976) and Admiral U. S. Grant Sharp's *Strategy for Defeat: Vietnam in Retrospect* (1978) emphasize the political restraints and impediments which hindered the military in Vietnam. Westmoreland is candid but philosophical; Sharp is more outspoken and bitter. Lieutenant Colonel Anthony Herbert's *Soldier* (1973) is bitter for different reasons. Herbert, the most decorated enlisted man of the

Korean War, became a critic of the Vietnam conflict; his protests of alleged war atrocities led to his involuntary retirement.

On a more analytic plane is the effort of retired Brigadier General Douglas Kinnard, veteran of two Vietnam tours, who mailed questionnaires to the 173 US Army general officers who held commands in Vietnam between 1965 and 1972. From the 64 percent who responded, some rough generalizations emerged. Kinnard's *The War Managers* (1977) found the generals satisfied with the professionalism of Army personnel and with theater-level military performance, but dissatisfied with Washington's managerial control of the war and with the overall combat effectiveness of the armed services. The generals were notably pessimistic about the quality of the forces and leadership of the Army of the Republic of Vietnam; they had little confidence that the ARVN could defend the country. Also, Kinnard found a consensus among the generals that media coverage of the war was irresponsible and disruptive.

At about the time of Kinnard's survey, the Fletcher School of Law and Diplomacy sponsored a symposium on "The Military Lessons of the Vietnamese War." Participants included academic scholars and such military and civilian policymakers as William Westmoreland, Edward Lansdale, Paul Nitze, Robert Komer, Barry Zorthian, Elmo Zumwalt, George Keegan, and Sir Robert Thompson. W. Scott Thompson and Donaldson D. Frizzell collected many of the papers and excerpts from the discussions in a book entitled *The Lessons of Vietnam* (1977), which, like Kinnard's study, addresses fundamental issues and provides candid assessments of errors and failures. Both books, compiled in the interim between the US troop withdrawal in 1973 and the fall of South Vietnam in 1975, are significant early assessments of the war experience.

Also a product of this interim period, Robert Gallucci's *Neither War Nor Peace: The Politics of American Military Policy in Vietnam* (1975) is a sophisticated study of the problems, pitfalls, limitations, and conflicts of the policymaking process. Beginning with the premise that the Vietnam entanglement represented unwise policy, Gallucci focuses upon the decisionmaking process, how the involvement in Vietnam continued, and why policy decisions did not accomplish their aims. The implications of this excellent study of bureaucratic politics go far beyond Indochina.

The war literature by ordinary participants is increasing. Tim O'Brien's *If I Die in a Combat Zone* (1973), Ron Kovic's *Born on the Fourth of July* (1976), Charles R. Anderson's *The Grunts* (1976), Philip Caputo's *A Rumor of War* (1977), and iconoclastic journalist Michael Herr's *Dispatches* (1977) are recent examples. C. D. B. Bryan's *Friendly Fire* (1976), the story of an Iowa farm family's search for the truth about how their son died in Vietnam, reveals a basic truth: the dearth of information about their son's death resulted from neither a conspiracy nor a cover-up; it was merely the product of the red-tape, bureaucracy, and inertia which plagued the larger war effort.

The postwar memoirs of Nguyen Cao Ky, Saigon politician Trans Van Don,

veteran Australian Saigon journalist Denis Warner, and victorious North
Vietnamese Generals Vo Nguyen Giap and Van Tien Dung, differ in lessons
and meanings of the Vietnam experience. *RN: The Memoirs of Richard Nixon*
(1978) turns from Watergate long enough to defend Vietnam policies. William
Colby's *Honorable Men* (1978), both memoir and apologia for the CIA,
concentrates on the several years that the former Director of Central
Intelligence spent in Vietnam. *White House Years* (1979) by Henry Kissinger, a
massive memoir of 1552 pages, addresses the critical period from 1969 to 1973.
The forthcoming memoir by Peter Arnett, a prize-winning Associated Press
reporter who was in and out of Vietnam from 1962 through 1975, should also
be instructive, while Stephen T. Hosmer's *The Fall of South Vietnam: Statements by
Vietnamese Military and Civilian Leaders* (1978) is a useful compendium of
proposed lessons.

A host of more specialized works also address lessons. These include Shingo
Shibata's *Lessons of the Vietnam War: Philosophical Considerations on the Vietnam
Revolution* (1973); Allan E. Goodman's *Politics in War* (1973); Abram Chayes et
al., *Vietnam Settlement: Why 1973, Not 1969?* (1973); Charles A. Joiner's *The
Politics of Massacre* (1974); Jeffrey S. Milstein's quantitative study on the
interrelationship of policy, public opinion, costs, and military strategy,
Dynamics of the Vietnam War (1974); Gareth D. Porter's anti-Vietnamese-
Government account of the Paris accords and aftermath, *A Peace Denied* (1975);
Robert Warren Steven's *Vain Hopes, Grim Realities: The Economic Consequences of
the War* (1976); Benjamin F. Schemmer's examination of the heroic but
abortive attempt to rescue the American POWs at Son Tay, *The Raid* (1976);
Herbert Y. Schandler's *The Unmaking of a President: Lyndon Johnson and Vietnam*
(1977); Gloria Emerson's Bancroft Prize-winning, *Winners and Losers* (1977);
Douglas Blaufarb's *The Counter-Insurgency Era* (1977); Stephen A. Garrett's
Ideals and Reality: An Analysis of the Debate Over Vietnam (1978); Gregory Palmer's
The McNamara Strategy and the Vietnam War (1978); and Jaya K. Baral's *The
Pentagon and the Making of U.S. Foreign Policy: A Case Study of Vietnam, 1960-1968*
(1978).

The number of memoirs by former prisoners of war continues to grow, with
the quality varying greatly, John Hubbell's *POW: A Definitive History of the
American Prisoner of War Experience in Vietnam, 1964–1973* (1977) is less
monumental than the overblown title would suggest, but at present it is the
most thorough work. The Center for POW Studies of the Naval Health
Research Center is conducting interviews with former prisoners of war which
should expand our knowledge. Navy Captain Douglas L. Clarke's *The Missing
Man* (1979) discusses the too-often overlooked men listed as missing in action.

The literature on the Vietnam-era draft is also extensive but mostly of
minimal value. Lawrence M. Baskir and William A. Strauss' *Chance and
Circumstance: The Draft, The War and The Vietnam Generation* (1978) attempts a
comprehensive overview. The saga of inequities, chaos, discrimination, and
ineptitude of the system details lessons that may increase in importance if the

draft is resurrected. Studies of the Vietnam veteran include Robert J. Lifton's *Home from the War – Vietnam Veterans* (1973); John Helmer's *Bringing the War Home* (1974); Paul Starr et al., *The Discarded Army* (1974); Jan Barry and W. D. Ehrhart's *Demilitarized Zones: Veterans After Vietnam* (1976); and Charles R. Figley, editor, *Stress Disorders Among Vietnam Veterans* (1978).

The spring of 1975, when America finally came to "the end of the tunnel," was a time for reflection and introspection. Perspectives on the final days before the fall and life in communist Vietnam differed greatly; the plight of the boat people and their accounts of present life in the Socialist Republic of Vietnam have continued the controversy. Eyewitness accounts of the fall and aftermath include John Pilger's pictorial *The Last Day* (1975), Tiziano Terzani's *Giai Phong: The Fall and Liberation of Saigon* (1976), Alan Dawson's *55 Days: The Fall of Vietnam* (1977), Wilfred Burchett's *Grasshoppers and Elephants: Why Vietnam Fell* (1977), and Earl S. Martin's *Reaching the Other Side: The Journal of an American Who Stayed to Witness Vietnam's Postwar Transition* (1978). Bernard and Marvin Kalb, Paul Steube, and Karl Jackson are all working on books dealing with the days before and after the fall of South Vietnam. Darell Montero and Marsha I. Weber's *Vietnamese Americans* (1978) and Gail P. Kelley's *From Vietnam to America* (1978) deal with the settlement of refugees in the US.

Robert F. Turner's *Vietnamese Communism* (1975) and Douglas Pike's brief *History of the Vietnamese Communist Party* (1978) are important updates of the earlier studies by Pike, Bernard Fall, P. J. Honey, Jean Lacouture, George Tanham, Joseph J. Zasloff, and Dennis Duncanson. Further work is progressing on communist strategic thinking, the Vietnamese Communist Party and its grass-roots ties in the south, the People's Army of Vietnam, the history of the National Liberation Front, Vietnamese communist leadership, Marxist doctrine in Vietnam in the 1950's, and Vietnamese peasant organizations.[3]

The most important book on the final days now in print is former CIA analyst Frank Snepp's controversial *Decent Interval* (1978). Among the last to leave beleaguered Saigon, Snepp witnessed the chaos and travesty of the final weeks and days. After the evacuation, Snepp sought permission to compile an after-action report, an account of the lessons of the experience. When his request was repeatedly denied, Snepp, in violation of his CIA oath of secrecy, wrote and published the book without authorization. Snepp argues that Ambassador Graham Martin and CIA Station Chief Thomas Polgar bear grave responsibility for the delayed and bungled evacuation because they misread the crisis and exercised poor leadership. While all Americans were safely evacuated, thousands of loyal Vietnamese employees were left behind, while sensitive files – including lists of Vietnamese with American intelligence affiliations – were abandoned intact. Without endorsing Snepp's actions, it can be acknowledged that this is a story which needed to be told. The book presents little threat to national security, but it is a devastating exposé of individuals and agencies.

The final days of Cambodia soon followed those of Vietnam. John Barron and Anthony Paul's *Murder of a Gentle Land* (1977) and François Ponchaud's *Cambodia: Year Zero* (1978) – originally published in French in 1976 – reveal the brutal genocide conducted by the conquering Khmer Rouge. While the Khmer Rouge bear total responsibility for their barbarism, British journalist William Shawcross's *Sideshow: Kissinger, Nixon and the Destruction of Cambodia* (1979) contends that US actions accelerated the communist takeover. The book is a slashing attack on Nixon and Kissinger's handling of Cambodian policy, particularly with regard to the Cambodian incursion of 1970. For Shawcross, "Cambodia was not a mistake; it was a crime"; it was a capsule repetition of the arrogance and errors of Vietnam which demonstrated that leaders had learned little from the earlier experience. The fall of Cambodia did not result from the cutoff of US aid in August 1973, according to Shawcross; it was set in motion three years earlier with the US incursion. The book touched some sensitive nerves – Henry Kissinger revised his memoir chapters on Cambodia to refute Shawcross' charges. Finally, Roy Rowan's *Four Days of the Mayaguez* (1975) and Richard G. Head's *Crises Resolution* (1978), a case study in crisis management, treat the *Mayaguez* incident.

After a decade of virtual consensus against the war and the institutionalization of many antiwar clichés, a mild revisionism is emerging which accepts the goals but questions the means. Some of the most entrenched stereotypes are being reexamined and new lessons posited. The most important book of this new genre, Peter Braestrup's *Big Story* (1977), may become one of the classics of Vietnam literature. Braestrup, a Korean War veteran who was the Saigon Station Chief for *The Washington Post* in 1968, addresses the question of why the Tet offensive was misinterpreted by the American press. Students now agree that the 1968 offensive resulted in the worst military defeat suffered by the communists during the war. Lyndon Johnson and the military claimed this at the time. Yet the American people received a much different picture, for the press portrayed the offensive as a decisive communist victory and a disaster for American and ARVN forces. This erroneous coverage contributed to the downfall of Johnson and complicated the entire American extrication process.

Braestrup pulls no punches in his outspoken account. He acknowledges that the awesome power of the press was not always employed responsibly in Vietnam; but considering the problems involved, he believes that the overall record was good. Most correspondents in Vietnam were not qualified for their positions as war reporters. They lacked military experience and did not comprehend the complexity of warfare. Although Vietnam appeared to be inundated with correspondents and journalists, individual bureaus were too understaffed to handle the constant demand for dramatic reportage. The trend toward news as entertainment exacerbated the situation. These demands and expectations led to hasty reports and overblown analyses. Compelled to pose as authorities "dominating what they described," television commentators were often speculative in their analyses, proclaiming more than they really knew or could know. Preoccupied with impact, television relied on short filmed vignettes as microcosms of the larger war, a technique that inevitably introduced distortion. Attempts by military information sources to orchestrate news flow further contributed to superficial assessments. Finally, Braestrup faults senior editors for their lack of leadership and guidance in moderating the natural overzealousness of the younger reporters caught up in the maelstrom of the war.

Even though the handling of Tet was an aberration, it could happen again, Braestrup warns; thus he considers it imperative to record the lessons of the experience. The book belongs in American journalism school curriculums and has much to contribute to the larger understanding of Vietnam and its lessons. Lawrence Lichty's forthcoming history of television coverage of war may prove a valuable companion piece.

The Irony of Vietnam (1979) by Leslie H. Gelb and Richard K. Betts ranks with *Big Story* as another of the most significant books on Vietnam of recent years. The authors challenge the liberal "quagmire" thesis that the US stumbled into Vietnam through miscalculation, inadequate policy process, and limited policy options. On the contrary, the authors argue that the decision process functioned well, providing varied options and assessments of the costs, probabilities for success, and the implications of the various alternatives. The problem did not come from the process but from the choices pursued by presidents and other policymakers. Kennedy and Johnson knowingly opted for limited-objective alternatives calculated as the minimal steps necessary not to lose. With the passage of time and gradual escalation, presidents, Congress, the press, and the public "both reinforced the stakes against losing and introduced constraints against winning." Washington attempted to wear down the enemy at least cost. This strategy led to the rejection of the more decisive recommendations of senior military advisors and the adoption of incremental escalation. Such an approach played into the enemy's hands, for their protracted war strategy was to drag out the conflict and make it increasingly costly to the US. Hanoi's total resolve and complete commitment to ultimate victory was never fully appreciated. The authors conclude that the basic lesson of Vietnam is the need for pragmatism rather than doctrines, formulas, ideologies, or structural changes in the decision process.

In its careful analysis of the peace process, Allan E. Goodman's *The Lost Peace* (1978) reiterates the themes of Gelb and Betts. Contray to critics' claims, Johnson and Nixon were fully committed to a negotiated settlement, one that preserved the status quo antebellum; but, Goodman claims, this minimal goal was never a real option. Committed to nothing less than total victory, Hanoi never compromised their objective. Washington sought the fruits of military victory without actually having to achieve one. North Vietnam realized that negotiating while fighting was in their interest and that the US would not penalize them for this tactic. Indeed, the longer the war dragged on, the greater were American concessions in each peace proposal. Hanoi skillfully manipulated the negotiating process, hinting at concessions in public while rejecting them in private. This tactic further eroded American public acceptance of the war and garnered new concessions, which in turn widened the breach between Saigon and Washington. The result was a peace treaty amounting to nothing more than a face-saving device for US extrication; only the most optimistic could hold any hope for the success of South Vietnam. The lessons of Goodman's study are clear.

The most controversial of the new revisionist accounts, Guenter Lewy's *America in Vietnam* (1978), has caused a storm among liberal reviewers. One responds: "Every war is fought twice – first militarily and then, especially among the losers, politically and intellectually. Guenter Lewy's book is the first salvo in the refighting of the Vietnam War."[4] Others have branded the work a whitewash, an apology for the war, and a selling of the war. Lewy, a respected political scientist and author of several highly acclaimed works primarily in political philosophy, is the first scholar to receive "historian's access" to the voluminous military records of the war. From his extensive work in these unclassified and declassified records, he concludes that American policy in Vietnam was unwise and inept – the conventional military approach to a revolutionary situation was a hopeless failure – but in contradiction to the claims of many antiwar critics, American actions were neither illegal under international law nor immoral. The author's extensive data and statistics well illustrate his thesis and refute the cherished stereotypes of leftist commentators.

Lewy is critical of academics who forsook their obligation to engage in dispassionate and rational scholarship to become ideologues and propagandists. He accuses many of his colleagues of exaggeration, reliance upon dubious sources of information, and commitment to prejudices and *a priori* assumptions rather than objective analysis of the evidence. Lewy's critics counter with the same charges against him. Lewy's book breaks new ground, provides new evidence, and has helped to revive the Vietnam debate. Along with the other postwar revisionist studies, it makes major contributions to the continuing search for the lessons of Vietnam.

Finally, as with most wars, Vietnam has inspired a large body of fictional literature, including some first-rate novels and short stories. *Free Fire Zone: Short Stories by Vietnam Veterans* (1973), edited by Wayne Karlin et al., and *Writing Under Fire: Stories of the Vietnam War* (1978), edited by Jerome Klinkowitz and John Somer, are interesting collections.[5] Hollywood was originally wary, the subject being considered box office anathema. But the passing of time has turned the pain and anguish into nostalgia, and a new generation which does not remember the trauma of the war is becoming increasingly interested in the subject. Several Vietnam movies in the last year have enjoyed critical acclaim and financial success, including the winner of the Academy Award for best picture of 1978, *The Deer Hunter*; runner-up, *Coming Home*; and the current extravaganza, *Apocalypse Now*. Other Vietnam movie productions are in progress. Julian Smith's book *Looking Away: Hollywood and Vietnam* (1975), attempts unsuccessfully to argue that war movies after World War II created a climate conducive to the American involvement in Vietnam.

In an oft-quoted maxim, George Santayana reminded us that "those who cannot remember the past are condemned to repeat it." Some would argue that Gaddis Smith's rejoinder is more applicable: "One of the most somber aspects of the study of history is that it suggests no obvious ways by which mankind could have avoided folly."[6] In either case, the search for knowledge, meaning, and the lessons of Vietnam will continue.

NOTES

1. William A. Williams, "History as a Way of Learning," in *The Contours of American History* (Chicago: Quadrangle, 1966), p. 19; Staughton Lynd, "A Profession of History," *The New Journal*, 12 November 1970, 12; Howard Zinn, "Introduction," in *New Deal Thought*, ed. Howard Zinn (Indianapolis: Bobbs-Merrill, 1966), p. xv.
2. Otis L. Graham, Jr., "New Deal Historiography: Retrospect and Prospect," in *The New Deal: The Critical Issues*, ed. Otis L. Graham, Jr. (Boston: Little, Brown, 1971), pp. 171-72; Adam Ulam, "On Modern History: Re-reading the Cold War," *Interplay*, 2 (March 1969), p. 51; Hans J. Morganthau, "Rejoinder," in *The Origins of the Cold War*, by Lloyd C. Gardner, Arthur Schlesinger, Jr., and Hans J. Morganthau (Waltham, Mass.: Ginn-Blaisdell, 1970), p. 119.
3. The references to forthcoming books noted at various points in the article are drawn from Peter Braestrup, "Vietnam as History," *The Wilson Quarterly*, 2 (Spring, 1978), 178-87, and Douglas Pike's letter to the editor in response, *The Wilson Quarterly*, 2 (Summer 1978), 191-92.
4. Michael Walzer, rev. of *America in Vietnam*, by Guenter Lewy, in *The New Republic*, 11 November 1978, pp. 31-34.
5. For a bibliography of novels and short fiction, see Philip D. Beidler, "The Vietnam Novel: An Overview, with a Brief Checklist of Vietnam War Narrative," *Southern Humanities Review*, 12 (Winter 1978), 45-55.
6. Gaddis Smith, *American Diplomacy During the Second World War: 1941-1945* (New York: Wiley, 1965), p. 177.

This article appeared in the December 1979 issue of *Parameters*.
A bibliography of Vietnam literature to that date was listed at the conclusion of the article.

II. THE STRATEGY AND NATURE OF THE VIETNAM WAR

4

A Strategic Perception of the Vietnam War

by HARRY G. SUMMERS, JR.

There is a famous Jules Feiffer cartoon in which one of the characters, having just made what he believes to be the telling point of a long and involved argument, is devastated by the riposte "Now let us define your terms." To avoid such a fate, it is best to define your terms in advance, and for this particular argument the main term to be defined is "strategic," for there is a fundamental difference between strategic perceptions of the Vietnam War and historical perceptions of that conflict.

Military strategy is officially defined as "the art and science of employing the armed forces of a nation to secure the objectives of national policy by the application of force, or the threat of force."[1] Strategic appraisal of the Vietnam War, therefore, would properly involve an examination of that war through the application of theoretical principles to both the military means employed and the political ends that were to be achieved, not only to account for success or failure but also to revalidate the principles themselves. Carl von Clausewitz, that master theoretician on the nature and conduct of war, labeled this process "critical analysis," a procedure that involves three different intellectual activities.

The first of these is "the discovery and interpretation of equivocal facts . . . historical research proper." Then there is "the tracing of effects back to their causes." Up to this point, historical and strategic analysis travel the same path, for most military historians would agree that these first two intellectual activities accurately describe the nature of their profession. But with the next intellectual activity the paths diverge. The third process is "the investigation and evaluation of means employed," and Clausewitz went on to say that "critical analysis is not only an evaluation of the means employed, but of *all possible means* . . . . One can, after all, not condemn a method without being able to suggest a better alternative."[2]

What this divergence of paths tells us is that while the test of a work of military history is the degree to which it accurately portrays precisely what happened and why, military theory is tested "by the application of theoretical truths to actual events." "Here," Clausewitz said, "theory serves history, or rather the lessons to be drawn from history."[3] Simply put, military history provides us with a set of answers. Military theory, on the other hand, provides what our current doctrinal manuals describe as "military planning interrogatories – a set of questions that should be considered if military strategy is to best serve the national interest."[4]

THE FIRST STRATEGIC QUESTION

In *On War* Clausewitz emphasized that

the first, the supreme, the most far-reaching act of judgment that the statesman and commander have to make is to establish . . . the kind of war on which they are embarking; neither mistaking it for, nor trying to turn it into, something that is alien to its nature. This is the first of all strategic questions and the most comprehensive.[5]

Practically from the beginning of our involvement in Vietnam, the received "theoretical truth" was that the conflict there was a *revolutionary* war. Sir Robert Thompson, British expert on insurgent warfare, explained how revolutionary war differed from conventional war:

Revolutionary war is most confused with guerrilla or partisan warfare. Here the main difference is that guerrilla warfare is designed merely to harass and distract the enemy so that the regular forces can reach a decision in conventional battles . . . . Revolutionary war on the other hand is designed to reach a decisive result on its own.[6]

With this "new kind of war," conventional military histories were deemed useless, and the classic theories and principles of war derived from these histories by Clausewitz, Jomini, Liddell Hart, J. F. C. Fuller, and others were considered irrelevant. They had been replaced by the works of Mao Tse-tung and Vo Nguyen Giap on revolutionary war and the theories of academic "counterinsurgency experts."

The model for such a war was not derived from our then-recent experience in Korea where we also had fought to contain communist expansion, but from the British experience in Malaysia. As British researcher Gregory Palmer noted:

The official view supported by the advice of Diem's British Advisor, Sir Robert Thompson, was that the appropriate strategy was counterinsurgency with emphasis on depriving the enemy of the support of the population by resettlement, pacification, good administration, and propaganda.[7]

Counterinsurgency doctrines thus channeled our attention toward the internal affairs of the South Vietnamese government rather than toward the external threat.

Clausewitz observed that "we see things in the light of their result, and to some extent, come to know and appreciate them fully only because of it."[8] If we apply the theoretical truths of revolutionary war to the actual events of the Vietnam War, we find that they do not fit. The Viet Cong did not achieve decisive results on their own. Instead, their actions fit Sir Robert Thompson's description of "guerrilla or partisan warfare" almost exactly – they harassed, distracted, and wore down the United States and South Vietnam so that by 1975 the regular forces of North Vietnam could reach a decision in conventional battles. In the Afterword to a collection of papers presented at a 1973-74 colloquium on "The Military Lessons of the Vietnam War" at the Fletcher School of Law and Diplomacy, where more than 30 distinguished military and civilian panelists discussed the merits of counterinsurgency, panel organizers Air Force Colonel Donald D. Frizzell and Professor W. Scott Thompson sadly concluded:

There is a great irony in the fact that the North Vietnamese finally won by purely conventional means, using precisely the kind of warfare at which the American army was best equipped to fight . . . . In their lengthy battle accounts that followed Hanoi's great military victory, Generals Giap and Dung barely mentioned the contribution of local forces.[9]

Only in retrospect is it obvious that the North Vietnamese used the smokescreen of revolutionary war to hide their true intentions. Part of this smokescreen was the so-called National Liberation Front, which was portrayed as an indigenous South Vietnamese organization leading the revolutionary war against the Saigon regime. With victory long since won, the North Vietnamese have not bothered to keep up this pretense and now freely admit that the NLF was their own creation. In a French television documentary broadcast on 16 February 1983, North Vietnamese Generals Vo Nguyen Giap and Vo Bam freely admitted their subterfuge. As reported by *The Economist*,

General Bam admitted the decision to unleash an armed revolt against the Saigon government was taken by a North Vietnamese communist party plenum in 1959. This was a year before the National Liberation Front was set up in South Vietnam. The aim, General Bam added, was 'to reunite the country'. So much for that myth that the Vietcong was an autonomous southern force which spontaneously decided to rise against the oppression of the Diem regime. And General Bam should know. As a result of the decision, he was given the job of opening up an infiltration trail in the south. The year was still 1959. That was two years before President Kennedy stepped up American support for Diem by sending 685 advisers to South Vietnam. So much for the story that the Ho Chi Minh trail was established only to counteract the American military build-up . . . . General Bam got his orders on May 19, 1959. 'Absolute secrecy, absolute security were our watchwords,' he recalled.[10]

It is not surprising that we were deceived, for many South Vietnamese members of the NLF were equally deluded. But now the denouements of former NLF leaders such as Truong Nhu Tang[11] provide valuable sources for "the discovery and interpretation of equivocal facts [and] the tracings of effects back to their causes." With such a reexamination it will become increasingly apparent that, unlike the First Indochina War between France and Viet Minh, which *was* a revolutionary war, the Second Indochina War between North Vietnam and South Vietnam was, in the final analysis, more a conventional war best understood in terms of classic military theories and principles. Among these are the principles of the *Objective*, and of *Mass*, *Maneuver*, and *Economy of Force*.[12]

THE OBJECTIVE

"No one starts a war," wrote Clausewitz, "or rather, no one in his senses ought to do so – without first being clear in his mind what he intends to achieve by that war and how he intends to conduct it."[13] Since 1921 this warning has been incorporated into the Army's doctrine as the first Principle of War – the principle of the Objective.[14] In the words of the current Army doctrine manual

As a derivative of the political aim, the *strategic military objective* of a nation at war must be to apply whatever degree of force is necessary to allow attainment of the political purpose or aim for which the war is being fought . . . . It is essential . . . that the political purpose be clearly defined *and* attainable by the considered application of the various elements of the nation's power. Not until the political purpose has been determined and defined by the President and the Congress can strategic and tactical objectives be clearly identified and developed. Once developed, the strategic objectives must constantly be subjected to rigorous analysis and review to insure that they continue to reflect accurately not only the ultimate political end desired, but also any political constraints imposed on the application of military force.[15]

As with our failure to determine accurately the nature of the war in Vietnam, the application of this strategic principle seems never to have been one marked by precision and consistency – as the actual events of American participation amply illustrate. Examining the *official* justifications most often cited from 1949 through 1967 for America's involvement in Indochina, Professor Hugh M. Arnold found that, compared to the *one* North Vietnamese objective of total control over all of Indochina, there were some 22 separate American rationales.[16] None of them focused on how the war was to be ended. When Secretary of Defense Clark Clifford took office in 1968, he complained that no one in the Defense Department could tell him what constituted victory. No one could tell him of a plan to win the war.[17] This confusion over objectives had a devastating effect on our ability to conduct the war. As Brigadier General Douglas Kinnard found in a 1974 survey of Army generals who had commanded in Vietnam, "Almost 70 percent of the Army generals who managed the war were uncertain of its objectives." Kinnard went on to say that such uncertainty "mirrors a deep-seated strategic failure: the inability of policy-makers to frame tangible, obtainable goals."[18]

Vietnam-era military theorists not only failed to set objectives, they also deliberately excluded the American public from the strategic equation. Theorists went so far as to say that military strategies ought to be pursued even when they are opposed by the American people.[19] This approach not only violated our American political and military heritage and both the intent and letter of the Constitution, it also violated a fundamental precept of war. Modern warfare, Clausewitz emphasized, consists of "a remarkable trinity" of the people, the army, and the government. "A theory that ignores any one of them . . . would conflict with reality to such an extent that for this reason alone it would be totally useless.''[20] As he would have predicted, the effect of the deliberate exclusion of the American people as a prime consideration in strategic planning was deadly. In the Vietnam War, unlike previous American conflicts, the American people were being asked to bear the cost of a war whose ''value'' had neither been fixed nor adequately justified by their government. One hundred fifty years earlier Clausewitz had warned:

Since war is not an act of senseless passion but is controlled by its political object, the value of this object must determine the sacrifices to be made for it in *magnitude* and also in *duration*.[21]

In words that seem to have been written to explain Vietnam, he went on to say, ''Once the expenditure of effort exceeds the value of the political object, the object must be renounced.''[22] Our failure to understand and apply the principle of the objective and the other fundamentals of war created a strategic vulnerability that was to prove fatal to American war efforts.

MASS, MANEUVER, AND ECONOMY OF FORCE

Faulty strategic thinking, not surprisingly, led to faulty military operations in the field. The primary principles that govern battlefield operations are *Mass* (the concentration of combat power at the decisive place and time), *Economy of Force* (the allocation of minimum essential combat power to secondary efforts), and *Maneuver* (the placing of the enemy in a position of disadvantage through the flexible application of combat power).[23] In theory, these three principles operate in concert against what Clausewitz called the enemy's center of gravity – ''the hub of all power and movement on which everything depends.'' The center of gravity can be a tangible, such as the enemy's army, its territory, or its capital, but it also can be something abstract, such as the community of interests of an alliance, the personality of a leader, or public opinion. Once identified, the center of gravity becomes the focal point against which all military energies should be directed.[24]

Because we failed to correctly identify the nature of the war, we also failed to identify the center of gravity for that war. Because we misperceived the Vietnam War as a revolutionary war, we saw the Viet Cong as the center of gravity. Our efforts were massed against this guerrilla enemy in search-and-destroy and pacification efforts, while we used an economy of force against the North Vietnamese regular forces. Contrary to popular opinion, these efforts against the Viet Cong had considerable military success. This was especially true during the Tet Offensive of 1968 in which the Viet Cong guerrillas surfaced, led the attacks on South Vietnamese cities, and were virtually destroyed in the process. Former NLF member Truong Nhu Tang called it ''a military debacle.'' ''The truth was,'' he said, ''that Tet cost us half of our forces. Our losses were so immense that we were simply unable to replace them with new recruits.''[25] But even after the Viet Cong were virtually eliminated, the war continued unabated for another seven years.

We had selected the wrong center of gravity. The key was not the Viet Cong or the allegiance of the South Vietnamese people. ''Like us, Hanoi failed to win the 'hearts and minds' of the South Vietnamese peasantry,'' Colonel Stuart Herrington wrote in his account of counterinsurgency operations. ''Unlike us, Hanoi's leaders were able to compensate for this failure by playing their trump card – they overwhelmed South Vietnam with a twenty-two division force.''[26] The results of the war clearly demonstrate that the primary enemy was the North Vietnamese regular army; the Viet Cong were never more than a secondary force. As Norman Hannah, the former State Department political advisor to the Commander-in-Chief, Pacific Command (the war's strategic commander), put it, ''We responded mainly to Hanoi's simulated insurgency rather than to its real, but controlled aggression, as a bull charges the toreador's cape, not the toreador.''[27] Our concentration on a secondary enemy frittered away our military resources on inconclusive military and social operations that ultimately exhausted the patience of the American people. Because we did not properly define our terms at the outset, we ended up defeating ourselves.

CONCLUSION

Through Clausewitzian ''critical analysis'' – i.e., by testing classic military theory against the actual events of the Vietnam War – one is left with a strategic perception of the Vietnam War that reveals, among other things, that much of the existing historical perception is faulty. This is not surprising, for scholars have always rightly been suspicious of works written in the heat of passion, which too often mirror the prejudices of the times.

But, ten years after the American withdrawal from Vietnam, passions are beginning to cool. In his examination of ''The New Vietnam Scholarship,'' Asian scholar and former Vietnam War correspondent Fox Butterfield called attention to

the emergence of a small group of scholars, journalists and military specialists who have started to look afresh at the war . . . . For most of these scholars, their re-examination is not to prove whether Vietnam was or was not a 'noble cause,' in President Reagan's phrase, but to find out what really happened and why.[28]

As noted earlier, military historians and military strategists share a common interest in finding out ''what really happened and why.'' To this end, the study of the military history of not only the Vietnam War but all past wars has been reintroduced into the entire Army educational system. But the study of military history is not an end in itself, only a means to the further end of ''providing a thinking man with a frame of reference.'' If it is to accomplish this task, military history must be subjected to what Clausewitz called ''an analytical investigation leading to a close acquaintance with the subject.'' As he said, ''It is precisely that inquiry which is the most essential part of any *theory.*" And it is only after such inquiry, he said, that theory "becomes a guide to anyone who wants to learn about war from books; it will light his way, ease his progress, train his judgment, and help him to avoid pitfalls."[29]

Strategic analysis of the war in Vietnam cannot change the tragic results of our involvement there. But if it can train our judgment and help us avoid such pitfalls in the future, our experience there will not have been totally in vain.

NOTES

1. *JCS Pub. 1: Dictionary of Military and Associated Terms* (Washington: The Joint Chiefs of Staff, 1979), p. 217.
2. Carl von Clausewitz, *On War*, ed. and trans. by Michael Howard and Peter Paret with introductory essays by Peter Paret, Michael Howard, and Bernard Brodie and a commentary by Bernard Brodie (Princeton, N.J.: Princeton Univ. Press, 1976), pp. 156, 161.
3. Ibid.
4. US Department of the Army, *The Army*, Field Manual 100-1 (Washington: GPO, 1981), p. 13.
5. Clausewitz, pp. 88-89.
6. Sir Robert Thompson, *Revolutionary War in World Strategy 1945-1969* (New York: Taplinger Publishing Co., 1970), pp. 16-17.
7. Gregory Palmer, *The McNamara Strategy and the Vietnam War: Program Budgeting in the Pentagon, 1960–1968*, (Westport, Conn.: Greenwood Press, 1978), pp. 99-100.
8. Clausewitz, p. 165.
9. W. Scott Thompson and Donald D. Frizzell, ed., *The Lessons of Vietnam* (New York: Crane, Russak & Co., 1977), p. 279.
10. "Vietnam: We Lied to You," *The Economist*, 26 February 1983, pp. 56-57.
11. Truong Nhu Tang, "The Myth of a Liberation," *New York Review of Books*, 21 October 1982, pp. 31-36.
12. For a complete critical analysis of the Vietnam War based on the principles of war, see my *On Strategy: A Critical Analysis of the Vietnam War* (Novato, Calif.: Presidio Press, 1982), chaps. 9-14.
13. Clausewitz, p. 579.
14. For a detailed analysis of the Principles of War, see John I. Alger, *The Quest for Victory* (Westport, Conn.: Greenwood Press, 1982).
15. Field Manual 100-1, p. 14.
16. Hugh M. Arnold, "Official Justifications for America's Role in Indochina, 1949-67," *Asian Affairs*, 3 (September-October 1975), 31.
17. Michael MacLear, *The Ten Thousand Day War, Vietnam: 1945-1975* (New York: St. Martin's Press, 1981), p. 216.
18. Douglas Kinnard, *The War Managers* (Hanover, N.H.: Univ. Press. of New England, 1977), p. 25.
19. Stephen Peter Rosen, "Vietnam and the American Theory of Limited War," *International Security*, 7 (Fall 1982), 85.
20. Clausewitz, p. 89.
21. Ibid., p. 92.
22. Ibid.
23. Field Manual 100-1, pp. 14-15.
24. Clausewitz, pp. 595-97.
25. Tang.
26. Stuart A. Herrington, *Silence Was a Weapon: The Vietnam War in the Villages* (Novato, Calif.: Presidio Press, 1982), p. 203.
27. Norman B. Hannah, "Vietnam: Now We Know," in *All Quiet on the Eastern Front*, ed. Anthony T. Bouscaren (New York: Devin-Adair, 1977), p. 149.
28. Fox Butterfield, "The New Vietnam Scholarship: Challenging the Old Passions," *The New York Times Magazine*, 13 February 1983, pp. 26-28.
29. Clausewitz, p. 141.

This article appeared in the June 1983 issue of *Parameters*.

5

Vietnam: The Debate Goes On

by JOHN M. GATES

At the start of 1983, veteran correspondent Fox Butterfield surveyed what he termed "the new Vietnam scholarship" in *The New York Times Magazine.* Examining the work of "a small group of scholars, journalists and military specialists who have started to look afresh at the war," he noted their challenge to "some of the most cherished beliefs of both the right and the left."[1] One member of the group identified by Butterfield is Colonel Harry G. Summers, Jr., research analyst at the Army's Strategic Studies Institute and an instructor at the United States Army War College. *Parade* magazine, not to be accused of understatement, claimed that "in military circles" Colonel Summers is "the man of the hour," saying that "in the upper echelons of the Pentagon" his book, *On Strategy*, "is considered 'must reading.'"[2] Rarely has a military intellectual received such widespread publicity, and no one engaged in the study of the Vietnam conflict can ignore his critique of American wartime strategy.

Summers has presented his argument in a variety of published works, including a recent article in *Parameters.*[3] According to Summers, Americans were misled by "the fashionable new model of Communist revolutionary war."[4] The work of such "counterinsurgency experts" as Sir Robert Thompson "channeled our attentions toward the internal affairs of the South Vietnamese government rather than toward the external threat" posed by the regular military forces of the Democratic Republic of Vietnam (DRV).[5] In addition to misperceiving the conflict as a revolutionary war, American leaders also failed to establish clear objectives to guide their country's military commanders in Vietnam. As a result of these errors in strategic analysis, American military forces in Southeast Asia engaged in "faulty military operations in the field."[6] Failing to identify the true center of gravity in the war, the Americans used the bulk of their power to attack a "secondary enemy," the Viet Cong guerrillas, leaving the enemy's real power untouched. Summers believes that the guerrilla war in South Vietnam was a diversion. The significant communist threat was the army of the DRV, particularly the units of that army held in strategic reserve north of the 17th parallel. Victory came for the DRV in 1975 when those regulars moved south to mount a successful conventional attack on the Republic of Vietnam (RVN).

Colonel Summers argues his case persuasively, and his innovative use of Clausewitz to analyze the war in Vietnam broadens our understanding of the conflict. Unfortunately, two of the basic premises underlying his argument appear to be flawed. First, considerable evidence supports the conclusion that the conflict in Vietnam was always a revolutionary civil war and not a conventional one. Second, a survey of the internal documents produced by the US government demonstrates that the American objective in Vietnam was much clearer than Summers would have one believe. One must thus look elsewhere for an explanation of the faulty military operations that took place there.

THE FIRST STRATEGIC QUESTION

According to Clausewitz, "the first, the supreme, the most far-reaching act of judgment that the statesman and commander have to make is to establish . . . the kind of war on which they are embarking; neither mistaking it for, nor trying to turn it into, something that is alien to its nature." Determining the nature of a conflict is thus "the first of all strategic questions and the most comprehensive."[7] Using these injunctions of Clausewitz as the starting point for his own argument, Colonel Summers asserts that the Vietnam War was not a revolutionary one. "If we apply the theoretical truths of revolutionary war to the actual events of the Vietnam war," wrote Summers, "we find that they do not fit. The Viet Cong did not achieve decisive results on their own."[8] He presents the fact that the DRV achieved victory in 1975 by a conventional attack on the forces of the RVN as evidence that the revolutionary war model was an improper one. In reality, however, the conventional outcome of the war in Vietnam is anticipated in the major writing of both Asian theorists of revolutionary war and Western "counterinsurgency experts." The fit between "actual events" and "theoretical truths" is really very close.

Mao Tse-Tung, Vo Nguyen Giap, and Troung Chinh all commented upon the need for revolutionaries to move from guerrilla to mobile warfare, and they also identified mobile or conventional warfare as the more important and necessary element for success. Mao, for example, wrote that regular forces were of "primary importance" and that mobile warfare was "essential." He called guerrilla warfare "supplementary" because it could not "shoulder the main responsibility in deciding the outcome."[9] In 1961, Giap had noted the progression in the Vietnamese "Resistance War" from guerrilla warfare to "mobile warfare combined with partial entrenched camp warfare," and his compatriot Troung Chinh had written even earlier that in the final stage of revolutionary conflict "positional warfare" would play "a paramount role."[10] In theoretical terms, the conventional attacks by DRV regulars in 1975 represented the revolution moving into its "final stage."[11] According to Thompson, the defeat of government forces by "*the regular forces of the insurgents*

. . . *in conventional battle"* constituted "a classical ending in accordance with the orthodox theory.''[12] Summers errs in concluding that the conventional DRV offensive in 1975 demonstrated the inapplicability of the revolutionary war model to the Vietnam War. Revolutionary war theory never implied that the Viet Cong would "achieve decisive results on their own."

More important than evidence of the close fit between revolutionary war theory and the war's end in a conventional military attack is the revolutionary nature of communist goals in Vietnam and their consistency. "The aim," as General Giap so cogently summarized it in 1961, "was to realize the political goals of the national democratic revolution as in China, to recover national independence and bring land to the peasants, creating conditions for the advance of the revolution of our country to socialism.''[13] Most important, the goals were to be achieved throughout the entire area of Vietnam, not only in the North, and the communist leadership of the Vietnamese revolution consistently sought the overthrow of any government standing in their way: the French, Ngo Dinh Diem, the American-supported regime that followed him.

From Ho Chi Minh's 1946 assurance that he considered the people of Nam Bo "citizens of Viet Nam" to the call of the Vietnamese Workers Party to "advance to the peaceful reunification of the Fatherland" in 1973,[14] the communist leaders in Vietnam neither swayed from their commitment to unification nor effectively hid that commitment. One thus wonders how non-communist leaders of the National Liberation Front (NLF) such as Troung Nhu Tang could have believed they "were working for Southern self-determination and independence – from Hanoi as well as from Washingon," as Summers assumes.[15] The ten-point program of the NLF, distributed throughout the world in February 1961, called for "peaceful reunification of the fatherland," and the communist-dominated front reaffirmed its goal of a unified Vietnam in subsequent statements. On 22 March 1965, for example, it spoke of "national unification" in strong, unambiguous language: "Vietnam is one, the Vietnamese people are one, north and south are one." A very long statement of the NLF political program broadcast in September 1967 observed that "Vietnam must be reunified," calling reunification "the sacred aspiration of our entire people," and a 1969 statement called "unity" one of "the Vietnamese people's fundamental national rights.''[16] The NLF consistently spoke of "peaceful" and "eventual" reunification; it did not promise independence or self-determination for the South. The communist commitment to a unified Vietnam could only have remained hidden from people such as Troung Nhu Tang because of their own naiveté, self-deception, or wishful thinking.

Similarly, if Americans were deceived as to the "true intentions" of Vietnam's communist leaders, they too were primarily victims of their own, not communist, dissembling. As Wallace J. Thies observed, "DRV leaders such as Le Duan and Nguyen Chi Thanh were deeply and passionately committed to the goal of completing the revolution in South Vietnam. It was a goal they had been pursuing for virtually all of their adult lives."[17] Pham Van Dong attempted to convey the importance of national unification to the United States when he met with Canadian diplomat Blair Seaborn in June 1964, using the French *drame* (signifying an intense unresolved crisis) in an attempt to capture the critical nature of such a "fundamental" issue.[18]

Rather than viewing North Vietnam as a complete nation, Vietnamese communists such as General Giap saw it as "a large rear echelon" of the army. It was "the revolutionary base for the whole country," and it would eventually supply the forces necessary for reunification.[19] American reports indicating the depth of the communist commitment to a truly national revolution were ignored in the Johnson years,[20] but the truth of that commitment kept emerging. The special assessment of the situation in Vietnam prepared for President-elect Richard Nixon at the start of 1969 noted that "Hanoi's ultimate goal of a unified Vietnam under its control has not changed."[21] Nor would it change. Like Troung Nhu Tang, Americans have little excuse for their ignorance of North Vietnam's "true intentions."

The real key to understanding the nature of a particular war is not an analysis of the way in which it is fought, but a study of the people involved and their reasons for fighting. If, as Summers admits, the First Indochina War "*was* a revolutionary war,"[22] then the claim that the Second Indochina War was not is illogical. The communist goal was the same in both wars: *revolution*, the overthrow of whatever noncommunist government might exist in any part of Vietnam and its replacement by the communist one headquartered in Hanoi. In the First Indochina War, a Vietnamese movement (led by Ho Chi Minh) fought throughout Vietnam and elsewhere in Indochina to create an independent, unified, communist state. Attempting to prevent the attainment of that goal were the French colonialists and their allies, some of whom hoped that they might eventually achieve independence under a noncommunist government. In the Second Indochina War, the parties on one side of the conflict had hardly changed at all. The movement led by Ho Chi Minh continued its attempt to achieve an independent communist state in a united Vietnam, having failed to achieve that goal in the First Indochina War. The United States and its Vietnamese allies, grouped in the South, sought to contain the communist revolution to the area north of the 17th parallel and create an independent, noncommunist state in the South. In Clausewitzian terms, the nature of the two wars was identical: a group seeking communist revolutionary ends was fighting against a group trying to prevent the spread of the revolution.

The communist goal in the Second Indochina War was clearly political, but the means used to implement it varied to fit the situation. Early in the conflict, when communist military power in the South was relatively meager, agitation, propaganda, and small guerrilla action predominated. As weakness appeared in the RVN, the communists used units infiltrated from the North to strengthen their military capability south of the 17th parallel, moving more than once toward mobile warfare. Later, as the war became stalemated, there was a lull in the fighting after unsuccessful communist offensives in 1968 and again in 1972, although communist cadres continued their work to undermine the South Vietnamese government. Finally, with the RVN left unsupported by the United States, the communists moved in for the kill in their final offensive, using everything available to them – what remained of their infrastructure in the South, guerrillas, and regular army units from the North.

Facing dedicated communist guerrillas and cadres determined to overthrow them, the leaders of the noncommunist government in Saigon found themselves involved in a struggle for survival. To counter the communist-led revolution, they had to build widespread support for their government, and that could not be done without pacifying the countryside. A conventional war response that would have contained the major elements of a communist military power within the confines of the northern base was necessary, but alone it was not sufficient to secure the RVN. Behind whatever shield might have been created to protect it, the Saigon government would need to engage in effective pacification operations to prevent the internal collapse of the RVN. One cannot abandon the model of revolutionary war without seriously distorting the nature of the conflict taking place in Vietnam.[23]

By the mid-1960s, however, many Americans, including Lyndon Johnson and his advisors, seemed to have abandoned the revolutionary war model. In a study of "Official Justifications for America's Role in Indochina," Professor Hugh M. Arnold found that the image of the United States engaged in "a simple response to aggression" was "overwhelmingly the most important justification used during the Johnson Administration." According to Arnold, the Johnson government sought to make clear to the American people that the war "was not a civil war or an indigenous rebellion, but an attempt to take over a nation by force of arms."[24] This view of the war is basic to Summers' argument also, but the conflict in Vietnam was not a contest between two sovereign states.

After the August revolution of 1945, the Viet Minh established their revolutionary government throughout Vietnam, although the combined action of the British and French, using Japanese forces in addition to their own, soon reestablished a French presence in the South. Nevertheless, as the Declaration of Independence of the DRV made clear, Ho Chi Minh saw himself and his government as representing "the entire people of Viet Nam," and that claim was confirmed by foreign observers at the time.[25] A year later, the Chief of the Division of Southeast Asian Affairs of the State Department, Abbot L. Moffat, affirmed the view that the DRV was a government for all Vietnam and not just the North.[26] The unity of Vietnam would be reasserted again and again throughout the war. From before the Geneva agreement, which stated clearly that the "military demarcation line" at the 17th parallel was "provisional and should not in any way be interpreted as constituting a political or territorial boundary,'' to after the Paris agreement of 1973, which reaffirmed that the parallel was ''only provisional and not a political or territorial boundary,'' leaders of the DRV repeatedly claimed that there was only one Vietnam, not two. Initially that was also the view of the non-communist leaders of the RVN.[27]

Believing a partitioned Vietnam to be preferable to an entirely communist one, Americans and many of their Vietnamese allies soon came to view the 17th parallel as a border between two sovereign states. As a result, American leaders created an illusory picture of the war, portraying the conflict as the result of the aggression of one sovereign state against another. In reality, it was a civil war between two Vietnamese parties, both of whom had originally claimed sovereignty over all of Vietnam. Although the United States often envisioned a Korea-like solution to the Vietnam problem, it could not create two sovereign states in Vietnam by rhetoric alone. Until the Americans and their allies in the RVN forced the DRV to abandon its goal of creating a revolutionary communist state in all Vietnam, the civil war would continue. From the communist point of view, what Americans called North Vietnamese ''aggression'' was nothing more than the attempt to complete the process of unifying Vietnam under a revolutionary government begun at the end of World War II.

Since the communist victory in 1975, a number of people, Colonel Summers among them, have spoken of the conquest of South Vietnam by ''North'' Vietnamese,[28] but that too is a distortion. Leaders in the governments of both the RVN and the DRV came from all over Vietnam, not only from the region in which their capital resided. The Diem government, for example, contained many Catholics who had migrated from the North in 1954, and later Vice President Nguyen Cao Ky provided a highly visible ''northern'' presence in the Saigon government. More important, however, was the ''southern'' presence in the highest ranks of the DRV leadership. Le Duan, the first secretary of the Central Committee of the Vietnamese Workers Party, was born in Quang Tri, just south of the 17th parallel. Pham Van Dong, the prime minister of the DRV, was born in Quang Ngai. Pham Hung, a vice-premier of the DRV and member of the Political Bureau since the late 1950s, was from Vinh Long; and Ton Duc Thang, who succeeded Ho Chi Minh as president of the DRV, was born in the Mekong Delta. Nguyen Chi Thanh, the DRV military commander in the South until his death in 1967, was also South Vietnamese. Such biographical information led one author to conclude that ''in terms of the birthplace of opposing leaders, it is evident that the Second Indochina War was more a civil war than was America's war of 1861-1865.''[29] However much Americans would like to believe it, the war did not end with a conquest of the RVN by alien ''northerners'' alone. It ended when the noncommunist Saigon government was destroyed by forces of the revolutionary communist government in Hanoi.

THE OBJECTIVE

In a number of critiques of American strategy in Vietnam, one finds the statement that American objectives were not presented clearly. As evidence for that conclusion Summers cited "some 22 separate American rationales" categorized by Professor Arnold, compared to "the *one* North Vietnamese objective of total control over all of Indochina." Summers also quoted General Douglas Kinnard's conclusion that "almost 70 percent of the generals who managed the war were uncertain of its objectives."[30] The survey data reported by Kinnard, however, do not indicate so great a problem as Summers would have one believe. Although 35 percent of the respondents to Kinnard's questionnaire classified American objectives in Vietnam as "rather fuzzy," 29 percent found them to be "clear and understandable."[31] The interpretation of the meaning of the statement "not as clear as they might have been," the response selected by 33 percent, is open to debate. To say that goals could be stated more clearly is not the same as saying one is "uncertain" regarding the objective.

The article by Professor Arnold is also not particularly supportive of the argument that American objectives were unclear. Although Arnold noted "22 separate rationales," he made clear that some of the "themes" he identified were "more concerned with means than ends." More important, a "rationale" is not necessarily an objective. One constant Arnold identified was "the Communism theme," stressed in both public and private contexts, "in every Administration, and in every year covered by this study." He concluded that "if one single reason for United States involvement in Indochina can be derived from the analysis, it would have to be the perceived threat of Communism."[32] That is particularly true when one separates statements that deal with the American objective in Vietnam from those that attempt to rationalize or explain that objective.

One sees the clarity of American objectives in the similarity of official statements made during different administrations at widely varying times during the war. In 1948, for example, the 27 September statement on Indochina by the Department of State presented the "long-term" objective of "a self-governing nationalist state which will be friendly to the United States and which, commensurate with the capacity of the peoples involved, will be patterned upon our conception of a democratic state as opposed to the totalitarian state which would evolve inevitably from Communist domination."[33] In 1951, the American goal for "the nations and peoples of Asia," as outlined in a 17 May annex to NSC 28/4, remained the same: "stable and self-sustaining non-Communist governments, oriented toward the United States."[34] A decade later, as the United States became more involved in the Vietnamese situation, statements of the US objective remained unchanged: "to prevent Communist domination of South Vietnam; to create in that country a viable and increasingly democratic society."[35] By 1964, with an even greater American commitment, the statement of goals had not altered; the United States still sought "an independent non-Communist South Vietnam."[36] Statements such as these, made throughout the war by the people involved with setting policy, should leave no doubt that any ignorance of the American goal in Vietnam did not result from a failure to set clear objectives.

As evidence of a lack of clarity in American policy, Summers observed that "when Secretary of Defense Clark Clifford took office in 1968, he complained that no one in the Defense Department could tell him what constituted victory."[37] In fact, in the source cited by Summers, Clifford made no such claim. What he did say was that he was startled "to find out that we had no military plan to win the war."[38] The difference is not unimportant. American leaders knew what would constitute victory – forcing the leaders of the DRV to accept the existence of "an independent non-Communist South Vietnam." The problem was how to achieve that goal.

Clifford himself was even exaggerating when he stated that the United States lacked a plan to "win the war," as seen by his own summary of the Pentagon's answers to his questions. Clifford was told that "the enemy will ultimately be worn down so severely by attrition that the enemy will eventually capitulate,"[39] a view that had been prevalent at least since 1965, when Secretary of Defense Robert McNamara reported to the President on his conversations in Honolulu with Ambassador Taylor, General Wheeler, Admiral Sharp, and General Westmoreland. "Their strategy for 'victory,' over time," said McNamara, "is to break the will of the DRV/VC by denying them victory."[40] Clifford was not really reacting to the absence of a plan, but to what he perceived to be its inadequacies. Since the war, the dissection of those inadequacies and the search for better alternatives has been an important focus of many works, Summers' among them, but one should not make the mistake of assuming that flaws in execution resulted from an absence of clear goals.

OPERATIONS

"Because we failed to correctly identify the nature of the war," argues Summers, "we also failed to identify the center of gravity." Seeing the conflict as a revolutionary war, Americans "saw the Viet Cong as the center of gravity" and "massed against this guerrilla enemy in search-and-destroy and pacification efforts." As a result, "our concentration on a secondary enemy frittered away our military resources on inconclusive military and social operations that ultimately exhausted the patience of the American people."[41] Critics of the American approach to the war who take what may be termed a counterinsurgency view would disagree. They have argued that the response of General Westmoreland and other military leaders was not the proper one for a revolutionary war. They are particularly critical of the military de-emphasis of pacification, relegating it to the category of "the other war," and engagement in counterproductive search-and-destroy operations instead. If the critics are correct, then a number of the faulty operations Summers deplores could not possibly have resulted from the military becoming overly involved in a campaign of counterinsurgency.[42]

Actually two centers of gravity existed. One was the Viet Cong guerrillas and communist cadres in the South; the other was the communist military power in the North. Success in attacking one would not assure the destruction of the other, and either could prevent the United States from achieving its goal. In the early 1960s, for example, the revolutionaries in the South had achieved considerable success without a high level of material aid from the North. In fact, the communists might well have achieved their aim without moving from guerrilla war to regular mobile warfare had it not been for the significant increase in American aid to the RVN. Although Summers is correct to argue that pacification and attacking the Viet Cong guerrillas were tasks that properly belonged to the South Vietnamese, the situation in the 1960s was such that the job could not be done without considerable help from the United States. The evidence that the RVN approached the point of collapse more than once before the commitment of DRV regulars to the war highlights the importance of the American ·contribution to pacification and nation-building. Without those efforts, the RVN might have fallen into communist hands much earlier.

By the 1970s, of course, the situation had changed. Then, despite some progress in pacification and the virtual destruction of Viet Cong military power in 1968 and after, the government of South Vietnam was still challenged by the communist military forces in North Vietnam. Containment of North Vietnamese military power, if not its outright destruction, was thus also necessary, and Summers is correct to identify that mission as a logical one for the American forces in the region. Neutralization of those forces and the communist will to use them to force the unification of Vietnam was essential if the American objective in Vietnam was to be achieved, but nothing in the revolutionary civil war model presented here or in the frequently stated American objective of establishing a secure noncommunist state in South Vietnam precluded the acceptance of the strategy advocated by Summers. Instead, it was prevented by the President's desire to keep the war limited, a desire shared by many other Americans during the course of the war.

Although Clausewitz believed that ''no matter what the central feature of the enemy's power may be . . . the defeat and destruction of his fighting force remains the best way to begin,'' he also recognized that in a civil conflict such as that in Vietnam the center of gravity might not be the enemy's military forces, but ''the personalities of the leaders and public opinion.''[43] In the RVN, the crucial element, in addition to the Viet Cong guerrillas, was the population at large, and of particular importance were the people in a position to give support and shelter to the guerrillas. Also important were the non-communists in the NLF and other opposition groups. Detaching them from the communists was essential if the RVN was to emerge as a viable and secure state, and the pacification program was crucial to that end. No strictly military approach would suffice.

The will of the communists throughout Vietnam was very strong, although a majority of the generals surveyed by General Kinnard admitted that it was "not sufficiently considered" by the Americans.[44] In retrospect, knowing the tremendous casualties taken by the communists in the course of their resistance since 1945, one cannot assume that the destruction of North Vietnamese military power would have ended the war. The history of conflict in Indochina and the continuation of the fighting long after the US withdrawal indicate that the conquest of the DRV base in the North might have been needed to destroy the communist will to continue the war. From the perspective of many Americans, communist determination in the face of such high costs may appear irrational, but people throughout the world, particularly revolutionaries, have demonstrated a capacity for such fanatical behavior too frequently for it to be ignored.

During and after the war, a number of people have argued against the limitations placed on the use of American forces in Vietnam, chiding civilian leaders for having taken counsel of their fears. As General Kinnard noted, however, the desire to limit the use of American power to avoid widening the conflict to include China, the Soviet Union, or both was one specific objective that the United States achieved.[45] More important, the critics provide no specific evidence that in the mid-1960s such limitations were unnecessary, while the Chinese commitment of some 30,000 to 50,000 "support troops" to the aid of the DRV after 1965 provides some evidence of the wisdom of the decision to limit the American response in Indochina.[46]

Judging the degree of risk inherent in any strategy after the fact is difficult, and one cannot know with certainty how China or Russia might have reacted in the 1960s to such forceful actions as the Linebacker bombing campaigns or the Cambodian incursion. In the 1950s and 1960s, when American leaders, including some military leaders, asked themselves whether the potential risks of a less-restricted war were worth the possible gains in Vietnam, they invariably answered no. Only after the international environment had changed significantly did the answer to the question also change. The diplomatic world in which Richard Nixon functioned appeared very different from that facing Eisenhower, Kennedy, and Johnson. In a nuclear world, caution is an important survival mechanism, and critics should think twice before advocating that American leaders act more boldly.

Given the willingness of military leaders to fight a limited war in Vietnam, despite their misgivings, rather than resign, the important question remains a military one. *Within the limitations set down*, what strategy was best to achieve the goal of destroying the enemy's will? Summers joins numerous other authors in a condemnation of the choices made during the war: controlled escalation, limited bombing of the North, counterinsurgency and a war of attrition in the South. But the course of action he and others have suggested, using American military power to isolate the communist base above the 17th parallel, was not possible within the context of the specific limitations set down by civilian leaders in Washington. Without a change of guidelines, the approach Colonel Summers advocates is not really an alternative to the flawed operations that took place.

The supreme irony of the war in Vietnam may be that despite all of the flaws in the American approach noted by a wide variety of critics, by 1969 the United States and the RVN were as well-positioned to attain their objectives as they had ever been. The forces of General Westmoreland had found and destroyed thousands of communist troops, both guerrillas and regulars, and the reorganized pacification program appeared to be making progress in the countryside. The leaders of the RVN may not have won the hearts and minds of the populace, but communist progress in that endeavor had been slowed or stopped. As American aid improved the economic situation in the countryside, the tolerance of people for the Saigon government also increased. Thus, even after all of the perceived failures of American policy and strategy in Vietnam, the war was not lost prior to 1973, nor was it being lost, except in the crucial American center of gravity, popular opinion. In the United States, on mainstreet and on Capitol Hill, ending the war had become more important than winning it.

Although Summers and others have deemed the American approach to the war strategically bankrupt, by 1968 the DRV had adopted essentially the same approach: to keep fighting until the enemy became frustrated and quit. The critical difference was that the American plan failed while that of the DRV succeeded. The United States hurt the communists, but not enough. In material terms the communists damaged the United States far less. More important was the psychological and political damage done by astute communist propaganda, American errors in applying force (particularly the highly visible reliance on firepower in the South), and specific events such as the Tet Offensive. Limited American military activity proved unable to achieve the objective before American will proved insufficient to sustain the nation in a protracted war. But the problem was not a faulty perception of the war's nature or unclear objectives. In fact, the major problem may not even have been flawed operations, given the absence in America of the kind of commitment to the war that sustained the communists.

The final outcome of the war was primarily the result of historical events outside the realm of strategic thinking. In the United States the anti-war movement created sufficient turmoil that the functioning of government was altered if not impaired, and the Watergate scandal, which must be seen as a war-related event to be understood fully, created an environment that doomed the President's Vietnam policy to failure.[47] Political weakness in the face of an assertive Congress and a population grown tired of the war prevented Richard Nixon from implementing a program for the protection of Vietnam based on the use of American firepower instead of manpower. The effects of the scandal could not be calculated in advance, but in the end they were decisive. Although clearly in the realm of speculation, the argument that without Watergate

President Nixon might have successfully defended the RVN through the continued use of American air power and aid cannot be easily dismissed.

CONCLUSION

The possibility that without Watergate the United States might have muddled through to a more favorable outcome in Vietnam should not prevent one from subjecting the wartime strategy to searching criticism. Summers' critique, however, does not provide an adequate model for future action. By stressing the need for a conventional military response, he diverts attention from the importance of the unconventional elements that remain primary in revolutionary struggles such as that in Vietnam. In the RVN, the problems of pacification and national development would have remained even if the United States had succeeded in containing the regular forces of the DRV above the 17th parallel. If those problems went unresolved, then internal collapse behind the American shield would have prevented the attainment of the US objective of creating a secure, noncommunist state in South Vietnam. At the very least, as happened more than once in the war, the threat of a collapse in the American rear would necessitate further American commitment and prolong the war, heightening the risk of a collapse of American will.

Any analysis that denies the important revolutionary dimension of the Vietnam conflict is misleading, leaving the American people, their leaders, and their professionals inadequately prepared to deal with similar problems in the future. The argument that faulty strategic assessment and poorly articulated goals doomed the American military to faulty operations in Vietnam only encourages military officers to avoid the kind of full-scale reassessment that failures such as that in Southeast Asia ought to stimulate. Instead of forcing the military to come to grips with the problems of revolutionary warfare that now exist in nations such as Guatemala or El Salvador, Summers' analysis leads officers back into the conventional war model that provided so little preparation for solving the problems faced in Indochina by the French, the Americans, and their Vietnamese allies. Such a business-as-usual approach is much too complacent in a world plagued by the unconventional warfare associated with revolution and attempts to counter it.

When Fox Butterfield surveyed the authors of the "new" Vietnam scholarship he implied that somehow they had managed to place themselves above the battle and engage in a truly objective analysis of the war. Building upon Butterfield's work, Summers implies that his contribution to scholarship is closer to the truth than previous accounts "written in the heat of passion which too often mirror the prejudices of the times."[48] One should be wary, however, of any author's claim to objectivity. Although Summers' analysis may lack passion, it is certainly what many people in the Army and the nation want to hear. With the responsibility for failure in Vietnam placed squarely on "academic counterinsurgency experts" and overly timid leaders in

Washington, significant military errors become a function of strategic or perceptual errors made at a higher, usually civilian level. In short, the military is absolved of virtually all responsibility for failure. A different analytical framework would make such a shirking of responsibility much more difficult, and readers should be wary of any institutional insider whose seemingly objective scholarship fits so well with what many other members of the institutions want to hear.

NOTES

1. Fox Butterfield, "The New Vietnam Scholarship," *The New York Times Magazine*, 13 February 1983, pp. 26-27.
2. "Man of the Hour," *Parade*, 14 August 1983, p. 9.
3. Harry G. Summers, Jr., "A Strategic Perception of the Vietnam War," *Parameters*, 13 (June 1983), 41-46, contains an excellent summary of Summers' argument, as does "Vietnam Reconsidered," *The New Republic*, 12 July 1982, pp. 25-31. A more extensive and detailed presentation is contained in Summers' book, *On Strategy: A Critical Analysis of the Vietnam War* (Novato, Calif.: Presidio, 1982).
4. Summers, "Vietnam Reconsidered," p. 25.
5. Summers, "A Strategic Perception of the Vietnam War," p. 42.
6. Ibid., p. 44.
7. Carl von Clausewitz. *On War*, ed. and trans. by Michael Howard and Peter Paret (Princeton: Princeton Univ. Press, 1976), pp. 88-89.
8. Summers, "A Strategic Perception of the Vietnam War," p. 42.
9. *Mao Tse-Tung on Guerrilla Warfare*, trans. by Samuel B. Griffith (New York: Praeger, 1961), pp. 56 and 113; *Mao Tse-Tung on Revolution and War*, ed. by M. Rejai (New York: Doubleday, 1970), p. 288.
10. Vo Nguyen Giap, *People's War, People's Army* (New York: Praeger, 1962), pp. 103-04; Truong Chinh, *The Resistance Will Win* in *Primer for Revolt* (New York: Praeger, 1963), p. 116.
11. Van Tien Dung, *Our Great Spring Victory*, trans. by John Spragens, Jr. (New York: Monthly Review Press, 1977), p. 12.
12. Sir Robert Thompson, *Revolutionary War in World Strategy, 1945-1969* (New York: Taplinger, 1970), p. 11. Italics in original. For an overview of revolutionary war strategy and a summary of its strategic phases including mobile warfare, see John J. McCuen, *The Art of Counter-Revolutionary War* (Harrisburg: Stackpole, 1966), ch. 2, pp. 37-44 in particular.
13. Vo Nguyen Giap, *People's War, People's Army*, p. 69.
14. "Letter from Ho Chi Minh to Compatriots in Nam Bo, May 31, 1946," in Gareth Porter, ed., *Vietnam: A History in Documents* (New York: New American Library, 1981), p. 45 and extract of article in *Hoc Tap* (April 1973) in Gareth Porter, ed., *Vietnam: The Definitive History of Human Decision* (New York: E. M. Coleman, 1979), p. 626.
15. Truong Nhu Tang, "The Myth of a Liberation," *New York Review of Books*, 21 October 1982, p. 32.
16. The 1961, 1965, and 1967 statements are from "NLFSV Position Statements" in Part VI B, Negotiations 1965-1967, *United States-Vietnam Relations, 1945-1967*, Book 12 (Washington: GPO, 1971), pp. 189, 197, and 233. The 1969 statement is from Appendix 17 of George McTurnan Kahin and John W. Lewis. *The United States in Vietnam* (revised ed.; New York: Dial Press, 1969), p. 513.
17. Wallace J. Thies, *When Governments Collide: Coercion and Diplomacy in the Vietnam Conflict, 1964-1968* (Berkeley: Univ. of California Press, 1980), p. 400.
18. George C. Herring, ed., *The Secret Diplomacy of the Vietnam War: The Negotiating Volumes of the Pentagon Papers* (Austin: Univ. of Texas Press, 1983), p. 31.
19. *The Senator Gravel Edition: The Pentagon Papers* (Boston: Beacon Press, 1971), I, p. 264.
20. Thies, *When Governments Collide*, p. 418.
21. *Congressional Record*, 10 May 1972, p. 418.
22. Summers, "Vietnam Reconsidered," p. 26. Italics in original.

23. Harry G. Summers, Jr., "An *On Strategy* Rejoinder," *Air University Review*, 34 (July-August 1983), 93, indicates that the author did not "intend to imply that counterinsurgency tasks like pacification and nation-building were unimportant." Unfortunately the structure, style, and force of his argument lead readers to that erroneous conclusion despite his intentions.
24. Hugh M. Arnold, "Official Justifications for America's Role in Indochina, 1949-1967," *Asian Affairs: An American Review*, 3 (September-October 1975), 42.
25. Porter, *Vietnam: A History in Documents*, pp. 30 and 34-35. See also Harold R. Isaacs, *No Peace for Asia* (New York: Macmillan, 1947), ch. 6.
26. Porter, *Vietnam: A History in Documents*, p. 47.
27. A copy of the Geneva agreement is in Ibid., p. 160. For the 1973 Paris agreement see Gareth Porter, *A Peace Denied: The United States, Vietnam, and the Paris Agreement* (Bloomington: Indiana Univ. Press, 1975), p. 322. RVN views appear in Porter, *Vietnam: The Definitive Documentation of Human Decisions*, I, 581, 656.
28. Summers, "Vietnam Reconsidered," p. 26.
29. James Pickney Harrison, *The Endless War: Fifty Years of Struggle in Vietnam* (New York: Free Press, 1982), p. 30.
30. Summers, "A Strategic Perception of the Vietnam War," p. 44.
31. Douglas Kinnard, *The War Managers* (Hanover, N.H.: Univ. Press of New England, 1977), p. 169.
32. Arnold, "Official Justifications for America's Role in Indochina," p. 48.
33. Porter, *Vietnam: A History in Documents*, p. 73.
34. Ibid., p. 105.
35. *The Senator Gravel Edition: The Pentagon Papers*, II, p. 642.
36. Ibid., p. 412.
37. Summers, "A Strategic Perception of the Vietnam War," p. 44.
38. Michael Maclear, *The Ten Thousand Day War – Vietnam: 1945-1975* (New York: St. Martin's Press, 1981), p. 216.
39. Ibid.
40. Porter, *Vietnam: A History in Documents*, p. 310.
41. Summers, "A Strategic Perception of the Vietnam War," pp. 44-45.
42. Richard A. Hunt and Richard H. Shultz, Jr., eds. *Lessons from an Unconventional War: Reassessing U.S. Strategies for Future Conflicts* (New York: Pergamon, 1982) make clear that the American approach in Vietnam was not in harmony with counterinsurgency theory. See also Douglas S. Blaufarb, *The Counterinsurgency Era: U.S. Doctrine and Performance, 1950 to the Present* (New York: The Free Press, 1977), p. 288 in particular. For a survey of the debate between "The Counterinsurgency School" and "The Hawks" see George C. Herring, "American Strategy in Vietnam: The Postwar Debate," *Military Affairs*, 46 (April 1982), 57-63.
43. Clausewitz, *On War*, p. 596.
44. Kinnard, *The War Managers*, p. 172.
45. Ibid., p. 161.
46. *The Senator Gravel Edition: The Pentagon Papers*, IV, p. 231.
47. Seymour M. Hersh, *The Price of Power: Kissinger in the Nixon White House* (New York: Summit Books, 1983), pp. 130, 195, and 637-38. See also P. Edward Haley, *Congress and the Fall of South Vietnam and Cambodia* (Rutherford, N.J.: Fairleigh Dickinson Univ. Press, 1982).
48. Summers, "A Strategic Perception of the Vietnam War," p. 45.

This article appeared in the spring 1984 issue of *Parameters*.

6

Vietnam War Diplomacy: Reflections of a Former Iron Curtain Official

by JÁNOS RADVÁNYI

Before becoming a US citizen, the author served for 19 years in the Hungarian Diplomatic Service. As Chief of Mission in the United States, he was personally involved in the negotiations between Washington and Hanoi over the Vietnam War, particularly in 1965-66. He gained worldwide attention in 1967 when he requested and was granted political asylum in the United States, becoming the highest ranking official then to have defected from a Warsaw Pact country.

* * *

Among the many misconceptions of our tragic involvement in Vietnam is the naive belief that the war was essentially an American-Vietnamese affair. It was not. The United States was but one of the players in an enormously complex and deadly encounter. Russia and China also had vital roles, while numerous lesser actors – like Poland and Hungary – were peripherally involved. The leaders in the Kremlin, for instance, pursued an "anti-imperialist struggle" against the United States by helping Hanoi to win the war militarily and diplomatically. At the same time, they waged a cold war against "the dogmatist, adventurist, and phrasemongering" Chinese Communists by weaning Ho Chi Minh away from Peking and by rendering the North Vietnamese increasingly dependent upon the supply of sophisticated Soviet weapons. Mao Tse-tung and his colleages also had axes to grind in Vietnam. They supported Hanoi's war effort substantially and left no stone unturned in attempting to eliminate US influence in the area. In addition, they persisted in their attempts to contain the expansionist "Soviet social imperialism." The arena of conflict thus ranged far beyond the battlefield proper, affecting the strategies, tactics, and power-relationships of the superpowers and widening the Sino-Soviet rift.[1]

Another misperception centers on the key figure of the war, Ho Chi Minh. While some Americans saw him as a charismatic leader, but nothing more, others regarded him as the devil's pawn, if not the devil himself. Inside the communist world, Stalin did not trust him and Khrushchev despised him, but Mao Tse-tung and Tito held him in high regard. Brezhnev was willing to take a chance with him. Some observers held that he was a staunch nationalist communist and that he was close to Moscow. Others maintained that his most intimate ties were with Peking. Some East Europeans held the view that Ho Chi Minh was a lucky man to have survived Stalin's blood purges – lucky to have been in China and in the Vietnamese jungles while his friends from the Far Eastern Bureau of the Comintern were liquidated one by one.

I met Ho in the spring of 1959 during a visit to Hanoi. My opinion was and is that he was a shrewd, ruthlessly ambitious, and highly intelligent Marxist colonial revolutionary. He effectively spread communism in Indochina, and under his leadership the Viet Minh guerrillas defeated both the Japanese and the French. This frail man with iron resolve was one of the few party leaders in the communist camp who presided over a Politburo and Central Committee that could claim an extraordinary record of cohesion and consensus. Moreover, he was one of few communist chiefs who, like Yugoslavia's Tito, had come to power after a long and successful guerrilla war rather than as an appointee of Moscow or Peking. And, like Tito, Ho remained neutral during the years of struggle between the two communist giants, and profited from that neutrality. In North Vietnam he installed a closely controlled communist regime, nationalized the banks and the factories, and collectivized the countryside. His secret police hauled off dissenters to lead mines and executed landlords and collaborators with the French colonialists. Ho Chi Minh totally discounted the possibility of a reunification of Vietnam through elections as stipulated in the 1954 Geneva Agreements. In his view, all parties concerned – the North and South Vietnamese, and the Americans as well – knew that an election would result in a communist victory; therefore, no election would be held. The reunification, he maintained, could be effected only through military means. He seemed to believe what he was saying. And indeed at the Fifteenth Plenum of the Central Committee of the Lao Dong Party in May 1959, Ho Chi Minh and his Politburo made the crucial decision to invade the South.[2]

Frankly, I did not expect that the Americans, having witnessed the bitter experiences of the French, would get involved in a ground war in Vietnam. Nor did I believe that Brezhnev would be interested in Vietnam, which had been abandoned by Khrushchev as a place where the Soviet Union should not waste money and energy. I also thought that neither of the superpowers would allow itself to become chained to the fortune of a small and relatively insignificant power in Southeast Asia. But I was wrong – things had gone too far for the superpowers to stay on the sidelines. Possibly my miscalculation was due to the fact that during the Khrushchev years, and even at the time of the Tonkin Gulf incident in August 1964, East European party and government officials, including the Hungarians, showed little interest in events in Southeast Asia.

The news of the clash between a US naval vessel and North Vietnamese torpedo boats caused hardly a ripple in Budapest and Warsaw, although it should have been obvious that the event portended a change in the character of the war. No one seemed to care about Hanoi's war, about America's role in it, or about the fact that it had become an issue in the American presidential campaign. (For instance, the Hungarian party boss, János Kádár, explained to me in private that he really did not care who was to be elected, Johnson or Goldwater. For him it was the same: they were both imperialists.)

But the indifference ended in 1965, when Soviet party leader Brezhnev put forth his "United Action" plan to support Ho Chi Minh. The Vietnamese, of course, were delighted; but not so the East Europeans, who felt little sympathy toward sponsoring Hanoi's expensive undertaking. Public opinion, however, is not a decisive factor in formulating foreign policy in that part of the world, and despite rising popular dissatisfaction, the Russian plan was endorsed by the governments of Eastern Europe. (The maverick Ceauscescu of Romania was the only one who dared to say no to Brezhnev. He sent his contribution to Ho's war directly to Hanoi.) Soon thereafter, food, hospital supplies, construction materials, etc were flowing by rail and sea from Eastern Europe to Vietnam. The military shipments were handled by the Soviets exclusively. As part of the "United Action" program, the Russians furnished the armed forces of North Vietnam with airplanes, tanks, coastal guns, warships, and other items of military hardware. Soviet specialists installed a web of antiaircraft rockets and conventional antiaircraft artillery around North Vietnamese cities and strategic points. They assisted in training pilots, rocket personnel, tank drivers, and artillerymen at Soviet bases. Further, the USSR routed extensive military and economic supplies through Hanoi to the National Liberation Front of South Vietnam, commonly known as the Viet Cong.

At the same time, the Kremlin stepped up its anti-Chinese attacks, accusing Peking of obstructing Soviet attempts to get help to Hanoi. According to the Soviets, Chinese advisors persuaded the Vietnamese that men are more effective than machines or weapons, and the electronic equipment sent by the Soviets for air defense batteries was consequently stored for a while in caves. Moscow also "disclosed" that Peking had refused to permit Soviet transport planes loaded with weapons to fly over Chinese territory. Soviet diplomats pointed out that although the Communist Party of the Soviet Union had repeatedly urged joint action by all socialist countries in support of North Vietnam, the Chinese had flatly and stubbornly rejected all such proposals. From this, Moscow affected to deduce that the Chinese leaders were trying to prolong the Vietnam War in order to perpetuate international tension and sustain the image of China as a besieged fortress. In addition, the Soviet leadership asserted that one of the goals of the Chinese with respect to Vietnam was "to originate a military conflict between the USSR and the United States . . . so that they may, as they say themselves, sit on the mountain and watch the fight of the tigers.''[3] One aspect of this "policy-evaluation persecution complex" was that the Soviet KGB and the Warsaw Pact intelligence agencies were directed to gather evidence of secret Chinese-American collaboration.

Not surprisingly, the Chinese Communists summarily rejected these Soviet charges and countered with charges of their own. They accused the Soviet leadership of "actively plotting new deals" with the United States and other "reactionary forces." They bluntly stated that there was no shade of difference between Brezhnev and Khrushchev on the questions of the international communist movement and relations with China; "Khrushchevism without Khrushchev" they repeated in their anti-Soviet propaganda. They blamed the "Soviet revisionists" for whipping up hysteria against China, claiming that what exists is what causes differences, and that which should be common is missing. Naturally, they threw responsibility for the Sino-Soviet tension upon the Soviet party leadership. As for Vietnam, Moscow's "United Action" plan was rejected as an attempt to "deceive the world"; the Soviet leadership was denounced for trying to tie the East European socialist countries to "the chariot of Soviet-United States collaboration" in behalf of world domination; and the Soviets were accused of using Vietnam as "an important counter" in their bargaining with the United States, and as a means to isolate, encircle, and attack China.[4]

The Vietnamese in Hanoi, of course, deplored the dissensions that divided Russia and China and expressed continuing concern over the tension created by the family feud. At the same time, they expressed gratitude for the generous and steadily increasing support of the Soviets and the East Europeans and thanked the Chinese for their assistance as well. Indeed, the Vietnamese were able to produce cleverly formulated and well-balanced statements of gratitude and solidarity all around.

Meanwhile, throughout the mounting rancor of the Sino-Soviet dispute, the Soviet press continued its steady castigation of the US role in Southeast Asia and endorsed North Vietnam's war aims as well as its four-point plan to end the war.[5] Leading Soviet political figures used every occasion that came their way to promise support for the North Vietnamese and the Viet Cong, repeatedly declaring that the Soviet Union was fully prepared to develop better relations between the USSR and the United States, if only the United States would abandon its policy of aggression in Vietnam.

The Chinese propaganda machinery also directed its heavy artillery against the US intervention in the Vietnam War. Its vicious attacks against the American "imperialists" were coupled with encouragement for Hanoi and the Viet Cong to wage an all-out, protracted "people's war." The Chinese leaders' public statements, as well as their opinions expressed in private, differed neither in tone nor in content from those so harshly reported in the news media.

Meanwhile, policymakers in Washington spent considerable time analyzing and judging the militant Chinese and hostile Russian attitudes and actions. Since they were concerned that an abrupt turn in the conduct of the war might trigger an irresponsible Chinese reaction, they tried to avoid any drastic change. They calculated that China would not enter the war unless there was an American invasion of the North beyond the 17th parallel or unless the Hanoi regime was in danger of being toppled. But Washington showed considerable anxiety over Chinese plans for world revolution. In a memorable article entitled, "Long Live the Victory of the People's War," Lin Piao, then heir-apparent to Mao Tse-tung, announced that China, while emphasizing self-reliance in any "revolutionary struggle," certainly would encourage the outbreak of revolutions among the newly emerging nations.[6] Several analysts have pointed out that the article reflected the author's concern over domestic power struggles; yet, in his advice to "encircle the cities from the countryside," he referred to North America, Japan, and the Soviet Union as the cities and the newly emerging nations of Africa, Asia, and Latin America as the countrysides. Naturally, the revolution in Vietnam was singled out as the most convincing application of this "encircling theory." Undersecretary of State George Ball considered the Lin Piao enunciation a "do-it-yourself kit" for global revolution, while Dean Rusk compared it to Hitler's *Mein Kampf*. President Johnson thought that it confirmed the notion that if Vietnam fell, others in Southeast Asia would follow.[7]

Peking, at the time, was also making much of a new "anti-American power axis" that was said to be shaping up between Djakarta, Hanoi, Peking, and Pyongyang. There was no doubt that something like cooperation was developing among Indonesia, North Vietnam, China, and North Korea, but the limited consensus among them was a far cry from an axis. Yet, to American eyes, China appeared to be the driving force behind North Vietnam's decision to militarize its strategy and resist any diplomatic solution to the war. This obviously simplistic view was not altered when the Peking-dominated "axis" disintegrated following the abortive coup of the Indonesian communists, nor when the Chinese revolutionary pronouncements were unfavorably received in the Third World and Lin Piao was liquidated as an agent of American imperialism. China watchers in the State Department and in many other quarters of the US diplomatic community still strongly believed that the United States and China were headed for a collision that neither wanted. Yet the plain truth was that Mao Tse-tung could not afford to go to war with the United States. His power base had so dwindled that he had to launch his Great Proletarian Revolution, marking his greatest power struggle since consolidating control over the Chinese Communist Party in the 1930's.

Just as Chinese intentions were misread in Washington, so were those of the Russians. It was widely believed that the Chinese were the extreme communists while the Soviets were the moderates, favoring a negotiated settlement. Several high officials in the Johnson and Nixon Administrations went so far as to infer that Moscow was "interested" in helping Washington extricate itself from the war. Some in the Western camp, including Ambassador J. Blair Seaborn of Canada, Prime Minister Harold Wilson of

Great Britain, and Foreign Minister Amintore Fanfani of Italy, believed that
the Russian peace feelers could lead to a negotiated settlement. Of course the
solution was not a simple one. On one side of the diplomatic equation stood the
North Vietnamese, with their obsessive determination to carry out their
aggression and win the war. On the other side stood the Americans, with their
aim to assure the survival of a free and independent South Vietnam.
Complicating the problem was the nature of the supporting cast – members of
the Soviet bloc, who were sending out their peace feelers but standing all the
while on Hanoi's side. Thus several questions arose: What was Moscow's true
intention – did the leaders in the Kremlin want to end the war with a
compromise, or was their real aim to feed the Americans misleading
information? Since the Russians and such minor players as the Poles,
Hungarians, and Rumanians appeared to act independently, how could the
US President or Secretary of State be sure who could be trusted – the Soviets,
the Hungarians, the Poles, the Rumanians, or none of them? Were, in fact, the
Soviets and their client states acting on behalf of Hanoi and telling fairy tales to
Washington?

Surely it would be misleading to state that US leaders were not aware of the
hazards and complexities that accompany any dealing with the Soviet Union
and its allies. Yet they had to learn the hard way that the Soviet bloc
meticulously followed the policy set forth by Ho Chi Minh and his successor,
Le Duan. The Soviets and their allies were ready to mediate between Hanoi
and Washington, not with the intent of bringing peace, but only of furthering
Hanoi's cause. First and foremost, their efforts were designed to stop the
American bombing of North Vietnam in order to provide time for the North
Vietnamese to recover and prepare for their next assault on the South. In
broader scope, the Soviet bloc was eager to make the American Government
appear to its own people and the world to be unwilling to make peace, when in
fact it was Hanoi which was committed to a purely military solution.

I was personally involved in one round of these "peace negotiations," which
started in the autumn of 1965 and ended in 1966. It was a bizarre adventure in
make-believe diplomacy, producing the longest bombing pause, a 37-day
Christmas cessation. In this extraordinary example of secret diplomacy,
Hungarian Foreign Minister János Péter, a former Calvinist bishop turned
communist diplomat, badly misled Secretary of State Dean Rusk. Pretending
to speak for Hanoi, he suggested that once the United States halted the
bombing, negotiations to end the war would begin. But this self-appointed
negotiator fabricated the "peace terms," raising false hopes where human lives
were at stake. This Hungarian mediation effort was only one of many peace
hoaxes. The KGB had successfully trapped Adlai Stevenson, U Thant, and
Eric Severeid with a bogus peace feeler.[8] Polish Foreign Minister Adam
Rapacki's mediation attempt, the so-called "Marigold Affair," resembled the
Péter mediation in some respects, but as a diplomatic ploy it was more
sophisticated and was masterfully executed.[9] He made a tempting offer to the

Americans to "prove North Vietnam's readiness for negotiation," while in fact he had nothing firm to offer. He then instigated prolonged Polish-US exploratory talks to obtain concessions from Washington that could be presented as an American position to Hanoi. And finally he made an effort to work out a package deal favorable to Hanoi for the settlement of the conflict.

Ironically, there were moments of candor, too, in the process of the deception game. For instance, Soviet Premier Kosygin once admitted to US Ambassador Llewellyn Thompson that mediators usually either complicate problems or pretend they are doing something when in fact they are not.[10] On another occasion, when Dean Rusk asked his Soviet counterpart Gromyko about the reliability of the East Europeans, the Russian answered bluntly that the United States should listen only to the Russians.[11] But to my knowledge, only once were the Soviets really helpful; in October 1968, Minister Counsellor Valentine Oberenko of the Soviet Embassy in Paris patched up differences over the shape of the conference table at the Paris peace talks.[12]

The four years of Nixon's diplomacy were no more successful than those of the previous administration. It was said that the President and his Secretary of State, Henry Kissinger, provided both the Russians and the Chinese with incentives for wanting the war settled. As Professor Morton A. Kaplan remarked: "Their relationship to Vietnam, their competition in Southeast Asia, the effects in Europe and elsewhere were important too in creating those incentives – so that both of them simultaneously put pressure on the North Vietnamese to come to terms with us."[13] Yet in retrospect it is clear that the new American "global strategy," or, as Kissinger called it, "the diplomatic revolution that had been brought about," had not been working in America's favor. It is true that a semiofficial diplomatic line of communication had been opened up between Washington and Peking. The antiballistic missile systems of Russia and the United States had been limited, and a strategic arms ceiling had been specified. Yet the original aim of Kissinger's "grand design" to resolve the Vietnamese conflict through "global strategy" had not been achieved. Neither the Russians nor the Chinese showed change in their attitudes toward Vietnam. Both communist powers stressed "unflinching" solidarity with the "just struggle" of the peoples of Vietnam, Laos, and Cambodia "for their freedom, independence, and social progress" until the very end of the war. And despite the Sino-Soviet rift, both powers unequivocally demanded the withdrawal of US troops from South Vietnam. In addition, even while negotiating with Washington, Peking and Moscow increased their military and economic assistance to North Vietnam to unprecedented levels. In short, Kissinger simply could not cash in on the differences between China and the Soviet Union; the new formula, the "balance of incentive," induced neither the Russians nor the Chinese to pressure Hanoi into ending the war. It was other elements that changed the diplomatic scenario and led to a ceasefire and later to the peace treaty: decisionmakers in Hanoi came to the view that the successful continuation of the war required a "negotiate and fight" period, considering diplomatic negotiation as only another means of achieving final victory; and those in Washington decided not to insist on the withdrawal of North Vietnamese troops from the South.

In January 1973, "An Agreement on Ending the War and Restoring the Peace in Vietnam" was signed in Paris and endorsed by the great powers, including Russia and China. The monitoring of the peace was entrusted to an International Commission for Control and Supervision, with 290 representatives each from Canada, Indonesia, Hungary, and Poland.[14] But after the withdrawal of American troops from South Vietnam and the return of the American POWs, the treaty was constantly violated by both Hanoi and Saigon.

By the end of 1974, the US Congress had cut back considerably appropriations to provide military aid to South Vietnam. At the same time, Moscow increased its arms shipments to North Vietnam, and the Soviet Government advised Hanoi to launch an all-out offensive against the South.[15] The chief of staff of the Soviet armed forces, General Kulikov, traveled to the North Vietnamese capital to review with his Vietnamese friends, Generals Giap and Dung, the details of the offensive. The rest is well known. The invading North Vietnamese Army crushed all resistance. The Thieu government collapsed like a house of cards. During the last weeks of the war, Hanoi could not believe that the United States would give up a place where it had invested billions of dollars. Through the commanding officers of the Hungarian military contingent of the International Commission for Control and Supervision, Hanoi sent word to the Americans that a last-minute political solution was a real possibility. This bit of make-believe diplomacy, however, was quickly forgotten by the initiators when Dung's tanks rolled onto the streets of Saigon.

Five years ago the helicopter carrying Ambassador Graham Martin left the rooftop of the American Embassy in Saigon. With this final act US direct involvement in the Vietnamese tragedy came to an end. But the United States continued to live under the pressure and humiliation of the lost peace. It engulfed itself in nationwide masochism and mourned about a war which it won militarily but lost politically and diplomatically. It insisted on believing that the villains were Americans themselves, not the "best and the brightest" of the other side. It embraced détente, wanting to believe that the leaders in the Kremlin were genuinely interested in relaxing international tensions, even while Moscow not only extended its sphere of influence all over the world but aided a number of Moscow-oriented communist parties to gain state power in Asia and Africa. The first protégé of the Kremlin was the communist Pathet Lao, which gained control over Laos in 1975. Next in line was the communist Popular Movement for the Liberation of Angola, which overpowered two other national Angolan parties in 1976. Then with Soviet, Cuban, and East German assistance, Colonel Mengistu Haile-Mariam eliminated his fellow-traveler colleagues and installed a staunch communist regime in Ethiopia in 1977. The same year, Marxist Samora Machel of Mozambique, supplied with Chinese and Soviet weapons, took over that African state. In 1978, two bloody Moscow-directed coups were carried out, one by the veteran communist Nur Muhammad Taraki in Afghanistan, the other by the communists in South Yemen, who eliminated their former ally, President Salim Rubay'i 'Ali, and established a stronghold on the tip of the Arabian peninsula. Finally, Hanoi, again with Soviet help, installed a puppet government in Cambodia. Meanwhile the United States, paralyzed by post-Vietnam trauma, was unable to respond to the Soviet advances and accepted the changes in the status quo as facts of life. Not until the Soviet invasion of Afghanistan did policymakers in this country express serious concern about the growing appetite of Soviet imperialism.

Perhaps now, after the events in Afghanistan and Iran, the Vietnam-rent American society will at last come together. Perhaps the severely damaged relations between the United States and a number of its allies will be repaired, and people around the world will come to count again on the strength and reliability of American commitments. Perhaps the era of the Vietnam syndrome will finally be over, and, in place of empty rhetoric, the US Government will demonstrate the force and resolve to counter communist expansion.

NOTES

1. Part of the material of this article appeared in somewhat different and more extended form in my book: *Delusion & Reality: Gambits, Hoaxes & One-Upmanship in Vietnam* (South Bend, Ind.: Gateway Editions, 1978).
2. See Chester A. Bain, *Vietnam, The Roots of Conflict* (Englewood Cliffs, N.J.: Prentice-Hall, 1967), p. 153; also George Carver "The Faceless Viet Cong," *Foreign Affairs*, 44 (April 1966), 347-472.
3. "Secret Letter Of The CPSU To Other Communist Parties Regarding The Split With The Chinese Communist Party," published by *Die Welt*, Hamburg, 21 March 1966, and quoted in "Text of Chinese Note to Russians and Excerpts from Soviet Letter to Parties," *The New York Times*, 24 March 1966, p. 14.
4. "Refutation of the New Leaders of the C.P.S.U. on 'United Action,'" *Peking Review*, 12 November 1965, pp. 10-21.
5. The four points were these: The US Government "must withdraw from South Vietnam US troops . . . . [It] must stop its acts of war against North Vietnam . . . . The internal affairs of South Vietnam must be settled by the South Vietnamese people themselves in accordance with the program of the NFLSV . . . . [And] the peaceful reunification of Vietnam is to be settled by the Vietnamese peoples in both zones, without any foreign interference" (Hanoi Radio broadcast, 13 April 1965).
6. Lin Piao, *Long Live The Victory of People's War* (Peking: Foreign Languages Press, 1965).
7. Background briefing by George W. Ball on 1 April 1971 at the Stanford Faculty Club. Transcript of the lecture deposited at the Institute of Political Studies, Stanford University.
8. See Eric Sevareid, "The Final Troubled Hours of Adlai Stevenson," *Look*, 30 November 1965, pp. 81-86.
9. The best documentary evidence of the "Marigold Affair" can be found in the so-called Diplomatic Volumes of "The Pentagon Papers" (*United States-Vietnam Relations 1945-1967*, Vol. 6.C.2), a copy of which is held in the US Army Military History Institute, Carlisle Barracks, Pa.

10. Ibid., Vol. 6.C.3, p. 19. See transcript of Ambassador L. Thompson's conversation with Premier A. Kosygin.
11. Personal recollection.
12. Some of the details of the Paris peace negotiations were given to me during my interview with Ambassador Averell Harriman at his Yorktown Heights home in the summer of 1975.
13. Morton A. Kaplan et al., *Vietnam Settlement: Why 1973, Not 1969?* (Washington: American Enterprise Institute for Public Policy Research, 1973), p. 41.
14. Kissinger and his aides assumed that Hanoi believed the Hungarians and the Poles could be reliably counted upon to follow Soviet directions and that the Soviets would in turn do nothing to frustrate or embarrass North Vietnamese intentions. And, of course, this assumption proved to be entirely correct. This opinion was expressed to the author in a letter-interview dated 29 September 1977 by Ambassador William H. Sullivan, chief negotiator of the US Government at the 1973 Paris Peace Conference.
15. US Congress, House of Representatives, Committee on International Relations, Special Subcommittee on Investigations, *Hearing, The Vietnam-Cambodia Emergency, 1975: Part III – Vietnam Evacuation: Testimony of Ambassador Graham A. Martin*, 94th Cong., 2d Sess., 27 January 1976, p. 540.

This article appeared in the September 1980 issue of *Parameters*.

7

On Strategy and the Vietnam War

by JEFFREY CLARKE

Although ten years have passed since the conflict in South Vietnam ended, Americans are still debating the significance of what Professor George Herring has labeled "America's longest war."[1] Much of the discussion centers on American strategy in Southeast Asia between 1961 and 1972. Current commentators such as Colonel Harry G. Summers, Jr., and General William E. DePuy argue that the war could have been won if Washington had followed a more decisive and comprehensive military strategy in Southeast Asia.[2] A formal declaration of war, mobilization of the reserves, the military occupation of the Ho Chi Minh Trail, and a naval blockade of Haiphong harbor and perhaps of Sihanoukville as well are all part of a recipe which, they feel, might have changed the outcome of the struggle. Like any historical hypothesis, their assertions are difficult to prove or refute. Yet many of their assumptions can be challenged. Despite the vast material on the Vietnam War pouring forth over the last twenty years, there are still document collections hitherto unexploited, memoirs yet to be written, and entire areas of the conflict that have been unaddressed. The US Army's official history of the period has still to see the light of day. Future revelations may ultimately change our perceptions of what took place in Vietnam and in turn affect our judgment of the war's lessons, some of which appear so self-evident today.

At first glance, the history of the American involvement in South Vietnam appears relatively straightforward. The overall policy of the United States government there was always clear – the preservation of an independent, non-communist government in Saigon. American military objectives, however, were less sharply defined. By 1964 the major threat to Saigon came from an internal insurgency patterned after Mao Tse-tung's three-phase "revolutionary warfare" experiences in China. Two phases, an organizational phase creating a clandestine political infrastructure and a guerrilla warfare phase stretching the military forces of the established government as thin as possible, were firmly in place; the third or conventional warfare phase seemed imminent. In response, the US government supported a three-pronged counterinsurgency or "pacification" campaign in South Vietnam. With American advice and assistance, the Saigon regime attempted to destroy the military forces of the insurgents, root out their normally clandestine governmental apparatus, and protect and fortify its own political, economic, and social institutions. Pacification was a strategy for both defeating the revolutionaries and strengthening the fledgling state of South Vietnam – what social scientists have called "nation building."

Prior to the commitment of US ground troops in 1965, American military participation was limited primarily to advising the South Vietnamese armed forces. In 1964 Saigon faced an insurgent army that ranged from hamlet militia and full-time guerrillas to conventional light infantry battalions and regiments. To defeat this diverse force, American and South Vietnamese leaders identified three purely military missions: "search and destroy" (engaging conventional or mobile enemy units); "clear and hold" (engaging enemy territorial companies and guerrillas); and "securing" (providing military security on a continuing basis so that the other pacification tasks could be carried out). The nonmilitary pacification tasks remained largely the province of Saigon's civil administrators and their American civilian advisers (with some help from US Army Special Forces teams operating in the hinterlands).

Despite the great increase in American military aid between 1961 and 1964, the early pacification effort was a failure. Major problem areas centered on the southern republic's lack of leadership, the over-centralization of power in Saigon, and South Vietnam's often xenophobic resistance to American advice if not American support. Other difficulties arose from the complex sequencing of the various military and nonmilitary tasks, and the division of American advice among a variety of agencies loosely coordinated by the American Ambassador. The tendency of Americans to compartmentalize military and nonmilitary tasks exacerbated such problems. In both Saigon and Washington, the task of providing local security, the "securing" mission, was often badly neglected, and the other, nonmilitary elements of pacification also received decreasing attention.

Sometime in 1965, and perhaps even earlier, the direct participation of both Hanoi and Washington in the war changed the thrust of American strategy. As American ground combat forces arrived in South Vietnam, the search and destroy effort became increasingly distinct from the other elements of pacification and, in the end, became separate unto itself, the strategy of attrition. The attrition strategy was relatively simple. It sought to inflict unacceptable casualties on the forces of the opponent and thereby force a successful outcome to the war. Although the American military Commander-in-Chief in South Vietnam, General William C. Westmoreland, never articulated the new strategy in any formal directive or campaign plan, he and most of his fellow generals consciously adopted it in mid-1965 as the best way to use American superiority in firepower and mobility. The attrition strategy had the virtue of bypassing the political turmoil of Saigon and dispensing with the extraordinarily complex politico-military strategy of pacification. American leaders made the assumption that the insurgency directed by Hanoi had little indigenous support in the South. Military attrition, they felt, could force the northern regime out of the war and dry up the southern insurgency.[3] A ground invasion of North Vietnam was unnecessary. General Earle G. Wheeler, Chairman of the Joint Chiefs of Staff, summed up American thinking, telling President Johnson in February 1967: ''If we apply pressure upon the enemy relentlessly in the north and in the south, ... the North Vietnamese would be unable effectively to support the war in the south'' and ''the war would essentially be won.''[4]

Late in 1965 Maxwell Taylor, a former Chairman of the Joint Chiefs of Staff who had also served as the US Ambassador to Saigon, voiced strong reservations over the attrition strategy. Taylor believed that Westmoreland's plans would soon place the major burden of the war effort on the arriving US ground combat forces. The results, he warned, would relegate the South Vietnamese troops to the background, dramatically increase American combat casualties, and fuel domestic opposition to the war effort.[5] Two years later Taylor's predictions seemed to have come true. In April 1967, with about 400,000 American troops in South Vietnam and no victory on the battlefield in sight, Westmoreland found his civilian superiors, President Lyndon Johnson and Secretary of Defense Robert McNamara, reluctant to send further reinforcements. Both demanded that he somehow squeeze more mileage out of Saigon's own military forces. The impression in Washington, explained General Wheeler, was simply that ''the South Vietnamese have now leaned back in their foxholes and are content for us to carry the major share of the combat activity.''[6] To counter such charges, Westmoreland conducted a press campaign to improve the image of the South Vietnamese soldiers, and he sponsored more combined operations between American and Vietnamese units. At the end of the year, he also suggested publicly that the steadily improving South Vietnamese forces might be able to replace some American ground troops within the next two years.[7] According to General Leonard F. Chapman, the new Commandant of the US Marine Corps, Westmoreland also agreed to curtail American search and destroy operations in the interior of South Vietnam and to increase the number of American combat units providing security for the pacification campaign.[8]

However, the MACV commander put off making any major changes in the roles and missions of his American troops. During the Tet Offensive of 1968, he requested over 200,000 more US troops; with these reinforcements, Westmoreland hoped to move into the Laotian panhandle and the southern portions of North Vietnam, seal off the borders of the southern republic, and engage the enemy in his cross-border sanctuaries.[9] To Westmoreland's chagrin, President Johnson's continued reluctance to expand the ground war in Southeast Asia or to mobilize America's reserves made such proposals unacceptable. The war seemed to have arrived at a stalemate.

Following the Tet Offensive of 1968, American military policy in Vietnam underwent a major transition. Although its specific origins are difficult to trace, this change clearly predated the inauguration of Richard Nixon in January 1969. Several months prior to the 1968 American presidential election, General Creighton W. Abrams, Jr., Westmoreland's successor, approved a new "one war" campaign plan that formally ended the division of missions between the armed forces of South Vietnam and those of the United States. Henceforth the ground components of both armies were to assume identical missions, and those missions were to support the old strategy of pacification.[10] Both Abrams and his pacification deputy, Ambassador Robert W. Komer, feared that the Paris peace talks might lead to an expedited settlement to the war based on territorial control. They also regarded the change in roles and missions as the best means of bringing the war to a successful conclusion if a peace agreement could not be reached. Thus, pacification, with its emphasis on territorial security, once again moved to the forefront. The strategy of attrition was dead.

Even as these plans went into effect, the Nixon Administration initiated the strategy of Vietnamization, an entirely new American approach to the war. Initial guidance to Defense Secretary Melvin Laird in April 1969 specified that the primary objective of Vietnamization was to replace US ground combat forces with similar South Vietnamese forces. American ground units were to be withdrawn from South Vietnam over three to four years, leaving some type of residual force to provide only advisory assistance, air support, and technical aid.[11] With these instructions, General Abrams concentrated on three military objectives between 1969 and 1972: increasing the capabilities of Saigon's defense establishment; supervising the drawdown of the American military forces; and maintaining pressure on the "residual" Viet Cong insurgency. He also kept a close watch on the larger North Vietnamese Army units, which, for the most part, had retreated to border sanctuaries just beyond the reach of American firepower, badly damaged but still capable of offensive action. American objectives during the Cambodian and Laotian cross-border excursions of 1970 and 1971 were limited to disrupting enemy base areas and logistical capabilities, representing little departure from existing policies. In the spring of 1972, after most American ground combat units had departed, North Vietnam launched an "Easter Offensive," the only real test of Vietnamization. When the smoke finally cleared several months later, two new factors were apparent. First, the internal insurgency was no longer a potent factor on the battlefield; the battles had been almost entirely conventional in nature. Second, the North Vietnamese offensive showed that with massive American air support directed by "advisers" like Major General James F. Hollingsworth, John Paul Vann, and many others, Saigon's armed forces were capable of beating back even the strongest enemy attack.[12] In this light, Vietnamization can be judged a success. Its life, however, was brief. The Paris peace accords, signed in January 1973, terminated the American advisory effort, drastically curtailed further American military assistance to Saigon, and brought an end to the gradual and orderly process known as Vietnamization. American leaders had not had time to prepare South Vietnam for a total withdrawal of direct US military advice and support. The agreement came as a shock to Saigon, and the ensuing collapse of the southern republic in 1975 had little to do with Vietnamization as it had been originally conceived in Washington.

Although perhaps superficially valid, this survey of American policy and strategy in South Vietnam may be too simplistic. Many issues remain. Some were identified during the course of the war, but few were resolved. At what point, for example, did the conflict cease to be primarily a ''low-intensity'' insurgency and become a conventional war? Was it in 1965 when regular North Vietnamese Army troops entered the contest? In 1968 when the insurgents decided to stand and fight at Hue and elsewhere? Or in 1972, when the North Vietnamese attempted a large conventional invasion? To what extent did the North control the insurgency in the South? To what extent was the struggle a contest between two sovereign states rather than rival Vietnamese governments or competing ideologies? Finally, was Vietnamization, beneath all the official fanfare, merely a ploy to cover an ignominious American withdrawal from a war that could not be won – or was it an innovative program for successfully pursuing America's objectives in Southeast Asia that somehow went astray? More to the point, was Vietnamization a strategy for winning the war or was it a means of solving domestic American political and economic problems that had little to do with Southeast Asia?

To Colonel Robert A. Guenthner, a division senior adviser in the South Vietnamese delta region, some answers in mid-1965 were clear enough: the local guerrillas posed no more than an occasional annoyance; the real threat came from the regular Viet Cong forces operating along the Cambodian border. In Guenthner's opinion, the war had already ''assumed the proportion of a military confrontation between two relatively sophisticated conventional military machines.'' Whatever side put the most military power in the field, he predicted, would win.[13] Another American adviser, Colonel Edward F. Brunner, who served in the same area one year later, seconded these views.[14] Elaborating on the same point in *On Strategy: The Vietnam War in Perspective*, Colonel Summers argued that American military leaders paid too much attention to pacification and the internal insurgency throughout the war; the heart of the enemy's effort could be found only in Hanoi. The pacification strategy addressed the manifestations of the problem rather than its cause. As long as North Vietnam remained virtually untouched, the United States could not engage the enemy effectively, let alone win the war.[15] For the United States to achieve its objectives in South Vietnam, more decisive military action against Hanoi was necessary. Taking Summers one step further, General DePuy recently suggested that placing the equivalent of seven US combat divisions astride the Ho Chi Minh Trail along the DMZ and into Laos might have effectively ended the war in the South. Like Summers, both he and retired Admiral Elmo R. Zumwalt, Jr., the Chief of Naval Operations between 1970 and 1974, felt that the weight of American combat power ought to have been directed against North Vietnam and that heavier air attacks on Hanoi and Haiphong also were necessary.[16] North Vietnam's response to the Linebacker bombing campaigns in 1972 seems to bear out their point.

General Westmoreland himself might find it easy to approve these judgments. As MACV commander, he had repeatedly but unsuccessfully urged his superiors to adopt such measures.[17] Other military spokesmen, however, have disagreed, holding that the United States placed too much emphasis on the conventional war effort between 1965 and 1968, and too little on the provision of population security or the advisory effort. Early in the war Ambassador Taylor and retired Lieutenant General James Gavin favored an "enclave strategy," in which American ground forces, operating from secure coastal enclaves, would back up the South Vietnamese forces that would continue to handle most of the fighting.[18] Retired General Bruce Palmer, Jr., later noted that "our number one military job was to develop South Vietnamese armed forces that could successfully pacify and defend their own country," but the United States never gave this critical task sufficient attention.[19] Thomas C. Thayer, Director of the Southeast Asia Office of the Assistant Secretary of Defense for Systems Analysis, 1966-1972, pointed out that only a small portion of US military expenditures in the war went for territorial security; the larger share was absorbed by US air interdiction and ground operations along South Vietnam's borders.[20] His detailed statistics challenge Summers' assumption that American military operations were too closely tied down to pacification-related tasks.

Others had different answers. Colonel Charles M. Simpson III, former deputy commander of the US Army 5th Special Forces Group, saw the Civilian Irregular Defense Group program, the effort to bring the South Vietnamese ethnic and religious minorities into the war effort, as a prototype for a larger, more effective advisory system that might have obviated the use of US combat troops.[21] The US Marine Corps generals were dissatisfied with Saigon's performance in pacification and wanted to commit their own forces more heavily to local security, gradually eliminating the insurgency in their rear areas along the coast before moving into the interior.[22] Sir Robert Thompson, a counterinsurgency expert who headed the British Advisory Mission to South Vietnam from 1961 to 1965, agreed with the Marines, advocating what has often been called the "spreading oil spot" strategy of pacification.[23] In his eyes, Westmoreland's military campaigns in the heavily forested, mountainous interior nullified America's sophisticated technological superiority and allowed the enemy a free hand in the populated coastal regions. More ambitious US military operations in the rugged Laotian wilderness to block the Ho Chi Minh Trail were too expensive and too risky, and Lam Son 719, South Vietnam's "raid" into Laos in 1971, supported this point. In addition, Army logisticians might have looked askance at any proposal to put a large American army in the Indochinese interior with no deep-water port in sight.[24]

The debate over American strategy continued throughout the Vietnam War and after, often at an earthy level. While some advocated "bombing the north back into the stone age" – suggesting that the decisive opponent was Hanoi – others favored "towing South Vietnam out into the middle of the Pacific and sinking it," implying that the war could be won in the South itself. But without any consensus regarding military objectives, there could be no consensus on military strategy. Obviously the earlier views of Taylor and Thompson were compatible with the Vietnamization policy of President Nixon and Secretary Laird. Vietnamization reaffirmed America's limited objectives in South Vietnam, and it emphasized the primary role that the Saigon government would have to play in ending the conflict. However, Vietnamization was not a strategy for fighting the war; it simply shuffled existing roles and missions between the allied participants. In the later years of the war, even as the fighting grew more conventional, the allied forces remained deployed in an area support configuration and continued to rely on firepower rather than mobility to defeat their opponents in battle. The conclusion that American and South Vietnamese leaders never resolved the question of whether they were pursuing a strategy of attrition or a strategy of pacification is inescapable, and it explains, in part, Saigon's inability to respond effectively to the final enemy offensive in 1975.

A final question involves the nature of the ground war itself. History may never produce an accurate assessment of North Vietnamese and Viet Cong operations because of deficient records and the extremely decentralized organization of the insurgents. But even on the American side, the picture is confusing. Throughout the conflict, different levels of enemy activity necessitated different responses from region to region and even from province to province. It is almost impossible to generalize on the nature of the war based on personal experiences. Although American officials compiled masses of statistics in an effort to pierce the dense fog of war, the results were often less than illuminating. In 1968, for example, military analysts noted the direct relationship between enemy offensive ground operations and American casualties, and they gloomily concluded that the enemy controlled the tempo of the war from nearly inviolate border sanctuaries.[25] However, the same statistical evidence can be used to show that the tempo of the war, if measured in terms of American combat deaths, was directly proportional to US ground troop levels in South Vietnam and thus, presumably, to US ground operations (obviously this relationship does not hold true for South Vietnam's Laotian operation in 1971 or the 1972 Easter Offensive). The more US ground combat troops in South Vietnam, the greater the number of American war casualties. Despite Abrams' announced changes in the employment of US ground forces after 1968, there was no appreciable diminution in the proportion of American losses. Either Westmoreland's search and destroy tactics that characterized

American combat operations prior to 1968 were not as hazardous as they had seemed, or the enemy had found new methods of inflicting casualties on the Americans after 1968.

Equally confounding were South Vietnamese casualty levels and rates. In most categories their losses were higher than American losses throughout the war. For example, in 1967, when South Vietnamese and American troop strengths were approximately equal, Saigon suffered 12,716 combat losses to 9,378 for the United States.[26] If the Vietnamese casualty reports are reliable, then obviously not all of the indigenous soldiers were leaning back in their foxholes. Confining the comparison to numbers of actual combat troops in the theater may resolve some of these anomalies (since the United States had a huge logistical apparatus), but it would also introduce new ones since the South Vietnamese militia-like territorial units had the highest casualty rates. Perhaps the "unconventional" war for the hamlets and villages was more hotly contested during Westmoreland's tenure than many believed. Indeed, it may be one of the great ironies of the war that as MACV geared up for the pacification effort with the establishment of Komer's Civil Operations and Revolutionary Development Support staff in 1967 and the Accelerated Pacification Campaign in 1968, the war was becoming increasingly conventional and, by 1972, its course much more susceptible to the kind of military power that the US armed forces were best able to project.

A recent review at the Center of Military History of a detailed draft manuscript treating combat operations in South Vietnam from 1966 to 1967 has thrown into question even deeper assumptions about the nature of the war. The study showed that Westmoreland's "search and destroy" attrition strategy may never have been implemented due to the enemy's unwillingness to engage larger American units. Large-scale operations in the Vietnamese interior were uncommon and those that were undertaken, like Junction City, were fairly ineffectual. Instead, most American ground combat operations, Army and Marine Corps alike, were small-scale affairs that took place along the Vietnamese coast, from the Delta waterways to the Bong Son plains, or in the adjacent forests and jungles that bordered these densely inhabited regions. The war of the "big battalions" may have been a myth. Such a reinterpretation of American combat activities may better explain why, for example, units of the American and 9th Divisions were continually operating in heavily populated areas from 1967 to 1969, why there was great confusion between US and South Vietnamese units over roles and missions, and why officers like Summers felt MACV paid too much attention to pacification. But other mysteries remain unsolved: the final results of the Westmoreland-CBS case were unsatisfying; an accurate appraisal of America's joint bombing campaign in Laos and North Vietnam continued to be elusive; and a serious debate over the performance of rotary-wing aviation in Lam Son 719 was never resolved. Indeed, the controversies surrounding the conflict have scarcely abated since 1975, making one more sympathetic to those, both inside and outside of the defense establishment, who would rather forget that America ever fought a war in Southeast Asia.

Until we achieve a better understanding of what took place in South Vietnam, Washington, and Hanoi, any discussion of alternative strategies raises more questions than it answers. Studying the roles and missions of American forces as well as those of their allies is critical to comprehending what US leaders felt were their objectives and how they sought to accomplish them. Disagreements in the allied camp over roles and missions only reflected deeper divisions over what had to be done and how best to do it. Almost all postmortems of the war attest to such differences over ends and means and the confusion that often ensued. The intentions and responses of the enemy are another story. As pointed out by one former Special Forces officer, there may never have been a clear dividing line between the conventional and unconventional aspects of the war, and the internal insurgency may have had more resiliency after 1968 than many pacification experts thought possible.[27] On the other hand, perhaps Viet Cong operations behind South Vietnamese lines after 1972 were no more than commando raids with little staying power and bore little resemblance to the deep-rooted insurgency that had characterized the earlier years of the war. At present, we simply do not have the answers.[28]

Like war itself, military strategy is inextricable from politics. In South Vietnam, the two were closely related with political considerations impinging on almost every major military decision, as we should have expected. To isolate military strategy may be a theoretical exercise with little practical application except to remind political decision-makers of the limits and requirements of military force. In the case of Vietnam, Washington never seriously considered expanding American participation in the ground war beyond the borders of South Vietnam. America's fighting strategy in 1972 represented a return to policies that predated the arrival of US ground troops in 1965. It is indisputable that America's participation in the war from 1965 to 1972 bought time for Saigon to reorganize and strengthen its political and military apparatus. However, it would be disingenuous to argue that this was an American military objective. Between 1965 and 1968, American leaders clearly hoped to settle the matter through the use of military force. The application of conventional military power, they felt, was the best way to win the war. Their degree of success is still a matter of conjecture. But any argument that even more conventional military power would have turned the tide must be judiciously qualified; Clausewitz would have been among the first to agree that such power has its limits. Only when those limits were reached did American leaders begin seriously to explore other options. To date, few studies have analyzed this search, but its examination in depth must dominate any critical assessment of the final years of the war.

NOTES

1. For example, see discussions in Peter Braestrup, ed., *Vietnam as History: Ten Years After the Paris Peace Accords*, Wilson Center Conference Report (Washington: Univ. Press of America, 1984); John Schlight, ed., *The Second Indochina War* (Washington: US Army Center of Military History, 1986); and a summing up of the various schools of thought in Gary R. Hess, "The Military Perspective on Strategy in Vietnam: Harry G. Summers's *On Strategy* and Bruce Palmer's *The 25-Year War*," *Diplomatic History*, 10 (Winter 1986), 91-106.

2. Harry G. Summers, Jr., *On Strategy: The Vietnam War in Perspective* (Carlisle, Pa.: US Army War College, 1981); William E. DePuy, "What We Might Have Done And Why We Didn't Do It," *Army*, 36 (February 1986), 23-40.

3. See William C. Westmoreland, *A Soldier Reports* (New York: Doubleday, 1976), p. 410.

4. Related in message, Wheeler JCS 1284-67 to Sharp and Westmoreland, 17 February 1967, Message File, Westmoreland Papers, Center of Military History (CMH).

5. Related in message, Wheeler JCS 450065 to Westmoreland, 201906 November 1965, Message File, Westmoreland Papers, CMH.

6. Message, Westmoreland HWA 1272 to Heintges, 19 April 1967, Message File, Westmoreland Papers, CMH, citing in toto Message, Wheeler, JCS 2861-67 to Westmoreland, 19 April 1967.

7. See message, Westmoreland MAC 10451 to Sharp, 030422 November 1967, subject: Amphibious Operations North of the DMZ, Message File, Westmoreland Papers; message, MAC 36743, COMUSMACV to subordinate commands, 090257 November 1967, subject: Improving the Image of ARVN Among the US Public, Westmoreland Papers, COMUSMACV Signature File 1967, Westmoreland Papers; and message, Westmoreland, HWA 3445 to Abrams, 26 November 1967, subject: Concept of Situation Portrayed During Recent Visit to Washington, History File, Tab 25-A45, Westmoreland Papers, all at CMH.

8. Memo, Chapman to president, 2 February 1968, subject: Strategy for the Conduct of the War in SEASIA, Box 127, Harold K. Johnson Papers, US Army Military History Institute, Carlisle Barracks, Pa.

9. Westmoreland, *A Soldier Reports*, pp. 350-60; Paul L. Miles, "The Origins of the Post-Tet 1968 Plans for Additional American Forces in RVN," 9 November 1970, an unpublished study prepared for General Westmoreland at CMH.

10. MACV/JGS, Combined Campaign Plan AB 144, 30 September 1968, pp. 6-8; *MACV Command History, 1969*, I, II-3.

11. National Security Study Memorandum 36, Henry Kissinger to Secretary of State, Secretary of Defense, and Director of Central Intelligence, 10 April 1969, subject: Vietnamizing the War.

12. Ngo Quang Truong's critical *The Easter Offensive of 1972* (Washington: US Army Center of Military History, 1980) and G. H. Turley's firsthand *The Easter Offensive: The Last American Advisors, Vietnam, 1972* (Novato, Calif.: Presidio Press, 1985) are good first cuts at a turbulent episode.

13. Letter, Guenthner, Senior Adviser, 7th (South Vietnamese) Division, to Director of Special Warfare, Deputy Chief of Staff for Military Operations, 22 July 1965, subject: Debriefing Report of Officers Returning from Field Assignments, p. 1, in CMH Vietnam War Records.

14. Interview with Brunner, 15 May 1985.

15. See Summers, pp. 53, 65; see also Summers' "Lessons: A Soldier's View" in Braestrup, pp. 109-14, and criticism by Russell F. Weigley, pp. 115-24 and Ernest R. May, pp. 125-28.

16. DePuy, pp. 36-39; Zumwalt lecture, "A View of Three Wars: Continuity and Change," presented at the US Army Center of Military History, 15 January 1986.

17. Westmoreland, *A Soldier Reports*, pp. 271-72, 410-12.

18. Ibid., pp. 129-30.

19. Bruce Palmer, Jr., *The 25-Year War: America's Military Role in Vietnam* (Lexington: Univ. Press of Kentucky, 1984), p. 179.

20. Thomas C. Thayer, *How to Analyze a War Without Fronts: Vietnam, 1965-72*, Journal of Defense Research Series B: Tactical Warfare, vol. 7B, No. 3, Fall 1975, pp. 782-84.

21. Charles M. Simpson III, *Inside the Green Berets: The First Thirty Years* (Novato, Calif.: Presidio Press, 1983), p. 216.

22. Jack Shulimson and Charles M. Johnson, *U.S. Marines in Vietnam: The Landing and the Buildup, 1965* (Washington: US Marine Corps History and Museums Division, 1978), pp. 115-16.

23. See Robert Thompson, *No Exit from Vietnam* (New York: McKay, 1969), especially ch. IX, "The Failure of American Strategy."

24. On the logistical problems of over-the-beach and port supply during the 1944 invasion of France, see Martin Van Creveld, *Supply in War* (New York: Cambridge Univ. Press, 1977), pp. 204-15; for Vietnam, see appropriate sections of Joseph M. Heiser, Jr., *Logistic Support*, Vietnam Studies (Washington: Department of the Army, 1974).

25. See Thayer, pp. 835-36. The contention is widely accepted; see Guenter Lewy, *America in Vietnam* (New York: Oxford, 1978), pp. 82-84, and George C. Herring, *America's Longest War: The United States and Vietnam, 1950-1975* (New York: Wiley, 1979), p. 154. But Thayer believed that North Vietnam lost this control after 1968.

26. Thayer, pp. 848-51. For all other years, South Vietnamese losses are much higher than American casualties.

27. Rod Paschall, "Low-Intensity Conflict Doctrine: Who Needs It?" *Parameters*, 15 (Autumn 1985), 33-45.

28. In Van Tien Dung, *Our Great Spring Victory: An Account of the Liberation of South Vietnam*, trans. John Sprangens (London: Review Press, 1977); and Tran Van Tra, *Vietnam: History of the Bulwark B2 Theater, Vol. 5: Concluding the 30-Year War* (Ho Chi Minh City: Van Nghe, 1982), reprinted by the Joint Publications Research Service, Arlington, Va., February 1983, the authors may have both political and personal reasons for either emphasizing or deemphasizing the role played by the guerrillas in the 1975 offensive.

This article appeared in the winter 1986 issue of *Parameters*.

III. THE CONDUCT OF WAR

8

American Planning for Ground Combat in Vietnam: 1952-1965

by ALEXANDER S. COCHRAN, JR.

A problem exists with current analyses of the Vietnam War, one that can be summed up best as a fascination with the "what if" theory. Many analysts assume that America's role in that unhappy conflict was reactive from its outset and they have developed the notion that this somehow explains why the United States "lost" the war. With guilt presumed, they then must simply present the corroborating evidence.[1]

The "what if" premise has also fostered a conceptualization that skews the analysis of the military planning that led to commitment of US ground combat troops to Vietnam in the spring and summer of 1965. Relying upon the mass of evidence released in the wake of the publication of *The Pentagon Papers* plus that gained through Freedom of Information queries, scholars such as military historian David Palmer, diplomatic historian George Herring, and political scientist Larry Berman view the planning for and the deployment of US combat units as hasty and reactive. Their judgments suggest inadequate American military strategic planning, leading one to ponder, What if the United States had been better prepared? Might its army have prevailed in 1965, thus "winning" the war? Or perhaps more to the point, might the United States not have committed ground combat units in 1965, thereby avoiding the "loss"? While their theory provides a useful counter to Leslie Gelb and Richard Betts, who imply that the whole matter can be understood best within the context of misguided bureaucracy, the "what if" questions suggested by Palmer, Herring, Berman, and others are serious enough to warrant a careful examination of their basic assumption.[2]

The origins of American military planning for the use of US combat troops in Vietnam can be traced to the days of American involvement in the Korean War and the French campaign against the Viet Minh. In 1952 the US Joint Chiefs of Staff gave serious thought to either aiding French units in the Red River Delta region or replacing them with eight American combat divisions to release the French to fight elsewhere in Indochina. The plan was vigorously opposed by Army Chief of Staff Matthew B. Ridgway, although not so much for its strategic implications as for its manpower ramifications. The proposed deployments would strip the active Army of all available resources and thus require partial mobilization of reserves if the Army were faced with another contingency. A major problem for Ridgway's planners at this stage was their reliance on the big-unit strategy that had been so successful on the northern European plains during the last year of World War II. That strategy ran counter to the New Look, a reliance upon nuclear weapons in lieu of large units ordered by President Dwight D. Eisenhower early in his administration. Ike, for diplomatic reasons, finally chose not to intervene in the Indochina War. Still, Army planners were painfully aware that the New Look also meant a lack of flexibility to cope with small, localized conflicts such as that in Vietnam, or as they soon would be called, limited wars.[3]

Another factor modified American military planning for Southeast Asia in the mid-1950s. With the conclusion of the Geneva Accords, the French withdrew their army from Vietnam, and the country was partitioned. American military planners now projected a limited war in Vietnam, patterned on their experiences in Korea, and envisioned a parallel series of events. They anticipated a North Vietnamese invasion of South Vietnam that might also involve the Chinese communist forces. They assumed that the enemy's objective would be reunification of the two nations, or perhaps even the more ambitious goal of communist domination over all of mainland Southeast Asia.[4]

The planners identified three invasion routes, all terminating at the capital city of Saigon. The most direct – and the most restrictive because of geography – followed Route One from North Vietnam along the South Vietnamese coast through Hue, Da Nang, Tuy Hoa, Nha Trang, and Phan Thiet to Saigon. The second avenue passed through the Laotian panhandle into the Central Highlands via Kontum, Pleiku, and Ban Me Thuot and then cut south along Highway Fourteen to Saigon. The third route ran through northern Laos and then east into Cambodia and along the Mekong River into the "rice bowl" of Southeast Asia, the Vietnamese Delta. American contingency plans placed US divisions in critical blocking positions along these invasion routes. As most of these forces would be deployed to Vietnam by sea and a few by air, and all would be resupplied through coastal ports, the security of major sea and air facilities in the South was critical. Thus American plans called for bases at Da Nang, Qui Nhon, Nha Trang, Vung Tau, Bien Hoa, and Tan Son Nhut.

Since two of the invasion routes involved neighboring countries, American military planners for the first time saw the threat to South Vietnam in a regional context. That realization led the United States to call for the establishment of a defense pact for the region, the Southeast Asia Treaty Organization (SEATO). At the same time, the US Military Assistance Advisory Group (MAAG) persuaded the South Vietnamese to design their plans so that their forces would occupy these blocking positions prior to the arrival of US combat units.

During the first phase of operations, the defense, American forces were to secure the coastal and inland bases and then move forward to blocking positions in the Hue-Pleiku-Kontum region and in areas to the north and west of Saigon. The initial American units to deploy were to be forces already stationed in the Pacific Command – the Okinawa-based Marines plus an Army airborne battle group from the 25th Infantry Division (redesignated in 1963 as the 173d Airborne Brigade) and the remainder of the 25th Infantry Division. Follow-up combat units from the continental United States included the 101st Airborne Division (to be airlifted) and the 1st Infantry Division (to be moved by sea).

The next phase, the counteroffensive, was to begin after the blocking forces had contained the North Vietnamese invasion. Harking back to the Korean War and MacArthur's Inchon strategy when he flanked the enemy with amphibious landings, American plans envisioned pushing back the communist forces with an ambitious joint airborne, amphibious, and ground attack into North Vietnam to seize the strategic objective of the Hanoi-Haiphong area. The ultimate objective was reunification of the two Vietnams under pro-Western (presumably South Vietnamese) leadership.

This strategic scenario began to change during the last year of the Eisenhower Administration. American military planning at that stage represented a synthesis of the military realities of the New Look with the Cold War strategy of containment. The defense of Vietnam thus was to be fought along conventional lines, to include the use of nuclear weapons. Whatever considerations that planners gave to guerrilla tactics were rudimentary, based upon limited knowledge of partisan warfare during World War II and experience with the North Korean stay-behind operations during the Korean War. With the formation of SEATO and the worsening Laotian crisis, American military planners began to shift emphasis to regional defense against communist expansion, primarily in Thailand. Thus their contingency plans for Vietnam by the early 1960s had become oriented more toward regional containment than national reunification.[5]

A second factor affecting plans was the increasing Viet Cong insurgency in South Vietnam. Interest by Army strategists and planners in counterinsurgency doctrine came largely at the insistence of President John F. Kennedy and his civilian advisers and proved only a superficial distraction to the military. In general, they had difficulty translating doctrine and strategy into plans and tactics for the use of American combat forces in Southeast Asia. As they were unsure how to deal conventionally with an insurgency, they tentatively proposed to train indigenous forces for this mission. Under this scheme, American units would move into blocking positions to stop the invading North Vietnamese forces while the Vietnamese would take on the Viet Cong.[6]

A different approach came from the President's Special Military Adviser, General Maxwell D. Taylor. After returning from an inspection trip to Vietnam in late 1961, he proposed the introduction of a "military task force" of American infantrymen and engineers into the Delta for flood relief. Once there, the units "would conduct such combat operations as are necessary for self defense, . . . provide an emergency reserve to back up the Armed Force of GVN, . . . [and] act as an advance party for such additional forces as may be introduced."[7]

While this idea of introducing US combat troops into Vietnam under the guise of missions other than combat was novel neither in Saigon nor in Washington, it was a bit too much for the American President, and he rejected the notion of US combat troops being committed to what might well turn into another Asian war.[8] Though distracted by the Bay of Pigs failure and concerned with the Berlin Wall crisis, he remained alarmed over the increased hostilities in Laos. To increase his options, he directed planners to "prepare plans for the use of US combat forces in Vietnam under various contingencies." So while it appeared that the Vietnamese were to fight their own war, American planners were left with the baffling question of how to deal with the Vietnamese insurgency using conventional and limited-war methods.[9]

February 1962 brought a step in the direction of resolving the uncertainty with the establishment of a new military headquarters in Vietnam, the Military Assistance Command, Vietnam (MACV). Its commander (COMUSMACV) now reported to the JCS through the Commander in Chief, Pacific (CINCPAC). Previously senior military officials in Vietnam often had dealt with Washington through State Department channels. This had become difficult when differences emerged between the Army and the State Department over strategy regarding Vietnam; those at Foggy Bottom wanted to emphasize civilian measures, while Pentagon officials favored military steps. More importantly, planning responsibilities in Saigon, which previously had been handled by the assistance-oriented MAAG, were now assigned to the operations-oriented MACV. One reason why planners had established MACV was to have a command and control headquarters in Vietnam in the event that US combat forces were deployed. Thus one of the initial tasks for the MACV planners was to update contingency plans.[10]

These plans were the multilateral SEATO schemes for the regional defense of Southeast Asia. A long-standing problem for American planners had been the unrealistic assumption that all SEATO countries would honor their commitments once the plan was implemented. To cope with this eventuality, they had developed a unilateral plan, OPLAN 32, in which the Americans shouldered the majority, if not all, of the responsibilities. One phase of this planning dealt with the defense of South Vietnam.

Though OPLAN 32 was new, the planning scenario for Vietnam was not. The same combat forces from the Pacific Command and the continental United States – a US Marine Expeditionary Force, the 173d Airborne Brigade, the 1st Infantry Division, and the 101st Airborne Division – were to deploy to the same entry points and areas of initial employment. However, their blocking missions were revised. US planners were now concerned with the escalating threat posed by the Viet Cong, who, with startling success, were exploiting the internal dissension that followed the assassination of South Vietnamese

President Diem. Now MACV envisioned that US ground combat forces would take over internal security missions previously assigned to Vietnamese forces. Their assumption was that the Vietnamese forces would then devote full attention to the Viet Cong insurgency. Also implicit was the premise that the US forces would be available to occupy the old blocking positions. Gone forever, however, were notions of reunification.[11]

Several factors worked to refine further American plans for possible large-scale operations in Southeast Asia. One was the earlier decision by Kennedy to forgo military action in Laos, a policy that served to make Vietnam the focus of American interest in Southeast Asia. With the increased success of the Viet Cong in 1964, and at the urging of the new COMUSMACV, General William C. Westmoreland, President Lyndon B. Johnson approved the deployments of numerous logistical and support units to Vietnam. Although they were supposedly to assist the Vietnamese, it was more than coincidental that many also were forces included in OPLAN 32.

A second factor was Washington's preoccupation with the use of air power to persuade the North Vietnamese to withdraw their support of the insurgency. Planners had many cogent reasons for this interest. Air operations were flexible, as easily intensified as terminated. Also, air strategists were anxious to demonstrate air power's potential. Most important, in a presidential election year, the President viewed air operations as more palatable politically, and he frequently reminded the JCS of that point. But the determination at the national level to rely upon air power did little to help the military planners in Saigon with the nagging question of how to deploy conventional forces in an insurgency. This problem became painfully evident late in 1964 when the Viet Cong hit the air strip at Bien Hoa with mortar fire; despite this provocation, no one in Saigon, Hawaii, or Washington entertained serious notions about the commitment of US ground troops.[12]

The final factor in 1964 was reluctance on the part of General Westmoreland and his MACV staff to ask for US combat troops. Although they were concerned for the security of American dependents and US facilities, they wanted to provide this security with military police units. There were good reasons for hesitancy in Saigon over committing US combat troops. Ambassador Taylor had reservations that should there be another change in Vietnamese national leadership, the new chief of state might well "uninvite" any committed US combat forces. General Westmoreland was worried that the presence of US combat troops might create anti-American sentiment. Critical, however, was the concern of the MACV staff that committing US combat troops would slow the improvement of South Vietnamese combat effectiveness. Most American advisers agreed that the South Vietnamese army would become effective militarily only when it took the offensive against the Viet Cong. They were rightly concerned that any introduction of US combat units would allow the Vietnamese forces to sit back and leave the hard fighting to the American soldiers. "After all," the

MACV argument concluded, ''we are supposed to be working our way out of business, not trying to win their war ourselves.''[13]

Though the MACV staff harbored reservations on the wisdom of committing US combat units, Saigon planners still were responsible for updating plans for that contingency, especially in the wake of the Washington decision to implement the bombing campaign early in 1965. They now identified specific enclaves to be secured by American units. This enclave concept, as developed for Vietnam, was a refinement of existing contingency plans, which called for troops to deploy to critical ports of entry such as Da Nang, Bien Hoa, and Vung Tau, there to await further development of the military situation and the possible relief by Vietnamese army units. By early in 1965, MACV had identified 12 specific enclaves to be secured by American ground units. Contrary to the suggestions in *The Pentagon Papers*, these MACV plans did not represent a dramatic change in strategy but rather continuing refinement of existing plans. There was no bitter debate between enclavists at the embassy and the ''search and destroyists'' at MACV. What was involved was a dialogue between MACV planners who were still concerned at the possible adverse effect upon Vietnamese combat effectiveness and Ambassador Taylor, who, along with General Westmoreland, expressed reservations about the suitability of American troops for static security missions in Southeast Asia. If anything, reluctance from Saigon emphasized the continuing problem over the role of conventional forces in an insurgency situation.[14]

A major step in resolving this problem came when the first American combat troops, the US Marines, deployed to the Da Nang enclave. Soon after the commencement of the sustained US bombing campaign in February 1965, military planners expressed concern that the enemy might well retaliate with either North Vietnamese air strikes or Viet Cong ground attacks on the critical American facilities at the Da Nang airfield. President Johnson ordered a Marine surface-to-air missile battalion plus combat units to protect Da Nang. This action cannot be viewed as reactive since the Marine deployment to Da Nang had long been part of OPLAN 32 scenarios.

Events worked to change the Marines' initial mission as planners nervously eyed two developments. One was the obvious new direction in Viet Cong strategy, which they demonstrated in their attacks on American facilities at Pleiku and Qui Nhon. For the first time, the measures were directed solely against US military installations. The second was increasing intelligence that the North Vietnamese were infiltrating regular army units into the South. Now MACV planners had to consider their offensive capabilities. Rightly concerned for the security of the Da Nang base and the safety of the HAWK battalion, they, along with the Commandant of the Marine Corps in Washington, now proposed to change the strictly defensive mission of the Marines to a more aggressive offensive role. They argued that the gradual expansion of the Da Nang perimeter would assure better security by denying the enemy staging areas from which to launch mortar attacks. President Johnson approved the change in mission in early April. Thus the Marine story at Da Nang is not one of radical change from defensive to offensive planning but rather a logical and pragmatic attempt by planners in Washington and Saigon to employ conventional forces in an unconventional situation.[15]

Over the next two months, decisions were made in Washington for the deployment of more combat forces to Vietnam, additional Marine units and an Army brigade. The groundwork for these deployments was laid during a visit to Vietnam by the Chief of Staff of the Army, General Harold K. Johnson. Representing a President who had become increasingly impatient over the lack of substantive results from the bombing campaign, General Johnson was empowered to determine just what more General Westmoreland needed to improve the situation. If this involved additional deployment of US combat units, then the President wanted to know how they would be used.[16]

Though General Johnson himself favored the deployment of three US Army divisions as a blocking force across northern South Vietnam and the Laotian panhandle, General Westmoreland's own views involved considerably less. In a Commander's Estimate of The Situation prepared by MACV planners for Washington, he concluded that US combat forces were required "to engage as necessary in the war against the Viet Cong in order to: a. Secure vital US installations and defeat Viet Cong efforts to control Kontum, Pleiku, Binh Dinh regions, and b. Secure critical enclaves in the coastal region." This concept of coastal enclaves and highland security was not new, having been part of previous planning scenarios. Neither was Westmoreland's specific request for troop deployments – Marines to reinforce the existing enclaves in the Hue-Da Nang areas and Army infantrymen to secure bases in the Bien Hoa-Vung Tau enclave.[17]

The differences between General Johnson's aggressive plan and General Westmoreland's more modest suggestion were resolved at a series of hastily called planning meetings in Honolulu during April 1965. Initially limited to only CINCPAC and MACV planners, the talks eventually brought together Secretary of Defense Robert McNamara, JCS Chairman General Earl Wheeler, CINCPAC Commander Admiral Ulysses Sharp, Presidential Special Assistant McGeorge Bundy, Ambassador Taylor, and General Westmoreland. From these deliberations emerged a series of recommendations for deployment of ground combat troops which were presented to the President by McNamara in late April. Also introduced was a new strategy, "to break the will of the DRV/VC by denying them victory." At stake here was "the critical importance of holding on and avoiding . . . a spectacular defeat of GVN or US Forces."[18] The scene was thus set for the final revision in strategic thinking.

It was several months before Washington decision-makers acted on the Honolulu proposals. Delays came from all quarters. In Saigon, Ambassador Taylor continued to preach caution with respect to American troop capabilities. In Hawaii, CINCPAC planners lobbied for more time to assess the efficiency of the bombing campaign. And in Washington, policymakers worried about strategic inflexibility once actual ground-unit deployments began. As a result, the units deployed sporadically, creating the illusion of hasty planning. Still, they were as familiar as their destinations – a US Marine task force to the Da Nang enclave, the 173d Airborne Brigade to the Saigon area, and the 2d Brigade of the 1st Infantry Division to the Cam Ranh Bay – Nha Trang complex. Nor had their missions been altered from those in OPLAN 32 development, as each unit was assigned the cautious task of enclave security, albeit with the expanded definition based upon the Marine experience at Da Nang.[19]

The major change in the planners' thinking came with the presidential decision in July 1965 to commit the 1st Cavalry Division (Airmobile) to Vietnam, a deployment which General Westmoreland had suggested in March as part of his Commander's Estimate of The Situation and which McNamara had seconded in April with the Honolulu recommendations. This deployment provided planners with an answer to their concern over conventional warfare in Vietnam. It also formed a distinct break in the continuity of their OPLAN 32 thinking. The division was ordered to An Khe, a base that had not figured in earlier contingency planning. It was to exploit the technology of organic airmobility, a concept which to date had received only limited application. But most importantly, its offensive mission was in the unpopulated Central Highlands where the enemy most likely to be encountered would be not main force Viet Cong units but regular North Vietnamese army regiments. (In fact, within a month of arrival, the division clashed with the North Vietnamese in the Ia Drang.) The planners' decision to deploy the 1st Cavalry Division to the Central Highlands was one designed to engage the North Vietnamese in a big-unit war of attrition. Thus they had come full circle in a route that began in the 1950s when they first pondered the problem of big-unit combat in war.[20]

In summary, the planning for the commitment of US ground combat troops to Vietnam in 1965 was not reactive. Those that were deployed had long been part of planners' existing contingencies, and their initial areas of operations had been specified the decade before. In retrospect, the most telling criticism against the planners was their necessity to come full circle on strategic thinking, in essence reinventing the wheel with respect to the big-unit war. What modifications they had made were the result of attempts to envision conventional combat in an insurgency. By the spring and summer of 1965, they had completed this task. Now it was up to the military troops deployed to be, in the words of General Westmoreland, "fire brigades."[21]

Centuries ago, Machiavelli counseled his prince "never to let his thoughts stray from the exercise of war: in peace he ought to practice it more than in war, which he can do two ways: by action and by study." With respect to planning for the use of US ground combat troops in Vietnam, the evidence shows that military planners did just that. Thus those who are still obsessed with the "whys" of a lost war must look elsewhere. But to those interested in analysis of complex planning, the period offers just what Machiavelli urged – a place to begin study.

NOTES

1. An earlier version of this paper was read at the Inter-University Seminar on Armed Forces and Society during the 1983 Southwestern Social Science Association Annual Meeting. I am indebted to my colleagues at the US Army Center of Military History for their comments and suggestions, in particular to Vincent H. Demma, David F. Trask, and Cathy A. Heerin.

2. David Richard Palmer, *Summons of The Trumpet* (San Rafael: Presidio Press, 1978), pp. 45-90; George C. Herring, *America's Longest War* (New York: Wiley, 1979), pp. 108-44; Larry Berman, *Planning A Tragedy* (New York: Norton, 1982), pp. 31-78; and Leslie H. Gelb and Richard K. Betts, *The Irony of Vietnam: The System Worked* (Washington: The Brookings Institute, 1979), pp. 227-45.

3. Ronald H. Spector, *Advise and Support: The Early Years, 1941-1960, The United States Army in Vietnam* (Washington: GPO, 1983), ch. 11; and "Evolution of The War: US and France's Withdrawal From Vietnam, 1954-1956," *United States – Vietnamese Relations, 1945-1967*, VI. A. 3 (Washington: GPO, 1971) (hereinafter *US-VN Relations*), and *Foreign Relations of The United States, 1952-1954, Volume XIII: Indochina* (Washington: GPO 1982).

4. Historical Division, Joint Secretariat, Joint Chiefs of Staff, *The Joint Chiefs of Staff and The War in Indochina: History of The Indochina Incident, 1940-1954, Volume I* (Wilmington: Michael Glazier, 1982).

5. "NATO and SEATO: A Comparison," *US-VN Relations*, VI. A. 1.

6. See, for instance, Oral History Interview with Joseph E. O'Connor, 9 February 1966, and General George H. Decker, 18 September 1968, both part of The John F. Kennedy Library Oral History Program, John F. Kennedy Library, Boston, Mass. (hereinafter JFKL). For difficulty in translating doctrine and strategy into plans and tactics, see Lesson Plan M 2300, "Introduction to Unconventional Warfare and Counterinsurgency Operations," Lesson Plans, School Years 1961 through 1965, on file at the US Army Command and General Staff College, Fort Leavenworth, Kans.

7. "Evolution of The War: The Kennedy Programs and Commitments, 1961," *US-VN Relations*, IV. V. 1.

8. Several months prior to the trip, military planners in Washington, at the urging of the senior military representatives in Vietnam, had considered the deployment of two Army divisions to the Pleiku area to assist in training Vietnamese troops. See Memorandum For The Vice President, Subject: Program for South Vietnam, 6 May 1961, and Memorandum to Members of Task Force on Vietnam, 29 April 1961, Box 193, Vietnam Country File, National Security File, JFKL; and Letter, General Lionel G. McGarr to General George C. Decker, 15 June 1961, on file at the US Center of Military History, Washington, D.C. (hereinafter CMH files).

9. Washington to Saigon, 06989, 14 November 1961, CMH files. Also see National Security Action Memorandum Number 111, 22 November 1961, CMH files.

10. George S. Eckhardt, *Vietnam Studies: Command and Control, 1950-1969* (Washington: GPO, 1974), pp. 1-46.

11. *A Study of Strategic Lessons Learned in Vietnam. Volume V: Planning The War* (McLean, Va.: BDM Corp., 1980), pp. 3-1 through 3-29.

12. "Evolution of The War: Military Pressures Against North Vietnam, November-December 1964," *US-VN Relations*, VI. C. 2. (c).

13. "The Advisory Buildup, 1961-1967," in Ibid., IV. B. 3, especially pp. 37-69.

14. "Phase I In The Buildup of US Forces: The Debate, March-July 1965, in Ibid., C.5, especially pp. 1-10.

15. Jack Shulimson and Charles M. Johnson, *US Marines in Vietnam: The Landings and The Buildup, 1965* (Washington: Headquarters, US Marine Corps, 1978), pp. 1-35.

16. William C. Westmoreland, *A Soldier Reports* (Garden City: Doubleday, 1976), pp. 125-27.

17. Commander's Estimate of The Military Situation in South Vietnam (March 1965), 26 March 1965, CMH files.

18. "US Ground Strategy and Force Developments, 1965-1967, Volume I," *US-VN Relations*,

IV. C. 6(a); and *A Study of Strategic Lessons Learned in Vietnam, Volume VI: Conduct of The War, Book 1: Operational Analyses* (McLean, Va.: BDM Corp., 1980), chs. 2 and 3.

19. Memorandum For The President, Subject: Vietnam, 21 April 1965, National Security File, Vietnam, Volume 33, Box 16, Lyndon B. Johnson Library, Austin, Tex.
20. John J. Tolson, *Vietnam Studies: Airmobility, 1961-1971* (Washington: GPO, 1973), pp. 51-85.
21. William C. Westmoreland, *Report on The War in Vietnam (As of 30 June 1968), Section II: Report on Operations in South Vietnam, January 1964-June 1968* (Washington: GPO, 1969), ch. III.

This article appeared in the summer 1984 issue of *Parameters*.

9

Senior Officers and Vietnam Policymaking

by MICHAEL W. DAVIDSON

Senior military officers carry many responsibilities within the broad arena of national security policymaking. Before the Vietnam era, one such responsibility had been to bring to the national security policymaking process an awareness of the inescapably high costs associated with go-to-war policy decisions. Confronting the costs of a proposed military commitment is a difficult task; it is an undertaking which requires a forceful advocate. Senior military officers formerly carried that advocacy, but by the early 1960s there was no properly positioned uniformed officer to compel a recognition of the high cost of a military solution in Vietnam. A gradual narrowing of the overall role of senior military officers as national security policymakers clouded that responsibility.

During his tenure as Chief of Staff of the Army from 1939 to 1945, General George C. Marshall established a role model for senior officers as national security policymakers. Marshall was one of Roosevelt's principal war policy advisers. In striking contrast to the position of Vietnam-era senior officers, Marshall was the direct agent of the President in the planning and conduct of military operations in World War II. He functioned without the numerous intermediary levels of civilian policymaking and coordination which by the time of the Vietnam War had become a norm.

Marshall's direct relationship with the President came about in the early stages of World War II as the enormity of the Army's wartime mission became apparent. Abandoning a horse-and-buggy organization carried over from World War I, Secretary of War Henry L. Stimson undertook a broad reorganization of the War Department in February 1942. The reorganization proposal was contained in a draft executive order sent by Stimson to President Roosevelt. The Stimson document specified duties for the Secretary of War and for several key military officers but was altogether silent on the role of the Army Chief of Staff.[1]

Roosevelt approved the Stimson proposal as submitted with the single exception that "paragraph 6 be rephrased to make it very clear that the

Commander in Chief exercises his command function in relation to strategy, tactics, and operations directly through the Army Chief of Staff.''[2] Roosevelt's exact language was adopted in the executive order as finally signed. That order was the primary legal authority defining the role of the Army Chief of Staff throughout the Second World War.

The Marshall model for senior military officers as primary policymakers remained largely intact until overtaken by the postwar implementation of service unification. Various unification proposals, the subject of much interservice politicking, eventually resulted in the adoption of the National Security Act of 1947. The 1947 act did not establish a Department of Defense but rather fashioned a National Military Establishment, something of a grand federation of the existing and still independent-minded military services. In part as a legislative compromise, the existing War and Navy Departments, and the newly autonomous Air Force, were left substantially intact under an additional coordinating level of civilian policymaking.

The federation approach of the National Military Establishment was not a notable success. To correct the shortcomings of the original legislation, Congress extended the responsibility and strengthened the authority of civilian policymakers at the renamed Department of Defense through legislative revisions to the original act in 1949, 1953, and 1958.[3] The increased authority and activity of DOD-level decision-makers had the practical result of placing increasing distance between senior military officers and final policy formulations.

A part of that distancing occurred by sheer weight of numbers. In 1945, General Marshall was accountable for an army of over eight million men and women engaged in a multi-theater war fought by a multinational alliance. He did so in a War Department that contained a total of eight undersecretary, assistant secretary, and special assistant secretary positions. In 1965, the Army Chief of Staff had to answer for an army of one million, a portion of which was fighting a single-theater war without the intensely complicating factor of substantial allied forces. The 1965 effort required the services of 50 undersecretaries, deputy secretaries, assistant secretaries, deputy assistant secretaries, and deputy undersecretaries at the Department of Defense and the Department of the Army.[4]

The postwar implementation of service unification also included the statutory formalization of the Joint Chiefs of Staff. During World War II, the Joint Chiefs were a loosely structured body established initially, in December 1941, as a protocol to facilitate combined planning with the British joint chiefs organization. In a bureaucratic oversight of monumental proportions, the wartime arrangement was apparently never reduced to writing. Operating under an informal structure, the wartime Chiefs dealt with the President as the responsible and accountable heads of relatively independent services. That relationship changed markedly after the statutory formalization of the Joint

Chiefs of Staff in 1947 when the senior officers of each service came to deal with the President primarily as members of an advisory corporate committee.

The legislative creation and revision of the position of Chairman of the Joint Chiefs of Staff further altered the policymaking base of senior military officers. The World War II forerunner was significantly different from the JCS chairmanship which has since evolved. During and after the war, Admiral William D. Leahy served as Chief of Staff to the Commander-in-Chief of the Army and Navy of the United States.[5] As such, he functioned primarily as a conduit for information between the President and the service Chiefs. General Dwight D. Eisenhower served as Chief of Staff of the Army under the Leahy arrangement and in a confidential analysis at the end of his tour viewed Leahy as "the Presidential Chief of Staff," more an extension of the presidency than the head of the service Chiefs.[6] As the Chairman's job developed after its statutory enactment in 1949, the officer occupying the chairmanship came to be the representative of the Joint Chiefs to the White House, meeting with the President most often without the other Chiefs present and expressing both the majority and minority views of the entire JCS.[7] The JCS chairmanship has been neither fish nor fowl, a titular pinnacle of limited direct authority.

The postwar implementation of service unification – by placing growing levels of civilian policymaking between the President and the senior officers of each military service, by formalizing military advice in a joint committee, and by centering that advice in the Chairman, JCS – held the potential for diluting both the counsel and the counseling ability of senior military officers.

Due to an unusual set of circumstances during the Eisenhower Administration, the full impact of the postwar unification restructuring was delayed and perhaps camouflaged. The White House was then occupied by a former general, a defense expert of great stature. Before assuming the presidency, Eisenhower had thoroughly viewed the process from the uniformed perspective by serving both as Army Chief of Staff and informally as Chairman, JCS, while that position was being considered by Congress.[8] As President, Eisenhower developed a committee-supported, staff-oriented National Security Council.[9] That was a decision-making forum comfortable to senior officers. Even when Eisenhower made national security decisions outside the formal NSC structure, his inner circle for such matters included several general officers.[10] Under those circumstances, it was unlikely that senior military officers and their counsel would be far removed from the Oval Office.

The features of the Eisenhower presidency which preserved a major policymaking role for senior officers were not present in the Kennedy and Johnson Administrations. During the Kennedy/Johnson period, the postwar statutory changes implementing service unification came to full effect and passed responsibility for the military aspects of national security policymaking to a civilian-dominated bureaucracy. In assessing the development of military strategy, a study conducted by the Congressional Research Service in 1982 concluded:

There was little competition from the OSD [Office, Secretary of Defense] staff for the first 14 years (1947-60), but skeptical civilians armed with new analytic tools began to advance alternatives soon after [Secretary of Defense] McNamara took office. They and their successors, more than the JCS, have been making U.S. military strategy ever since.[11]

That shift in policymaking responsibility came about because, in addition to the statutory changes which vested when Eisenhower departed the White House, the Kennedy Administration adopted a process for decision-making in national security matters which substantially excluded senior military officers. Kennedy was not himself expert in the defense area, nor was he particularly comfortable in dealing with senior military officers.[12] Kennedy moved away from the existing National Security Council structure in favor of multiple ad hoc decision-making forums.[13] The increasingly aggressive White House staff and the activist management onslaught of Secretary McNamara within the Pentagon provided alternatives to the waning Marshall model for senior military officers as national security policymakers.

President Kennedy's lack of enthusiasm for his uniformed counselors was evident in his recalling former Army Chief of Staff Maxwell D. Taylor to active duty to serve on the White House staff as the Military Representative of the President. The naming of a Military Representative at least initially caused concern among members of the Joint Chiefs who, with some justification, may have viewed themselves as already serving in that capacity.[14]

A harbinger of the Kennedy approach to national security matters was evident at a very early stage in the Administration's Vietnam policymaking. Barely a week after taking office, President Kennedy assembled an ad hoc group of counselors at the White House for a Saturday morning meeting to consider Vietnam. The only military officer present was an Air Force brigadier general who was in favor at the time with the New Frontiersmen of the Kennedy inner circle. The accuracy of the military counsel given the President, at least at that early meeting, is suspect. As justification for a proposed increase in the troop level of the Army of the Republic of Vietnam, the President was told that "a very high proportion of total Vietnam forces was now penned on the front facing a Viet Minh force of 300,000."[15] More authoritative estimates later placed the Viet Cong force level at that time at 5500.[16] There was, of course, no front for the ARVN to be penned on. While a single meeting does not indict the Administration's overall Vietnam position, the practice of relying on civilian ad hoc committees for the development of detailed military policy alternatives remained the norm of the Kennedy presidency.

The trends which narrowed the role of senior military officers in national security policy formulation during the Kennedy Administration continued during the Johnson years. A further restriction of that role occurred as a result of a sharp reduction in the number of decision-makers privy to Vietnam policymaking. The US commitment in Southeast Asia hardened during the last half of 1964 and the first half of 1965 through the sustained bombing of North Vietnam and the decision to deploy conventional American combat forces to South Vietnam. That period also included a presidential election and a Johnson Administration initiative to pass Great Society legislation in Congress. To maintain confidentiality and control of the growing military crisis in Vietnam, President Johnson severely restricted the decisionmaking circle dealing with the war. The core group of decision-makers consisted primarily of the President, the Secretary of Defense, the President's National Security Adviser, and the Secretary of State.[17]

In both the Kennedy and Johnson Administrations, the policymaking role given senior officers was not one which was likely to foster the clear, direct counsel which Vietnam required. With the service Chiefs largely excluded from final policy deliberations, the JCS Chairman became the focal point of military counsel. The roles given the two Chairmen most concerned, Maxwell Taylor and Earle Wheeler, may in fact have lessened the likelihood of forceful, independent counsel.

Taylor started on Vietnam from the admittedly patchwork position of an active-duty general officer on the White House staff, put in place as an alternative to the Joint Chiefs. Taylor was there to bridge the chasm between the Kennedy New Frontiersmen and uniformed military officers. After becoming JCS Chairman, Taylor's role continued to require that he be a member in good standing of each camp. Taylor's additional active policymaking involvement as Ambassador to Vietnam and as a special consultant to President Johnson had him counseling from all points of the compass, sometimes in uniform and sometimes not. Taylor's ability and expertise on Vietnam were clear, and the varied assignments he undertook may have been necessary. But the bureaucratic straddling imposed on him did little to promote clear, singular military counsel on Vietnam.

The postwar legislative dimensions of the JCS chairmanship made that officer the emissary of the Joint Chiefs to the White House. During the Johnson presidency, General Wheeler also came to function as a peacemaker and consensus-builder for the White House among the Joint Chiefs.[18] General Wheeler was called upon to function as a two-direction diplomat, keeping the bureaucratic process running.

The tasks which fell to Generals Taylor and Wheeler were difficult and, given the nature of Vietnam policymaking, probably necessary. Both officers brought unquestioned ability to their roles and, by and large, were successful in their assigned efforts. But the very roles given them, the most senior and influential military officers involved, diverted uniformed military policymakers from what arguably should have been their primary function, offering clear and accurate military counsel to the President. Having focused military counsel in the JCS chairmanship, that position became a bureaucratic centerpiece subject to the tugs and pulls of the surrounding bureaucracy.

The sustained crisis in Vietnam would have taxed the best of relationships among US civilian and military policymakers. The relationship between the Joint Chiefs and the civilian officials of the Johnson Administration may not have been up to the strain. At a meeting of the President with his senior civilian Vietnam policymakers in late 1965, a meeting attended by the President, Dean Rusk, Robert McNamara, McGeorge Bundy, George Ball, and Jack Valenti, the advisability of a bombing pause was considered. According to notes of the meeting, the President reflected that "the Chiefs go through the roof when we mention this pause." Secretary McNamara responded,

I can take on the Chiefs . . . . The Chiefs will be totally opposed . . . . We decide what we want and impose it on them. They see this as a total military problem – nothing will change their views . . . . I know exactly what the arguments of the Chiefs are. Before you decide, I cannot deliver. After you decide, I can deliver.[19]

It would appear that, anticipating opposition from the Joint Chiefs, the Secretary favored excluding them until the President had reached a final decision. At a minimum, the Secretary's expressions suggest that the close give-and-take relationship which should exist between civilian and military policymakers on war and war-risk decisions did not exist on the Vietnam issue in 1965.

Whether this unfortunate state of affairs came about through a lack of ability on the part of the Joint Chiefs as policymakers or through a lack of perspective on the part of civilian officials is perhaps less important than the fact that such a state existed. That poor relationship eroded the independence and objectivity of the military counsel produced. General Harold K. Johnson, Army Chief of Staff from 1964 to 1968, recounts of Vietnam policymaking,

There was, I felt, an unfair, unreasonable, and illogical effort on the part of many of the assistants to Mr. McNamara to get the services – and this was especially so as far as the Army staff was concerned – to get the Army staff to submit recommendations that had been prepared in the office of the Secretary of Defense. I think this is wrong.[20]

In the bureaucratic alternative which supplanted the Marshall model, the accountability which should accompany a decision to commit American combat power was blurred. Speaking of the legislative change of 1958 which put the Secretary of Defense in the military chain of command, a change which fostered the active participation of a burgeoning number of civilian secretarial and staff assistants in military decisionmaking, General Johnson observed, "It created civilian command, but without an assumption of the intangible and abstract obligations and responsibilities that accompany command."[21]

Thus the broad role of Marshall-era military officers as policymakers had been sharply restricted by the early 1960s. The narrowing of that policymaking role impaired the United States' national security policy formulation process by removing from it a forceful recognition of the costs of the contemplated military commitment in Vietnam.

Under the Marshall model, and under its extended effect during the Eisenhower presidency, senior officers could and did make their views on the likely costs of proposed war policies forcefully known to the President. In 1954, serious consideration was given to a proposal to commit American combat units to Vietnam to aid the French colonial forces fighting there. Army Chief of Staff Matthew B. Ridgway bucked the New Look wave of policymakers, both military and civilian, and confronted President Eisenhower with the inevitably high costs of an American war in Vietnam. Ridgway's strong and continued pressing of that issue contributed to a rethinking and eventual abandonment of the proposed deployment.[22]

By contrast, when similar issues concerning Vietnam arose in the mid-1960s, senior military officers occupied a significantly curtailed role in the process of national security policymaking. From that diminished position, senior officers were less likely to initiate the development of Ridgway-like cost assessments and less able to make such costs a part of final policy consideration.

Leslie Gelb and Richard Betts have written an analysis of US policymaking concerning Vietnam titled *The Irony of Vietnam: The System Worked*. Gelb and Betts argue that the policymaking process worked approximately as intended and about as well as could be expected. They recognize a telling exception to their general proposition:

If the decision making system failed, it did so in ways that were not unique to the issue of Vietnam but only seem so because the consequences were so horrendous . . . . Perhaps it is most significant that the system did not force a definitive early decision on what the tolerable limits of eventual total costs would be.[23]

To the extent that military counsel was involved in addressing the costs of a proposed military solution in Vietnam before deploying major American combat units, such counsel appears to have been contained most directly in a memorandum prepared in 1961 in response to the Taylor study mission to Vietnam. A draft memorandum prepared for the President specifically represented the views of the Secretary of Defense, the Undersecretary of Defense, and the Joint Chiefs of Staff on the costs of the proposed commitment of American forces to Vietnam. The draft DOD memorandum was dated 8 November and argued for a recognition and acceptance of the high costs of sending combat forces to Vietnam prior to any such deployment. On 11 November the National Security Council adopted a redrafted joint memorandum offered by the Department of Defense and the State Department. The redrafted version of the memorandum sidestepped or deleted altogether the provisions regarding a recognition and acceptance of the eventual high costs of a war in Vietnam. The very difficult issue of the costs of a commitment was avoided, perhaps to reach a bureaucratic consensus.[24]

As the decision to deploy American units to combat in Vietnam reached its final stage, the Joint Chiefs had an eleventh-hour opportunity to offer counsel. Several days before the deployment was to be announced to the public,

Secretary of Defense McNamara tasked the JCS Chairman to form a study group to work with Assistant Secretary of Defense John McNaughton to gauge the chances of success of a conventional force commitment. McNaughton sent a memorandum to the study group which severely limited the scope of the inquiry and which, as a practical matter, largely determined its outcome. McNaughton excluded from consideration the issues of a reserve call-up, extended in-country tours beyond one year, and escalating the air war. He assumed that the government of South Vietnam could not raise additional forces in a timely manner and that it could not provide stable governmental leadership. He defined victory as not losing.[25] Thus constrained, it is not surprising that the Joint Chiefs endorsed the program that was already underway. The process of decisionmaking is illustrative. It was not a process likely to foster independent and objective counsel on the fundamental issue of whether Americans fighting a war in Vietnam would be successful. It is difficult to imagine an assistant secretary so constraining George Marshall or Matthew Ridgway.

One must ask why senior officers did not promote their views with a louder, more decisive voice. No officer upset the policymaking apple cart as General Ridgway had in 1954. In a system of government where the concept of civilian control of military policymaking is so deeply ingrained in both the civilian and military participants, it is difficult to fault military officers who follow civilian leads. Despite that fact, senior officers under the Kennedy and Johnson Administrations allowed themselves to be co-opted into a national security policymaking bureaucracy. When that occurred, the independence and objectivity of their counsel was lessened. Without forceful counsel on the costs of a war in Vietnam, the United States embarked on a military policy that eventually cost more than the American public was willing to pay.

Rather consistently, the opinion of the Joint Chiefs on the issue of sending troops to Southeast Asia was that, if the decision was for war, then the ultimate costs of that decision should be faced prior to deployment. Hindsight shows that to have been good counsel, but it was counsel neither forcefully offered nor seriously heeded.

Even the limited involvement of military officers which was a part of the process was ineffective. General Bruce Palmer, knowing Maxwell Taylor's ability and influence, wonders: "The nagging question, though, remains – why was he not more successful in bringing about a sounder strategic approach to the war?"[26] The answer, and it applies equally to General Wheeler, lies in the attenuated position within a shifting bureaucracy from which senior officers operated.

If there was or is an imbalance in the role of military officers as policymakers, civilian officials must be the ones to recognize that imbalance and they must be the ones to take steps to correct it. There is no guarantee that senior officers could have met the additional burden of greater policymaking responsibility in the 1960s. What is clear is that senior civilian policymakers could have been better informed on the costs of a military solution in Vietnam.

The Joint Chiefs structure of the Vietnam era did not produce the clear, cogent counsel which was needed. That structure essentially is with us still. The ability of the Joint Chiefs to offer military advice to the President, to the Secretary of Defense, and to the National Security Council has been seriously questioned by a series of reviews and studies. A consistent criticism has been the consensus-building, corporate tendencies of the JCS and its coordinating chairmanship. In a consensus, corporate environment, hard advocacy on difficult issues, such as the cost of going to war, is less likely. And officers who will go against the policymaking grain and forcefully bring bad news to the President become an endangered species. It remains to be seen whether the present defense reorganization legislation taking shape will cure the problem.

The appraisals and reappraisals of the American experience in Vietnam have been largely and properly free of recriminations. Asking the question "Who lost Vietnam?" makes little sense. What does make great sense is to look to the policymaking structures and the Vietnam policies they produced to find areas for improvement. That is not a matter of affixing blame for the past but, rather, one of informing ourselves for the future.

NOTES

1. Henry L. Stimson, draft Executive Order, 20 February 1942, George C. Marshall Research Foundation, Xerox 923, GCM-COAS-CO: Relationships, George C. Marshall Research Library, Lexington, Va.
2. Franklin D. Roosevelt, Letter, 26 February 1942, George C. Marshall Research Foundation, Xerox 923, GCM-COAS-CO: Relationships, George C. Marshall Research Library, Lexington, Va.
3. *1949 U.S. Code Congressional and Administrative News*, pp. 590-97; *1953 U.S. Code Congressional and Administrative News*, pp. 892-93; *1958 U.S. Code Congressional and Administrative News*, pp. 592-602.
4. *United States Government Manual, 1945*, First Edition, (Washington: GPO, 1945), p. 248; *United States Government Organization Manual, 1965-66* (Washington: GPO, 1965), pp. 129-31, 144-46.
5. William D. Leahy, *I Was There* (New York: Whittlessey House, 1950), pp. 96-97.
6. James F. Schnabel, *The History of the Joint Chiefs of Staff: The Joint Chiefs of Staff and National Policy 1945-1947*, 3 vols. (Wilmington, Del.: Michael Glazier, 1979), 1, 4-5; Louis Galambos, ed., *The Papers of Dwight D. Eisenhower*, 9 vols. (Baltimore: Johns Hopkins Press, 1978), IX, 2245-46.
7. George H. Decker, recorded interview by Dan H. Ralls, 18 December 1972, section IV, pp. 36-37, US Army War College Senior Officers Debriefing Program, US Army Military History Institute, Carlisle Barracks, Pa.; Earle G. Wheeler, recorded interview by Dorothy Pierce McSweeny, 21 August 1969, pp. 7, 14-15, Lyndon Baines Johnson Library, Austin, Tex.
8. Stephen E. Ambrose, *Eisenhower, Volume One: The General* (New York: Simon and Schuster, 1983), p. 487.
9. I. M. Destler, "National Security Advice to Presidents: Some Lessons From Thirty Years," *World Politics*, 29 (January 1977), 152.
10. Stephen E. Ambrose, *Eisenhower, Volume Two: The President* (New York: Simon and Schuster, 1984) pp. 242, 509.
11. John M. Collins, *U.S. Defense Planning: A Critique* (Washington: Congressional Research Service, 1982), pp. 68-69.

12. Maxwell D. Taylor, recorded interview by Elsbeth Rostow, 21 June 1964, p. 12; Roswell L. Gilpatric, recorded interview by Dennis J. O'Brien, 12 August 1979, p. 117, John F. Kennedy Oral History Program, John F. Kennedy Library, Boston.

13. Stanley L. Falk, "The National Security Council Under Truman, Eisenhower, and Kennedy," *Political Science Quarterly*, 79 (September 1964), 429.

14. Maxwell D. Taylor, recorded interview by Elsbeth Rostow, 26 April 1964, p. 12, John F. Kennedy Oral History Program, John F. Kennedy Library, Boston.

15. Assistant National Security Adviser Walt W. Rostow, Memorandum to McGeorge Bundy, 30 January 1961, the Papers of President Kennedy, National Security Files, Box 193, countries: Vietnam, 1/61-3/61, John F. Kennedy Library, Boston.

16. U. S. G. Sharp and William C. Westmoreland, *Report on the War in Vietnam (As of 30 June 1968)* (Washington: GPO, 1968), p. 77.

17. National Security Adviser McGeorge Bundy, Memoranda to the President, 27 January 1965, 26 March 1965, 14 April 1965, microfilm holdings, The War in Vietnam, reel 2, Univ. of Louisville, Louisville, Ky.

18. Bruce Palmer, Jr., *The 25-Year War* (Lexington: Univ. Press of Kentucky, 1984), pp. 28, 35.

19. Meeting Notes File, Box 1, 17 December 1965. Lyndon Baines Johnson Library, Austin, Tex.

20. Harold K. Johnson, recorded interview by Rupert F. Glover, 6 March 1973, section II, p. 9, US Army War College Senior Officers Debriefing Program, US Military History Institute, Carlisle Barracks, Pa.

21. Ibid., p. 3.

22. Matthew B. Ridgway, Memoranda, 21 April 1954, 17 May 1954, Ridgway Papers, US Army Military History Institute, Carlisle Barracks, Pa.; Matthew B. Ridgway, *Soldier: The Memoirs of Matthew B. Ridgway* (New York: Harper & Brothers, 1956), p. 276; "What Ridgway Told Ike," *U.S. News & World Report*, 24 June 1954, pp. 30-32.

23. Leslie H. Gelb and Richard K. Betts, *The Irony of Vietnam: The System Worked* (Washington: Brookings Institution, 1979), p. 3.

24. *The Pentagon Papers: The Defense Department History of United States Decisionmaking on Vietnam*, the Senator Gravel Edition, 5 vols. (Boston: Beacon Press, 1971), II, 108-17.

25. Ibid., IV, 291-93.

26. Palmer, *The 25-Year War*, p. 45.

This article appeared in the spring 1986 issue of *Parameters*.

10

Communist Offensive Strategy and the Defense of South Vietnam

by HUNG P. NGUYEN

Throughout the Vietnam War, the most mysterious figure among the communist military high command was a man known by his *nom de guerre*, Tran Van Tra. Rarely appearing in public, although known to American intelligence services, General Tra was believed to be responsible for the planning of both the 1968 Tet Offensive and the 1972 drive toward Saigon that was contained at An Loc.[1] Beyond that, not much was known with certainty about Tra's role and responsibility in the communist southern command.

The mysteries surrounding Tra's war career were lifted, however, with the publication of his memoirs, *Ending the Thirty Years' War*, in 1982.[2] During the First Indochina War, General Tra began his long and extraordinary career in guerrilla and mobile warfare as commander of Vietminh forces in French Cochinchina (basically the Mekong Delta). After the Geneva agreement in 1954, he was regrouped to the north, like many of his comrades in the southern command, leaving behind the political and military infrastructure of the Vietminh. In 1963, with the insurgency movement in the south on the rise, Tra was sent back to the south by Ho Chi Minh to command all Viet Cong forces in South Vietnam. He was responsible for organizing the Viet Cong into main force units and securing their bases. During the next two years, Tra conducted a mobile war against the South Vietnamese army which threatened to bring down the Saigon regime until American ground troops were introduced in 1965. With the much heavier involvement of large North Vietnamese units in the war, Hanoi reorganized communist forces into four different commands: the Tri-Thien region (the two provinces south of the DMZ, including Hue); the Central Highlands; the coastal lowlands from Da Nang to Cam Ranh Bay; and COSVN (the Central Office for South Vietnam), comprising the southern half of South Vietnam. While the other three regions were placed under the direct control of Hanoi, COSVN retained substantial independence in planning and operations. COSVN was placed under the command of General Nguyen Chi Thanh, a rising star in the Politburo and chairman of the Central Military-Party Committee until he died in 1967, reportedly in a bombing raid. From then until 1975, General Tra commanded COSVN forces and became the guiding hand behind the communist offensives of 1968, 1972, and 1975.[3]

The point of examining Tra's career is to appreciate his unique perspective on the war. Here is a man truly experienced in both guerrilla and conventional warfare, one who spent 12 years at COSVN – the mobile and elusive southern command that allied troops never managed to track down, even during Operation Junction City in 1967 and the Cambodian incursion in 1970. As the military commander at COSVN, Tra was responsible for the conduct of the big-unit war in the jungles and mountains as well as the guerrilla war in the Mekong Delta, an experience quite unlike his colleagues' in the other commands. Tra was thus in a unique position to enunciate and execute a form of warfare in Vietnam whose character and underlying principles have baffled strategists.

Unlike Giap's turgid tracts on revolutionary war, Tra's memoirs were written in a vibrant literary style, replete with accounts of the planning and conduct of the war in his theater of operations. Tra also presented in his book the clearest statement yet by the communists of the basic principles underlying their strategy and operational art during the war. Most importantly, Tra's special relationship with the southern cadres, as well as his intimate knowledge of the thinking of the central command in Hanoi, gives one a rare look at the viewpoints of the different participants on strategies for the war. Here one can find a spectrum of opinions that correspond remarkably to the debates among American strategists about the character of the war. Some communist officials in the south advocated a protracted guerrilla war against the Americans and South Vietnamese and saw the gaining of control of the rural areas as the vital step before victory, and the populated lowlands and river deltas as the main battlefields. Others, especially members of the North Vietnamese General Staff and some field commanders in the other regions, viewed the war in an essentially conventional light, i.e., as an attrition struggle between two armies. Tra makes clear in his book that he, together with some leading figures in the Politburo, held a third, quite different, position. Tra presents his views in the form of a series of debates at crucial points of the war and on the strategic rationales for the planning of each campaign. Although the focus of the book is on the 1973-75 period, Tra constantly harks back to the lessons that he learned in earlier campaigns in trying to come up with an offensive plan in 1974-75.

This article examines the basic principles of communist strategy and operational art as enunciated by Tra and others in the communist high command.[4] Their statements on this subject will be compared and contrasted with the perceptions and analyses of American and South Vietnamese participants in the war. Tra's own assessment of American and South

Vietnamese strategy and its effectiveness will also be analyzed and compared to alternative strategies suggested but not implemented during the war.

PRINCIPLES OF COMMUNIST STRATEGY

Long after it ended, the Vietnam War still eludes neat categorization. A common view is that the war is a variant, albeit unique, of Mao's concept of revolutionary war. In this view, revolutionary war can be conceived as a military crescendo consisting of three phases: organization and political mobilization, guerrilla warfare, and the final climactic confrontation, where guerrilla units are converted into big units to defeat the enemy's conventional forces. The first phase, in which the primary objective is to build up an underground organization and infrastructure in the outlying areas, is essentially defensive in character. The second phase sees a rising tempo of guerrilla warfare to push for more control of the countryside up to a point of equilibrium, where the insurgents gain enough control of the surrounding countryside to threaten the cities and the connecting lines of communication. The last phase is entirely offensive and the most decisive, when the insurgents concentrate their forces for a military or political decision.[5]

This model contains a fair resemblance to what happened in South Vietnam during 1959-64, before the massive introduction of US combat troops into the war. In fact, it was the realization that the communists were about to move into this final phase (with the help of the political turmoil in 1963 and North Vietnamese regular regiments) that prompted the American action. What happened afterward, however, represents a substantial and qualitative departure from Mao's model of a conflict rising in intensity and stakes. Throughout 1965-75, large-scale battles occurred simultaneously with small-scale guerrilla attacks, at times with equal intensity. In fact, there is a consensus among American analysts that the Vietnam War was a "double war" of two components: the big-unit war and the "other war" – the war for population control – with the corresponding strategies of attrition and pacification. The disagreement among these analysts is on the timing and emphasis of these two strategies, not on the characterization of the war as such.[6]

This compartmentalization of the war clearly is not shared by Tra, or for that matter, by the leadership in Hanoi. They look at the Vietnam War as a war of syntheses (*chien tranh tong hop*).[7] Of these syntheses, the most crucial, in military terms, were:

• The synthesis of the three types of forces, deployed both in the front and the rear of the enemy.

• The synthesis of operations in the three stategic areas: the jungles and mountains, the lowlands and river deltas, and the cities.

• A unique version of the blitzkrieg, which stressed the *synchronization* of an offensive on the basis of the two spatial syntheses to create the conditions for a total collapse of the enemy.

The Synthesis of the Three Types of Forces

The first synthesis involved main, local, and guerrilla forces. Main forces were regular troops organized in regiments and divisions, which could break up and disperse or regroup depending on the circumstances. Sometimes they could even fight in small units as guerrillas. As a rule, these troops were under the control of COSVN or a military subregional command.[8] Local forces were usually organized in companies and battalions, under the direct control of provincial committees, and were similarly deployed flexibly in combat. These forces could be employed to support guerrillas in their usual missions or main force units in their operations. They could thus be used to counter pacification or for conventional battles. Guerrillas, besides performing their classic missions, constituted a source of manpower for local and main forces.[9]

The strategic disposition (*chien luoc*) that allowed this synthesis to develop its effects fully is called the *cai rang luoc*. This untranslatable term evokes the image of a comb with its teeth sinking deep into a lock of hair. At the forefront of this deployment are the guerrilla units and the party cells, usually interspersed with the enemy in an intricate pattern. The smallest unit at each locality forms a link with – and can rely on the support of – a chain of larger units, all the way up to battalions or even larger formations. These mutually supporting links in the chain extend all the way from the "liberated" to the contested and the "enemy-controlled" areas. These units, according to Tra, form

a system which cannot afford to lose a single link in the chain. This is the magical formation of our people's revolutionary war, causing the enemy to suffocate, creating tension and fear in him night and day, so that he sees a need to create a defense and a strong military force everywhere before he can become confident.[10]

Once established, this system would allow the main, local, and guerrilla forces to function in a mutually supporting manner. Lacking motorized and air transport and the control of the main lines of communication, especially in the populated lowlands, for example, the main force units could not move around en masse at will and thus would have to rely on a chain of supply put in place by the supporting political and military infrastructure.[11] Besides fulfilling this supporting function, local and guerrilla forces could also play a crucial role in offensive operations and participate directly in attacks on critical targets behind the front line of the battle, in coordination with a frontal assault by main forces. On the other hand, local guerrilla units, benefiting from the continuous support of local (and sometimes main force) units familiar with the local terrain and the appropriate tactics, could provide a counterforce to the pacification strategy. It was this coordination between main, local, and guerrilla forces that would prove so intractable to the pacification strategy. An area could be secure one day and become insecure, practically on the next day, because of the mobility of the local and main force units operating in support of the guerrillas. This successful infiltration of main force units would reduce the effectiveness of government territorial units and tie down ARVN divisions in territorial security missions. As South Vietnamese General Ngo Quang Truong pointed out, the reverse was also true, because "when the shield or screen provided by ARVN and US units on the outside was solid and reliable, allowing no chance for enemy main force units to penetrate, then the Regional and Popular forces were most effective."[12]

This system led ARVN to station forces everywhere to maintain security, tying down large numbers of troops in contested and even Saigon-controlled areas, neutralizing the South Vietnamese advantage in number. Moreover, guerrilla operations, always with the suspected support of larger units behind them, could ring up "false alarms," forcing large sweep operations that turned up with nothing, compounding the frustration and exhaustion of ARVN units responsible for confronting the VC or NVA main forces.[13] All in all, this strategic disposition and system of coordination was intended to create maximum uncertainty and insecurity and to tie down the bulk of government forces in territorial security missions, thus inducing all the elements of friction that eventually wear down a much larger military machine.

How was this basic synthesis and strategic disposition put into practice by Tra and other communist commanders? Their different reactions to the new situation in South Vietnam after the Paris peace agreement in 1973 illuminate the difficulty of maintaining it without strong and viable local and guerrilla forces. For example, General Tra attributed the stalemate in the Quang Tri and Hue area south of the DMZ after 1973 to the failure to adhere to this basic strategy.[14] Instead of maintaining the usual three zones ("liberated," contested, and "enemy controlled"), the regional commander willingly pulled back his force to the agreed line to consolidate his rear and thus unwittingly created a war with fronts. In the process, he risked being pushed back when the balance of conventional forces swung to ARVN's favor. What Tra neglected to mention was the fact that the Viet Cong guerrillas and infrastructure, together with their mini-bases (*lom*) in the region, were effectively rooted out by the successful pacification campaigns from 1969 to 1972. During that period, communist main forces were put at bay far beyond the populated areas by the solid shield of US and ARVN forces, thus cutting the connections between these three types of forces and disrupting their coordination.[15] On Tra's part, he favored this forward deployment so much that he allowed local commanders in the Mekong Delta to continue pushing back government forces in the contested areas and insisted that the system of 60 or so guerrilla bases around Saigon be preserved at all costs. Without the maintenance of this system, Tra thought, the repenetration of the NVA and VC into the Delta in 1974 would not have been possible and Thieu would have consolidated his strategic defense in the Mekong and Saigon areas.[16] On this point, General Cao Van Vien, the

South Vietnamese chairman of the Joint General Staff, lamented, "The standstill ceasefire thus gave the Communists a chance to stay mixed with the South Vietnamese positions in an intricate pattern which had always been the enemy scheme."[17] Moreover, "the Communists would certainly try, as soon as the ceasefire was announced, to break down into small units and penetrate our villages and hamlets."[18]

Likewise, after the decimation of the VC ranks during Tet in 1968, Tra was willing to disperse main force units into the Mekong Delta to preserve the VC infrastructure. Tra cited the example of Long An province, the focal point of pacification in 1968-69, and a strategic area linking Saigon with the Mekong Delta. To preserve the VC infrastructure and guerrilla movement in the province, Tra sent in a main force regiment (with continuous reinforcements for losses) to fight as guerrillas to protect the infrastructure and as regrouped units to counter the US and South Vietnamese campaign of pacification. Despite the heavy losses, Tra felt that the survival of the infrastructure in a strategically important area was worth the price. As a result, although the VC overtly controlled only four percent of the population in Long An, the VC infrastructure there was still intact.[19] This nucleus of organization would become the seed of a new guerrilla movement after 1972. In 1975, the three to four local force regiments there formed a surprise prong of attack against the southern defense line of Saigon during the final offensive.[20]

Heavy as the cost of preserving the infrastructure may have been, it was even more costly and difficult, Tra pointed out, to reenter an area once the infrastructure was lost.[21] Whenever communist forces were withdrawn from a contested area, together with the VC infrastructure, whether it was on their own initiative or not, recreating their bases and infrastructure was "much more difficult than to do so in areas where the infrastructure was previously nonexistent."[22] This surprising assessment implies that if pacification was to be successful, priority should have been given to permanently rooting out the VC infrastructure in an area (even if defended by main force units). This task, once accomplished, would have yielded far more results than a large sweep operation lasting a few days, leaving local defense to territorial units after government big units had left.[23] Simply put, the destruction of the VC infrastructure and the associated mini-bases was a much greater loss to the Viet Cong in terms of their future effectiveness than the casualties suffered by the local combat troops, which could be offset by the influx of main force units.

We have seen how the three types of communist forces were used together to counter the pacification strategy and tie down the bulk of government forces in territorial security missions. On the other hand, this synthesis of forces also helped communist main forces in their big-unit war by preventing South Vietnamese infantry divisions from massing in one place for a prolonged operation without endangering the security of their usual area of responsibility. Since territorial security was not their primary mission, communist main forces could mass in their predetermined zone of operation and strike at the South Vietnamese weak points.[24]

To appreciate the dilemma posed to military planners in Saigon by this strategy, one can look at the example of the ARVN 22nd Division in the populated, coastal Binh Dinh province adjoining the strategic Central Highlands. In 1964, the division was deployed as a counter-guerrilla force and concentrated on small-unit operations for pacification. As General Westmoreland pointed out, as "progress began to become evident, two main-force enemy regiments debouched from the hills and virtually destroyed the spread-out South Vietnamese units in detail, making a shambles of the pacification program. It took well over a year to recover what was lost."[25] He used this case to argue against the Marines' emphasis on pacification and the view that "the real war is among the people and not among these mountains."[26] On the other hand, in 1972 the 22nd Division was redeployed to help stem the communist Easter offensive in the Central Highlands, and thus left behind a large gap for the local Viet Cong and NVA main force units to exploit. A large part of Binh Dinh province was occupied by communist forces for more than two months before government units, released from the Central Highlands front, could drive the communists from the area. In general, ARVN infantry divisions could not be extricated from their territorial missions to serve as a mobile reserve because they acted as the "primary forces that kept territorial security from deteriorating."[27] In 1975, the 22nd Division was again pinned down in an indecisive struggle for control of Binh Dinh province and thus was unable to reinforce government troops in the Central Highlands.

The Synthesis of Operations in the Three Strategic Areas

The above argument about where the "real war" was brings one naturally to an extremely important principle underlying communist strategy: the synthesis of operations in the three strategic areas – the jungles and mountains, the lowlands and river deltas, and the cities.[28] In the communists' view, their strategy had always been offensive in character, and a strategic offensive posture was assumed in all three strategic areas. In this offensive strategy, the main forces decided the war. Since the jungles and mountains formed a natural terrain for the massing of troops and the establishment of their bases and sanctuaries, it was there that the war would be decided. Tra rejected the view that the war could only be decided once the populous plains and river deltas had been "liberated." In his view, this strategy of "using the countryside to surround the towns" would put the communist main forces, the decisive forces, at a disadvantage.[29] From "plenty of experiences," he knew that the increasingly mechanized communist main forces could not mass effectively for large-scale battles in the river deltas because of the muddy terrain and the lack of control by communist forces of the main lines of communication. It was difficult for infantry units to advance without using the roads, let alone tanks. For that reason, the best way to deploy main forces in the deltas was to form them into light infantry regiments without heavy artillery.[30] The jungles and mountains, therefore, became the decisive strategic area, because that was where the mechanized main forces could mass into divisions and maximize their effectiveness. Only twice during the war, in 1962 and in 1974, did the river deltas become the primary strategic objectives in the communist offensive plans.[31] These two periods, one notices, immediately preceded the years Hanoi was planning the final offensives to decide the war. The purpose of designating the populous river deltas and lowlands as the primary strategic objective was to disperse and tie down ARVN forces in counter-guerrilla efforts, thus preventing them from massing effectively against communist main force units during the final offensive.

The way Tra targeted the river deltas as the primary strategic objective during the 1973-74 dry season also illuminated the principle of the second "synthesis." Targeting the deltas here, Tra explained, did not mean that COSVN main forces should be committed to the Mekong Delta on a large scale, because of the reasons discussed above.[32] Rather, Tra would order the divisional commanders to quickly organize and train a number of companies and battalions to reinforce the military sub-regional commands. In the region west of the Mekong River, because of heavy government pressures there, he would detach one whole regiment from a main force division to be sent there. The timing and intensity of the COSVN forces' offensive were to be closely coordinated with other forces in the river deltas to prevent the concentration of ARVN forces and the mobile reserve units in operations in the Mekong Delta.[33] Two COSVN divisions, therefore, would come out from their bases in War Zone C and War Zone D for a probing attack against the Iron Triangle and an area northeast of Saigon. Thus the offensive would both tie down the III Corps forces, preventing them from reinforcing those in the plains and river deltas, and punch holes in the middle defense line of Saigon.[34] In the IV Corps area, Tra would deploy one understrength NVA division and sapper units to the Plain of Reeds to tie down the efficient ARVN 9th Division. This would leave only the weakened ARVN 21st Division in the area west of the Mekong, together with its territorial units, to combat the combined main and local forces there.

The success of the anti-pacification campaign during the dry season of 1973-74 (from December to May) caused the Central Military-Party Committee in Hanoi (headed by Giap) to issue a resolution in April 1974 calling for a step-up of this campaign to push for more control of the plains and river deltas.[35] Specifically the command of the Tri-Thien region south of the DMZ was asked to recreate the "three zones formation," disrupting "the enemy's front-line formation," while tying down the two marine and airborne divisions there to prevent them from being redeployed elsewhere.[36] In the IV Corps area, the remaining ARVN division in the Mekong Delta had to break up into battalion-sized units to help defend the outposts, many of which were overextended in VC-controlled areas. At the end of 1974, government forces had to abandon many of these overextended outposts and tried to defend only company-sized ones.[37] This had a tremendous psychological effect on the population of the area, because to them "the outpost was the symbol of governmental authority, an indication of the government's determination to stay with them and provide protection."[38] The result of this offensive, Tra claimed, was to push communist control of the population in the COSVN area nearly back to the level achieved before Tet in 1968.[39]

The key to understanding Tra's dry-season plan in 1973-74 lies in Sun Tzu's discussion of the actions of two instruments of force at the disposal of the generals: the normal, direct, or *cheng*, force and the extraordinary, indirect, or *ch'i*, force.[40] The normal force fixes or distracts the enemy, and the extraordinary force strikes when and where it is not expected. Thus,

the force which confronts the enemy is the normal; that which goes to his flanks the extraordinary . . . . *I make the enemy conceive my normal force to be the extraordinary and my extraordinary to be the normal.* Moreover, the normal may become extraordinary and vice versa . . . . Generally, in battle, use the normal force to engage; use the extraordinary to win.[41]

Tra used the main force divisions in War Zone C and War Zone D as normal forces to fix and distract Saigon forces and to engage ARVN's strongest divisions, whereas the local and guerrilla forces (reinforced by some main forces) acted as the extraordinary forces to gain their strategic objective in the Mekong Delta. Judging by the deployment of ARVN units, it seems that Saigon thought the reverse was true. In 1975, the main force divisions did reverse their role and became the extraordinary forces, the forces of "decision," and the guerrillas the normal, the forces of "distraction." Bogged down in their territorial security missions in the Mekong Delta, the ARVN divisions there were unable to redeploy to defend Saigon.[42]

The Tet Offensive serves as another example of the working of this synthesis. Throughout 1967, most American forces were drawn into fighting in the jungled mountains of South Vietnam, from Khe Sanh and the DMZ to Dak To in the Central Highlands and the Iron Triangle and War Zone C in the III Corps area.[43] Thus, the North Vietnamese and Viet Cong divisions in this strategic area acted as normal forces fixing the bulk of allied combat troops to allow the Viet Cong guerrillas and local forces (or main forces in regiment-sized or smaller units) to strike at the cities for a decision.[44] The towns and cities of South Vietnam were certainly the weakest links in the defense. Only 10 to 20 percent of ARVN forces were estimated to be present in their garrisons when the attacks began, almost simultaneously, throughout South Vietnam.[45]

Hanoi's Blitzkrieg Theory

Hanoi's war strategy had a temporal aspect as well. In this theory, an offensive should be synchronized to maximize its effects, to prevent the concentration of allied defense forces in any one place or in any enclave and thus spread them as thin as possible throughout the country. Throughout the war, the communists carried out their general offensives simultaneously over the length of South Vietnam in order to defeat the allied forces in detail by not allowing units from one region to reinforce another or mass for a concentrated defense. Moreover, this principle of synchronization was dictated because, although communist main forces were engaged in "an entirely mobile mode of combat, they were only mobile within a specific region and coordinated closely with the localities," and thus they were "never mobile throughout the theater of operations or detached from the localities."[46] Therein lay the communist advantage, because "all localities were guided and coordinated closely from the center in a united fashion." Therefore, the success of an offensive depended critically on whether the planned disposition of communist forces allowed them to achieve an overwhelming superiority over the enemy in the objective area while at the same time preventing enemy reinforcements from the other regions from reversing this situation. In this scheme, forces-in-place, striking simultaneously at their predetermined targets, could win a rapid victory entirely by themselves if some strategic objectives had been achieved that created the conditions for the total collapse of the enemy. Here Tra distinguished between an offensive for "total annihilation" and one for "total collapse." To strike for "total collapse" meant:

> There will still be a *coup de main* to rapidly undermine the enemy so that he no longer possesses the will and capability to resist or counter-attack, thus leading him to total collapse, total defeat – despite the fact that his troops are still numerous and well-equipped. This *coup de main* does not necessarily mean the destruction of the bulk of enemy vital forces but only certain parts of them. It also means the occupation of certain localities with strategic significance. This *coup de main* thus creates a decisive situation causing the enemy to lose his morale and will to fight, to become chaotic, and when he faces a relentless offensive and uprising will collapse in parts and then in totality.[47]

This strike for total collapse lay behind the Tet Offensive in 1968, but the communists could not achieve that goal because, Tra thought, the strategic objectives established by Hanoi were far beyond the capabilities of his available forces, despite "marvelous planning and execution." The objectives, Tra pointed out, were due mainly to "illusions based on subjective wishes." However, Tet was a "realistic and large-scale exercise" to enable the communists to refine their offensive principle and understand "the enemy's laws of action."

Tet was thus the first manifestation of Hanoi's version of the blitzkrieg (*than toc*, or "lightning speed"), which stressed the synchronization of an offensive undertaken by forces-in-place to achieve rapid victory through the total collapse of the enemy. The emphasis was on the *disruption* of the enemy's defensive plans rather than the *destruction* of enemy forces. The speed of an offensive was attained by the operational successes of forces-in-place, over a large span of territory. On this point, Tra states that *than toc* meant:

covering a wide space in a short time, lightning actions in combat, in operations and, more importantly, in a strategic period, in the way of ending a war. Don't think of it as a lightning offensive from afar with the use of mobile main forces because, then, one would never comprehend its working.[48]

Even the 1975 offensive fell into this pattern because the attacks on the Central Highlands occurred at the same time as other communist actions in the northern quarters, the central coastal lowlands, and COSVN. In fact, the offensive on Saigon started on 10 March, roughly the same time as the attack on Ban Me Thuot, with COSVN forces making probing attacks around the northern and western defense lines. After the fall of Da Nang at the end of March, Hanoi allowed Tra to use the NVA division held in reserve and two other divisions to attack Xuan Loc, a strategic town guarding the approaches to Bien Hoa and Saigon from the Central Highlands in the north and the coastal lowlands in the northeast. Under direct order from Le Duan and Giap, Tra was to use these three divisions to attack Xuan Loc to clear this choke point for NVA divisions rushing down from the north and the northeast.[49] At the same time, the rest of COSVN was to try to cut off Route 4 connecting Saigon with the Mekong Delta.[50] Thus, Hanoi's objective was to isolate and cut off Saigon defense forces from the Delta and defeat them in detail. Another objective was to prevent a retreat of Saigon forces to the Mekong Delta to create an enclave defense. It was only three weeks later that the bulk of the NVA invasion forces could arrive in the Saigon area, together with their supplies, for a final assault.[51]

In addition to the coordinated strikes of forces-in-place in different areas of operations (i.e., over the whole theater), there was also, at the operational level, strict coordination between forces striking deep inside the operational depth of the enemy and the main assault forces on the front line. During Tet in 1968, the seizure of key military and political targets inside Saigon was carried out by specialized forces and small raiding detachments in conjunction with attacks on the major defensive strongholds on the outskirts of Saigon. This principle of "attacking on the rear to collapse the front" (or, more metaphorically, "blossoming lotus") was also applied to the offensive in the Central Highlands in 1975. It was the reason Hanoi chose to attack Ban Me Thuot in the rear of Kontum and Pleiku to collapse ARVN forces in the front, in conjunction with communist forces poised on the outside.[52] In the battle of Ban Me Thuot, the disruption of South Vietnamese defense in depth was achieved not only through the actions of forward detachments and specialized forces, but also by the use of tank forces to complete the breakthrough and deeply penetrate the operational depth in conjunction with these forward units.[53]

In summary, the principles underlying Hanoi's strategy during the war encompassed the two spatial syntheses and a unique version of the blitzkrieg in its timing. Each of these syntheses contained inseparable components which relied on each other for support. To maintain the integrity and maximize the effectiveness of each part of the syntheses required the preservation of all of their components. To prevent the working of these syntheses, then, one needed to sever the connections between each component, since the sum total of the parts was much less than the whole. To concentrate solely on the big-unit war or on population control, therefore, was to allow these syntheses to continue without disruption.

ALTERNATIVE COUNTER-STRATEGIES

Tra's assessment of allied strategy follows directly from the logic of communist theory about the war. The greatest common mistake on the American and South Vietnamese side, Tra stated, was the strategy of "defending the whole country," trying to secure and control every nook and cranny of South Vietnam.[54] This strategy played right into the hands of Hanoi, because the essence of communist strategy was to "stretch and pull" allied defense forces as thin as possible and then to strike on the weak links at a time and place of their own choosing.[55] Therefore, throughout the war allied strategy allowed the basic forward deployment and strategic disposition of communist forces and in turn prevented the development at any one place of a coherent, consolidated defense line, i.e., a war with fronts.

Search and Destroy Strategy

To some extent, it can be argued that General Westmoreland's search and destroy strategy did succeed in pushing communist main forces from their bases of operations in the jungled mountains of South Vietnam after 1968 and thus severed the links between them and local forces in the populated areas in the lowlands. Together with the decimation of the Viet Cong ranks in 1968, the solid shield of American and South Vietnamese divisions along the border with Cambodia and Laos allowed an unprecedented period of security in the countryside. Yet the Viet Cong infrastructure, the political wing of the Viet Cong, continued its activities and thus formed a nucleus for future guerrilla operations. As it turned out, "the elimination of the VCI proved to be a task much more difficult than the destruction of enemy combat units."[56] It was only a matter of time before the communist main forces tried to reenter South Vietnamese territories from their bases in Cambodia and Laos to reestablish their links with the lowlands. In fact, this was precisely what the communists had in mind during the 1972 offensive, as Tra himself admitted. Again, the offensive in the jungles and mountains along the length of South Vietnam drew away government forces and left a gaping hole in the countryside for the communist anti-pacification campaign to exploit. This basic objective explained the communist method of attacking on all three fronts at once, since it allowed the reestablishment of the intricate formation Hanoi had always desired. Had Hanoi wanted to occupy as much territory as possible for a negotiated partition of South Vietnam, then it would have made sense for communist divisions to concentrate their attacks in the northern quarters.[57]

Although search and destroy operations from 1968 to 1971 did succeed in temporarily disrupting communist bases of operations, they could not prevent the infiltration of small units into the deltas to support guerrillas there. Moreover, they failed to stop communist main forces from returning to their former sanctuaries when insufficient allied forces were stationed there to prevent it. Operations Cedar Falls and Junction City in 1967 against the Iron Triangle and War Zone C amply demonstrated this fact. According to Tra himself, whose COSVN forces and command center were the key targets of this campaign, his favorite tactic when faced with such an imminent massive assault was to disperse his large units from the area to reassemble at a chosen time and place for a counteroffensive.[58] To harass and slow the assaulting forces right at the edges of his sanctuaries, Tra would leave behind snipers and light infantry units. To preserve whatever they could of their logistic channels, logistic units would stay behind together with the VC infrastructure to undertake their own defense while holding onto these channels. Tra claimed that these tactics allowed COSVN forces to mount a prompt counteroffensive against units of the 1st and 25th Infantry, and the 1st Cavalry, Divisions, as well as the Tet Offensive in 1968 – Tra's answer to General Westmoreland.[59] According to General Hay of the Big Red One, COSVN forces were not destroyed because it was "extremely difficult" to establish an impenetrable seal against infiltration by VC units "thoroughly familiar with the dense jungle terrain."[60] His assistant, General Rogers, also noted that the option to fight belonged to the enemy because of this, and that soon afterward, "the Iron Triangle was again literally crawling with what appeared to be Viet Cong."[61] Bringing the war to the jungle thus meant fighting the communist main forces in terrain entirely favorable to them.

In 1970, the Cambodian incursion again succeeded only in temporarily disrupting COSVN bases near the border, moving their sanctuaries into northeastern Cambodia.[62] Pushing the communist main forces from their bases along the jungled mountains of South Vietnam so that pacification could proceed successfully in the lowlands and deltas was an entirely laudable goal. But it could be achieved only at enormous costs in providing firepower and logistic support for combat units, and it required overwhelming superiority in manpower.[63] When this superiority could no longer be achieved, then the mobile, big-unit war could be continued only at the expense of territorial security in the rear.

In fact, Hanoi viewed "this contradiction between population and territorial control and mobile combat" as a common affliction for both the Americans and the South Vietnamese.[64] This assessment of allied strategic weakness was a recurrent motif during the war. Nevertheless, superior US firepower and mobility helped alleviate this "contradiction," for, as South Vietnamese General Cao Van Vien pointed out, these were "the very things that helped maintain *tactical* balance against an enemy who held the initiative.''[65] In fact, General Vien added, ''the ability to hold territory [South Vietnamese strategists] felt, was a direct function of aid level.''[66]

After 1973, with the withdrawal of US air and combat support and the steep reduction in the mobility and firepower of ARVN, this ''contradiction'' reached an acute phase. In Tra's view, Thieu's strategy of ''trying to hold onto every hamlet and village'' to deny the communists control of any populous area spread his forces too thin throughout the country and kept them on the defensive.[67] Moreover, this strategy gave rise to a serious depletion of a mobile strategic reserve to counter communist probes around Saigon and the repenetration of the NVA and VC main forces into the Delta in 1974. It also prevented the massing of enough forces to attack the enemy in any one direction without the fear of being exposed in another.[68] And when a weak spot in the defense was overrun, like the case of Phuoc Long at the end of 1974, there were no reserves left to rescue the defenders. As a result, throughout 1974, along the entire length of South Vietnam, there was no consolidated enclave of defense to prevent communist infiltrations and probings.

The Strategy of Defense with Mobile Regional Forces

The South Vietnamese solution to this problem of depleting a mobile reserve due to the commitment to hold territory was to upgrade the Regional Forces to carry out a dual function. According to General Vien, the plan was to establish:

mobile regional group commands, each capable of controlling from two to four Regional Force battalions and one four-piece artillery battery relieved from territorial duties . . . . The JGS [Joint General Staff] plan called for the activation of twenty-seven such groups by June 1975. This effort was intended to free regular divisions from territorial concerns and give the military regions a sizable combat force to confront enemy territorial units.[69]

These mobile regional groups, therefore, would be involved in both territorial security missions and mobile combat to support or reinforce the ARVN divisions in the military region. However, General Truong considered the plan as being implemented too late:

This should have been done in 1971, when most U.S. infantry divisions had been withdrawn and the enemy was grouping the local forces into battalions and regiments and preparing for mobile conventional warfare . . . . If we had achieved this at that time, then ARVN infantry divisions would not have found themselves overextended when replacing U.S. units being redeployed. They could have become more mobile and would have constituted a formidable deterrent to invasion.[70]

The creation of such dual forces proficient in both anti-guerrilla and mobile conventional warfare clearly was not an easy task, especially when these battalion-sized units were previously used for defending outposts and in guard duties. However, the peculiar form of warfare in Vietnam, with the three types of communist forces, called for such intermediate forces on the South

Vietnamese side. In fact, these mobile regional groups were similar in concept to the French *Groupement Mobile* during the First Indochina War. Jean Ferrandi, the French G-2 officer in Hanoi during the war, saw these forces as General De Lattre's response in 1951 to the new "mobile warfare stage" that Giap's forces were entering. In De Lattre's conception, these units would be flexible and mobile enough to be capable of "being engaged at any point in the territory and then ensuring incessantly growing security on our rear."[71] He also ordered the construction of a series of fortified outposts around the perimeter of the Red River Delta – the famous De Lattre Line – to control Vietminh infiltration into the Delta and create an enclave of defense. The "mobile groups" would be available for reinforcement anywhere an attack should occur.

The Enclave Strategy

De Lattre's concept brings one to another alternative strategy proposed during the war by General James Gavin in 1965-66. The idea was "to hold several enclaves on the coast, where sea and air power can be made fully effective. By enclaves I suggest Cam Ranh Bay, Da Nang, and similar areas where American bases are being established."[72] Otherwise, he argued, presciently, in almost the same words that Tra would use years later, "we are stretching current U.S. resources beyond reason in our endeavors to secure the entire country of South Vietnam from the Vietcong penetration. This situation, of course, is caused by the growing Vietcong strength."[73] According to Gavin's biographer, he also envisioned highly mobile defense forces which would move out from their enclaves on the coast to patrol the periphery, secured against attacks by the use of new weaponry and systems.[74]

General Tra himself mentioned what he called "the Gavin plan," designating a strategy of gradual retreat from overextended territories to set up an enclave defense around the Mekong Delta, in the worst circumstances.[75] In fact, what the communist high command and leadership feared most about Thieu's counterplan in 1974, Tra revealed, was a resort to an enclave strategy to consolidate a defense line around the Mekong Delta, with the back of the enclave facing the coast, close to the support of American naval air power.[76] This was exactly what some leaders in South Vietnam envisioned early in 1974 when it became clear that US support for the war would be on the wane. Prime Minister Khiem and General Vien began to push for "truncation," which eventually would involve a pullback from the Central Highlands and the northern coastal provinces and an evacuation of the population in the areas concerned.[77] Thieu rejected the plan outright only to come back to it in March 1975 after the fall of Ban Me Thuot, when, according to both the communist General Tra and the South Vietnamese General Vien, that strategic retreat was already too late.

The communist leaders in Hanoi were sufficiently concerned about this plan to order a step-up in the anti-pacification campaign in the Delta even during the rainy season of 1974 and to push communist control of the area back to the 1968 level.[78] Tra clearly felt that the anti-pacification efforts during 1973-74 had paid off well enough to the communists to foil the development of the enclave strategy. By the time Thieu tried to implement this strategy in late March 1975, Tra's forces were already locked deep in the Mekong Delta because of their earlier successes in repenetrating and expanding areas under their control in 1974. In 1973-74, despite his realization that the Mekong Delta campaigns were "essential to the survival of South Vietnam," Thieu could not commit enough forces to root out communist bases of operations and solidify control there, especially in the swampy areas west of the Mekong River. Moreover, having lost the outer defense line in northern War Zone C to Tra's forces, Thieu should have tried to close the gaps in the middle defense line north and west of Saigon, two areas Tra repeatedly exploited to tie down the bulk of III Corps forces there. The defense of the northern quarters pinned down South Vietnam's best divisions and depleted her mobile strategic reserves, leaving them in a position to be cut off from the south. The faulty disposition of South Vietnamese forces thus made them vulnerable to Hanoi's strategy in 1975, which did not aim at a frontal attack to win by attrition but a decisive strike on the rear to collapse the front. In 1975, an offensive for "total collapse" completely foiled any hope for the realization of a "Gavin plan" by South Vietnam in 1975.[79]

The success of an enclave defense, therefore, depended on the ability by the defense forces to defeat this principle of "attacking in the rear to collapse the front," first in parts and then in totality. In terrain unfavorable for the deployment of large units and lacking control of the lines of communication (such as the Mekong Delta, and during the First Indochina War, the Red River Delta), communist main force units were adept at breaking into smaller units to infiltrate through the outer defense line and then regroup for a strike at a command center or a town. This usually was done in conjunction with bigger units poised on the outside. This method lay behind communist offensives against the deltas and cities during the Vietminh campaign against the southern edge of the Red River Delta in 1951, Tet in 1968 against the cities, and the final offensive in 1975 against Ban Me Thuot and Saigon. The Day River Campaign in 1951 against the De Lattre Line illustrated the success of an enclave strategy against such tactics. Achieving a measure of surprise, two Vietminh divisions attacked two strong outposts on the southern edge of the De Lattre Line to allow the 320th Division, commanded by General Van Tien Dung, to infiltrate into the southern part of the Delta to occupy the Catholic diocese of Phat Diem and disrupt French control of the area together with two Vietminh regiments previously infiltrated. The 320th Division, then, was to regroup and push back for an attack on the outer line. The offensive was foiled because *Groupement Mobile* reinforcements prevented the taking of the two strong outposts and the exposed 320th Division was cut up by another such mobile group.[80] General Van Tien Dung again applied this "blossoming lotus" principle in Ban Me Thuot in 1975, this time with more success because of overwhelming superiority. The Day River Campaign, however, pointed out the importance of rooting out the internal infrastructure that allowed infiltrated main force units to roam about and regroup through its support. Moreover, the shield on the outside had to be solid and constantly reinforced by a mobile defense force. The lines of communication had to be well protected through a series of fortified outposts, as the success against NVA main force units in the Mekong in 1975 indicated. Last but not least, there had to be dual-function mobile groups to deal with both the guerrillas and the regrouped main force units inside the shield, in addition to more conventional forces to counter the big units on the outside. It is interesting to note that De Lattre's strategy foiled Giap's offensive on the Red River Delta in 1951, until he decided to bring the war to the mountains in 1952, which allowed the 320th and 316th Divisions to infiltrate again and occupy a swath of land posing as a dagger toward Hanoi.[81]

If Saigon had managed to realize its enclave strategy before the communist offensive in 1975, the question remains as to whether this truncated version of South Vietnam would have survived a determined communist onslaught. Some of the discussions that Tra had with the Politburo at the beginning of 1975 shed some light on the issue. According to Tra, Le Duc Tho, Kissinger's counterpart at the Paris peace talks, told him that Hanoi's materiel reserves were extremely thin, that because of the "complicated internal and external situations" they could not be much increased, and hence that an offensive for a decisive victory must take place by 1976 because Hanoi "should not and cannot prolong the war like before."[82] The most important objective, Tho said, was to prevent the successful development of an enclave strategy.[83] One can infer that Hanoi feared that the enclave strategy would involve a stalemate, which it wanted to avoid at all costs. In a following meeting with the Politburo, Truong Chinh, currently the second-ranked member of the Politburo, expressed concerns about the "enemy's tendency towards an enclave strategy centered around large cities," and he was afraid the communist forces could not penetrate these consolidated defense lines, especially with American support from the air, even on a limited level.[84] The optimists, represented by Le Duan and Le Duc Tho, discounted the possibility of American intervention after Watergate. The offensive in 1975 was then approved.

IN CONCLUSION

If only one lesson were to be learned from the Vietnam War, then the thesis convincingly argued by Tra deserves to be remembered: America and South Vietnam lost the war *because their military strategy was wrong*. Stark and direct as this message may be, coming as it does from an experienced protagonist, it should not be taken lightly. And if one believes that the war constituted a new "mode" of warfare, as the other side seems to believe, then one should look at the war from now on through this new lens.

To repeat, it was a war of "syntheses": a synthesis of the three types of forces on the one hand and the three strategic areas on the other. These syntheses worked, in the final analysis, to shape South Vietnamese force dispositions for the final strike for "total collapse." Even though the big-unit war in the jungles and mountains was decisive, Hanoi clearly considered the revolutionary war in the lowlands as *indispensable* to the success of the former.

The importance of the war in the lowlands can be seen by the way Hanoi sent its own best and brightest into the two Indochina wars. The ones who eventually rose to the top were the commanders in the lowlands. General Van Tien Dung, the commander of the 320th Division haunting the southern Red River Delta, became Giap's replacement. Likewise, General Le Duc Anh, the little-known commander of communist forces in the areas west of the Mekong River, directed the Vietnamese forces that invaded Cambodia in 1978 and became an important Politburo member. Hanoi clearly valued the skills of generals who could apply the three types of forces to fight this peculiar form of warfare. On this point, Tra had the final word:

A general in the current era, an era of revolution and science ... not only has to know how to deploy his available forces in the most sensible formation but also to create his forces, organize them into different types of forces with different modes of combat. He needs to know how to combine every type of forces, military and political, internal and external. He has to know not just to deploy his forces for a frontal assault but also to strike the enemy in the rear.[85]

NOTES

The author would like to thank Professor Michael Vlahos, co-director of Conflict Management and Security Studies at the School of Advanced International Studies, Johns Hopkins University, for his valuable comments and suggestions on this article.

1. Walter S. Dillard, *Sixty Days to Peace: Implementing the Paris Peace Accords, Vietnam 1973* (Washington: National Defense Univ. Press, 1982), p. 58.

2. General Tran Van Tra, *Ket Thuc Cuoc Chien Tranh 30 Nam (Ending the Thirty Years' War)* (Ho Chi Minh City: Literature Publishing House of Ho Chi Minh City, 1982).

3. After 1975, Tra became the commander of Vietnamese forces around Saigon and the areas near the border with Cambodia. In March 1978, he became Vice Minister of Defense, whereas his deputy, General Le Duc Anh, later would command the invasion forces in Cambodia. Tra was made a member of the Central Military-Party Committee in 1979, as well as Deputy Chief of General Staff in 1980, until his removal from the Central Committee in 1982, reportedly over differences on policies toward Cambodia.

4. In addition to Tra's book, a number of articles on the Vietnam War written by other senior commanders have recently appeared in a military journal designed for an audience of middle- and high-ranking officers. The most notable articles include General Hoang M. Thao's account of the 1972 offensive in the Central Highlands, "Planning a Battle," *Tap Chi Quan Doi Nhan Dan* (Journal of the People's Army – hereinafter *TCQDND*) (May 1983); General Pham H. Son, "Several Problems Concerning Warfare in Jungled Mountain Terrain," *TCQDND* (February 1983); and an account of the air defense of Hanoi during the Christmas bombing in 1972 by General Hoang V. Khanh, "Creativity: An Important Cause for the Victory," *TCQDND* (November 1982).

5. For a concise discussion of revolutionary war, see Sir Robert Thompson, *Revolutionary War in World Strategy 1945-1969* (London: Secker and Warburg, 1970), pp. 16-17.

6. *Some Lessons and Non-Lessons of Vietnam: A Conference Report*, (Washington: Woodrow Wilson International Center for Scholars, 1983), pp. 32-38.

7. Tra, pp. 90, 136; see also the articles signed by Q. S., "Military Strategy," *TCQDND* (September 1981); and "Operations and Operational Art," *TCQDND* (November 1981).

8. For a discussion on communist military organizations in Vietnam, see Colonel Hoang Ngoc Lung, *Intelligence* (Washington: Indochina Monographs, US Army Center of Military History, 1976), p. 87.

9. After Tet, North Vietnamese troops became fillers to reinforce local guerrillas rather than the reverse.

10. Tra, p. 62.

11. Ibid., pp. 136-39.

12. General Ngo Quang Truong, *Territorial Forces* (Washington: Indochina Monographs, US Army Center of Military History), p. 90.

13. Phan Nhat Nam, *Doc Duong So 1 (Along Route 1)* (Saigon: Dai Nga Publishing House, 1970). This war diary by an ARVN paratroop officer contains many interesting anecdotes and incidents that tell volumes about the way US and South Vietnamese troops fought the VC and NVA. His chapter about a joint operation with the US Marines, for example, highlighted the inappropriate tactics used against the VC by these American units in 1967. Marines would march in assault formation in inappropriate terrain. Landing zones for supplies became easy targets for VC mortars. In short, they did so many predictable things that the VC easily learned the habits of action of these units to lure them into traps and sniper fire. On the South Vietnamese side, every time a bridge near a district headquarters was destroyed by sappers, the military region would send down a reserve paratroop battalion for a fruitless sweep of the area for fear of a wider attack plan behind it.

14. Tra, pp. 61, 70, and 72.

15. Truong, pp. 90-94.

16. Tra, p. 88.

17. General Cao Van Vien, *The Final Collapse* (Washington: US Army Center of Military History, 1983), p. 29.

18. Ibid., p. 20.

19. Richard A. Hunt, "Strategies at War: Pacification and Attrition in Vietnam," in *Lessons from an Unconventional War*, eds., Richard A. Hunt and Richard H. Schultz, Jr. (New York: Pergamon Press, 1982), p. 42.

20. Tra, p. 260.

21. Ibid., p. 63.

22. Ibid.

23. Tra noted that a famous tactic by the 3rd Brigade of the US 9th Division, known to the local VC as "hop and probe," was to use small units on low-flying helicopters, suddenly swooping down on the suspected VC infrastructure or guerrilla activities and raining fire on them, then taking off quickly to escape. Tra sent his main force regiment to Long An to protect the VC infrastructure against such pacification campaigns. General Ewell (commander of the US forces in Long An and other provinces in the III Corps area) was skeptical of pacification operations because they yielded lower body counts than search and destroy sweeps. (Quoted in Hunt, p. 42.) Had he known that Tra was under direct order from Hanoi to try to protect the Long An VC infrastructure, he might have thought otherwise.

24. On this point, Tra stated that good generalship consisted of "deploying available forces in a cohesive strategic disposition ... to allow them to exploit the opportunity to divide and disperse the enemy forces so that when strong they become weak and when many they become few." See Tra, pp. 169-70.

25. Quoted in Jack Shulimson, *U.S. Marines in Vietnam: An Expanding War, 1966* (Washington: History and Museums Division, Headquarters, US Marine Corps, 1982), p. 12.

26. Comment by General Krulak, Commander of Marine Forces in the Pacific, cited in Shulimson.

27. Truong, p. 21.

28. Tra, pp. 90, 136.

29. Ibid., p. 91.

30. Ibid., p. 90.

31. Ibid.

32. Ibid., p. 92.

33. Ibid., p. 95.

34. Ibid.

35. Ibid., pp. 134-35.

36. Ibid.; also see the chapter on Westmoreland in Robert Pisor, *The End of the Line: The Siege of Khe Sanh* (New York: W. W. Norton and Company, 1982). The month before Tet, 50 percent of US combat troops were drawn to the I Corps area because Westmoreland was concerned about the threat there posed by NVA divisions, particularly in Khe Sanh.

37. Ibid., p. 111.

38. Truong, p. 82.

39. Tra, p. 218.

40. Sun Tzu, *The Art of War*, trans. and with an introduction by Samuel B. Griffith (New York: Oxford Univ. Press, 1963), pp. 91-92.

41. Ibid., p. 91.

42. Vien, pp. 138-40. Similarly, the 22nd Division in Binh Dinh was unable to redeploy to stem the communist offensive in the Central Highlands.

43. Pisor.

44. Although Tra admitted that the VC suffered heavy losses during Tet, he still considered it ''a strategic turning point,'' at which ''American limited war strategy was defeated,'' forcing the US to deescalate. Tra, p. 47.

45. Lung, p. 145.

46. Tra, p. 147, also p. 206.

47. Ibid., p. 206; see also pp. 57-58 and p. 101 for comments on Tet.

48. Ibid., p. 147.

49. Ibid., pp. 228, 258. In their rush to move down the Central Highlands and along the coast toward Saigon, the NVA divisions experienced a tremendous logistical headache. Units would arrive without their ammunition; tanks ran out of fuel; and artillery units were short of shells! Hardly the picture of a blitzkrieg army in the usual sense.

50. Tra was unhappy with this order by Le Duan and Giap. He thought that the muddy terrain there and the strongly fortified outposts on Route 4 put his light infantry divisions in the Mekong at a disadvantage. In fact, the communists were pushed back from Route 4, suffering heavy casualties. Tra, p. 230.

51. By then the battle was almost decided. Tra had his artillery units with their deadly 130mm guns within range of Saigon and the airport, which were surrounded except from the south and southeast.

52. Ibid., pp. 182-83. Originally, the General Staff's plan in Hanoi was to concentrate the NVA offensive on the Central Highlands but did not envision an attack on Ban Me Thuot. Tra was dismayed when he found out during a discussion on the forthcoming plan in Hanoi that the offensive was centered on Kontum and Pleiku, the defensive strongholds of the ARVN in the Central Highlands. These defense positions were stationed extremely close to the NVA infiltration routes from the Ho Chi Minh Trail. The intention of the General Staff in Hanoi was to engage these defense forces in an attrition battle, since the NVA had numerical superiority and the advantage of an interior line of communication, whereas reinforcements for ARVN units could be blocked off on Route 19. Doing so, Tra argued, would play right into the hands of Saigon because the ARVN positions were strongly defended and well stocked. Moreover, the plan reflected a ''conventional war'' mentality, whereas the communist forces should have exploited the ability to infiltrate into the rear by bypassing Kontum and Pleiku to strike at Ban Me Thuot, and thus indirectly collapse the front. According to Tra, he interceded with Pham Hung, the southern party secretary, to dissuade the Politburo from approving this plan. At the last moment, when the final Central Military-Party Committee meeting was taking place to hammer out the offensive plan, Politburo member Le Duc Tho entered with an explicit order to focus the attack on Ban Me Thuot.

53. During the 1975 offensive, these tank units could achieve a speed of advance of up to 50 to 60 kilometers a day and thus disrupted the efforts by South Vietnamese forces to reorganize and consolidate their defense. See Colonel Le X. Kien, ''The Potential for Rapid Attack by Tank Forces in Modern Offensive Operations,'' *TCQDND* (August 1982).

54. Tra, p. 112.

55. Ibid., pp. 110-12.

56. General Tran Dinh Tho, *Pacification* (Washington: Indochina Monographs, US Army Center of Military History), p. 11.

57. General Cao Van Vien, the South Vietnamese chief of the Joint Staff, stated that South Vietnam "would have been much better off with a reduced but not infested territory ... two clean-cut zones instead of the purulent spots of the 'leopard skin.'" See Vien, p. 81.
58. Tra, p. 105.
59. These attacks occurred mainly in October 1967, a few months after the end of Junction City. They included an ambush against a battalion of the Big Red One, an attack on Phuoc Long, and a division-sized attack on Loc Ninh, a district capital north of An Loc. The last attack was later considered a trial run for Tet to test combat tactics against towns and cities.
60. General Bernard W. Rogers, *Cedar Falls-Junction City: A Turning Point* (Washington: Department of the Army, 1974), p. 155.
61. Ibid., pp. 157-58.
62. General Tran Dinh Tho, *The Cambodian Incursion* (Washington: Indochina Monographs, US Army Center of Military History, 1978), p. 175.
63. According to General Murray, the US logistic chief in Vietnam in 1974, at the height of the US involvement in Vietnam there were 433 allied combat battalions fighting 60 enemy combat regiments (somewhat larger than an allied battalion). In 1974, ARVN had 189 battalions against 110 enemy regiments; see *Some Lessons and Non Lessons*, p. 38.
64. Tra, p. 188.
65. Vien, p. 7.
66. Ibid.
67. Tra, pp. 97, 111.
68. Ibid., pp. 105, 110.
69. Vien, p. 43.
70. Truong, p. 45.
71. Jean Ferrandi, *Les Officiers Français Face au Vietminh, 1945-1954* (Paris: Fayard, 1966), p. 152.
72. General James M. Gavin, "A Communication on Vietnam," *Harper's*, 232 (February 1966), 17.
73. Ibid.
74. Bradley Biggs, *Gavin: A Biography of General James Gavin* (Hamden, Conn.: Archon Books, 1980), pp. 148-49.
75. Tra, p. 145.
76. Ibid.
77. Frank Snepp, *Decent Interval* (New York: Random House, 1977), pp. 104, 109, and 156.
78. Tra, pp. 128, 160.
79. Ibid., p. 146.
80. Ferrandi, p. 167.
81. Ibid., p. 182.
82. Tra, p. 161.
83. Ibid.
84. Ibid., p. 188.
85. Ibid., p. 170.

This article appeared in the winter 1984 issue of *Parameters*.

11

Mobilization for the Vietnam War: A Political and Military Catastrophe

by JOHN D. STUCKEY and JOSEPH H. PISTORIUS

The United States has relied extensively on its militia, National Guard, and Reserves in every major war in its history, except for the Vietnam War. That only a diminutive mobilization occurred for the Vietnam War was a remarkable departure from American military history. This article briefly reviews the reliance on the citizen-soldier in major American wars, then examines the extent to which the President and his civilian and military advisers considered mobilization during the first three years of the Vietnam ground war and the rationale behind nonmobilization during that period. We then focus on the 1968 call-up of Army National Guard and US Army Reserve forces for the Vietnam War and the characteristics and problems of that partial mobilization.

The United States has never maintained nor seriously considered maintaining during peacetime a Regular Army of sufficient size to meet the needs of war. The United States has engaged in nine major wars, and extensive reliance has been placed on the citizen-soldier in the first eight of them. That reliance is made clear in the following table.[1] The first column of figures shows the strength of the Regular Army at the beginning of the wars listed; the second column shows the number of militia, Army National Guard, and Army Reserve troops mobilized for each.

	Initial strength	Mobilized
Revolutionary War[2]	0	250,000
War of 1812	6,744	458,000
Mexican War	7,365	73,532
Spanish-American War	28,183	170,954
World War I	127,588	208,000
World War II[3]	187,893	377,000
Korean War	591,487	382,900
Vietnam War	970,000	22,786

The proposition that the National Guard and Reserve would be called into

123

active federal service had been proven prior to Vietnam in every major war. Even the Berlin Crisis of 1961 had witnessed the call-up of 119,622 Guard and Reserve members. Because of this historical perspective, there was an unquestioned readiness to believe that mobilization of the Guard and Reserve would provide citizen-soldiers for the Vietnam War.

NONMOBILIZATION IN 1965

The first momentous year of the Vietnam War regarding Army manpower was 1965, when 44 combat battalions of the United States and its allies were deployed to South Vietnam, beginning 8 March. When this buildup of ground combat forces began, the Army National Guard (ARNG) and US Army Reserve (USAR) had a Ready Reserve paid strength of 695,000, organized into 23 divisions, 11 separate brigades, and some 8000 units.[4] The Regular Army had a strength of about 970,000 (with 42 percent of its personnel deployed overseas), organized into 16 divisions, four regimental combat teams, seven separate brigades, and seven special forces groups.[5]

During the first three years of the Vietnam ground war (1965-67), mobilization of the National Guard and Reserve was a major topic of consideration by President Johnson and his military and civilian advisers. From the onset of the buildup of ground combat forces in South Vietnam, mobilization was favored by the Secretary of Defense, the entire Joint Chiefs of Staff (JCS), the National Security Adviser, the Secretaries of the military departments, many members of Congress, the National Guard and Reserve leadership, and others.

On 2 April 1965, the JCS asked the Secretary of Defense in JCSM 238-65 for an increased ability to wage the war by removing "all administrative impediments that hamper us in the prosecution of this war." This request included authority to extend military terms of service and to conduct consultations with Congress on mobilizing the Guard and Reserve.[6]

Paul H. Nitze, Secretary of the Navy, reported that both he and Secretary of Defense McNamara favored mobilization in 1965: "We also thought that there should be a greater commitment of support by Congress, and that the way you could get that would be to put a bill into the Congress asking for the power to call up the Reserves."[7]

On 15 July 1965, Secretary McNamara stated that if increased numbers of American troops were to be sent to South Vietnam, "it will be necessary to consider calling up reserves, extending tours, and increasing the draft."[8] Two days later, Deputy Secretary of Defense Vance informed Secretary McNamara (by cable since the Secretary was in South Vietnam) that President Johnson was favorably disposed to the call-up of reserves and extension of tours of active duty personnel.[9]

Secretary McNamara returned to Washington on 20 July and reported immediately to the President. Among his recommendations was one to ask

Congress for the authority to call up 235,000 members of the National Guard and Reserve. He also proposed increased recruitment, larger draft calls, and extensions of tours to raise the size of the regular armed forces by 375,000.[10]

The President considered McNamara's proposals very carefully: he met with his top advisers at the White House on 21 July; with the JCS and Secretaries of the military departments the following day; and with other advisers on 22 July at the White House and on 25 July at Camp David. The President assembled the National Security Council on 27 July and laid out five options. In his own words,

We can bring the enemy to his knees by using our Strategic Air Command, I said, describing our first option. Another group thinks we ought to pack up and go home.

Third, we could stay there as we are – and suffer the consequences, continue to lose territory and take casualties. You wouldn't want your own boy to be out there crying for help and not get it.

Then, we could go to Congress and ask for great sums of money; we could call up the Reserves and increase the draft; go on a war footing, declare a state of emergency. There is a good deal of feeling that ought to be done. We have considered this. But if we go into that kind of land war, then North Vietnam would go to its friends, China and Russia, and ask them to help. They would be forced into increasing aid. For that reason I don't want to be overly dramatic and cause tensions. *I think we can get our people to support us without having to be too provocative and warlike* [emphasis added].

Finally, we can give our commanders in the field the men and supplies they say they need.

I had concluded that the last course was the right one. I had listened to and weighed all the arguments and counterarguments for each of the possible lines of action. I believed that we should do what was necessary to resist aggression but that we should not be provoked into a major war. We would get the required appropriation in the new budget, and we would not boast about what we were doing. *We would not make threatening scenes to the Chinese or the Russians by calling up Reserves in large numbers* [emphasis added]. At the same time, we would press hard on the diplomatic front to try to find some path to a peaceful settlement.

I asked if anyone objected to the course of action I had spelled out. I questioned each man in turn. Did he agree? Each nodded his approval or said "yes."[11]

The President also reported in his memoirs that even then (27 July 1965) the nonmobilization decision was not final. He next met with leaders of Congress on the evening of the same day. Following these sessions with key civilian and military advisers, the President held a press conference on 28 July at which he explained the US commitment of ground combat forces to resist communist aggression in South Vietnam. In his prepared statements he said:

First, we intend to convince the Communists that we cannot be defeated by force of arms or by superior power. They are not easily convinced. In recent months they have greatly increased their fighting forces and their attacks and the number of incidents. I have asked the Commanding General, General Westmoreland, what more he needs to meet this mounting aggression. He has told me. We will meet his needs.

I have today ordered to Vietnam the Airmobile Division and certain other forces which will raise our fighting strength from 75,000 to 125,000 men almost immediately. Additional forces will be needed later, and they will be sent as requested. This will make it necessary to increase our active fighting forces by raising the monthly draft call from 17,000 over a period of time to 35,000 per month, and for us to step up our campaign for voluntary enlistments.

After this past week of deliberations, I have concluded that it is not essential to order Reserve units into service now. If that necessity should later be indicated, I will give the matter more careful consideration and I will give the country due and adequate notice before taking such action, but only after full preparations.[12]

Whatever was personally felt by the political, military, and intelligence players in 1965, and by observers, they all had one thing in common: they recognized that deploying 44 combat battalions to Vietnam in 1965 was the crossing of an important threshold and the beginning of a major new course whose end was not in sight. General Westmoreland's plans called for increasing the troops in Vietnam and included the expectation that the war would last well beyond a year. The authors of *United States-Vietnam Relations* ("The Pentagon Papers") made the following conclusion pertaining to mobilization and the length of the war in the 1965 period:

> The decision not to call up the Reserves, which was made some time during the week just prior to the President's press conference of 28 July, indicated that the President also expected the war to last in Vietnam well beyond a year. No doubt the Secretary of Defense told him that without a declaration of national emergency – a move the President found politically unpalatable – the Reserves as an asset would be fully expended in one year, leaving the military establishment in worse shape than before if the war still continued.[13]

US military contingency plans for Indochina, which were being drafted as early as the 1950s, were based upon the campaign in Korea, upon the fundamental concept of the massive use of force – air power, naval power, and ground power – and upon concurrent mobilization of the Guard and Reserve. Mobilization was a cornerstone of the planning. Douglas Kinnard wrote that "contingency planning viewed the Active Army and Reserves as one force, and war plans were drawn up accordingly."[14] James Gavin, who was Chief of Plans of the Army Staff in the mid-1950s, wrote about war planning for Vietnam, "We believed it would be necessary to call up the Army Reserve and National Guard."[15] General Donald V. Bennett, Director of Strategic Plans in the Joint Staff, reported that he was probably the most shocked man in the world upon hearing of the 1965 decision not to mobilize.[16]

Even though the President rejected the recommendations of his Secretary of Defense, the Joint Chiefs of Staff, and others, the Department of Defense nevertheless clung to a hope that mobilization would occur for the Vietnam War. The President did not foreclose that possibility. In August 1965, Secretary McNamara reported to Congress that "the buildup of the active Army and the improvement of the readiness of a portion of the Reserve Components were necessary to offset planned deployments to Southeast Asia, to provide additional forces for possible new deployments, and to be able to deal with crises elsewhere in the world."[17]

President Johnson presented only one reason for nonmobilization in 1965: his fear that such a warlike action might trigger a greater war with China and Russia. Doris Kearns tells of other reasons:

> In private conversation, Johnson admitted two other considerations: His fear of "touching off a right-wing stampede" and his concern for the Great Society. Convinced that McCarthyism was dormant but not defeated, Johnson feared that if the full extent of our difficulties in Vietnam were known, the political right – a force of undetermined size whose power Johnson almost certainly

overestimated – would seize the initiative and demand an invasion of North Vietnam and the bombing of Hanoi. Johnson was much more concerned with the kind of furor that men like John Stennis, Richard Nixon, Gerald Ford, and others might have created than he was about any dove opposition. This reflected his knowledge of the sources of congressional power. Dissembling was the only way to keep the stampede from beginning. By pretending there was no major conflict, by minimizing the level of spending and by refusing to call up the Reserves or ask Congress for an acknowledgement of acceptance of the war, Johnson believed he could keep the levers of control in his hands.[18]

Chester L. Cooper wrote that the nonmobilization decision was a balance between military requirements in Vietnam versus political consequences at home:

> The announced increase to 125,000 men was almost certainly substantially less than either the Joint Chiefs or Westmoreland had requested and expected. Johnson was determined to fight the war with minimum disruption at home, and the troop increase was not based on the estimated number required, but rather on the maximum number that could be deployed without having to call up the Reserves. Doling out additional forces with a view to balancing off military requirements in Vietnam and political consequences at home typified the President's approach. He wished to avoid giving the impression that the United States was, in fact, "at war."[19]

Another, similar explanation of the President's decision is given by Kearns: "Johnson recoiled from the dramatic display of presidential action of a presidential declaration, asking Congress for higher taxes to pay for the war, and ordering a mobilization. The alternate strategy – which was Johnson's strategy – was to tell Congress and the public no more than absolutely necessary."[20]

David Halberstam's analysis of President Johnson's decision not to mobilize in 1965 is also particularly revealing:

> If there were no decisions which were crystallized and hard, then they could not leak, and if they could not leak, then the opposition could not point to them. Which was why he was not about to call up the reserves, because the use of the reserves would blow it all. It would be self-evident that we were really going to war, and that we would in fact have to pay a price. Which went against all the Administration planning: this would be a war without price, a silent, politically invisible war. The military wanted to call up the Reserves.
>
> He was against a call-up of the Reserves for other reasons as well. It would, he thought, telegraph the wrong signals to the adversaries, particularly China and the Soviet Union (frighten them into the idea that this was a real war) and Hanoi, which might decide that it was going to be a long war (he did not intend to go into a long war), and he felt if you called up the Reserves you had to be prepared to go the distance and you might force your adversary to do the same. He also felt that it would frighten the country, and he had just run as a peace candidate; similarly, he felt it would be too much of a sign that the military were in charge and that the civilians would turn over too much responsibility to the military. Finally, and above all, he feared that it would cost him the Great Society, that his enemies in Congress would seize on the war as a means of denying him his social legislation.[21]

John K. Mahon has written that there were three major reasons for President Johnson's refusal to mobilize the Guard and Reserve in 1965: (1) to conceal America's military commitment in Vietnam from the American people; (2) to avoid sending a belligerent message to the North Vietnamese, Chinese, and Soviets; and (3) to preserve the reserves for other contingencies.[22]

Whatever President Johnson's motivations were not to mobilize the Guard and Reserve in 1965, one of his objectives is now clear: he wished to conceal the expanded American participation in Vietnam from the public at large, from Congress, and from most of his own government. This policy of concealment was made explicit in National Security Action Memorandum 328, 6 April 1965.[23] Calling up the National Guard and Reserve would have destroyed the duplicity.

NONMOBILIZATION IN 1966 AND 1967

By the autumn of 1965, the infiltration of North Vietnamese units into South Vietnam had increased substantially. General Westmoreland requested additional forces on 22 November 1965, and following another trip to South Vietnam, Secretary McNamara recommended troop deployments totaling 74 battalions and 400,000 US personnel by the end of 1966, with possibly 200,000 more in 1967.[24] The Joint Chiefs continued to advocate a call-up of the reserves. They believed that commitments to NATO and elsewhere, as well as General Westmoreland's troop requirements for Vietnam, could not be met without a mobilization. The JCS also felt that only a massive deployment of troops and firepower would end the war in the least time and with the least cost. They did not share with President Johnson any illusionary wishful thinking about the length of the war or its requirements.

On 1 March 1966, the JCS forwarded their recommendation regarding 1966 deployments (Phase II A [R] forces – later named Phase 3) to Vietnam and reconstituting the Strategic Reserve. They stated that to satisfy further force requirements in Vietnam and to reconstitute the Strategic Reserve would require "a selective call-up of Reserve units and personnel and extension of terms of service." The JCS also recommended that if the reserves were not called up nor terms of service extended, then the deployments for 1966 (Phase 3) should be extended into 1967. On 10 March 1966, the Secretary of Defense rejected this advice and directed the JCS to plan for deployment of forces without either a call-up or extension of terms of service.[25]

On 7 October 1966, the JCS forwarded to the Secretary of Defense their analysis of the worldwide US military posture in light of meeting the 1966 and 1967 deployment requirements for Vietnam. This analysis concluded that without a call-up of reserves, with no change in rotation policy (from the one-year tour), and assuming that resources for the proposed 1967 deployment to Vietnam would be taken from existing US worldwide structure, the Army would have a force deficiency of three and two-thirds active divisions.[26]

In November 1966, the President made his decision on force deployments for Vietnam through FY 1967 (Program 4). The forces programmed were to be significantly less than requested by the field commander: a ceiling of 470,000 to be reached by June 1968, as opposed to the request for 542,000 by the end of calendar year 1967. However, there would not be a mobilization of the Guard and Reserve.[27] The Program 4 decision met with disagreement, for various reasons, on Capitol Hill and in the press. Many political leaders spoke out against the restricted force levels. Senator John Stennis, chairman of the Armed Services Committee, argued for meeting General Westmoreland's troop requests "even if it should require mobilization or partial mobilization." The JCS also sharply disagreed with the ceiling of 470,000.[28]

In May 1967, considerable attention was focused on determining capabilities of the services to provide troops and units without calling the reserves or a further drawing down of units in Europe. A Systems Analysis Office study of 5 May concluded that the services could provide only 66,000 of the additional 186,000 troops requested by MACV, and only 19 combat battalions of the 42 requested.[29]

Significant attention was devoted in the fall of 1967 to accelerate deployments of Program 5 and to find new approaches to military operations in Vietnam. Calendar year 1967 ended with the Program 5 combat elements either closing in Vietnam or on their way there, with mobilization continuing to be a major issue, and with a continuing presidential decision not to mobilize.

EVENTS AND MOBILIZATION IN 1968

When calendar year 1968 began, American Army combat units had been fighting in Vietnam for 34 months (since March 1965), and no mobilization had been permitted by the President. The approved force levels in Program 5 totaled 525,000, with an Army portion of 351,618, which was a net increase of 26,983 over Program 4.[30]

In January 1968, the Army National Guard and Army Reserve had a combined Ready Reserve unit strength of approximately 680,000, organized into some 7,000 units, plus an Individual Ready Reserve (IRR) strength of over 540,000. The force structure of these Army reserve components included eight combat divisions, 13 training divisions, 21 separate combat brigades, two engineer brigades, seven support brigades, 250 separate combat battalions, and other units. The Regular Army structure in January 1968 included 19 numbered divisions, with a total active Army strength of about 1.5 million: five divisions were located in the United States, two in Korea, five in Europe, and seven were in the Republic of Vietnam.[31]

On 25 January 1968, President Johnson directed, by Executive Order, a partial call-up of some Guard and Reserve units as a result of the USS *Pueblo* incident. He refrained from declaring a national emergency, which would have permitted him to bring up to one million Ready Reservists on active duty for a period of up to one year. The legal authority actually used by the President for the mobilization was Public Law 89-687 (the 1967 DOD Appropriation Act), which included the following key language: "Notwithstanding any other provision of law, until June 30, 1968, the President may, when he deems it necessary, order to active duty any unit of the Ready Reserve of an armed force for a period of not to exceed twenty-four months."[32]

Twenty-eight units involving 14,801 unit members were mobilized under the January order: six units with 593 Navy Reserve members; 14 units having 9340 members of the Air National Guard; and eight units having 4868 Air Reserve members. No Army National Guard, Army Reserve, Marine Corps Reserve, or Coast Guard Reserve units or individuals were called. Although the 25 January mobilization was not ordered at the time specifically for Vietnam, four of the Air National Guard units (tactical fighter squadrons) were deployed to RVN in May 1968. All six of the activated Naval Reserve units were demobilized by the end of calender year 1968, as were seven of the eight Air Reserve units. By December 1969, all of the units mobilized under the 25 January 1968 order were deactivated.[33]

Although the 25 January 1968 mobilization did not include Army reserve components, the Army Staff nevertheless began formal planning for a partial mobilization of the ARNG and USAR on 25 January in response to a directive from the Secretary of the Army to do so. The Army had developed in 1962 a Partial Mobilization Plan, based on the experience of the limited mobilization in 1961 during the Berlin Crisis, but the plan was not kept current following the 1965 decision not to mobilize the reserve components for the Vietnam War. The Army conducted no serious mobilization planning between 1965 and 1968.[34]

The new planning in 1968 was oriented initially toward the buildup of US Army forces in Korea and reconstitution of the Strategic Army Forces but later was expanded to include the need for additional Army forces in Vietnam.[35] The Army mobilization planning phase lasted from 25 January to 10 April 1968 and consisted of two types of planning: (1) intensive, specific, close-hold planning characterized by minimal guidance, restriction to a few selected persons on the Army Staff, short suspense dates, lack of staff coordination, changes in the type of units and strength of the force which might be authorized, and secrecy; and (2) general planning, which included a review of the 1961 mobilization during the Berlin Crisis, updated personnel procedures, and preparation of a congressional information plan. This general planning was well coordinated within the Army Staff and with US Continental Army Command (CONARC) headquarters.[36]

The first type of planning (intensive, close-hold) focused on developing troop lists and lasted 11 weeks (25 January to 10 April). This planning was actually accomplished in two distinct subperiods: the period 25 January to 9 February concentrated on developing plans to reinforce the Eighth US Army in Korea and to reconstitute the Strategic Army Forces; during the period 10 February to 10 April, planning for deployment of additional forces to South Vietnam was added to the task. Approximately 75 force packages were developed during the 11-week period. Revisions in lists of selected units occurred almost daily. There was no coordination in developing troop lists among the full Army staff, CONARC headquarters, the Continental US Armies, State Adjutants General, or Reserve commands.[37]

Planning was thus restricted and hampered. Further, the Army Guard and Army Reserve were undergoing substantial reorganizations that began 1 December 1967 and were not completed until 31 May 1968. Current unit readiness data were not available at HQDA because the readiness reporting system of reserve components had been suspended by the Undersecretary of the Army in 1966.[38]

The enemy's Tet Offensive began on 31 January 1968, only eight days after the USS *Pueblo* was seized. As the large-scale Tet operations continued, Secretary McNamara asked the JCS on 9 February to provide plans for emergency reinforcements. A formal request by General Westmoreland for reinforcements was made on 12 February.[39]

President Johnson met with his advisers (Rusk, McNamara, Clifford, Wheeler, Taylor, Helms, and Reston) on 12 February to discuss General Westmoreland's request for reinforcements. Calling up reserves was discussed. The President approved reinforcements but again rejected mobilization. President Johnson wrote of the 12 February mobilization question: ''Wheeler was in favor; McNamara was opposed. I asked them to study the problem further and to agree on a recommendation.''[40] The meeting continued the following day, and the President reported the following in his memoirs about the discussion:

> My advisers still disagree on whether Reserves should be called, and, if so, how many and in what categories. I told McNamara and Wheeler there were many questions I wanted them to answer. I remember the complaints about the call-up of Reserves during President Kennedy's administration and, more recently, the failure to use effectively those who had been called up during the *Pueblo* crisis.
>
> Why, I asked, is it necessary to call up Reserve units at this time? If we decided on a call-up, how large should it be? Could we reduce the numbers by drawing on forces stationed in Europe or South Korea? Could we avoid or at least postpone individual Reserve call-ups? If Reserves were called, where would they be assigned? How long would they serve? What would be the budgetary implications? Would congressional action be necessary? I said that I would take no action until I received satisfactory answers to these and several other questions.[41]

On 13 February, the reinforcement decision of the day before was being implemented, to consist of the deployment of one brigade of the 82d Airborne Division and one Marine regimental landing team, for a total emergency reinforcement of 10,500 men. Responding to this decision, the JCS immediately forwarded their recommendations for a call-up of reserve forces: the minimum call-up, which would replace deploying forces, would require 32,000 for the Army, 12,000 for the Marine Corps, 2300 Navy Reserves, and none for the Air Force. In addition, the Joint Chiefs stressed that it would be both prudent and advisable for a larger mobilization of 136,650: 58,000 Army, 51,000 Marines, 5150 Navy, and 22,500 Air Force. The Joint Chiefs of Staff also reiterated their recommendation that legislation be sought for mobilization and extension of terms of service.[42]

General Westmoreland also saw the need for a mobilization at that time in order to provide reinforcements and to increase the Strategic Reserve. He reported, however, that General Wheeler had informed him on 24 March, under the President's direction, that "making a major call-up of Reserves and contesting the enemy's geographical widening of the war was politically infeasible."[43]

On 29 February, Secretary of Defense designate Clark Clifford (sworn in as Secretary on 1 March) initiated, at the order of the President, a complete reexamination of US strategy in Vietnam which became known as the "A to Z" reassessment. The last week of February and first week of March 1968 were characterized by frantic preparation, discussion, consultation, and writing. On 4 March, the President was presented with the "A to Z" reassessment, which contained a recommendation to mobilize 262,000 Guardsmen and Reservists for the war.[44]

MOBILIZATION DECISIONS AND POLICIES

On 13 March, the President made the decision to have a mobilization, but the specific size of the mobilized force was not then decided. The Office of the Secretary of Defense began planning on 14 March for a call-up of 96,000 personnel, of which 43,500 were to be deployed to Vietnam.[45]

On 28 March, the President made the decision that mobilization would be limited to about 24,500 personnel. On 2 April, the final troop list submitted by the Army to the JCS totaled 54,000. Two days later, the Secretary of Defense decreed that 54,000 was too high because of cost.[46] It is pathetic that after all the debate and arguments about the need for a mobilization, all the planning and consideration about the size and composition of the mobilized force, despite the requirements for forces to be deployed and to reconstitute the Strategic Reserve, and regardless of the money spent on the war over the previous several years, in the end the size of the mobilized force was decided by financial and political considerations and not operational requirements.

On 31 March 1968, President Johnson addressed the nation on television. He summarized his efforts to achieve peace in Vietnam over the years and made the following brief comment about a call-up of the Reserves:

> In order that these forces [the 10,500 emergency reinforcements] may reach maximum combat effectiveness, the Joint Chiefs of Staff have recommended to me that we should be prepared to send – during the next five months – support troops totalling approximately 13,500 men.
> A portion of these men will be made available from our active forces. The balance will come from Reserve Component units which will be called up for service.[47]

The President then reiterated US objectives in Vietnam and closed his address with the startling announcement, "I shall not seek, and I will not accept, the nomination of my party for another term as your President."[48] Thus, two of the major decisions of the Johnson presidency were made in March 1968. It is interesting to speculate on the possible linkage of these two decisions, although there is no recorded evidence of any.

President Johnson signed an Executive Order (No. 11406) authorizing the mobilization for the Vietnam War. The actual mobilization authority exercised by the President (and delegated to the Secretary of Defense) was contained in the 1967 DOD Appropriations Act, which was the same authority utilized for the 25 January 1968 partial mobilization resulting from the USS *Pueblo* incident. The mobilization was based neither on a declaration of emergency nor on a declaration of war.[49]

At 10.00 hours on 11 April 1968, Secretary of Defense Clifford announced at a news conference that 24,500 men in some 88 units from the reserve components of the Army, Navy, and Air Force and 3600 members of the Individual Ready Reserve (IRR) would be mobilized.[50] The mobilization order was dated that same day and directed the call-up to occur on 13 May (M-Day). Seventy-six ARNG and USAR units, with a strength of 20,034, were actually mobilized. In addition, 2752 members of the IRR were called up. There were two objectives for the 13 May 1968 mobilization: (1) to provide troops for actual deployment to Vietnam, and (2) to provide troops to build up the strategic reserves in the United States. Forty-three units were deployed to Vietnam, and 33 units remained in the United States.[51]

Selection of the 76 ARNG and USAR units to be mobilized was made by the Assistant Chief of Staff for Force Development in frantic consultation with the Chief, National Guard Bureau, and the Chief, Army Reserve. No other Army staff, major Army commands, or states were involved in the unit selection determination.

Although 74 of the 76 needed types of units were in the Selected Reserve Force (SRF) in 1968, or had recently been in the SRF, only 59 units were selected from the SRF category for mobilization.[52] Thus, the primary criterion of highest operational readiness was applied to only 66 percent of the unit selection. Other criteria which influenced selection were geographic distribution (34 states provided units), proportionate contribution by the ARNG and USAR (68 percent and 32 percent, respectively), and the civil disturbance threat (no state was denuded of its ARNG).[53]

Because the mobilization of units was small, only 3069 enlisted IRR fillers were required. From a total IRR paper strength of 540,000, only 4132 of its members were eligible for call-up because the 1967 DOD Appropriations Act prohibited calling up IRR members who had completed two or more years of active service and those who had fulfilled their statutory military obligations. No officers in the IRR were recalled because the number eligible was too small to deal with; only 93 were eligible from an initial projection of 2400. The number of IRR personnel actually mobilized was 2752, which was only one-half of one percent of the IRR. Of these, 1060 were assigned to the active Army and 1692 went to mobilized ARNG and USAR units.[54]

HQDA attempted from the onset to manage mobilized personnel (unit members and nonunit members) in the same manner and under the same regulations as Regular Army personnel. It didn't work. Personnel actions and problems associated with the 1968 partial mobilization for Vietnam included reassignments, promotions, delays, exemptions, deferments, separations, medical exams, proficiency pay eligibility, personnel accounting, reporting, and control.[55] These problems and issues had occurred with every mobilization in US history.

As was the case with mobilization planning in general, the preparation of stationing plans did not begin until 25 January 1968. Considerable difficulty was encountered because of the many changes in the type and number of units in the troop lists during the mobilization planning period of 25 January to 10 April. Developing stationing plans was difficult also because the planners did not know what units would be mobilized, when the mobilizations would occur, what active Army deployments would be made, or the length of time between alert and movement to mobilization stations.[56]

Determining the Army's capability to equip mobilized ARNG and USAR units was impossible during the mobilization planning period. In addition to problems similar to the ones encountered by those attempting to develop stationing plans, the DA staff did not know the true equipment status of the units that were on the final list to be mobilized.

The incredible assumption was made that units scheduled for deployment were in a combat-ready status. In fact, every one of the 76 mobilized units was rated C-4 (not combat-ready) in equipment readiness. In many cases the DA analysts did not know the TOE under which the mobilized units were organized. Following M-Day there were serious problems with assumptions, equipment status reporting, distribution, and redistribution. A consistent feature of every mobilization in US history has been the requirement to provide equipment for the mobilized units.[57]

Unit training at mobilization stations was adversely affected by the large number of personnel who were not branch- or MOS-qualified, by understrength units, by equipment shortages, and by the issuance of equipment not previously used by the ARNG and USAR. The major reorganization of the reserve components immediately before the mobilization degraded readiness, as had the inclusion of civil disturbance training in the Guard's inactive-duty training program. The requirement to conduct individual training as well as unit training to overcome these problems resulted in an extension of the postmobilization training beyond that prescribed in the Army Training Program for 58 of the 76 mobilized units.[58]

That mobilized units had to undergo a complete unit training program in 1968 to achieve deployability readiness was no different from the experience of earlier mobilizations. Whenever mobilized units have a readiness condition of C-4 in equipment, which all had in 1968, a post-mobilization training program will be required. Whenever units are less than C-1 (combat-ready, no deficiencies) in personnel, which all were in 1968, a postmobilization training program will be necessary. Even if mobilized units were C-1 in both personnel and equipment, the question of operational readiness from a training perspective would arise. The historical experience with mobilizations demands the realization that postmobilization training will be mandatory, and that it will take at least several weeks to achieve operational readiness. Peacetime training and the peacetime equipment status of the Army National Guard and Army Reserve have never, in US history, been sufficient for immediate deployment.

The question of how to use mobilized units of the Guard and Reserve has historically been an issue and became controversial again during the Vietnam War. Unit integrity was not maintained either with the units that deployed to Vietnam or those that were not deployed. For example, of the 12,234 mobilized Army National Guardsmen, 2729 reported to Vietnam with their Guard units, but many were subsequently transferred to other units. Of the 9505 Guardsmen whose units remained in the United States, 4311 were sent to Vietnam as fillers.[59]

Unit history and unit integrity are matters of great pride and intense concern within the National Guard and Reserve. Those forces have been built on the basis of units, beginning with the initial militia system. Training, equipment, organization, tactics, and readiness are all based on cohesion of units. Using unit members as fillers and individual replacements always causes considerable dissatisfaction, and the use of the reserve component units as some sort of individual recruiting preserve is neither proper nor wise.

The mobilization of reserve components, however large or small the call-up, is never a routine matter. In addition to strategic considerations and purely military events and activities in conducting the mobilization, there will always be political and public affairs implications – particularly with partial mobilizations. The media, Congress, and the public will rightfully direct a barrage of inquiries to the White House and the Pentagon. There will initially be considerable excitement and attention to the topic, and if DOD is properly prepared for the inquiries, the public attention may soon wane. Of the many questions asked about mobilization, the most important one to answer is "Why?" The next questions will be: "Where are the mobilized troops now and what are they doing?" Three months after the January 1968 mobilization, the media reported that mobilized Reservists were "just waiting around," which was mostly true. The same can be said of the May 1968 mobilization. The charge of unsuitable use of mobilized reserves will always occur when the mobilized units are not deployed and when unit integrity is violated.

The 76 units mobilized on 13 May 1968 served on active duty between 14 and 19 months. During the first half of that time, many unit personnel were assigned to other units as fillers, resulting in their being scattered all over the world. During the last half of the period, the Army attempted to plan and execute a system to reestablish unit integrity in order to demobilize the units.

Demobilization of units was accomplished by 12 December 1969, after which one unit was eliminated from the structure and three were reorganized. The Army's demobilization was characterized by poor planning, inefficiency, disinterest, terrible policy, poor execution, and ill-timing. Nearly everything about the demobilization was cause for complaint. Of the numerous problems, the most serious was the loss of unit integrity. The strong feeling was widespread within the Guard and Reserve that a breach of good faith had been committed by the Army.[60] Thus, after years of neglect and receipt of equipment which was not considered appropriate for active Army use, the Guard and Reserve forces were shunted even further into the background of full and equal treatment as a viable component of the national force structure.

PURPOSE AND MEANING OF MOBILIZATION

Mobilization is a military and a political event of crucial importance. The purpose and meaning of mobilization to the military can be expressed concisely: the central concept of strategy is force; the central concept of force is manpower; and the central concept of manpower is mobilization. Mobilization increases the options and the capabilities of the Defense Department to carry out national military policy, and it directly affects the timing, size, and composition of deployments to a theater of war. In addition, mobilization affects other potential theaters, as well as the strategic reserves. The decision to mobilize is vital to actual and potential military operations and capabilities, as well as to policy, strategy, and tactics.

The other element of mobilization can be stated as a fundamental proposition: mobilization is an act of political will. It makes commitment and determination real and visible to friends and foes alike. It is a conscious, concrete demonstration of firm resolve to achieve political objectives over a recognized and acknowledged enemy or threat.

As an unambiguous political statement, mobilization is immensely significant to the American people. The response to a mobilization by Americans will be immediate: it may be negative, but then it may be gratifying to the decision-makers; in any event, it will be illuminating and not oblique.

Mobilization is a symbol of commitment, and symbolism is often as important as substance. Mobilization is also a substantive act, and therefore it is a political and military event having mutually supportive purpose and meaning. It follows without amplification that nonmobiliztion for a war is also of critical importance and may be viewed as a disregard for military and political prudence.

Thirty-eight months after the ground war began for the United States in South Vietnam, President Johnson made the belated decision to mobilize a small portion of the National Guard and Reserve. Never before in US history had a president refused to use early in a major war the military force of the reserve components. And never before had a mobilization for a major war been so miniscule. The 13 May 1968 mobilization for the Vietnam War occurred far too late and was far too small to be of any political or military significance.

The mobilization itself, once ordered by the Commander in Chief, was conducted by OSD and HQDA in a manner of gross ineptitude: the preparation for a mobilization was impudently unsuitable; the conduct of the mobilization was contemptuous; the demobilization was a comedy of errors. And once the forces were mobilized, countless problems were inflicted by the Regular Army – as has been true throughout US history.

NOTES

This article is drawn from the authors' larger study "Mobilization of the Army National Guard and Army Reserve: Historical Perspective and the Vietnam War," published by the Strategic Studies Institute, US Army War College, 7 September 1984.

1. The Civil War is omitted from the table owing to its uniqueness.
2. The mobilized number includes the Continental Army. Statistics that show the number serving who were not members of the Organized Militia are unavailable.
3. Strength of the Regular Army was as of September 1939, when President Roosevelt declared a "limited national emergency" and began increasing the strength of the Regular Army as a result of war in Europe.
4. US Department of Defense, *Annual Report of the Secretary of Defense on Reserve Affairs* (Washington: GPO, FY65) (hereinafter referred to as *Annual Report*); US Department of the Army and the Air Force, *Annual Report of the Chief, National Guard Bureau* (Washington: GPO, FY65), pp. 28-29 (hereinafter referred to as *Annual Report CNGB*); US Department of Defense, *Annual Report of the Secretary of Defense and of the Secretary of the Army, Secretary of the Navy, and Secretary of the Air Force* (Washington: GPO, FY65), p. 406 (hereinafter referred to as *DOD Report*).
5. *DOD Report*, FY65, pp. 116, 131, 394; *Annual Report*, FY65, pp. 116-25.
6. US Department of Defense, *United States-Vietnam Relations, 1945-1967*, (Washington: GPO, 1971) Book 4, Part IV C. 5., p. 16. (Popularly known as "The Pentagon Papers.")
7. Paul H. Nitze, "The Evolution of National Security Policy and the Vietnam War," in W. Scott Thompson and Donaldson D. Frizzell, eds., *The Lessons of Vietnam* (New York: Crane, Russak, 1977), p. 7.
8. Chester L. Cooper, *The Last Crusade* (New York: Dodd, Mead, 1970), p. 280.
9. *United States-Vietnam Relations*, Book 4, Part IV C. 5., pp. 31, 110.
10. Lyndon Johnson, *The Vantage Point* (New York: Popular Library, 1971), p. 146.
11. Ibid., p. 149.
12. *United States-Vietnam Relations*, Book 4, Part IV C. 5., p. 31; Johnson, pp. 151-53.
13. *United States-Vietnam Relations*, Book 4, Part IV C. 5., p. 121.
14. Douglas Kinnard, *The War Managers* (Hanover, N.H.: University Press of New England, 1977), p. 118.
15. James M. Gavin, *Crises Now* (New York: Random House, 1968), p. 48.
16. BDM Corporation, *A Study of the Strategic Lessons Learned in Vietnam* (McLean, Va.: BDM, 1980-81), V, 3-24.
17. *DOD Report*, FY66, p. 175. Accordingly, the Army created the Selected Reserve Force (SRF) to enhance premobilization readiness of a portion of the ARNG and USAR.
18. Doris Kearns, *Lyndon Johnson and the American Dream* (New York: Harper and Row, 1976), pp. 295-96.
19. Cooper, p. 286.
20. Kearns, p. 294.
21. David Halberstam, *The Best and the Brightest* (New York: Random House, 1969), pp. 593-94.
22. John K. Mahon, *History of the Militia and the National Guard* (New York: Macmillan, 1983), p. 242.
23. Philip Geyelin, "Vietnam and the Press – Limited War and an Open Society," in *The Legacy of Vietnam*, ed. Anthony Lake (New York: New York Univ. Press, 1976), pp. 166-93.
24. *United States-Vietnam Relations*, Book 5, Part IV C. 6. (a)., pp. ii and 25.
25. Ibid., pp. 38-41.
26. Ibid., pp. 79-80.
27. Ibid., pp. 101-27.
28. Ibid., Book 5, Part IV C. 6. (b)., pp. 22-24.
29. Ibid., p. 133.

30. Ibid., p. 213.
31. *DOD Report*, FY67, pp. 21-22; *DOD Report*, FY68, pp. 150-57; *Annual Report*, FY67, pp. 8-9; *Annual Report*, FY68, pp. 8-10, D-6.
32. *United States Code Congressional and Administrative News* (St. Paul: West Publishing Co., 1967), I, 1160-61; *Annual Report*, FY68, p. A-11.
33. *Annual Report*, FY68, appendix C.; *Annual Report CNGB*, FY68, p. 10; Mahon, p. 243.
34. J. Heymont and E. W. McGregor, *Review and Analysis of Recent Mobilization and Deployments of US Army Reserve Components* (McLean, Va.: Research Analysis Corporation, October 1972), Ch. 5; Richard P. Weinert, *CONARC and the 1968 Reserve Mobilization* (HQ, US Continental Army Command, Fort Monroe, August 1970), pp. 8-14.
35. US Department of the Army, Assistant Chief of Staff for Force Development, *After Action Report, Mobilization of Reserve Forces, 1968* (Washington: GPO, 1971), pp. 1-1, 1-2 (hereinafter referred to as *After Action Report*).
36. Ibid.
37. Ibid., pp. 1-2, 1-3.
38. The first readiness report for the ARNG and USAR after suspension in 1966 of previous reporting was not established until April 1969. Ibid.; *Annual Report*, FY69, p. 41.
39. William C. Westmoreland, *A Soldier Reports* (New York: Dell, 1976), p. 462.
40. Johnson, p. 386.
41. Ibid., p. 387.
42. *United States-Vietnam Relations*, Book 5, Part IV C. 6., (c), pp. 6-12.
43. Westmoreland, pp. 467-72.
44. For a detailed treatment of the Clifford Task Force reassessment, see Herbert Y. Schandler, *The Unmaking of a President* (Princeton: Princeton Univ. Press, 1977), ch. 7; and *United States-Vietnam Relations*, Book 5, Part IV C. 6. (c), pp. 16-64.
45. *United States-Vietnam Relations*, Book 5, Part IV C. 6. (c), pp. 51-52, 71-73.
46. Ibid., pp. 76-78; *After Action Report*, p. 1-5.
47. *United States-Vietnam Relations*, Book 5, Part IV C. 6. (c), pp. 80-85.
48. Johnson, ch. 17; Kearns, ch. 12; *United States-Vietnam Relations*, Book 5, Part IV C. 6. (c), p. 90.
49. *United States Code Congressional and Administrative News*, 1968, III, 4698.
50. "Army Reserve Units Respond to Call-Up," *The Army Reserve Magazine* (May 1968), p. 6.
51. *After Action Report*, p. 2-1; Heymont and McGregor, ch. 5.
52. The Selected Reserve Force (SRF) was created in 1965 to increase greatly the readiness of selected units to mobilize within seven days after alert and enter active duty at 93 percent. The initial ARNG and USAR contribution to the SRF was 976 units. The SRF was abandoned on 30 September 1969.
53. *After Action Report*, pp. 1-7, 1-8, 3-15.
54. Ibid., pp. 2-2, 2-3, 2-4, 3-3, 3-10, 3-11.
55. Ibid., chs. 2, 3, and 4.
56. Ibid., pp. 4-14, 1-15, 1-16.
57. Ibid., ch. 3; Heymont and McGregor, p. 1-4; Joseph M. Heiser, Jr., *Vietnam Studies: Logistics Support* (Washington: GPO, 1974), pp. 27-29.
58. *After Action Report*, ch. 3.
59. *Annual Report, CNGB*, FY69, p. 9.
60. US Department of the Army, Assistant Chief of Staff for Force Development, *After-Action Report on Demobilization of Reserve Component Forces, 1969* (Washington: GPO, 1 August 1970), pp. 3-4, 3-7, 9-15; *Annual Report*, FY69, p. C-2; Heymont and McGregor, pp. 5-10, 5-11; *Annual Report*, FY69, p. C-2; *Annual Report*, FY70, p. A-8.

This article appeared in the spring 1985 issue of *Parameters*.

IV. THE LESSONS OF WAR

12

Some Political-Military Lessons of the Vietnam War

by GUENTER LEWY

Whether the American disengagement from Vietnam is to be regarded as a military defeat or not is largely a matter of semantics. It is rather clear that the United States did not achieve its key objective, the creation of a free and independent South Vietnam. If America wants to prevent similar failures in the future, it is essential that we find out as precisely as we can why, despite the sacrifice of almost 50,000 American lives on the field of battle, the expenditure of $112 billion, and much dedication and good will, the outcome was such a fiasco. To be sure, the final battle in 1975 was lost by the South Vietnamese, but this fact merely leads to a rephrasing of the question. The South Vietnamese armed forces (RVNAF) had been equipped and trained by the United States during 20 long years. They had been taught the American way of war. Why, then, did they collapse so ignominiously?

I

The cuts in aid imposed by a war-weary Congress in 1973 and 1974 created shortages in RVNAF military equipment and ammunition and led to a feeling of abandonment. But there is reason to conclude that internal weaknesses on the part of the RVNAF alone would have been sufficient to cause defeat. During the years of Vietnamization and again in late 1972, the United States had provided RVNAF with large quantities of sophisticated equipment which the South Vietnamese proved as yet unable to maintain properly. There were not enough skilled managers and technicians, and technical manuals translated into Vietnamese were in short supply; the importance of routine and preventive maintenance was poorly understood. Weatherproof storage, the keeping of accurate inventories, and the distribution of repair parts were handled badly, and transportation, like the entire logistical system, suffered from bureaucratic inertia and excessive red tape. As a result, much expensive equipment was sitting around rusting or could not be used for want of repair parts buried in mountains of crates in some faraway warehouse. Planes were grounded not only because of a shortage of fuel but also because they had not been properly maintained and therefore could no longer fly. RVNAF, concluded the US Defense Attaché in Saigon in his final assessment, had not achieved "sufficient maturity, technical expertise and managerial capabilities to completely maintain, operate and logistically support their communications systems and equipment resources."[1]

Just as equipment suffered from lack of adequate maintenance, the performance of the troops was impaired by insufficient attention to the value of training and continuous drilling in combat techniques. Training exercises by units in the field were rare. More fundamentally, leadership in many RVNAF units was woefully inadequate. While there had been improvement in the quality of the lower-ranking ARVN officers, division and corps commanders all too often were still weak leaders. Critical combat and staff assignments were given to incapable or outright corrupt officers. To please the Americans, President Thieu occasionally would fire one of the more notorious offenders, but usually the culprit would merely be transferred to some other important post. Some of the 116 Vietnamese generals evacuated from Vietnam arrived in the United States with nothing because they had nothing, but others are able to live a life of leisure, made possible by illictly gained wealth. Colonel Nguyen Be, a maverick figure who for a long time headed the pacification training center at Vung Tau, probably summed it up well when he told *The New York Times'* Fox Butterfield: "Under our system, the generals amassed riches for their families, but the soldiers got nothing and saw no moral sanction in their leadership. In the end they took their revenge."[2]

The crucial importance of leadership for the efficient functioning of an army in combat is, of course, well known. As General Matthew B. Ridgway, former US commander in Korea, pointed out in 1971: The building of an effective combat force requires "leadership, weapons, and training, and in that order of importance, for without leadership from the top down the other two factors will be nullified."[3] In Vietnam, the significance of the abundance of equipment owned by the armed forces of Vietnam was negated by inadequate training and leadership. The German Army in World War II could survive tremendous setbacks, losses, and long retreats and remain until the end a functioning combat instrument in large measure because of the quality of its leadership. The state of Israel occupies an extremely unfavorable geographic position, surrounded on three sides by hostile neighbors, and the Arab-Israeli conflict since its inception has been highly asymmetrical in human resources and military equipment; yet such weaknesses can be compensated for by superiority in leadership. The armed forces of the Republic of Vietnam in 1975, on the other hand, were outgunned *and* lacked effective leadership. The incompetence demonstrated by Thieu and his high command in the final days of the war, including in prominent place the ill-prepared evacuation of the central highlands and the removal of the First Airborne Division from the northern front, might have been enough to imperil the survival of even a well-disciplined and well-led army. Given the fragility of the ARVN, it is hardly surprising that these tragic mistakes proved irreversible and that they led to the quick unraveling of any remaining discipline in the officer corps and the rank-and-file.

The failure of RVNAF morale was linked to certain weaknesses of the South Vietnamese society whose contribution to the final collapse is difficult to assess in precise terms, but which undoubtedly played a significant role. In addition to leadership and a sense of comradeship, a soldier's effectiveness and combat morale are sustained by his belief in the basic legitimacy of the society of which he is a member and for which he is asked to risk his life. The South Vietnamese soldier, in the end, did not feel that he was part of a political community worth the supreme sacrifice; he saw no reason to die for the government of South Vietnam. The country lacked political leadership that could inspire a sense of trust, purpose, and self-confidence. It remained a society divided by geographic regionalism, ethnic minorities, and religious differences, and governed by cliques of politicians and generals. Thieu himself assuredly was not the kind of person who, like in some ways Diem before him, could function as a widely respected leader, a symbol of national unity. His government, despite belated reforms like the Land-to-the-Tiller program, had been unable to mobilize mass support in the countryside. In a series of moves in 1972 and 1973, Thieu once again seriously weakened local self-government by abolishing authority for the election of hamlet chiefs, authorizing district chiefs to appoint members of the village and hamlet administration committees and putting local militia forces under the control of military officers instead of village chiefs. This removal of local officials from public accountability was bound to reduce the credibility of government decisions and programs and probably further weakened popular acceptance of the legitimacy of the national government in Saigon. Many members of the educated urban elite, on the other hand, looked with disdain upon Thieu and his officers, who were serving as province and district chiefs, and regarded them as mere military men who did not merit their active backing and loyalty.

The inability of the Thieu regime to generate popular commitment was reinforced by the widespread corruption permeating the system. Revulsion at this corruption created a feeling on the part of the populace that the government lacked "virtue" and the "mandate of heaven" necessary in order legitimately to govern the country. As long as the Americans were there, corruption had been seen by many as tolerable, for the fat often came off Uncle Sam; now, on the other hand, it affected the dwindling income of ordinary Vietnamese and increased the unpopularity of the South Vietnamese government (GVN). In April 1974, the country was said to have 95,371 disabled veterans, 168,472 widows, and 231,808 orphans entitled to social welfare benefits,[4] but corruption often made it difficult for these war victims to receive their meager allowances. Corruption also worked direct benefits for the Viet Cong, thus further increasing popular disgust. VC purchasing agents could obtain supplies in the cities of South Vietnam; GVN officials and officers sold war material and food to the enemy; and members of the VC could buy positions as hamlet and village chiefs, as they did in Vinh Binh province for example.[5] It was well known that VC agents had infiltrated the highest levels of government and of the armed forces, creating an atmosphere of suspicion and distrust.

In July 1974, 300 Catholic priests had organized the People's Front Against Corruption, which quickly attracted support from other political opposition elements. In response to demands from this anticorruption movement, Thieu fired or reassigned a large number of officials accused of corruption – 10 cabinet ministers, 14 generals, 151 senior province or district officials, 870 village and hamlet officials, some 1000 national policemen and 550 military officers. But people had witnessed periodic purges of corrupt officials many times before and therefore had developed a strong sense of cynicism about the real improvements that could be expected from such reshuffles. Moreover, serious charges had also been leveled against President Thieu and his family, and many agreed with the statement of a leader of the Buddhist Reconciliation Force: "If Thieu wants to eliminate corruption in the army he must fire himself first."[6] At a time when the enemy stood at the gates and threatened the very survival of a noncommunist political order, these opposition forces hesitated to press their attack on Thieu too forcefully, but the corrosive effect of such charges, nevertheless, was undoubtedly pronounced.

The deep-seated internal weaknesses in South Vietnamese society – most of them of very long standing – had proven impregnable to repeated American proddings for reform. This leads to the first important conclusion and lesson of the Vietnam experience: Despite often-heard charges that the South Vietnamese were American puppets, in fact the United States lacked the leverage necessary to prevent its ally from making crucial mistakes. As a result of anticolonialist inhibitions and other reasons, the United States refrained from pressing for a decisive reorganization of the South Vietnamese armed forces and for a combined command, as America had done in Korea under the mantle of a UN mandate. Similarly, in regard to pacification and matters of social policies generally, America sought to shore up a sovereign South Vietnamese government and therefore, for the most part, limited itself to an advisory and supporting role, always mindful of the saying of Lawrence of Arabia: "Better they do it imperfectly than you do it perfectly, for it is their country, their war, and your time is limited." Western aggressiveness and impatience for results, it was said, ran counter to oriental ways of thinking and doing things and merely created increased resistance to change and reform.

But if internal weaknesses in the South Vietnamese society and the high level of corruption were factors as important in the final collapse as the evidence seems to suggest, might a radically different approach perhaps have been indicated? Should the United States initially have accepted full responsibility for both military and political affairs, as suggested by experienced Vietnam hands like John Paul Vann, and only gradually have yielded control over the conduct of the war to a newly created corps of capable military leaders and administrators? Should America have played the role of the "good colonialist" who in this way slowly prepares a new country for viable independence? At the very least, should the United States have exerted more systematic leverage on its Vietnamese ally? The former chief of pacification, Robert W. Komer, has written that the long record of American failure to move the GVN in directions which in retrospect would clearly have been desirable, for the people of both South Vietnam and America, suggests "that we would have had little to lose and much to gain by using more vigorously the power over the GVN that our contributions gave us. We became their prisoners rather than they ours – the classic trap into which great powers have so often fallen in their relationships with weak allies."[7]

II

Yet even if the United States had succeeded in making the South Vietnamese follow our lead and counsel, would this have assured victory? Did the United States know how to fight the kind of revolutionary war it faced in Vietnam? An American officer who had commanded a brigade in Vietnam wrote in 1968 that it was one of the tragedies of Vietnam that the services refused to recognize the realities of a people's war and clung to the illusion that this was a war that troops could win. "A political revolution is something quite different from a conventional military campaign, and yet we persist in viewing Vietnam as a war which will be won when we bring enough power and force to bear."[8] This criticism remained largely pertinent until the end of the war.

Despite much talk about "winning the hearts and minds," the United States never really learned to fight a counterinsurgency war and used force in largely traditional ways. The military, like all bureaucracies encountering a new situation for which they are not prepared and in which they do not know what to do, did what they knew to do. That happened to be the inappropriate thing. "The Vietnamese Communist generals," Edward G. Lansdale has written, "saw their armed forces as instruments primarily to gain political goals. The American generals saw their forces primarily as instruments to defeat enemy military forces. One fought battles to influence opinions in Vietnam and in the world, the other fought battles to finish the enemy keeping tabs by body count."[9] As it turned out, the enemy's endurance and supply of manpower proved stronger than American persistence in keeping up the struggle. Communist losses in most major engagements were far higher than those suffered by the Americans, but General Giap regarded these efforts worth the price. "His is not an army that sends coffins north," wrote a former American intelligence officer in 1968, "it is by the traffic in homebound American coffins that Giap measures his success."[10]

American forces, applying classic Army doctrine of aggressively seeking out the enemy and destroying his main force units, fought numerous bloody battles in the rough terrain along the DMZ and in the jungles of the highlands. A Marine Corps study in late 1967 pointed out that these engagements provided the enemy with a double bonus: They took allied forces away from the pacification effort and, in addition, involved them in combat under conditions favorable to the enemy. The NVA/VC benefitted from short supply lines and nearby havens across the border which enabled them to ambush, defend briefly, and withdraw. They also could fight under the protective cover of thick jungle, which created low visibility and weakened the effectiveness of allied airpower and other heavy support weapons.[11] The classic case of such a fight was the battle for Dong Ap Bia ("Hamburger Hill") in the A Shau Valley in May 1969. The Americans won most of these battles but lost the war.

Most fundamentally, the American strategy of attrition – seeking to cause the enemy more casualties than he could replace through infiltration or recruitment – ignored the crucial fact that the enemy whom it was essential to defeat was in the hamlets and not in the jungles. Without the support of the VC infrastructure in the villages, the communist main force units were blind and incapable of prolonged action – they could not obtain intelligence and food or prepare the battlefield by prepositioning supplies.

In 1965 and 1966, when newly created VC main force units and North Vietnamese regulars threatened the collapse of the South Vietnamese Army, a major quasi-conventional military response was probably unavoidable. Large operations against the enemy's main force units were necessary to provide a shield behind which pacification and the struggle against the guerrillas in the villages could proceed. However, these large search and destroy operations soon became an end in themselves, and the tautology that "the destruction of the enemy would bring security to the countryside" obscured the more basic question of who and where the enemy really was. As Francis J. West, Jr., a former Marine Corps officer and an astute analyst of American strategy and tactics in Vietnam, has written:

The rationale that ceaseless US operations in the hills could keep the enemy from the people was an operational denial of the fact that in large measure the war was a revolution which started in the hamlets and that therefore the Viet Cong were already among the people when we went to the hills. The belief that American units would provide a shield ("support for pacification") behind which the rural GVN structure could rebuild itself assumed that the hills threatened the hamlets.

West illustrates the irrelevance to pacification of much of the big-unit war by this episode:

In November of 1967 two officers from an American division visited the senior adviser to the district which abutted their division headquarters in order to be briefed on the local situation. The adviser said the situation was terrible, with the VC in control and the GVN unsure even of the district town. So bitter was the adviser that the visiting officers grumbled about his "negativism," pointing out that their division had the NVA units in the hills on the run and had killed over 500 of them in the past month . . . .

The officers returned to their headquarters for dinner and that same night a team of enemy sappers from a local force unit leveled the district headquarters and killed the adviser.

In October of 1968 I revisited that district and both the assistant district chief for security and the senior subsector adviser told me that the situation had not improved, that the VC still controlled the district, and that the division was still out in the hills bringing them security.[12]

While American large units prowled around to thwart enemy main force units, the pacification of the countryside often became a sideshow. After American troops had cleared an area of enemy main force units, Vietnamese troops, police, and pacification cadres were supposed to move in to root out the VC infrastructure and provide permanent security and development help to the hamlets. Unfortunately, the implementation of this plan was achieved late in the war and even then only spottily.

A study of the problems faced in Vietnam commissioned by the Army Chief of Staff and completed by a group of officers after eight months' work in 1966, known as the PROVN study, suggested a substantial revision of priorities and argued that pacification should be designated unequivocally as the major US/ GVN effort. "Victory" could be achieved only through bringing the individual Vietnamese, typically a rural peasant, to support willingly the GVN. The critical actions, the PROVN study argued, were those that occurred at the village, district, and provincial levels. This is where the war had to be fought and won. The military destruction of the communist regiments was not the solution to the complex challenge presented by the Vietnam conflict. "Present US military actions," PROVN maintained, "are inconsistent with that fundamental of counterinsurgancy doctrine which establishes winning popular allegiance as the ultimate goal."[13] American field commanders, for the most part, failed to heed these pleas.

The damage done to Vietnamese society by allied military operations constituted another liability. It was difficult to convince villagers that the Americans had come as their protectors if in the process of liberating them from the communists allied troops caused extensive harm to Vietnamese civilian life and property. The American command from the very beginning realized the potentially damaging effect of the great firepower of American combat forces, and it therefore issued rules of engagement governing ground and air operations that were designed to minimize the destruction of property and the loss of life among non-combatants. In addition, Westmoreland repeatedly reminded his commanders that "the utmost in discretion and judgment must be used in the application of firepower" and that noncombatant casualties resulting from the application of air power and artillery had "an adverse effect on the rural reconstruction effort and the attainment of the GVN national goals."[14] In a statement to the press handed out on 26 August 1966, Westmoreland acknowledged the special nature of the war in Vietnam, a conflict "fought among the people, many of whom are not participants in, or even closely identified with the struggle. People more than terrain, are the objectives in this war, and we will not and cannot be callous about those people."[15]

And yet, these sensible ideas ran head-on against the mind-set of the conventionally trained officer, who, seeing the war in the perspective of his own expertise, concentrated on "zapping the Cong" with the weapons he had been trained to use. There also was the understandable endeavor of commanders to minimize casualties among their troops. Ever since the huge losses of life caused by the human wave assaults of World War I, the military had embraced the motto "Expend Shells not Men." Hence when American troops encountered a VC company dug into a Vietnamese hamlet or in the fighting in Saigon and Hue during the Tet Offensive of 1968, the tempting thing to do was to employ all of the powerful military instruments developed by the leading industrial, technology-conscious nation of the world – artillery, tactical air power, naval gunfire, aerial rocket artillery, helicopter gunships. "The unparalleled, lavish use of firepower as a substitute for manpower," wrote an American officer in early 1968, "is an outstanding characteristic of US military tactics in the Vietnam war."[16]

The practice of the VC/NVA to "clutch the people to their breast" added to the difficulty of protecting the civilian population. The enemy liked to make the villages and hamlets a battlefield because in the open valleys and coastal lowlands the villages contained much natural cover and concealment. The hamlets also offered the VC a source of labor for the building of fortifications; their spread-out arrangement afforded avenues of escape; and, lastly, the VC knew that the Americans did not like to fire on populated areas.

A few American commanders in Vietnam realized the provocative nature of these VC maneuvers and argued against using friendly weapons to accommodate the enemy. "I have witnessed the enemy's employment of this tactic for the past 10 years," wrote John Paul Vann in 1972, then senior American adviser in II Corps, a man generally acknowledged to have been one of the most experienced and effective Americans to serve in Vietnam. He continued:

His specific objective is to get our friendly forces to engage in suicidal destruction of hard-won pacification gains. Invariably, he is successful since in the heat of battle rational thinking and long term effects usually play second fiddle to short term objectives.

In the last decade, I have walked through hundreds of hamlets that have been destroyed in the course of battle, the majority as the result of the heavier friendly fires. The overwhelming majority of hamlets thus destroyed failed to yield sufficient evidence of damage to the enemy to justify the destruction of the hamlet. Indeed, it has not been unusual to have a hamlet destroyed and find absolutely no evidence of damage to the enemy. I recall in May 1969 the destruction and burning by air strike of 900 houses in a hamlet in Chau Doc Province without evidence of a single enemy being killed . . . . The destruction of a hamlet by friendly firepower is an event that will always be remembered and practically never forgiven by those members of the population who lost their homes.

In view of the fact that the occupation of few places in Vietnam was truly essential to allied objectives, Vann argued, much the best move in a situation where all courses of conduct were unsatisfactory was to leave the enemy force in possession of the hamlet until it left again of its own accord. "While this course of action does not satisfy most natural emotions, it is a course of action which does not aid and abet the enemy in accomplishing his objectives."[17] Vann's counsel was seldom followed.

If we add to the balance sheet villagers killed in free-fire zones, the misery of the large number of refugees generated by allied operations and the destruction of crops – detailed by this author in another place – we can begin to understand why the American way of war proved so counterproductive. "Modern wars are not internecine wars in which the killing of the enemy is the object," it was stated in US War Department General Order No. 160, dated 24 April 1863. "The destruction of the enemy in modern wars, and, indeed modern war itself, are means to obtain that object of the belligerent which lies beyond the war." In Vietnam, "the object . . . which lies beyond the war," the PROVN study had argued, was the allegiance of the people of South Vietnam to their government,[18] yet this basic insight all too often was ignored. Military engagements were being fought without regard to their effect on the long-range political goals of the war.

There is much evidence to show that the way in which both the Americans and the South Vietnamese carried out the effort to suppress the communist insurgency alienated the population of the countryside. The record does not bear out charges of genocide or indiscriminate killings of civilians and wholesale violations of the laws of war. However, the strategy and tactics of the allied counterinsurgency, especially the lavish use of firepower, and the consequent suffering inflicted on large segments of South Vietnam's rural population during long years of high-technology warfare created a widespread feeling of resignation, war-weariness and an unwillingness to go on fighting against the resolute opponent from the North. It is also well to remember that revulsion at the fate of thousands of hapless civilians killed and maimed by the deadly arsenal of a modern army may undercut the willingness of a democratic nation to fight communist insurgents, and that reliance on high-technology weapons in an insurgency setting therefore may be counterproductive on still another level.

Another important lesson of Vietnam, therefore, is not Professor Richard A. Falk's legally incorrect assertion that the methods of large-scale counterinsurgency warfare with high-technology weapons necessarily amount to crimes under international law,[19] but that these tactics in such a setting frequently do not work. Technological superiority in such a war, in other words, is not unlawful, but it may be irrelevant to victory and indeed may play a positively negative role. The fact that the tactics employed by the allies were not forbidden by the laws of war and did not intentionally aim at inflicting casualties on the civilian population remains morally significant. Yet in any future guerrilla conflict in which the United States may become embroiled, it will be well to remember that the loss of civilian life caused by modern heavy weapons is not just legal and yet regrettable, it is largely unnecessary and self-defeating.

South Vietnam was finally defeated in an onslaught with heavy conventional weapons and not in a people's revolutionary war. But the ignominious collapse of ARVN was due not only to ARVN's inferiority in such weapons and the shortage of ammunition; in considerable measure it was also the result of lack of will and morale. Hanoi launched the 1972 and 1975 invasions, it has been suggested, because the VC had been defeated in the guerrilla phase of the war. This probably is only a half-truth, for the VC in many parts of the country were far from destroyed, and the internal weaknesses of the GVN were blatant – the losses of the VC had not been the government's gains.[20] It could therefore be argued with equal justice that greater allied success in the years prior to these conventional invasions, when the struggle still was for the allegiance of the people of South Vietnam, might have dissuaded Hanoi from launching these attacks. A stronger and more cohesive national community in the South thus could have brought about a different denouement to this tragic conflict. Weapons alone, after all, are never decisive. It is fighting morale, resolution, and the able leadership of an army which make possible the effective use of weapons and which win wars.

III

Many of America's military leaders argue to this day that their ability to conduct a winning strategy was hamstrung by overly restrictive rules of engagement, designed to protect civilian life and property, and by political constraints imposed on them for fear of a collision with communist China and the Soviet Union. In particular, the graduated application of air power in the bombing of North Vietnam during the years 1965-68, code-named Rolling Thunder, interrupted by frequent bombing halts, has been held up as a misuse of military assets. "Gradualism," former Chairman of the Joint Chiefs Admiral Thomas H. Moorer has written, "forced airpower into an expanded and inconclusive war of attrition."[21]

This argument no doubt represents sound military logic, and the North Vietnamese themselves have acknowledged that the slow escalation of the bombing, imposed on the United States because of an unfavorable "balance of international forces," helped them to ride out the storm.[22] But the decision for "gradualism" was made primarily because of fear of Chinese intervention, and whether the likelihood of such an intervention was overrated will never be known. By the spring of 1966 China had dispatched some 50,000 military personnel – engineer, railroad construction, and antiaircraft divisions – who engaged in combat and served as living proof of the seriousness of China commitment.[23] The threshold that US bombing could not pass without precipitating a major Chinese involvement was not known and unfortunately could not be known even within a wide margin of error. As George W. Ball put it in a memorandum for President Johnson in January 1966 which counseled extreme caution in this regard: "Unhappily we will not find out until after the catastrophe."[24] The miscalculation of Chinese intentions in the Korean War served as a vivid reminder that this was not an irrational and unfounded fear.

Moreover, it can be stated with some assurance that even if the military had received permission for a "sharp blow" strategy, this would not have prevented North Vietnam from sending men and supplies to the South or forced Hanoi to sue for peace. Damage initially would have been higher and American losses lower, but after a while North Vietnam most likely would have adjusted. The theory of either strategic or interdiction bombing assumed attacks on highly industrialized nations producing large quantities of military goods to sustain armies engaged in intensive warfare. The nature of North Vietnam's economy and the sporadic attacks launched by the VC/NVA in the South did not fit this model, and North Vietnam therefore was an extremely poor target for a sustained air campaign. The country was predominantly agricultural and had little industry and a rudimentary transportation system. North Vietnam's small industrial plant had been built by a poor country over many years and at considerable sacrifice, yet the assumption that destroying or threatening to destroy this industry would pressure Hanoi into abandoning its drive to take over over the South proved mistaken. The bombing caused manpower dislocations but did not limit North Vietnam's ability to maintain essential services in the North and to infiltrate ever larger numbers of men into the South. In view of experience with both interdiction and strategic bombing in World War II and Korea, none of this should have come as a surprise.

During Operation Strangle in the spring of 1944, the US Air Force flew 34,000 sorties and dropped 33,000 tons of bombs on German lines of communication in northern Italy; yet while this heavy bombing caused disruption, fuel and supplies were never at a critical level, and damage caused was quickly repaired.[25] Results were similar in the Korean War. Between June 1950 and July 1953 the US Air Force flew 220,168 interdiction and armed reconaissance sorties, which were reported to have destroyed 827 bridges, 869 locomotives, 14,906 railroad cars, and 74,589 vehicles.[26] Yet this massive damage failed to destroy the North Korean supply effort. Helped by the availability of large quantities of both lumber and laborers, roads and rail lines were repaired faster than US planes could destroy them; supplies were secreted in caves and tunnels and then moved at night; extensive and skillful use was made of bypasses and underwater bridges; trucks, oxcarts, horse-drawn wagons, and even pack animals provided shuttle service between break points. "The rate of construction and repair of rail and highway bridges by enemy forces in Korea," wrote an American officer at the time of the air campaign, "has been little short of phenomenal."[27] The official history of the American air war in Korea acknowledges that by December 1951 the contest between skilled pilots with expensive aircraft and unskilled coolie laborers armed with picks and shovels had become a stalemate. Air action did delay and diminish the flow of supplies, but it did not stop them or place an intolerable burden on the supply effort.[28]

In his testimony before the Stennis committee in 1967, Defense Secretary McNamara drew upon the failure of the interdiction campaign in Korea. He pointed out that the nature of combat in Vietnam, without established battle lines and with sporadic small-scale enemy action, reduced the volume of logistical support needed. The geography of Vietnam, too, was far less favorable to interdiction. In Korea the entire and relatively narrow neck of the peninsula had been subject to naval bombardment from either side and to air strikes across its width. The infiltration routes into South Vietnam, on the other hand, were far more complex and were protected by dense jungle and frequent cloudiness not to mention the use of the territory of adjoining countries at least in part immune from air attack.[29]

In the light of experience with population bombing in World War II, the failure of Rolling Thunder to demoralize the people of North Vietnam and make them rise up against their rulers who exposed them to the hardships of the American bombing also should not have come as a surprise. This is not to say that morale bombing in World War II stiffened the will to resist, as has been claimed by some critics of American policy in Vietnam. The US Strategic Bombing Survey, a careful study of all available evidence carried out in 1945, reported that "the morale of the German people deteriorated under aerial attack." The bombing caused vast suffering among German civilians, and the "bombing appreciably affected the German will to resist. Its main psychological effects were defeatism, fear, hopelessness, fatalism, and apathy."[30] To be sure, while the bombing of Germany succeeded in lowering morale, its effect on actual behavior was less decisive. Workers, by and large, continued to work efficiently – out of habit, discipline, the fear of punishment by a powerful police state, and the lack of alternative courses of action. The bombing of German cities severely depressed the mood of the people, but it did not stop the war machine. That was accomplished by the precision bombing of essential industries such as oil production and transportation during the last year of the war. In short, the strategic bombing of Germany in World War II demonstrated that bombing focused on the will to resist is unable to accomplish its goal. The far more concentrated and intense bombing of Japan, culminating in the use of two atomic bombs on the cities of Hiroshima and Nagasaki, supports this conclusion.[31]

It was estimated that Rolling Thunder caused North Vietnam about $600 million worth of damage in terms of destroyed military facilities, loss of capital stock, and lost production. However, between 1965 and 1968 North Vietnam received over $2 billion of foreign aid. As to the other side of the ledger, the bombing campaign cost the United States about $6 billion in destroyed aircraft alone.[32] This was a rather unfavorable financial balance sheet, to which one had to add heavy political costs. The bombing of North Vietnam strained US relations with other noncommunist nations and greatly exacerbated domestic tensions. The accusations of indiscriminate bombing of civilian targets can now be shown to have been utterly false, but during the years of the air war they were widely believed, and they seriously impaired the moral authority of the United States. Instead of bringing North Vietnam to the conference table, the bombing helped erode support for the war here at home. The intensive propaganda campaign against the bombing waged by Hanoi and her friends all over the world therefore was not necessarily a sign that the bombing really threatened the ability of the North to continue the war. Despite discomfort and dislocations, the bombing brought valuable political dividends.

The greatly intensified resumed bombing of North Vietnam in 1972, given the code names Linebacker I and II, does not disprove this negative assessment. In addition to destroying war-related resources and interdicting the movement of men and supplies to the South, Linebacker I had the aim of reducing or restricting North Vietnam's receipt of assistance from abroad. Unlike the case of Rolling Thunder, the military this time had far more tactical flexibility. Field commanders could pick targets from a validated list and strike them when they wanted. Targets in the key areas around Hanoi and Haiphong were authorized much sooner than during Rolling Thunder. By 22 October, when Linebacker I ended, ten MiG bases, six major thermal power plants, and almost all fixed POL storage facilities had been hit, which required strikes within ten miles of the center of both cities. Most importantly, a new family of "smart bombs" consisting of TV- and laser-guided bombs had become available that provided pilots with a new and unprecedented bombing accuracy.[33] Several important railroad bridges and tunnels near the Chinese border could now be struck without fear of political complications. The Thanh Hoa Bridge, which had survived numerous attacks during Rolling Thunder, was felled with several laser-guided bombs on 13 May. Aircraft losses were held down through improved electronic countermeasures.

The improved tactical ability of American planes meant that fewer sorties and less bombing tonnage, accompanied by a lower loss rate, during seven months of Linebacker I in 1972 were able to cause more serious damage to North Vietnam than had been scored during the high point of Rolling Thunder in 1967. The shipment of goods through Haiphong and other ports was virtually eliminated, railroad traffic from China was seriously crippled, and most imports were now coming down by truck and on waterways which were under continuous attack. According to estimates, the flow of imports into North Vietnam and the movement of supplies to the South by September 1972 had been reduced to between 35 and 50 percent of what they had been in May of that year.[34]

Linebacker II, which began on 18 December, lasted 12 days, though the weather was clear enough for visual bombing for only 12 hours. During these 12 days there were 729 B-52 sorties and about 1000 fighter-bomber attack sorties; 20,370 tons of bombs were dropped over all of Vietnam. A total of 26 planes were lost, including 15 B-52s. The bombing was concentrated on targets in the Hanoi and Haiphong complexes and included transportation terminals, rail yards, warehouses, power plants, airfields, and the like. When the bombing halted on 29 December, North Vietnam's electrical power supply was crippled, and extensive damage had been caused to all other targets as well.

North Vietnamese air defenses were shattered, and during the last few days American planes roamed the skies with virtual impunity.[35]

On 30 December 1972 the White House announced at a special press briefing that the President had called a halt in the bombing of the North Vietnamese heartland. "As soon as it was clear," the spokesman declared, "that serious negotiations could be resumed at both the technical level and between the principals, the President ordered that all bombing be discontinued above the twentieth parallel."[36] On New Year's Day the talks in Paris resumed, by 9 January the cease-fire agreement was essentially completed, and on 23 January 1973 it was initialed by Kissinger on behalf of the United States and by Le Duc Tho on behalf of North Vietnam. Did the intense bombing of December 1972 bring about this settlement and thus belatedly vindicate the decisiveness of airpower?

"I am convinced that Linebacker II served as a catalyst for the negotiations which resulted in the ceasefire," Admiral Moorer has stated. "Airpower, given its day in court after almost a decade of frustration, confirmed its effectiveness as an instrument of national power – in just 9 1/2 flying days."[37] Two Air Force legal officers have argued the same position: Linebacker II "was designed to coerce a negotiated settlement by threatening further weakening of the enemy's military effort to maintain and support his armed forces. It is our firm belief that this threat of continued and further destruction of military objectives produced the political settlement."[38]

It may well be that the heavy bombing of targets in the Hanoi and Haiphong complexes, the threat of more such punishing attacks, and the unwillingness or inability of the Soviet Union and communist China to prevent these bombings induced Hanoi finally to sign a cease-fire agreement, just as the intensive bombings during Linebacker I may have contributed to the breakthrough in the negotiations in October. However, to consider this result to be conclusive proof of the decisiveness of air power, one would have to be convinced that North Vietnam, in signing the Paris agreements, put itself at a serious disadvantage, and the evidence for this assumption is lacking. The cease-fire terms – the unanimity principle adopted for the inspection machinery, which virtually guaranteed that supervision of adherence to the agreements would be ineffective and the legitimation of the presence of NVA forces in the South – hardly represented an American victory; as subsequent events were to demonstrate, the Paris agreements did not impede North Vietnam's military drive to take over the South. Within little more than two years of the signing of the alleged "peace with honor," South Vietnam had fallen to North Vietnamese troops that had never left the South and to massive reinforcements which the meaningless inspection provisions of the Paris agreement could not prevent from entering South Vietnam.

To be sure, as Nixon assured Thieu in November 1972, the Administration believed that peace in Vietnam would depend not on the specific clauses of an agreement but on the willingness of the United States to enforce a cease-fire.

The events of Watergate, which seriously weakened the ability of the United States to react to the North Vietnamese violations of the Paris accords, could not have been foreseen. And yet the United States quite clearly had had to settle for a compromise; the Nixon Administration obviously would have preferred more advantageous terms that did not leave peace in Vietnam dependent solely on the threat of the reintroduction of American air power. Linebacker II helped bring about a cease-fire, but it failed to achieve a settlement that could be considered a victory for either South Vietnam or the United States. By December 1972 there were few military targets left in North Vietnam, and short of the complete obliteration of the country, it is likely that even a continuation of the bombing would not have induced North Vietnam to withdraw her forces from the South or to make other important concessions. In this sense, then, the argument for the decisive effectiveness of strategic air power in the Vietnam conflict – air power within the limits set by international law and Western public opinion – remains unproven.

The bombing of North Vietnam caused extensive damage to the country's war-making capacity, but at no point did it seriously hamper Hanoi's drive against the South. Neither Rolling Thunder nor Linebacker were able to wring decisive concessions from the North Vietnamese. The use of a ''sharp blow'' approach and less regard for civilian casualties might have reduced American losses at the beginning of the air campaign but, short of the use of nuclear weapons, seem unlikely to have led to different results.

The costs to America of the air war over North Vietnam were extremely high – both financially and politically. The bombing also helped the communist rulers of North Vietnam to organize their country on a war footing. But probably the most damaging consequence of the bombing of North Vietnam was that it diverted attention from the real hub of the Vietnam problem – the Southern battlefield – where the war was going to be won or lost. As presidential adviser John P. Roche wrote in a memorandum for Johnson on 1 May 1967: ''What has distressed me is the notion (expressed time and again by the Air Force boys) that air power would provide a *strategic* route to victory; and the parallel assumption that by bombing the North we could get a cut-rate solution in the South and escape from the problems of building a South Vietnamese army.''[39] President Johnson finally accepted the logic of this argument and the bombing of North Vietnam was ended. The Nixon Administration belatedly began a program of Vietnamization. The bombing of the North was resumed only in response to the 1972 Easter invasion and under far more favorable international political circumstances which allowed the imposition of a blockade, a crucial complementary measure to the air war. That this bombing did not bring final victory is no reflection on the true importance of air power, only a refutation of the illusions of air power enthusiasts.

The related argument that a more aggressive ground strategy, including disregard of enemy sanctuaries beyond the borders of South Vietnam, would have assured victory, is similarly less than persuasive. Military action in Laos and Cambodia at an early stage of the war, seeking permanently to block the Ho Chi Minh Trail, would have made the North Vietnamese supply effort far more difficult, but basically an expansion of the conflict would not have eased the American task. Certainly, an invasion of North Vietnam only would have magnified the difficulties faced.

Back in 1962 President Kennedy is supposed to have called the infiltration of communist cadres from the North a built-in excuse for failure in the South. In the same way, the collapse of the South Vietnamese Army in the face of still another large-scale invasion from the North, preceded by drastic cuts in aid to South Vietnam imposed by the US Congress after the Paris Agreement of 1973, has tempted both the last leaders of South Vietnam and most of the US military to avoid facing the fundamental reasons for this defeat. The South Vietnamese, and indeed American soldiers earlier, it is argued, could have won the war had they not been frustrated by political constraints in the United States and the collapse of the home front. There is no denying that the reductions in US aid did weaken the South Vietnamese ability to resist the well-equipped Northern divisions, and war-weariness and anti-war sentiment in America were widespread. However, the nonachievement of US goals in Vietnam had other and deeper reasons. To ignore these basic causes in favor of a facile stab-in-the-back legend will give rise to more illusions. In the long run, even more damaging to America's position in the world than the actual failure to achieve our objectives in Vietnam could be the unwillingness and inability of the military institution to understand and learn the real lessons of the Vietnam debacle.

NOTES

1. US Embassy Saigon, Defense Attaché Office, RVNAF Final Assessment, 15 June 1975, p. 10-18.
2. Fox Butterfield, "How South Vietnam Died – By the Stab in the Front," *The New York Times Magazine*, 15 May 1975, p. 35.
3. Matthew B. Ridgway, "Indochina: Disengaging," *Foreign Affairs*, 49 (1971), 588.
4. Special Assistant to the Ambassador for Field Operations, "Statistical Trends: Security Situation, April 1974," Center of Military History.
5. MACCORDS-PSG, "Trip Report Through the Delta by James H. Holl and Lee Braddock," 10 January 1973, p. 5.
6. Cited by Allan E. Goodman, "South Vietnam: War Without End?" *Asian Survey*, 15 (1975), 82.
7. Robert W. Komer, *Bureaucracy Does Its Thing: Institutional Constraints on U.S.-G.V.N. Performance in Vietnam* (Santa Monica, Calif.: Rand Corporation, 1973), p. 35.
8. William F. Long, Jr., "Counterinsurgency Revisited," *Naval War College Review*, 21 (November 1968), 7.
9. Edward G. Lansdale, in W. Scott Thompson and Donaldson D. Frizzell, eds., *The Lessons of the Vietnam War* (New York: Crane Russak, 1977), p. 42.
10. Patrick J. McGarvey, *Visions of Victory: Selected Vietnamese Military Writings, 1964-1968* (Stanford, Calif.: Hoover Institution Press, 1969), p. 43.
11. OASD (SA), *SEA Analysis Report*, January 1968, pp. 19-20.

12. F. J. West, Jr., *Area Security: The Need, the Composition, and the Components*, P-3979 (Santa Monica, Calif.: Rand Corporation, 1968), pp. 1-3.
13. US Department of the Army, Office of the Deputy Chief of Staff for Military Operations, "A Program for the Pacification and Long Term Development of South Vietnam" (short title: PROVN), 1 March 1966, p. 53.
14. Westmoreland message, "Minimizing Non-Combatant Casualties," 7 July 1965, "Conduct of the War in Vietnam" (short title: COWIN), a report commissioned in 1971 by the US Army Deputy Chief of Staff for Military Operations, Ref. Doc. 8.
15. Ibid., Ref. Doc. 20.
16. Robert M. Kipp, "Counterinsurgency from 30,000 Feet: The B-52 in Vietnam," *Air University Review*, 19 (January-February 1968), 17.
17. Memo, Senior Adviser's Policy for Combat in Populated and/or Built-up Areas, 4 April 1972, Center of Military History.
18. PROVN, p. 100.
19. Falk, in Peter D. Trooboff, ed., *Law and Responsibility in Warfare: The Vietnam Experience* (Chapel Hill, N.C.: Univ. of North Carolina Press, 1975), p. 37.
20. Compare Stuart A. Herrington, *Silence Was a Weapon: The War in the Villages* (Novato, Calif.: Presidio, 1982), p. 94. The same point is made by William J. Duiker, *The Communist Road to Power* (Boulder, Colo.: Westview, 1981), p. 319.
21. Thomas H. Moorer, "Recent Bombing in the North," *Air Force Policy Letter for Commanders*, Supp. no. 2 (February 1973), 12.
22. "General Van Tien Dung on Some Great Experiences of the People's War," McGarvey, p. 156.
23. Allen S. Whiting, *The Chinese Calculus of Deterrence: India and Indochina* (Ann Arbor, Mich.: Univ. of Michigan Press, 1975), pp. 186-87.
24. *Pentagon Papers* (Beacon Press ed.), IV, 52.
25. Robert E. Schmaltz, "The Uncertainty of Predicting Results of an Interdiction Campaign," *Aerospace Historian*, 17 (1970), 150-53.
26. Gregory A. Carter, *Some Historical Notes on Air Interdiction in Korea*, P-3452 (Santa Monica, Calif.: Rand Corporation, 1966), p. 2.
27. Felix Kozacza, "Enemy Bridging Techniques in Korea," *Air University Quarterly Review*, 5 (Winter 1952-53), 49.
28. Robert Frank Futrell, et al., *The United States Air Force in Korea: 1950-1953* (New York: Sloan and Pearce, 1961), p. 443.
29. US Senate, Committee on Armed Services, Preparedness Investigating Subcommittee, *Air War Against North Vietnam*, Hearings, 90th Cong., 1st sess., part 4, 25 August 1967, pp. 274-82.
30. US Strategic Bombing Survey, *Summary Report (European War)* (Washington: GPO, 1945), p. 4, and *Over-All Report (European War)* (Washington: GPO, 1945), p. 95.
31. Compare Bernard Brodie, *Strategy in the Missile Age* (Princeton, N.J.: Princeton Univ. Press, 1959), p. 138.
32. Alain C. Enthoven and K. Wayne Smith, *How Much is Enough? Shaping the Defense Program 1961-1969* (New York: Harper and Row, 1971), p. 304.
33. A. J. C. Lavalle, ed., *The Tale of Two Bridges and the Battle for the Skies over North Vietnam*, USAF SEA Monograph Series (Washington: GPO, 1976), pp. 79-83.
34. Guenter Lewy, *America in Vietnam* (New York: Oxford Univ. Press, 1978), p. 411.
35. Ibid., p. 412.
36. Quoted in Marvin and Bernard Kalb, *Kissinger* (Boston: Little, Brown, 1974), p. 418.
37. Thomas H. Moorer, "The Decisiveness of Airpower in Vietnam," *Air Force Policy Letter for Commanders*, Supp. no. 11 (November 1973), 9.
38. Norman R. Thorpe and James R. Miles, in Trooboff, p. 145.
39. Reprinted in Morton A. Kaplan, et al., *Vietnam Settlement: Why 1973, Not 1969?* (Washington: AEI, 1973), p. 153.

This article appeared in the spring 1984 issue of *Parameters*.

13

Reflections on Vietnam: Of Revisionism and Lessons Yet to Be Learned

by PAUL M. KATTENBURG

More than ten years have now passed since we withdrew our forces from Vietnam, and many feel that new "Vietnams" are again looming on the horizon. In what follows I look first at the meaning of our Vietnam experience as perceived at the time and in the more standard interpretations, as well as in the revisionist so-called "new scholarship" now emerging. I relate some impressions gleaned during my recent return to the area after an absence of some eight and a half years. Second, I try to examine what has been called the Vietnam Syndrome in American foreign policy and how that syndrome seems to have affected our policy between the collapse of Vietnam in 1975 and the present. Finally, I attempt to gauge the broader meaning of the term Vietnam in world politics as a whole, for it is evident that the Vietnam phenomenon is by no means something the United States alone is forced to consider, but has much broader implications for world affairs.

The new scholarship on America's Vietnam War, in the pithy words of Melvin Maddocks, "calls Vietnam . . . a war that might have been won if only we had thrown a little more fire in the lake, one more time."[1] The more conservative of the revisionist works blame our failure variously on insufficient use of military power, on our overzealous pressure for democratic reforms in South Vietnam (particularly those leading to the fall of President Diem in 1963), and on inaccurate reporting and media bias, which allegedly turned domestic opinion against the war.[2] These revisionists also allege that our failure in Vietnam had disastrous international consequences.

The more "pragmatic revisionist" works[3] allege, variously, that there are no lessons to be learned from the Vietnam War; that a different mix of means (particularly less reliance on excessive military power and more on socioeconomic reform) might have brought a different result; that although the war may have been a mistake and the manner in which it was fought counterproductive, it was not therefore immoral or unjustified, even in its later stages; and especially that the terrible events in Indochina since the communist victories there provide a retrospective justification for the war.

Much of the so-called new scholarship thrashes dead horses. It is no really great discovery, for example, that the National Liberation Front (NLF) enjoyed only a modicum of autonomy in the South or that almost all of the important strategic and political decisions on the communist side during the war were made by the Politburo and its dependencies in Hanoi. Among those of us in the US policymaking community who opposed some of the major decisions of the mid-1960s, such as the policy of graduated escalation of bombing against North Vietnam ("Rolling Thunder") or the direct entry of US combat forces, no one I can recall had any illusions on that score. Also, only a few rather insignificant and largely discredited figures in the anti-war movement seemed to believe in the exemplary virtues of Hanoi or in the overwhelming popularity of the Viet Cong. On this last point, however, one must retain a measure of skepticism: popular sympathies of the masses in Vietnam, especially in the countryside, were well and appropriately dissimulated during the war, as they most likely are and have to be again today.

Those who argued against graduated escalation, against the deepening of our involvement in 1965-66, against invading Cambodia and broadening the war under the guise of ending it in 1969-72, and in favor of immediate negotiations based on a willingness to accept coalition government even at the strong risk of eventual communist control in all Vietnam, those who argued these views during that long, seemingly endless period were arguing not only that it was morally wrong to destroy a country in order to save it from itself but also that it would not work. "You can't fight something with nothing" is the way Stanley Hoffman put it in his letter to the editor responding to Fox Butterfield's 13 February 1983 cover story in *The New York Times Magazine* on "The New Vietnam Scholarship."[4] There was never, in South Vietnam, at least after Diem, a genuine political counter to the nationalist communism of the Hanoi-led revolutionary forces, North or South. At best, the Republic of Vietnam must be considered to have been an empty quasi-administrative structure dominated by an untrustworthy and generally inept military.

Nor did any of the war's more sophisticated or knowledgeable opponents believe that Tet 1968 had been a great victory for the communists, although to this day it seems virtually impossible to convey to some Americans – particularly in the military and possessing a genuine and apparently very American difficulty in apprehending the meaning of the term "political objective" – that if certain political objectives were accomplished it hardly matters whether the means used to achieve them were "successful" in any traditional military sense. The revisionism of some of the "new Vietnam scholars" regarding Tet reveals continued and obdurate ignorance of both the purposes and tactics of revolutionary war.

What the new scholarship on Vietnam has been doing for the most part, as Hoffman says, is to refute the myths of some of the more deluded, romantic, or ideological wings of the anti-war movement. In so doing, it presents and argues some new myths of its own: that an electronic barrier in the middle of Vietnam might have stopped communist resupply, for example; or that B-52 air strikes were really "surgical" (I invite those who so argue to fly over the crater-dotted Kampuchean countryside!); or that because elements of the peace movement such as Senator Eugene McCarthy were perhaps less effective in changing US policies than at first believed, one therefore can deflate the notion that US public opinion opposed the war after 1968 or neglect the extraordinary rise of congressional skepticism about the war and its eventually strong dissent from it. That certainly did reflect American popular sentiment, and it lies at the root of today's vastly increased congressional power in foreign affairs.

There is a specific issue, however, on which the new scholarship has valuable views, and that is on the question of whether the US military was falsely blamed for some of the decision-making and whether it took what may be called a bum rap for the war. One "new scholar," Colonel Harry G. Summers, an instructor at the US Army War College, in fact blames our military in Vietnam in his *On Strategy* for all manner of sins in its conduct of the war – failures in essence stemming from ignoring classic, Clausewitzian doctrines of war – for which I think they can indeed be blamed, though not in my view held responsible. A point which is stressed in my *Vietnam Trauma*, and with which I believe most military revisionists including Summers would agree, is that all the *key* decisions relating to the American war in Vietnam were made by the civilian national security managers. These "civilian militarists" had no trouble keeping the military out of their charmed so-called national security decision-making circle – a circle in which the military had long since invited the civilians to play the key role because of their own abdication of military-political responsibility in favor of single-minded concentration on the technocratic aspects of war. It is encouraging to hear some military and retired military leaders today speaking out loudly on the political conditions and circumstances that they consider prerequisite to US military intervention anywhere.

All this leads us to some key aspects of our Vietnam involvement, issues which lie at the source of our failure and made it inevitable, so to speak. One of the most significant of these was the open-ended nature of our effort, its lack of a clear objective or clear terminal point, and its basically negative character: to prevent the loss of South Vietnam to communism without much thought or analysis about any of the many factors implied in that statement. What was this communism in terms of its specific nature and of its link with nationalism; what was South Vietnam in terms of an entity with genuine, legitimate political existence and will; who was to prevent this "loss," and if this was the South Vietnamese, how did they envisage the war's objective and who truly represented them?

These unanswered questions played a vital role in conferring to our effort its aptly named character of a stalemate machine, a term originally coined by Daniel Ellsberg: each President involved refusing to do what was necessary to move beyond the stalemate, and doing just enough to prevent a loss which each felt would have intolerable domestic political consequences. In the end, therefore, the real objective of our war in Vietnam was to keep any American president from being tarred domestically with the brush of having lost another round to communism. This should be clearly realized when the allegedly frightful consequences of Marxist-Leninist victories in other situations are presented to the American public today.

Among the many aspects that made Vietnam such a frustrating and unsuccessful experience for the United States, some of the more salient included the disporportionality of means and ends and the moral dilemmas this gave rise to, particularly in the later (so-called disengagement) stages of the war; the apparent absence of politics and diplomacy from the arsenal of American instruments of foreign policy, a point which still seems to be plaguing us in Central America (and other areas) today; and our single-minded civilian as well as military concentration on technocratic approaches, such as input-output models of nation-building and counterinsurgency, war by statistical body counts, so-called internal defense plans resting on static pacification methodologies, etc. – *in toto*, a sort of systems theory approach to politics which is, God help us, being revived on government contracts even today in obscure corners of certain schools of business administration and in certain remote institutions of the US military.

This rather mindless concentration during the American Vietnam War on what may be called ''effective motivation'' – that is on how to do it and do it better, rather than on what it is that should be done and why – this sort of mechanical emphasis on action, served us very poorly. Combined with the stalemate-machine approach, it gave the United States ''winning without winning'' and ''losing without losing,'' an undecipherable mix of programmatic approaches; unbridled technocracy and managerialism; and the triumph of systems analysis and business-school theories over politics, diplomacy, *and* strategy.

VIETNAM TODAY

The new revisionism on Vietnam also engages in the dubious business of judging the past from the present. Vietnam was then, as it remains today, a highly nationalistic, proud, and independent country; its communist leadership won out, as David Marr very correctly pointed out at a revisionist-sponsored conference held in January 1983,[5] because from the start it was draped in the mantle and championed the cause of nationalism; and no matter the trials and tribulations of the present, there is little doubt that the Vietnamese overwhelmingly wanted the victory of the revolution and the defeat of the imperialists. If they were today given a free chance to change the war's verdict, even given all that has happened, I doubt most sincerely that they would reverse it. For one thing, the North has just gone on living much as it had ever since 1954: levels of want and poverty are just so high that a lack of amelioration is barely noticed; outright starvation has thus far been avoided, and in fact a slight improvement in agricultural production (if in nothing else) has taken place.

As to the South, although hundreds of thousands of ethnic Chinese and urban bourgeois Vietnamese were no doubt severely hurt by the change of regime, with many thousands who worked for the previous government unfortunately still left in so-called reeducation camps even today, it must be recalled that there was and is an overwhelmingly larger number of rural Vietnamese, village and small-town dwellers, who have not (at least not yet) suffered grievously in the redistributive changes that have slowly taken place. Recall also that the bulk of the ethnic Chinese, in both North and South, who wanted to leave were encouraged to do so, constituting by far the greatest number of the boat people of the late 1970s and early 1980s of whom we heard so much. As collectivization slowly spreads to the South, and the bourgeois incentive systems are progressively eliminated from the economy, more and more Vietnamese are likely, as the saying goes, to "vote with their feet" for freedom. But in many instances what is sought is not so much freedom as we know it, but escape from the hardships and deprivations of the austere economy being established under Vietnam's brand of socialism.

One should not and, indeed, cannot minimize the current problems of poverty, backwardness, and continued hardships faced by the Vietnamese, and which have been aggravated so severely since 1979 by the continuing security threat perceived as coming from the Chinese, leading to the outbreak of serious hostilities on at least two occasions over the past four years.[6] In a continuation of the United States's evident incapacity to understand and communicate with this Vietnamese people, something that has apparently plagued us since immediately after World War II, we hold exactly the reverse perceptions of the current political-military situation from theirs. Whereas we see their invasion of Kampuchea in January 1979 as aggressive expansionism and their continued military occupation there as threatening Thailand, they on the other hand feel that they had no real choice, given the inescapable trap built for them by the Chinese through the Pol Pot regime to "bleed them" in Kampuchea; and they feel that Thailand, with China's active backing and connivance, is threatening them by way of the Pol Pot and related dissident Kampuchean forces which Thailand and China (backed by ASEAN and the United States) support on the Thai-Kampuchean border. The Vietnamese see this as necessitating their continued occupation of Kampuchea. They know Chinese hostility first-hand: twice in four years they have been invaded along their northern frontier, and the sense of threat and fear in Hanoi is enormous. In their view, the United States is being naively taken in by China; they regard our current Southeast Asia policy as, in their words, "made in Beijing."[7]

The essential point here is that, ill-prepared as they are to engage in still another war with still another great power after so many years of war already against so many great enemies (Japanese, French, Americans, and now

Chinese), the Vietnamese are indeed once again prepared to suffer and shoulder the burdens of what they regard as the inevitable cost of maintaining their independence. This in my view underscores the extraordinary determination and commitment to independence, the nationalism, of the Vietnamese. If we doubt today, as some of the revisionists do, that they really had their hearts in it in the 1960s and early 1970s, ignoring some of the most incredible experiences of mankind (such as the survival of certain personnel in tunnels for literally decades[8]), then how can we possibly explain their behavior in still resisting the Chinese today? I believe it can be stated, as the Vietnamese themselves are the first to admit, that they are far better warriors than economic managers; but in no sense does this justify a belief that they are imperialistic in Kampuchea by choice or joy, or that the Soviets, whose aid is barely adequate, called the shots that pushed them into this adventure. In conversations with Americans, they readily concede the priority needs of domestic construction and of concentrating on the alleviation of a poverty-stricken economy that only peace can bring. They are not in Kampuchea by choice and profess their eagerness for peace. But it is obvious, to them at least, that the security threat is real, and obvious too that the present only confirms a proper judgment of the past — that is, that Vietnam fought then and fights now for its conception of freedom with extraordinary persistence and determination.

A final point raised by the new scholarship is the question, could we have won? Contrary to what may perhaps be surmised from Butterfield's article on the new scholarship, winning in my view was not the essential point that Colonel Summers stressed in his book, particularly given the inflexible limiting parameters under which the war was fought, both under Johnson and Nixon. In this, Summers is quite at odds with General Westmoreland, who seems to view it all as a question of more willpower and more wherewithal. Summers' point was rather that in the absence of clear objectives, a clear strategy, and honest support from Congress for understood military purposes, we should not even have tried. Summers rightly suggests that poor policy squanders military power, to which we may add the corollary that a prime objective of diplomacy, properly employed, must be to harness military power for important purposes, purposes palpably and directly related to the security of the United States.

In this regard, despite recent revisionist efforts to make it appear as if the domino theory had addressed itself to Laos and Cambodia, which have now both fallen under effective Vietnam control, the fact was and is that Eisenhower and Dulles, when they invented dominoes way back in 1953, were thinking not about these, then not even independent countries and always in the recent past parts of Indochina, but about the rest of the Southeast Asian countries. The latter, the real dominoes, did not fall after 1975 or even after Vietnam seized Kampuchea in 1979. Take Singapore as an example. During the Vietnam War, no one more than the sycophantic leader of the Republic of Singapore, Lee Kwang Yu, implored LBJ to stay in Vietnam in order to keep his country free of the communist menace. And, since the communist victory in Vietnam, no country in Southeast Asia has fared better than the Republic of Singapore, one of the world's great success stories, and still under Lee's leadership. Perhaps the true domino in this instance was the United States, which became the victim of the so-called Vietnam Syndrome immediately after its Vietnam withdrawal.

THE VIETNAM SYNDROME IN US FOREIGN POLICY

Let us turn then to the question of the so-called Vietnam Syndrome, which led us, it is said, away from world engagement and into a headlong retreat from power, as a result of which we allegedly grew weak and pusillanimous as the Soviets grew strong, confronting us with challenges at every turn. We should first try to get as straight as possible what really did happen during the heyday of our so-called Vietnam Syndrome, after the 1975 fall of South Vietnam.

There is, in my view, little doubt that we were pusillanimous during the hostage crisis in Iran, for which error I think we are paying a large price in terms of the unwarranted bellicosity into which American popular reaction to US weakness has permitted the Reagan Administration to indulge. There is little doubt also that the Soviet Union did use the 1970s to catch up, more rapidly than it might otherwise have, particularly in certain areas of nuclear weaponry, and largely because the United States (not being particularly fearful during this period) allowed it to do so. Détente, fundamentally premised on a tripolar rather than on the tight bipolar outlook that had prevailed previously, opened the way for the significant arms control agreements (and, more broadly, conflict management and disarmament measures) that were reached in the 1970s.

Regrettably, this process came to a halt with the refusal of the Senate to ratify SALT II, or perhaps more properly stated, the refusal of President Carter to politick the treaty through the Senate after his pollsters had informed him, subsequent to his return from the Vienna Summit with Brezhnev in late spring 1979, that strongly nationalistic and anti-Soviet currents pulsating through US public opinion and reverberating in Congress cast doubt on the political wisdom of fighting for the treaty in a pre-election year. Virulent American nationalism, which was exacerbated further and finally brought to fever pitch by the Iran hostage crisis beginning in late 1979, was essentially hyped up by the media and by groups like the Committee on the Present Danger, which had been, from the very beginning of the Carter Administration, unwilling and unprepared to live with a policy of détente in US-Soviet relations.

Debatable though this is, subsequent events have, in my view, shown that these groups tended to exaggerate the degree of influence that the Soviets or Soviet surrogates had acquired over areas like Angola, Mozambique, South Yemen, or in the Horn of Africa – or at least that they grossly overstated the significance of such influence. Even if, as these elements suggested, Soviet influence exercised through surrogates increased in these areas (which also include Vietnam and Kampuchea) during that period, it is equally true that Soviet influence suffered dramatic reversals during the same period in other areas that are probably intrinsically more important to the United States – such as Egypt, the Middle East generally, Eastern Europe and specifically Poland, and in Western Europe after the Russians invaded Afghanistan.

As far as public opinion in Western Europe is concerned, it certainly did not turn anti-US to the extent that it has since the Reagan Administration took office because of any alleged Vietnam Syndrome of a less-interventionist US foreign policy. Quite to the contrary, it is the excessive reengagement of the Reagan Administration in the eyes of the Europeans, its confrontational attitude in such regions as Central America, its stridency in Southwest Asia earlier and in the Near East later, its unwillingness for a long time to come forward with any really constructive arms control proposals, and its revival of nuclear war-fighting fears by way of advocating changes in fundamental, long-held, and virtually universally accepted nuclear deterrence doctrine that have perceptibly weakened the world and specifically the European position of the United States – not the so-called Vietnam Syndrome.

Despite a probably healthy, if heavily overdone reemphasis on defense expenditures, the imprudent, rash manner in which the United States has tended to act internationally and tried to shed the Vietnam Syndrome, far more than that syndrome itself, has since 1981 given reasons for concern. Among such reasons are the following:

•Despite the restraints that a much higher degree of congressional involvement imposes on our foreign policy, we again tend quite unselectively and unilaterally to be too far "up front" in too many world crises, whether in Europe, the Middle East, Central America, Africa, or even East Asia.

•As a result, we may again be led into situations in which we are viewed by wide segments of world opinion to be lined up on what appears to be the morally wrong side. The side seen as the less worthy, or as morally wrong, by the principal actors on the ground in given situations is likely, as in Vietnam, to be the side that loses in the end, no matter how strongly it is supported by outsiders.

•Placing so much emphasis in our defense buildup on additional nuclear capability may have the unintended effect of reducing both our domestic and our international military credibility, since in the end our budgets are still insufficient to reflect our *real* military needs (almost all in the conventional area). Moreover, our nuclear gamesmanship leads to excessive responses, both at home and abroad, such as demands for unilateral nuclear disarmament measures that may well run counter to our best strategic interests, but which are fanned by the irrational peace movements which irrational nuclear bellicosity inevitably brings forth.

Finally, in regard to the Vietnam Syndrome, one might add that it seems to have lasted for only a very short time in US foreign policy. It seems to have broken the ongoing foreign policy consensus only for the short period 1969 to

1979 or so, when continuity in confrontational containment of the Soviets resumed – the break point possibly occurring when Secretary of State Vance resigned his office. Historical determinists would argue that continuity of this type in US foreign policy was foreordained, but others might be permitted to believe in the capacity of statesmen to influence events and affect history. There are those who are patiently awaiting that statesman, in American political life, who will be able to persuade us that selective engagement in foreign affairs, premised on clear perceptions of where our interests and values lie and on honest acceptance of limitations on our power, is not a sign of weakness or lost virility but of maturity and wisdom.

VIETNAM IN WORLD POLITICS

Looking finally at the meaning of the Vietnam experience from the even broader vantage point of world politics as a whole, an essential aspect of that experience seems to have been the demonstration of the limits imposed on US power by the slowly changing configuration of world politics in the 1960s and 1970s. Among principal factors contributing to this evolution we may list: the advent of substantial nuclear equivalence between the superpowers; the Sino-Soviet conflict and the ensuing Western perception of polycentrism in the so-called communist bloc, which in turn requires a more complex analysis of world affairs than the rather crude white-versus-black, good-versus-evil American perception during the high Cold War; the slow reemergence in world politics of Eastern as well as Western Europe, both able to interpose constraints on the complete freedom of maneuver of the superpowers, even in their contiguous zones, and along with this the resurgence of Japan and of other middle powers possessed of latitude to maneuver between the giants; and finally the rise of Third World demands, of the North-South gap, and especially of increasingly less tolerable socioeconomic-political circumstances in Third World societies where the rising expectations of the masses clash head-on with the entrenched rule of traditional oligarchies of wealth and power.

Under these circumstances, neither the Soviet Union, hemmed-in by the same factors, nor the United States has complete freedom of action and especially not the freedom to act unilaterally, even in what we may regard as the contiguous zone of greatest interest to each superpower. It does little good to say that the Soviet Union, which has thus seen itself constrained in Poland, has contradicted this proposition by intervening headlong in Afghanistan; look rather at the resistance encountered by the Soviet Union in Afghanistan and which provides perhaps the supreme example of the larger meaning of Vietnam: that a militantly aroused people which mobilizes in defense of its shared values can hold even the greatest powers at bay no matter how apparently remote or insignificant it may seem on world maps of power.

Ultimately, the great "lesson of Vietnam" is that given these constraints on the great and superpowers in late-20th-century world politics, policymakers in these powers must strive infinitely hard to become issue-specific and not tie their fate to globalistic notions of interlinkage which fail to judge consequences of local developments in local, issue-specific terms. As I have suggested elsewhere,

Turning this to present dilemmas in any of the numerous crises the US faces almost daily in international affairs, the US should not regard involvement here or there as bad because it was bad, or wrong, in Vietnam. That is what history now seems to prescribe; and if statesmen are allowed to take the easy course, they will. The right questions to ask are: Who is engaged in this conflict and what strengths and forces do they represent? What is the justice of this issue as seen by the people who are themselves most directly involved? What are the actual situations in all their local perplexities? Once answers to these questions are obtained, one can then ask: What are our interests, if any, and why? What are our capabilities and the limits to them in affecting this issue? What is sufficiently clearly right to such an overwhelming number of Americans that there can be no question later on if much larger sacrifices are called for?[9]

Such judgments will have to be made in the light of an ever-fluid international conjuncture, of ever-shifting value patterns, shifting as generations and institutions evolve, and as a function of changing leadership; they must not be made in some frozen perception of the national interest. Our national interest is not today, any more than previously, concerned with arranging regions of the world in some static geopolitical pattern, founded on the armed means of the last great war that the United States or others fought. It has everything to do instead with domestic values and with accurate perceptions reflecting them, with a view of security as absence of fear, and with the use of analysis and of diplomacy as means of adaptation in a rapidly changing world of ever-fluctuating moods.

Applying these general principles to a specific situation like that in Central America today, Vietnam would seem inescapably to teach several lessons. First, we should not tie our security and future to generically weak and repudiated regimes, as already suggested above. The side we support in every given instance should be the right side, that is, the morally acceptable one in consonance with US dedication to the advancement of human rights. In this regard, the side favoring private enterprise is not always necessarily right because it advocates a form of freedom, not if that form leads in practice to results as oppressive as those reached by the Marxist-Leninists.

Second, we should not fear mechanically imagined consequences. For example, rather than reasoning in dominoes, we need to ask specifically, not rhetorically, what would be the consequences to us (and also to Mexico) of a series of Marxist-Leninist regimes in Central America? Would these consequences be better or worse than those of a continuation of the prevailing explosive socioeconomic situations there, leading to potentially uncontrollable instability and the almost inevitable intervention of foreign powers in the region?

Third, we are not omnipotent or up to every task and should not undertake those we are not certain we can conclude successfully: technoprogrammatic approaches to war, as in the calamitous resurrection today of so-called internal defense plans for Third World countries from the dusty shelves of the Pentagon, are likely to squander our military power in impossible tasks.

Fourth, we should always strive first to give diplomacy a chance, precisely in order to conserve military power. What deals can we make, or can be made for us, that square with our moral standards and basic values? What fluidity, what novel elements, can be introduced by diplomacy and dialogue in these difficult situations? The essence of the deal we should seek in Central America must be that we would accept living with any type of regime that a country there establishes internally, even if such a regime is odious in our eyes (as the Marxist-Leninist regime in Cuba has been for the 20-plus years that we have coexisted with it); and in return we would exact conditions which would guarantee prevention of the establishment of new Soviet or Cuban military bases or positions in the region. If this means a Marxist regime in El Salvador, or the continuation of the Sandinists in power in Nicaragua, so be it, provided they do not allow Soviet bases aimed at the United States or Mexico and remain genuinely nonaligned. We started out by assuming that an extension of Soviet or Cuban influence would be the automatic outcome in both countries, and in the process of acting upon that assumption, we tended of course (as in Vietnam over a period going all the way back to the end of World War II) to make it come true. This is known in foreign policy as a "self-fulfilling prophecy" and is a fateful pitfall to be avoided.

A policy automatically upholding the status quo without consideration of its local merits, such as we followed in Vietnam, stems from misperceived notions of the national interest like the Domino Theory, or mechanistic conceptions of interlinkage such as that our power must be "credible" everywhere or it is "incredible" anywhere; or it stems from good-versus-evil casts of world politics in which we as well as our enemies construct ideological Frankensteins who then tend to devour us. The deemphasis of ideology in world politics is long overdue. It is not social revolutionary change that we must fear, even change openly directed at Marxist-Leninist goals, or above all change itself. What we must fear, and defeat, is our incapacity to adapt to change, whether desirable or inevitable change, to recognize it, and to move with it. This, if we cannot correct it, will in the end lead us into newer, larger, and worse Vietnams.

NOTES

1. Melvin Maddocks, "Appraising Some Reappraisals of Vietnam," *The Christian Science Monitor*, 28 February 1983, p. 22.
2. For example, W. Scott Thompson and Donald D. Frizzell, eds., *The Lessons of Vietnam* (New York: Crane, Russak, 1977); Denis Warner, *Certain Victory* (Mission, Kans.: Sheed Andrews and McMeel, 1977); BDM Corporation, *Strategic Lessons Learned in Vietnam* (Washington: BDM Corp., 1981).
3. The term was coined by Jerome Slater in an unpublished paper on "Misconceptions About the Vietnam War" (SUNY, Buffalo, 1983). Works he cites as belonging in this category include those by Guenter Lewy, *America in Vietnam* (New York: Oxford Univ. Press, 1978);

Leslie Gelb and Richard K. Betts, *The Irony of Vietnam: The System Worked* (Washington: Brookings, 1978); Douglas S. Blaufarb, *The Counterinsurgency Era* (New York: Free Press, 1977); Harry G. Summers, Jr., *On Strategy: A Critical Analysis of the Vietnam War* (Novato, Calif.: Presidio Press, 1982); and even my own *Vietnam Trauma* (New Brunswick, N.J.: Transaction, paper, 1982) although it strongly denounces the continuation of the war after 1968 as immoral.

4. "Letters," *The New York Times Magazine*, 20 March 1983, p. 110.
5. *Some Lessons and Non-Lessons of Vietnam Ten Years After the Paris Peace Accords* (Washington: Woodrow Wilson International Center for Scholars, 1983).
6. See my "'So Many Enemies': The View From Hanoi," *Indochina Issues*, No. 38, Washington, Center for International Policy, Indochina Project, June 1983.
7. P. M. Kattenburg, "Living With Hanoi," *Foreign Policy*, No. 53 (Winter 1983-84) pp. 131-149.
8. See J. P. Harrison, *The Endless War: Fifty Years of Struggle in Vietnam* (New York: Free Press, 1982).
9. Kattenburg, *Vietnam Trauma*, pp. 320ff.

This article appeared in the autumn 1984 issue of *Parameters*.

14

Lessons of History and Lessons of Vietnam

by DAVID H. PETRAEUS

One of the few unequivocally sound lessons of history is that the lessons we should learn are usually learned imperfectly if at all.

> – Bernard Brodie[1]

Trying to use the lessons of the past correctly poses two dilemmas. One is the problem of balance: knowing how much to rely on the past as a guide and how much to ignore it. The other is the problem of selection: certain lessons drawn from experience contradict others.

> – Richard Betts[2]

Of all the disasters of Vietnam, the worst may be the "lessons" that we'll draw from it .... Lessons from such complex events require much reflection to be of more than negative worth. But reactions to Vietnam ... tend to be visceral rather than reflective.

> – Albert Wohlstetter[3]

Of all the disasters of Vietnam the worst could be our unwillingness to learn enough from them.

> – Stanley Hoffman[4]

In seeking solutions to problems, occupants of high office frequently turn to the past for help. This tendency is understandable; potentially, history is an enormously rich resource. What was done before in seemingly similar situations and what the results were can be of great assistance to policymakers. As this article contends, however, it is important to recognize that history can mislead and obfuscate as well as guide and illuminate. Lessons of the past, in general, and the lessons of Vietnam, in particular, contain not only policy-relevant analogies, but also ambiguities and paradoxes. Despite such problems, however, there is mounting evidence that lessons and analogies drawn from history often play an important part in policy decisions.[5]

Political scientists, organizational psychologists, and historians have assembled considerable evidence suggesting that one reason decision-makers behave as they do is that they are influenced by lessons they have derived from certain events in the past, especially traumatic events during their lifetimes. "Hardly anything is more important in international affairs," writes Paul Kattenburg, "than the historical images and perceptions that men carry in their heads."[6] These images constitute an important part of the "intellectual baggage'' that policymakers carry into office and draw on when making decisions.

Use of history in this way is virtually universal. As diplomatic historian Ernest May has pointed out, ''Eagerness to profit from the lessons of history is the one common characteristic in the statecraft of such diverse types as Stanley Baldwin, Adolf Hitler, Charles de Gaulle, and John F. Kennedy.'' Each was ''determined to hear the voices of history, to avoid repeating the presumed mistakes of the past.''[7] President Reagan appears to be similarly influenced by the past. His ''ideas about the world flow from his life,'' *The New York Times'* Leslie Gelb contends, ''from personal history . . . a set of convictions lodged in his mind as maxims.''[8]

Perceived lessons of the past have been found to be especially important during crises. When a sudden international development threatens national security interests and requires a quick response, leaders are prone to draw on historical analogies in deciding how to proceed. Indeed, several studies have concluded that ''the greater the crisis, the greater the propensity for decision-makers to supplement information about the objective state of affairs with information drawn from their own past experiences.''[9]

The use of historical analogies by statesmen, however, frequently is flawed. Many scholars concur with Ernest May's judgment that ''policy-makers ordinarily use history badly.''[10] Numerous pitfalls await those who seek guidance from the past, and policymakers have seemed adept at finding them. Those who employ history, therefore, should be aware of the common fallacies to which they may fall victim. As Alexis de Tocqueville warned, misapplied lessons of history may be more dangerous than ignorance of the past.[11]

The first error that policymakers frequently commit when employing history is to focus unduly on a particularly dramatic or traumatic event which they experienced personally.[12] The last war or the most recent crisis assumes unwarranted importance in the mind of the decision-maker seeking historical precedents to illuminate the present. This inclination often is unfounded. There is little reason why those events that occurred during the lifetime of a particular leader and thus provide ready analogies should in fact be the best guides to the present or future. Just because the decision-maker happened to experience the last war is no reason that it, rather than earlier wars, should provide guidance for the contemporary situation.[13]

The fallacy of viewing personal historical experience as most relevant to the present – without carefully considering alternative sources of comparison – is compounded by a tendency to remove analogies from their unique contextual circumstances. Having seized on the first analogy that comes to mind, in too many instances policymakers do not search more widely. Nor, contends Ernest May, ''do they pause to analyze the case, test its fitness, or even ask in what ways it might be misleading.''[14] Historical outcomes are thus absorbed without paying careful attention to the details of their causation, and the result is lessons that are superficial and overgeneralized, analogies applied to a wide range of events with little sensitivity to variations in the situation.[15] The result is policy made, in Arthur Schlesinger's words, through "historical generalization wrenched illegitimately out of the past and imposed mechanically on the future."[16]

Finally, once persuaded that a particular event or phenomenon is repeating itself, policymakers are prone to narrow their thinking, seeing only those facts that conform to the image they have chosen as applicable. Contradictory information is filtered out. "As new information is received," observes Lloyd Jensen, "an effort is made to interpret that information so that it will be compatible with existing images and beliefs."[17]

In sum, lessons of the past are not always used wisely. Proper employment of history has been the exception rather than the rule. Historical analogies often are poorly chosen and overgeneralized. Their contextual circumstances frequently are overlooked. Traumatic personal experiences often exercise unwarranted tyranny over the minds of decision-makers. History is so often misused by policymakers, in fact, that many historians agree with Arthur Schlesinger's inversion of Santayana: "Those who *can* remember the past are condemned to repeat it."[18]

THE LESSONS OF VIETNAM

It is not surprising that lessons taken from America's experience in Indochina have influenced the views and advice of US military leaders on virtually all post-Vietnam security crises in which the use of force was considered. This has been particularly evident in those cases where the similarities to US involvement in Indochina have been perceived to be most striking, such as the debate over American policy toward Central America.[19]

The frustrating experience of Vietnam is indelibly etched in the minds of America's senior military officers, and from it they seem to have taken three general lessons. First, the military has drawn from Vietnam a reminder of the finite limits of American public support for US involvement in a protracted conflict. This awareness was not, of course, a complete revelation to all in the military. Among the 20th-century wars the United States entered, only World War II enjoyed overwhelming support.[20] As early as the 19th century, Alexis de Tocqueville had observed that democracies – America's in particular – were better suited for "a sudden effort of remarkable vigor, than for the prolonged endurance of the great storms that beset the political existence of nations." Democracies, he noted, do not await the consequences of important undertakings with patience.[21]

After World War II, General George C. Marshall echoed that judgment, warning that "a democracy cannot fight a Seven Years' War."[22] Yet such prescient observations as de Tocqueville's and Marshall's were temporarily overlooked; and, for those in military, Vietnam was an extremely painful reaffirmation that when it comes to intervention, time and patience are not American virtues in abundant supply.

Second, the military has taken from Vietnam (and the concomitant repercussions in the Pentagon) a heightened awareness that civilian officials are responsive to influences other than the objective conditions on the battlefield.[23] A consequence has been an increase in traditional military suspicions about politicians and political appointees. This generalization, admittedly, does not hold true across the board and has diminished somewhat in the past few years. Nonetheless, while the military still accepts emphatically the constitutional provision for civilian control of the armed forces,[24] there remain from the Vietnam era nagging doubts about the abilities and motivations of politicians. The military came away from Vietnam feeling, in particular, that the civilian leadership had not understood the conduct of military operations, had lacked the willingness to see things through, and frequently had held different perceptions about what was really important.[25] Vietnam was also a painful reminder that the military, not the transient occupants of high office, generally bears the heaviest burden during armed conflict. Vietnam gave new impetus to what Samuel Huntington described in the 1950s as the military's pacifist attitude. The military man, he wrote, "tends to see himself as the perennial victim of civilian warmongering. It is the people and the politicians, public opinion and governments who start wars. It is the military who have to fight them."[26] As retired General William A. Knowlton told members of the Army War College class of 1985: "Remember one lesson from the Vietnam era: Those who ordered the meal were not there when the waiter brought the check."[27]

Finally, the military took from Vietnam a new recognition of the limits of military power in solving certain types of problems in world affairs. In particular, Vietnam planted doubts in many military minds about the ability of US forces to conduct successful large-scale counterinsurgencies. These misgivings do not in all cases spring from doubts about the capabilities of American troops and units per se; even in Vietnam, military leaders recall, US units never lost a battle. Rather, the doubts that are part of the Vietnam legacy spring from a number of interrelated factors: worries about a lack of popular support for what the public might perceive as ambiguous conflicts;[28] the previously mentioned suspicions about the willingness of politicians – not just those in the executive branch – to stay the course; [29] and lurking fears that the respective services have yet to come to grips with the difficult tasks of developing the doctrine, equipment, and forces suitable for nasty little wars.[30]

These lessons have had a chastening effect on military thinking. A more skeptical attitude is brought to the analysis of possible missions. "We've thrown over the old 'can do' idea," an Army Colonel at Fort Hood told *The New York Times'* Drew Middleton. "Now we want to know exactly what they want us to do and how they think we can accomplish it." Henceforth, senior military officers seem to feel, the United States should not engage in war unless it has a clear idea why it is fighting and is prepared to see the war through to a successful conclusion.[31]

Vietnam also increased the military inclination toward the "all or nothing" type of advice that characterized military views during the Eisenhower Administrations' deliberations in 1954 over intervention at Dien Bien Phu and the Kennedy Administration's discussions over intervention in Laos in 1961. There is a conviction that when it comes to the use of force, America should either bite the bullet or duck, but not nibble.[32] "Once we commit force," cautioned Army Chief of Staff General John Wickham, "we must be prepared to back it up as opposed to just sending soldiers into operations for limited goals."[33] Furthermore, noted Wickham's predecessor, General Edward C. Meyer, before his retirement in 1983, commanders must be "given a freer hand in waging war than they had in Vietnam."[34] In this view, if the United States is to intervene, it should do so in strength, accomplish its objectives rapidly, and withdraw as soon as conditions allow.

Additionally, the public must be made aware of the costs up front. Force must be committed only when there is a consensus of understanding among the American people that the effort is in the best interests of the United States.[35] There is a belief that "Congress should declare war whenever large numbers of U.S. troops engage in sustained combat," and that the American people must be mobilized because "a nation cannot fight in cold blood."[36] Since time is crucial, furthermore, sufficient force must be used at the outset to ensure that the conflict can be resolved before the American people withdraw their support for it.[37]

Finally, Vietnam has led the senior military to believe that in the future, political leaders must better define objectives before putting soldiers at risk. "Don't send military forces off to do anything unless you know what it is clearly that you want done," warned then-Chairman of the Joint Chiefs General John Vessey in 1983. "I am absolutely, unalterably opposed to risking American lives for some sort of military and political objectives that we don't understand."[38]

In short, rather than preparing to fight the last war, as generals and admirals are often accused of doing, contemporary military leaders seem far more inclined to avoid any involvement overseas that could become another Vietnam. The lessons taken from Vietnam work to that end; military support for the use of force abroad is contingent on the presence of specific preconditions chosen with an eye to avoiding a repetition of the US experience in Southeast Asia.

USING THE LESSONS OF VIETNAM

The lessons of Vietnam as drawn by American military leaders do, however, have their limitations. While they represent the distillation of considerable wisdom from America's experience in Indochina, they nonetheless give rise to certain paradoxical prescriptions and should not be pushed beyond their limits. As this section will show, total resolution of the paradoxes that reside in the lessons of Vietnam is not possible, nor should it be expected given the nature of world events and domestic politics. Nonetheless, awareness of the limitations of the lessons of Vietnam is necessary if they are to be employed with sound judgment.

Users of the lessons of Vietnam should, first of all, recognize and strive to avoid the general pitfalls that await anyone who seeks useful analogies in the past. Most important, the fact that Vietnam was America's most recent major military engagement is no reason that it, rather than earlier conflicts, should be most relevant to future conflicts. Senior officials should remember the contextual circumstances of American involvement in Vietnam – the social fragmentation there, the leadership void, the difficult political situation, the geostrategic position, and so forth. They would be wise to recall Stanley Karnow's reminder that each foreign event "has its own singularities, which must be confronted individually and creatively. To see every crisis as another Vietnam is myopic, just as overlaying the Munich debacle on Vietnam was a distortion."[39] Hence specific guidelines for the use of force that draw on Vietnam, such as those discussed earlier and those announced by Secretary of Defense Weinberger,[40] should be applied with discrimination to specific cases and their circumstances, rather than in the rote manner that one-line principles of war are sometimes employed.

Policymakers employing the lessons of Vietnam, or the lessons of any other past event, should resist the American tendency for over-generalization.[41] For if nothing else, Vietnam should teach that global, holistic approaches do not work.[42] In short, when drawing on the lessons of Vietnam, senior officers would do well to recall the advice of Mark Twain:

> We should be careful to get out of an experience only the wisdom that is in it – and stop there; lest we be like the cat that sits down on a hot stove lid. She will never sit down on a hot stove lid again – and that is well; but also she will never sit down on a cold one.[43]

Beyond recognizing such general pitfalls that can snare users of historical analogies, military leaders also should be aware of the paradoxes that reside in certain of the prescriptions derived from the lessons of Vietnam. In particular, the guidelines taken from America's experience in Vietnam contain a significant dilemma about when to use force, appear to embody a potentially counterproductive approach to civil-military relations, and create a quandary over counterinsurgency doctrine and force structuring.

As explained earlier, many military leaders have concluded on the basis of the Vietnam experience that the United States should not intervene abroad militarily unless: there is support at home; there are clear political and military objectives; success appears achievable within a reasonable time; and military commanders will be given the freedom to do what they believe is necessary to achieve that success. The problem with such guidelines, as Robert Osgood has observed, is that "acting upon them presupposes advance knowledge about a complicated interaction of military and political factors that no one can predict or guarantee."[44]

Still, making judgments about such factors has always been part of decisions to use military force. Statesmen and soldiers have always had to assess the time and force required for success, the likelihood of public support, and the potential gains and losses associated with any particular intervention or escalation. Eliminating the uncertainty inherent in such determinations has never been completely possible. But Vietnam and the relative decline in US power (and hence America's margin for error in international politics) over the past two decades have heightened the importance of these judgments and made them more problematic. The normal response to this kind of uncertainty is – and has been – caution and restraint.

Restraint rests uneasily, however, alongside another lesson of Vietnam: that if the United States is going to intervene it should do so quickly and massively in order to arrive in force while the patient still has strong vital signs.[45] But getting there faster next time implies making the decision to intervene in force early on. It requires overwhelming commitment from the outset so that, as George Fielding Eliot prescribes, "we shall . . . look like military winners from the start of hostilities" and thereby "win popular support at home and confidence abroad." The American effort, therefore, should be designed to raise immediate doubt that the United States will permit a war to become protracted.[46]

Eliot does not specify, however, how long the appearance of winning will satisfy the American public in the absence of actual victory. Furthermore, getting there earlier next time is more easily said than done. Several post-Vietnam (and post-Watergate) developments – the 1973 War Powers Act, the decline of the "imperial presidency," increased congressional involvement in national security policy, and public wariness over involvement in another quagmire – pose obstacles to swift American action. Coupled with the short-term focus of political leaders and the constitutional separation of powers, these new phenomena (at least in post-World War II terms) make it difficult for the United States to decide early to intervene in any but the most clear-cut of circumstances. It usually takes what can be presented as a crisis before the United States is able to swing into action. The result is the oft-heard judgment that America is good at fighting only crusades.

Military leaders are, of course, well aware of the obstacles to early intervention. They realize that these obstacles, together with America's general inclination against involvement in situations that pose only an indirect threat to US interests, have the potential for incomplete public backing. As a result, senior military officers tend toward caution rather than haste, all the while cognizant of the dilemma confronting them: the country that hesitates may miss the opportune moment for effective action, while the country that acts in haste may become involved in a conflict that it may wish later it had avoided.

Another difficulty posed by the lessons drawn from the Vietnam experience centers on the issue of civil-military relations. During the Vietnam era, the traditional military suspicions of civilians hardened into more acute misgivings about civilian officials. This feeling lingers despite the apparently close philosophical ties on the use of force between the incumbent Secretary of Defense, Caspar Weinberger, and the Joint Chiefs of Staff.[47]

Yet such misgivings pose potential risks. Two post-World War II developments at either end of the so-called "spectrum of conflict," the advent of nuclear weapons and the rise of insurgencies, have made close civil-military integration more essential than ever before.

Counterinsurgency operations, in particular, require close civil-military cooperation. Unfortunately, this requirement runs counter to the traditional military desire, reaffirmed in the lessons of Vietnam, to operate autonomously and resist political meddling and micro-management in operational concerns. Military officers are of course intimately aware of Clausewitz's dictum that war is a continuation of politics by other means; many, however, do not appear to accept fully the implications of Clausewitzian logic. This can cause problems, for while military resistance to political micro-management is often well founded, it can, if carried to excess, be counterproductive. As Eliot Cohen has noted:

Small war almost always involves political interference in the affairs of the country in which it is waged; it is in the very nature of such wars that the military problems are difficult to distinguish from the political ones. The skills of manipulation which successful coalition warfare in such circumstances requires are not only scarce, but in some measure anathema to the American military. The desire of the American military to handle only pure "military" problems is . . . understandable in light of its Vietnam experience, but unrealistic nonetheless.[48]

Hence, particularly in such "small wars," military leaders should not allow the experience of Vietnam to reinforce the traditional military desire for autonomy in a way that impedes the crucial integration of political and military strategies. The organizational desire to be left alone must not lead those who bear the sword to lose their appreciation for the political and economic context in which it is wielded. For while military force may be necessary in certain cases, it is seldom sufficient.[49]

Another paradox posed by the lessons of Vietnam concerns preparations for counterinsurgency warfare. The Vietnam experience left the military leadership feeling that they should advise against involvement in counterinsurgencies unless specific, perhaps unlikely, circumstances obtain. Committing US units to such contingencies appears a starkly problematic step – difficult to conclude before domestic support erodes and potentially so costly as to threaten the well-being of all of America's military forces (and hence the country's national security), not just those involved in the actual counterinsurgency. Senior military officers remember that Vietnam cost not only tens of thousands of lives, but also a generation of investment in new weapons and other equipment.[50] Morale plummeted throughout the military, and relations between the military and society were soured for nearly a decade.

A logical extension of this reasoning is that forces designed specifically for counterinsurgencies should not be given high priority, since if there are no sizable forces suitable for counterinsurgencies it will be easier to avoid involvement in that type of conflict.[51] An American president cannot commit what is not available. Similarly, along this line of thinking, plans for such contingencies should not be pursued with too much vigor.[52]

There are two problems with such reasoning, however. First, presidents may commit the United States to a conflict whether optimum forces exist or not. President Truman's decision to commit American ground troops to the defense of South Korea in 1950, for example, came as a surprise to military officers, who expected to execute a previously approved contingency plan that called for withdrawal of all American troops from the Korean peninsula in the event of an invasion. The early reverses in the ensuing conflict resulted in large measure from inadequate military readiness for such a mission.[53] So, prudence requires a certain flexibility in forces, especially if the overall national strategy opens the possibility of involvement in operations throughout the spectrum of conflict (as it presently appears to do). If commitment to counterinsurgency operations is possible, the military should be prepared for it.

The second problem posed by such reasoning is that American involvement in counterinsurgencies is almost universally regarded as more likely than involvement in most other types of combat – more likely, for example, than involvement in high-intensity conflict on the plains of NATO's Central Region (though, of course, conflict in Europe potentially would have more significant consequences).[54] Indeed, the United States is already involved in counterinsurgencies, albeit not with US combat troops. American military trainers in El Salvador are assisting an ally combatting an insurgency, and, depending on one's definitions, US military elements are also providing assistance to a number of other countries fighting insurgents, among them Chad, Colombia, Ecuador, Honduras, Morocco, Peru, the Philippines, Sudan, and Thailand.

The senior military is thus in a dilemma. The lessons taken from Vietnam would indicate that, in general, involvement in a counterinsurgency should be avoided. But prudent preparation for a likely contingency (and a general inclination against limiting a president's options) lead the military to recognize that significant emphasis should be given to counterinsurgency forces, equipment, and doctrine. Military leaders are thereby in the difficult position of arguing for the creation of more forces suitable for such conflicts, while simultaneously realizing they may advise against the use of those forces unless very specific circumstances hold.[55]

Until recently the inclination against involvement in counterinsurgencies seemed to outweigh the need for a sufficient counterinsurgent capability. Relatively little emphasis was given to preparation for this form of conflict, either in assisting other governments to help themselves or in developing American capabilities for more direct involvement.

There has been developing, however, gradual recognition that involvement in small wars is not only likely, it is upon us. It would seem wise, therefore, to come to grips with what appears to be an emerging fact for the US military, that American involvement in low-intensity conflict is unavoidable given the more assertive US foreign policy of recent years and the developments in many Third World countries, particularly those in our own hemisphere. It would be timely to seek ways to assist allies in counterinsurgency operations, ways consistent with the constraints of the American political culture and system, as well as with the institutional agendas of the military services.[56] One conclusion may be that in some cases, contrary to the lessons of Vietnam, it would be better to use American soldiers in small numbers than in strength to help a foreign government counter insurgents. Indeed, given the example of congressional limits on the number of trainers in El Salvador, the Army in particular should be figuring out how best to assist others within what might be anticipated as similar limits in other situations, while always remembering that it is the host country's war to win or lose.

Given that conclusion, the military should look beyond critiques of American involvement in Vietnam that focus exclusively on alternative conventional military strategies that might have been pursued. For all their value, such studies seldom address important unconventional elements of struggles such as Vietnam (although, of course, what eventually defeated South Vietnam was a massive invasion by North Vietnam forces) and several contemporary theaters. As Professor John Gates wrote in a 1984 *Parameters* article,

Any analysis that denies the important revolutionary dimension of the Vietnam conflict is misleading, leaving the American people, their leaders, and their professionals inadequately prepared to deal with similar problems in the future . . . . Instead of forcing the military to come to grips with the problems of revolutionary warfare that now exist in nations such as Guatemala or El Salvador, [such an] analysis leads officers back into the conventional war model that provided so little preparation for solving the problems faced in Indochina by the French, the Americans, and their Vietnamese allies. Such a business-as-usual approach is much too complacent in a world plagued by the unconventional warfare associated with revolution and attempts to counter it.[57]

The most serious charge leveled at the lessons of Vietnam is made by those who perceive them as promising national paralysis in the face of international provocation. This contention is also the most difficult to contend with because of its generality. The argument is that insistence upon domestic consensus before employing US forces is too demanding a requirement – that if it were rigorously applied it would, in the words of former Secretary of Defense James Schlesinger, "virtually assure other powers that they can count on not facing American forces." Schlesinger goes on to explain:

The likeliest physical challenges to the United States come in the third world – not in Europe or North America. If the more predatory states in the third world are given assurance that they can employ, directly or indirectly, physical force against American interests with impunity, they will feel far less restraint in acting against our interests. Americans historically have embraced crusades

– such as World War II – as well as glorious little wars. The difficulty is that the most likely conflicts of the future fall between crusades and such brief encounters as Grenada and Mayaguez. Yet these in between conflicts have weak public support. Even . . . with national unity and at the height of our power public enthusiasm for Korea and Vietnam evaporated in just a year or two. The problem is that virtually no opportunity exists for future crusades – and those glorious wars are likely to occur infrequently. The role of the United States in the world is such that it must be prepared for, be prepared to threaten, and even be prepared to fight those intermediate conflicts – that are likely to fare poorly on television.[58]

As Schlesinger was quick to acknowledge, however, there is no ready solution to the perplexities he described. Nor are there clear-cut solutions to the other ambiguities that reside in the lessons of Vietnam. The only certainty seems to be that searching reflection about what ought to be taken from America's experience in Vietnam should continue, for only with further examination will thoughtful understanding replace visceral revulsion when we think about America's difficulties in Vietnam.

CONCLUSIONS

History in general, and the American experience in Vietnam in particular, have much to teach us, but both must be used with discretion and neither should be pushed too far.[59] In particular, the Vietnam analogy, for all its value as the most recent large-scale use of American force abroad, has limits. The applicability of the lessons drawn from Vietnam, just like the applicability of lessons taken from any other past event, always will depend on the contextual circumstances. We should avoid the trap of considering only the Vietnam analogy and not allow it to overshadow unduly other historical events that appear to offer insight and perspective.

Nor should Vietnam be permitted to become such a dominant influence in the minds of decision-makers that it inhibits the discussion of specific events on their own merits. It would be more profitable to address the central issues of any particular case that arises than to debate endlessly whether the situation could evolve into "another Vietnam." In their use of history politicians and military planners alike would do well to recall David Fischer's finding that "the utility of historical knowledge consists . . . in the enlargement of substantive contexts within which decisions are made, . . . in the refinement of a thought structure which is indispensable to purposeful decisionmaking."[60]

Thus we should beware literal application of lessons extracted from Vietnam, or any other past event, to present or future problems without due regard for the specific circumstances that surround those problems. Study of Vietnam – and of other historical occurrences – should endeavor to gain perspective and understanding, rather than hard and fast lessons that might be applied too easily without proper reflection and sufficiently rigorous analysis. "Each historical situation is unique," George Herring has warned, "and the use of analogy is at best misleading, at worst, dangerous."[61]

NOTES

1. Quoted in Ole R. Holsti and James N. Rosenau, *American Leadership in World Affairs* (Boston: Allen and Unwin, 1984), p. 25.
2. Richard K. Betts, *Soldiers, Statesmen, and Cold War Crises* (Cambridge: Harvard Univ. Press, 1977), p. 164.
3. Quoted in *No More Vietnams?* ed. by Richard M. Pfeffer (New York: Harper and Row, 1968), p. 4.
4. Ibid., p. 6.
5. The best of the works that establish the influence of history on decision-makers is Ernest R. May's *"Lessons" of the Past* (New York: Oxford Univ. Press, 1978). Others include: Richard E. Neustadt and Ernest R. May, *Thinking in Time* (New York: Free Press, 1986); Robert Jervis, *Perceptions and Misperceptions in International Politics* (Princeton: Princeton Univ. Press, 1976), especially chapter six, "How Decision-Makers Learn From History"; Alexander L. George, *Presidential Decisionmaking in Foreign Policy: The Effective Use of Information and Advice* (Boulder, Colo.: Westview Press, 1980), pp. 42-53, 60-61; Stanley Karnow, "Vietnam As an Analogy," *The New York Times*, 4 October 1983, p. A27; and Holsti and Rosenau, pp. 3-10.
6. Paul M. Kattenburg, *The Vietnam Trauma in American Foreign Policy, 1945-1975* (New Brunswick, N.J.: Transaction Books, 1980), p. 317.
7. Quoted in George, *Presidential Decisionmaking in Foreign Policy*, p. 45.
8. Leslie H. Gelb, "The Mind of the President," *The New York Times Magazine*, 6 October 1985, p. 28.
9. Glenn D. Paige, "Comparative Case Analysis of Crisis Decisions: Korea and Cuba," in *International Crises: Insights From Behavioral Research*, ed. Charles F. Hermann (New York: The Free Press, 1972), p. 48. Paige's finding was confirmed in Michael Brecher, with Benjamin Geist, *Decisions in Crisis* (Berkeley: Univ. of California Press, 1980), p. 343.
10. May, *Lessons" of the Past*, p. xi.
11. Cited in Holsti and Rosenau, *American Leadership in World Affairs*, p. 8.
12. See, for example, Abraham Lowenthal, *The Dominican Intervention* (Cambridge: Harvard Univ. Press, 1972), p. 161.
13. Jervis, *Perception and Misperception in International Politics*, p. 281.
14. May, *"Lessons" of the Past*, p. xi.
15. Jervis, *Perception and Misperception in International Politics*, p. 281.
16. Arthur M. Schlesinger, *The Bitter Heritage: Vietnam and American Democracy, 1941-1946* (Greenwich, Conn.: Fawcett Crest, 1967), p. 98.
17. Lloyd Jensen, *Explaining Foreign Policy* (Englewood Cliffs, N.J.: Prentice-Hall, 1982), p. 39. See also May, *"Lessons" of the Past*, p. xi; Lowenthal, *The Dominican Intervention*, p. 162; and John D. Steinbruner, *The Cybernetic Theory of Decision* (Princeton: Princeton Univ. Press, 1974), pp. 65-71.
18. George Santayana, *The Life of Reason* (New York: Charles Scribner's Sons, one-volume edition, 1953), p. 82. Schlesinger, *The Bitter Heritage*, p. 102.
19. See William J. Taylor and David H. Petraeus, "The Legacy of Vietnam for the American Military," in *Democracy, Strategy and Vietnam,* ed. George Osborn et al. (Lexington, Mass.: Lexington Books, forthcoming 1987). See also: Richard Halloran, "Vietnam Consequences: Quiet From the Military," *The New York Times*, 2 May 1983, p. A16; Drew Middleton, "U.S. Generals Are Leery of Latin Intervention," *The New York Times*, 21 June 1983, p. A9; Walter S. Mossberg, "The Army Resists a Salvdoran Vietnam," *The Wall Street Journal*, 24 June 1983, p. 22; Joanne Omang, "New Army Chief Doesn't See Widening Latin Involvement," *The Washington Post*, 9 August 1983, p. A10; Philip Taubman, "General Doubts G.I. Role in Salvador," *The New York Times*, 2 August 1984, p. A3; Richard Halloran, "General Opposes Nicaragua Attacks," *The New York Times*, 30 June 1985, p. A3; and George C. Wilson, "Generals Who Contradict the Contras," *The Washington Post*, 13 April 1986, p. C2.

Military advice on the Marine peacekeeping mission in Lebanon also appeared to be influenced by the experience in Vietnam. See, for example, Steven V. Roberts, "War Powers Debate Reflects Its Origin," *The New York Times*, 2 October 1983, p. E4; Bill Keller, "Military Reportedly Opposed Use of U.S. Marines in Beirut," *The New York Times*, 22 August 1985, p. A6; Patrick J. Sloyan, "Lebanon: Anatomy of a Foreign Policy Failure," *Newsday*, 8 April 1984, pp. 4-5, 34-39; Roy Gutman, "Division at the Top Meant Half-Measures," *Newsday*, 8

April 1984, pp. 36-37; and William Greider, ''Retreat from Beirut,'' an episode in the Public Broadcasting System series *Frontline*, shown on 26 February 1985.

20. See John E. Mueller, *War, Presidents and Public Opinion* (New York: John Wiley, 1973), pp. 42-65, 168-75.
21. Alexis de Tocqueville, *Democracy in America* (New York: Vintage Books, 1945), I, 237.
22. Maurice Matloff, *Strategic Planning for Coalition Warfare, 1943-1944* (Washington: Department of the Army, 1959), p. 5.
23. See, for example, Andrew F. Krepinevich, Jr., ''Past As Prologue: Counterinsurgency and the U.S. Army's Vietnam Experience in Force Structuring and Doctrine,'' in *Vietnam: Did It Make A Difference?*
24. The overwhelming acceptance of civilian control is illustrated in ''A *Newsweek* Poll: The Military Mind,'' *Newsweek*, 9 July 1984, p. 37.
25. See, for example, Victor H. Krulak, *Organization for National Security* (Washington: US Strategic Institute, 1983), pp. 81-102; Stephan P. Rosen, ''Vietnam and the American Theory of Limited War,'' *International Security*, 7 (Fall 1982), 100-03; Krepinevich, ''Past As Prologue''; and Frank A. Burdick, ''Vietnam Revisioned: The Military Campaign Against Civilian Control,'' *Democracy* 2 (January 1982), 36-52.
26. Samuel P. Huntington, *The Soldier and the State* (Cambridge: Harvard Univ. Press, 1957), pp. 69-70.
27. William A. Knowlton, ''Ethics and Decision-Making,'' address delivered at the US Army War College, Carlisle Barracks, Pa., 22 October 1984, p. 28 of transcript (cited with permission of General Knowlton). Similarly, a ''senior officer'' told *The New York Times*'s Richard Halloran: ''We were the scapegoats of that conflict. We're the ones pulling back on the reins on [Central America].'' Halloran, ''Vietnam Consequences: Quiet From the Military,'' *The New York Times*, 2 May 1983, p. A16.
28. Thus retired General Maxwell Taylor described the ''great difficulty in rallying this country behind a foreign issue involving the use of armed force, which does not provide an identified enemy posing a clear threat to our homeland or the vital interests of long time friends.'' See his ''Post-Vietnam Role of the Military in Foreign Policy,'' in *Contemporary American Foreign and Military Policy*, ed. Burton M. Sapin (Glenview, Ill.: Scott, Foresman, 1970), pp. 36-43. For similar views expressed by General John Vessey before his recent retirement from the post of Chairman of the Joint Chiefs of Staff, see Richard Halloran, ''Reflections on 46 Years of Army Service,'' *The New York Times*, 3 September 1985, p. A18.
29. As former Secretary of State Alexander Haig wrote: ''The Joint Chiefs of Staff, chastened by Vietnam ... resisted a major commitment in [Central America]. I sensed, and understood, a doubt on the part of the military in the political will of the civilians at the top to follow through to the end on such a commitment.'' See Haig's *Caveat* (New York: Macmillan, 1984), p. 128.
30. There appears to be a muted debate under way, particularly within the Army, over whether American forces should be used in counterinsurgency operations at all, and if so, how they should be structured. Some officers feel that US forces are not well suited for such operations. As one senior officer who commanded a battalion in Vietnam advised: ''Remember, we're watchdogs you unchain to eat the burglar. Don't ask us to be mayors or sociologists worrying about hearts and minds. Let us eat up the burglar in our own way and then put us back on the leash.'' Quoted in George C. Wilson, ''War's Lessons Struck Home,'' *The Washington Post*, 16 April 1985, p. A9. Similar sentiments were expressed by a Navy Admiral who advised the US Military Academy's 1985 Senior Conference that the primary task of the military is to put ''ordnance on target.'' See John D. Morrocco, ''Vietnam's Legacy: U.S. More Cautious In Using Force,'' *Army Times*, 1 July 1985, p. 42. See also the letter to the editor of *Military Review* by Francisco J. Pedrozo, 66 (January 1986), 81-82. Others worry that the American people will not support extended US involvement in a ''small war.'' Lastly, there remain a few military officers who cling to the notion that no special capability is needed because big units can invariably handle small wars – that, in the words of General Curtis LeMay (Air Force Chief of Staff in the early 1960s), ''If you can lick the cat, you can lick the kitten'' (attributed to LeMay in William W. Kaufmann, ''Force Planning and Vietnam,'' in *Vietnam: Did It Make a Difference?*).
31. Drew Middleton, ''Vietnam and the Military Mind,'' *The New York Times*, 10 January 1982, p. 90. See also Richard Halloran, ''For Military Leaders, the Shadow of Vietnam,'' *The New York Times*, 20 March 1984, p. B10.

One may ask whether American military leaders have not always held such views, and question, therefore, whether the so-called lessons of Vietnam are really anything new. This was the reaction of retired General Edward C. Meyer, former Army Chief of Staff, to a draft paper that discussed the lessons of Vietnam in a similar vein (Taylor and Petraeus, "The Legacy of Vietnam for the American Military"). Other senior officers have expressed similar sentiments when queried by journalists about the impact of Vietnam. General John Vessey on several occasions maintained that "his attitudes toward the use of military force were largely unaffected by the U.S. experience in Vietnam." See P. J. Budahn, "Vessey Sees Need to Ease Up-or-Out Policy," *Army Times*, 16 September 1985, pp. 4, 26; and Harry G. Summers, Jr., "American Military in 'A Race to Prevent War,'" *U.S. News and World Report*, 21 October 1985, p. 40.

32. Paraphrased from Richard K. Betts, "Misadventure Revisited," *The Wilson Quarterly*, 7 (Summer 1983), 99.

33. George C. Wilson, "War's Lessons Struck Home," *The Washington Post*, 16 April 1985, p. A9.

34. George C. Wilson, "Top U.S. Brass Wary on Central America," *The Washington Post*, 24 June 1983, p. A20.

35. Bruce Palmer, *The 25-Year War* (Lexington, Ky.: Univ. Press of Kentucky, 1984), p. 204. See also the quotation of General Frederick C. Weyand in Harry G. Summers, Jr., *On Strategy: The Vietnam War in Context* (Carlisle Barracks, Pa.: US Army War College, 1981), p. 25.

36. Palmer, *The 25-Year War*, p. 194; and Wilson, "Top U.S. Brass Wary on Central America." In fact, it appears that senior Army leaders since Vietnam have sought an active component force that makes, in the words of former Army Chief of Staff Meyer, "except for the most modest contingency, a callup of Reserves ... an absolute necessity." See the collection of General Meyer's speeches and articles published by the Department of the Army in 1983, p. 314. On this see also Michael R. Gordon, "The Charge of the Light Infantry – Army Plans Forces for Third World Conflict," *National Journal*, 19 May 1984, p. 972; and Summers, *On Strategy: The Vietnam War in Context*, p. 113.

37. Richard Halloran, "Reflections on 46 Years of Army Service," *The New York Times*, 3 September 1985, p. A18.

38. Richard Halloran, "A Commanding Voice for the Military," *The New York Times Magazine*, 15 July 1984, p. 52.

39. Stanley Karnow, "Vietnam As An Analogy," *The New York Times*, 4 October 1983, p. A27. On this point, see Hans Morgenthau, *A New Foreign Policy for the United States* (New York: Praeger, 1968), p. 144. For an illustrative, though now somewhat dated, analysis of the differences between El Salvador and Vietnam, see George C. Herring, "Vietnam, El Salvador, and the Uses of History," in *The Central American Crisis*, ed. Kenneth M. Coleman and George C. Herring (Wilmington, Del.: Scholarly Resources, 1985), pp. 97-110.

40. In a November 1984 speech titled "The Uses of Military Power," Secretary of Defense Weinberger outlined six tests that he said would apply when deciding whether to send military forces into combat abroad. His six tests are very similar to the lessons drawn by the military from Vietnam. See "Excerpts From Address of Weinberger," *The New York Times*, 29 November 1984, p. A5; and Richard Halloran, "U.S. Will Not Drift Into A Latin War, Weinberger Says," *The New York Times*, 29 November 1984, pp. A1, A4.

41. A recent article by George F. Kennan contained a similar admonishment. See his "Morality and Foreign Policy," *Foreign Affairs*, 64 (Winter 1985/86), 205-18.

42. Paul Kattenburg makes a particularly good case for this in *The Vietnam Trauma in American Foreign Policy, 1945-1975* (New Brunswick, N.J.: Transaction Books, 1980), p. 321.

43. Mark Twain (Samuel L. Clemens), *Following the Equator: A Journey Around the World* (New York: Harper and Brothers, 1899), p. 125.

44. Robert E. Osgood, *Limited War Revisited* (Boulder, Colo.: Westview Press, 1979), p. 50.

45. See, for example, George Fielding Eliot, "Next Time We'll Have to Get There Faster," *Army*, 20 (April 1970), 32-36.

46. Ibid., pp. 32-33.

47. The best example of these close philosophical ties is Secretary Weinberger's November 1984 speech, "The Uses of Military Power." See note 40.

48. Eliot A. Cohen, "Constraints on America's Conduct of Small Wars," *International Security*, 9 (Fall 1984), 170. Richard Betts has observed that American military leaders in Vietnam "recognized the political complexity of the war but insisted on dividing the labor, leaving the

politics to the civilians and concentrating themselves on actual combat." See his *Soldiers, Statesmen, and Cold War Crises* (Cambridge: Harvard Univ. Press, 1977), p. 138.

49. Phrase suggested by Lieutenant Colonel Daniel J. Kaufman.

50. This sentiment is clearly evident, for example, in Halloran, "Vietnam Consequences: Quiet From the Military."

51. There is some evidence of such feelings. A recent article by Tom Donnelly in *Army Times* (1 July 1985, pp. 41-43), for example, was descriptively titled "Special Operations Still a Military Stepchild." See also "A Warrior Elite For the Dirty Jobs," *Time*, 13 January 1986, p. 18.

52. Some journalists reported that the military was slow in planning for contingencies in Central America. See George C. Wilson, "U.S. Urged to Meet Honduran Requests," *The Washington Post*, 20 June 1983, p. A4; and Doyle McManus, "U.S. Draws Contingency Plans for Air Strikes in El Salvador," *The Washington Post*, 13 July 1984, p. A27.

53. Joseph C. Goulden, *Korea: The Untold Story of the War* (New York: Times Books, 1982), pp. 57-58; and T. R. Fehrenbach, *This Kind of War: A Study of Unpreparedness* (New York: MacMillan, 1963). Senior military men took from Korea the necessity to have a force structure flexible enough to respond to such unanticipated decisions. See the comments of Lieutenant General Vernon Walters on this in Summers, *On Strategy: The Vietnam War in Context*, p. 120.

54. Among the many sources that make this point, see Robert H. Kupperman and William J. Taylor, eds. *Strategic Requirements for the Army to the Year 2000* (Lexington, Mass.: Lexington Books, 1984), esp. pp. 51-69, 125-42, and 171-86; Fred K. Mahaffey, "Structuring Forces to Need," *Army*, 34 (October 1984), 204-16; and Richard H. Shultz, Jr., and Alan N. Sabrosky, "Policy and Strategy for the 1980s: Preparing for Low Intensity Conflict," in *Lessons From an Unconventional War*, ed. Richard A. Hunt and Richard H. Shultz, Jr. (New York: Pergamon Press, 1982), pp. 191-227.

55. These tensions are well described in Tom Donnelly, "Special Operations Still a Military Stepchild," *Army Times*, July 1985, pp. 41-43.

56. As this article was being completed several steps in this direction were taken. The most significant were: a high-level conference on low-intensity conflict conducted 14-15 January 1986 at Fort McNair, Washington, D.C.; a joint study of low-intensiy conflict undertaken by the US Army's Training and Doctrine Command; announcement of Army and Navy plans to build up their special operations capabilities over the next five years; and announcement of a joint Air Force and Army examination of their ability to deal with low-intensity conflict. See Daniel Greene, "Conferees Face Challenges of Low-Level Wars," *Army Times*, 27 January 1986, pp. 2, 26; Larry Carney, "Army Plans 5-Year Expansion of Special Operations Forces," *Army Times*, 30 December 1985, p. 4; "Navy's SEAL Force to Grow to 2,700 by 1990," *Army Times*, 2 December 1985, p. 50; and Leonard Famiglietti, "Army-Air Force Team to Study Low-Intensiy Conflict," *Army Times*, 9 December 1985, pp. 59, 60.

57. John M. Gates, "Vietnam: The Debate Goes On," *Parameters*, 14 (Spring 1984), 24-25.

58. "Excerpts from Schlesinger's Senate Testimony," *The New York Times*, 7 February 1985, p. A14.

59. George Herring advanced a similar conclusion in "Vietnam, El Salvador, and Uses of History," p. 108.

60. David H. Fischer, *Historians' Fallacies* (New York: Harper and Row, 1970), p. 157.

61. Herring, "Vietnam, El Salvador, and Uses of History," p. 110.

This article appeared in the autumn 1986 issue of *Parameters*.

V. THE AFTERMATH OF WAR

15

Vietnam and Southeast Asia: The Neglected Issue

by W. W. ROSTOW

The United States' involvement in Vietnam and greater Southeast Asia evidently had and still has, both in that region and at home, many dimensions: military and economic, social and political, human and moral. I tried to evoke the multiple facets of that involvement in my book *The Diffusion of Power*. In the present article, however, I will focus on one important and largely neglected aspect of the subject: the strategic significance of Southeast Asia to all the countries with a stake in the disposition of power in the region.

In their serious effort to analyze the US involvement in Vietnam, Leslie Gelb and Richard Betts take as their central thesis the following proposition:

US leaders considered it vital not to lose Vietnam by force to communism. They believed Vietnam to be vital, not for itself, but for what they thought its 'loss' would mean internationally and domestically.[1]

George Herring's interesting historical assessment, *America's Longest War: The United States and Vietnam, 1950-1975*, contains a brief, accurate passage evoking the reasons for anxiety about Southeast Asia in Washington in the wake of the communist takeover of China in 1949;[2] but so far as my reading revealed, there is no further discussion of the strategic importance of Vietnam or Southeast Asia.

The general view of those who opposed US policy toward Southeast Asia in the 1960s is quite well captured by J. K. Galbraith's bon mot of April 1966: "If we were not in Vietnam, all that part of the world would be enjoying the obscurity it so richly deserves."[3] Or, take the following passage from an August 1968 interview with Eugene McCarthy in *The New York Times*:

I [interviewer] asked him [McCarthy] the final question about Vietnam: 'How are we going to get out?' He said 'Take this down. . . . [T]he time has come for us to say to the Vietnamese, We will take our steel out of the land of thatched huts, we will take our tanks out of the land of the water buffalo, our napalm and flame-throwers out of the land that scarcely knows the use of matches. We will give you back your small and willing women, your rice-paddies and your land.' He smiled. 'That's my platform. It's pretty good, isn't it?'[4]

At first glance, there would appear to be some evidence for the view that the US government did not regard Vietnam of intrinsic importance; for example, neither in office nor in his memoirs did Richard Nixon or Henry Kissinger discuss Southeast Asian policy except as an inherited burden and a responsibility that had to be honored if the credibility of US guarantees elsewhere were to be sustained. As I shall note later, John Kennedy and Lyndon Johnson (but not all members of their Administrations) took a different view. And the fact is that over the past 40 years nine successive Presidents – from Franklin Roosevelt to Ronald Reagan – have made serious strategic commitments to the independence of Southeast Asia, in every case with some pain and contrary to other interests.

The story begins, in a sense, with this passage from Cordell Hull's memoirs – which is where the Pentagon Papers should have begun but didn't:

> Japanese troops on July 21 [1941] occupied the southern portions of Indo-China and were now in possession of the whole of France's strategic province, pointing like a pudgy thumb toward the Philippines, Malaya, and the Dutch East Indies . . . .
> When Welles telephoned me, I said to him that the invasion of Southern Indo-China looked like Japan's last step before jumping off for a full-scale attack in the Southwest Pacific . . . .
> On the following day the President, receiving Nomura, proposed that if the Japanese Government would withdraw its forces from French Indo-China, he would seek to obtain a solemn declaration by the United States, Britain, China, and The Netherlands to regard Indo-China as a 'neutralized' country, provided Japan gave a similar commitment. Japan's explanation for occupying Indo-China having been that she wanted to defend her supplies of raw materials there, the President's proposal took the props from under this specious reasoning. A week later the President extended his proposal to include Thailand.
> Indicating our reaction to Japan's latest act of imperialist aggression, the President froze Japanese assets in the United States on July 26 . . . . All financial, import, and export transactions involving Japanese interests came under Government control, and thereafter trade between the United States and Japan soon dwindled to comparatively nothing . . . .
> From now on our major objective with regard to Japan was to give ourselves more time to prepare our defenses. We were still ready – and eager – to do everything possible toward keeping the United States out of war; but it was our concurrent duty to concentrate on trying to make the country ready to defend itself effectively in the event of war being thrust upon us.[5]

It was, in fact, the movement by the Japanese from northern to southern Indochina in July 1941 and Roosevelt's reaction to it which made war between Japan and the United States inevitable, despite Roosevelt's deep desire to avoid a two-front conflict. The story continues down to the more familiar commitments in Southeast Asia, from Truman to Nixon, to the less well-known fact that on four separate occasions the Carter Administration, in the wake of the communist takeover of South Vietnam in April 1975, reaffirmed the nation's treaty commitment to the defense of Thailand;[6] and, on 6 October 1981, President Reagan said this to the Prime Minister of Thailand on the occasion of his visit to Washington:

> I can assure you that America is ready to help you, and ASEAN, maintain your independence against communist aggression. The Manila Pact, and its clarification in our bilateral communiqué of 1962, is a living document. We will honor the obligations it conveys.[7]

That is where we are. With large Vietnamese forces in Kampuchea, just across the shallow Mekong from Thailand and dominating Laos as well; with the Soviet Navy based in the installations we built in Cam Ranh Bay, the Soviet Air Force based in the airfields around Da Nang, and a major port in Kampuchea being enlarged for Soviet strategic purposes – all just across the South China Sea from the US bases in Subic Bay and Clark Field – Southeast Asia is not likely soon to disappear from the national security agenda of the United States government. I doubt, however, that there is a wide awareness in the United States of how tightly drawn the confrontation is along the Mekong and across the South China Sea. Nor do I believe there is a wide awareness of the commitments reaffirmed in the region by President Carter and President Reagan. But, for the present, my point is this: We cannot understand what we have experienced in Asia over the past two generations, nor can we formulate and sustain a workable policy in Asia, until we as a nation come to a widespread understanding of the strategic importance of Southeast Asia to our own security and to the security of the other powers concerned.

I shall begin, therefore, by trying to evoke the character of the strategic interests at work in Southeast Asia; point out the linkages of Vietnam to the rest of the region; outline the strategic evolution of Southeast Asia since 1940; and, finally, reflect on the implications of the story for US policy, past and future.

THE STRATEGIC INTERESTS OF THE POWERS

At some risk of oversimplification, I shall now try to define the major strategic interests of each of the principal powers concerned with Southeast Asia.

Japan. The Japanese have three abiding interests in Southeast Asia: First, a straightforward security interest that Southeast Asia (and thus the South China Sea) not be controlled by a potentially hostile power, with all that would imply for the sea approaches to the Japanese islands. Second, trading access to the countries of Southeast Asia that have been and remain major sources of raw materials and major markets for Japanese exports, markets notably expanding in recent decades. Third, an interest that the Straits of Malacca remain reliably open for Japanese trade with the rest of the world, an interest greatly heightened by the remarkable emergence of Japan as a global trading nation and its heavy reliance on an unobstructed flow of Middle East oil.

Japan sought to achieve these objectives by creating the Greater East Asia Co-Prosperity Sphere in 1940-45. When that effort failed, it fell back on reliance on the United States (and, to a degree, its own diplomacy and defense forces) to assure these vital interests.

China. China has an enduring interest that Southeast Asia not be dominated by a potentially hostile major power. Such dominance would threaten it both over land and via the South China Sea, where Vietnamese bases could bring pressure against important coastal cities. China has pursued these interests since 1949 by contesting vigorously Soviet efforts to dominate Southeast Asian communist parties, notably the Vietnamese; by leading the 1964-65 effort to collapse noncommunist resistance in Southeast Asia, in association with Hanoi and Sukarno and Aidit in Indonesia; and, after the Cultural Revolution, by establishing relations with the United States and by contesting independently what the Chinese regard as Soviet efforts to encircle and isolate China.

USSR. Russia has had a continuing interest that Vladivostok remain open as a trading port and a naval base. And, since the trans-Siberian railway went through in the 1890s, that nation has been a recurrent contestant for power in Northeast Asia, notably vis-à-vis Japan and China. In the post-1949 period the Soviet Union moved out from this regional role to broader vistas of Asian and global power. Its contest for power developed two new dimensions: the struggle with the Chinese communists, which was initially confined to contention for leadership of Asian (and other) communist parties but in early 1958 became a cold war between the two countries; and the thrust, based on the radically expanded Soviet Navy, to develop a string of alliances from Southeast Asia through the Indian Ocean to the Arabian Peninsula and East Africa. (I shall have more to say later about this policy, which can be formally dated from June 1969.) The Soviet air and naval bases in Indochina are, evidently, fundamental to this strategy both to neutralize the US bases at Clark Field and Subic Bay, which have hitherto dominated the South China Sea, and to guarantee Soviet access to the Indian Ocean through the Malacca Straits.

India. Aside from an Indian Ocean open freely to commerce and not dominated by a single potentially hostile power, India's concern with Southeast Asia is that the countries of the region – Burma, above all – remain indepenent. It is an interest that parallels, for example, India's concern for an independent Afghanistan – a concern only recently articulated by Mrs. Gandhi.

India's interest in Southeast Asia is rarely discussed in public by its political leaders. Nevertheless, the fundamental strands of Indian policy toward the region have been consistent and deeply rooted in memories of the Japanese occupation of Burma and the possibility of a recurrence of danger on India's northeast frontier.[8] For this reason India supported Burma and Malaya against communist guerrilla movements in the 1950s.

Australia. The abiding interests of Australia in Southeast Asia are dual: that its sea routes to the United States, Europe, and Japan (now its most important trading partner) remain open; and that Southeast Asia – above all, Indonesia – remain independent of any major power and not hostile. The Australians are not likely to forget what a close call it was in 1942 when they were saved from Japanese invasion by the American victories in the Coral Sea and at Guadalcanal. And, unlike most Americans, they remember how close to a communist takeover Southeast Asia was, including, especially, Indonesia, in July 1965 when Johnson made his decision to introduce large US forces into Vietnam[9].

In the changing circumstances since 1965, Australian foreign and military policy has continued steadily to support the independence of Southeast Asia.

The United States. US policy in Asia began, of course, with a simple concern for the maintenance of trading access in the face of special interests developed by Western powers operating in the region. From, say, the ambiguities of the Open Door notes of 1900 and Theodore Roosevelt's tilt toward the Russians in 1905 at Portsmouth in the wake of the Russo-Japanese War, a strategic dimension to US policy emerged parallel to that which emerged during the First World War in Europe, namely, a US interest that a balance of power be maintained in Asia and that no single power dominate the region. A power with hegemony in Asia would command the resources to expel US naval power in the Pacific back to Hawaii at least, just as a hegemonic power in Europe could dominate the Atlantic, as German submarines twice came close to demonstrating. The United States has acted systematically on that principle for some 80 years when the balance of power in Asia has seemed under real and present danger. At various times, that instinctive policy has brought us into confrontation in Asia with Japan, China, Russia or their surrogates; and, at various times, it has brought us into association with Russia, China, and Japan.

As is evident from this brief review, Southeast Asia is a critical element in the balance of power in Asia because of its relation to sea routes and the exercise of sea and air power, because of its resources, and because of its location with respect to China, India, and Japan. For the United States, Southeast Asia has a quite special meaning as an area of forward defense of the Pacific – a relationship vividly demonstrated after the loss of the Philippines to Japan in 1942. But for victory in the Battle of Midway, we might, at best, have held Hawaii.

In addition, the United States shares to a significant degree the specific interests in Southeast Asia of its allies and others whose security would be threatened by the hegemony of a single power in Asia; that is, at the moment we share to a significant degree the interests of Japan, China, India, and Australia, as outlined earlier. It is, essentially, a negative interest satisfied, as all the Presidents from Roosevelt to Reagan have stated, by an independent, neutral Southeast Asia.

Southeast Asia. Excluding the three states of Indochina, Southeast Asia contains some 300 million people, a population approximating that of Latin America or Africa. They are diverse in their racial origins, historical experiences, degrees of modernization, and forms of government. History has also given them territorial and other deeply rooted conflicts to overcome. What they share is a desire to modernize their societies in their own way, true to their own cultures, traditions, and ambitions; and to be left in peace and independence by all the external powers. They do not wish to be run from Tokyo or Washington, New Delhi or Beijing, Moscow or Hanoi. They also shared an astonishing economic and social momentum in the 1960s and 1970s, including an annual per capita growth rate in real income averaging about four percent and a manufacturing growth rate of about 10 percent, as well as high rates of increase in foreign trade. They export about 83 percent of the world's natural rubber, 80 percent of its copra, palm, and coconut oil, 73 percent of its tin, and a wide range of other agricultural products and raw materials. Their literacy rates, which ranged from 39 percent to 72 percent in 1960, now range from 60 percent to 84 percent.

Out of their several and collective experiences as objects of the strategic interests of others, strongly encouraged by Lyndon Johnson (who made Asian regionalism a major, consistent theme of his policy), and conscious that the US role in Asia was likely to diminish with the passage of time, the five Southeast Asian countries beyond Indochina – Thailand, Malaysia, Singapore, Indonesia, and the Philippines – created the Association of Southeast Asian Nations (ASEAN) in 1967. It is an organization committed to economic and technical cooperation, to the peaceful settlement of its inner disputes, and, above all, to the pursuit of "stability and security from external interference in any form or manifestation."[10]

ASEAN moved forward slowly, building up the habit of economic cooperation and political consultation.

When the communists took over Vietnam in April 1975, ASEAN, alarmed by the turn of events, moved forward rather than backward. At a historic, carefully prepared session of the chiefs of government at Bali in Feburary 1976, they strongly reaffirmed a 1971 declaration calling for a Zone of Peace, Freedom, and Neutrality in Southeast Asia. And they have subsequently sought widened international support for this objective. Specifically, they have led the international effort to achieve the withdrawal of Vietnamese troops from Kampuchea and have fostered the negotiated establishment of a new national coalition of Kampuchean leaders committed to the authentic independence of their country. Although the countries of ASEAN command neither individually nor collectively the military power to deter or defeat a Vietnamese thrust into Thailand or to assure control over the critical sea lanes that surround them and link them to each other, the sturdy unity that they have managed to maintain for 15 years makes ASEAN an element to be reckoned with in the Asian equation of diplomacy.[11]

To sum up this review of various strategic perspectives on Southeast Asia, one can assert two propositions:

•The legitimate interests of all the powers concerned with the region would be satisfied by a neutral Southeast Asia left to develop in independence, with its sea lanes and strategic straits open by international consensus.

•The fundamental character of the various interests at stake in the region decrees that the effort of any one power to achieve dominance in the region will confront serious and determined opposition from multiple directions.

VIETNAM AND SOUTHEAST ASIA

Vietnam has tended to be discussed in isolation by Americans. Yet none of the nine Presidents caught up in Southeast Asia thought in such terms, not even

Nixon, who was the most reticent about articulating the importance of the region as a whole and the US interest in its fate.

Rather than taking Vietnam's strategic importance for granted as part of Southeast Asia, it is worth briefly specifying both its intrinsic importance and the nature of its linkages to the rest of the region.

A glance at a map of Southeast Asia suggests the various strategic roles of Vietnam.

First, its geography places it on the Chinese frontier; its ports and air bases make it of strategic importance with respect to both south China and the international sea lanes of the South China Sea. Thus, the Soviet naval and air bases in Cam Rahn Bay and Danang are a very serious matter, indeed, for China, Japan, the United States, every country in noncommunist Southeast Asia, and every country with an interest in the independence of Southeast Asia.

Second, easy overland access to Laos and Cambodia from Vietnam makes it likely that those in power in all of Vietnam would quickly gain control of all of Indochina. And that likelihood is increased by the extremely difficult logistical problems that an outside power would face (for example, the United States or China) in bringing its forces to bear in defense of Laos or Cambodia against an overland thrust from Vietnam. Further, control of Cambodia by an outside power would substantially increase the capacity of that power to bring air and naval forces to bear across the air and sea lanes of the South China Sea. For example, the destruction of the British battleship *Prince of Wales* and the battle cruiser *Repulse*, critical for the defense of Singapore, was accomplished by Japanese bombers in December 1941 based on a hastily constructed airfield in Cambodia.

Third, and most important for American policy in the 1950s and 1960s, a power emplaced in Vietnam, Laos, and Cambodia would confront Thailand across the long line of the shallow Mekong. The frontier is not only long and virtually indefensible against a massive attack by well-armed conventional forces, but the Mekong is also a long way from the Thai ports. As I have explained at length elsewhere, this is why John Kennedy in 1961 made the decision to defend Thailand and the rest of Southeast Asia by seeking via diplomacy the neutralization of Laos and by fighting the battle for Southeast Asia in Vietnam.[12]

Thailand is, ultimately, critical to Southeast Asia because of its geographical relation to Burma, on the one hand, and to Malaysia and Singapore, on the other. If a single major power were to control all of Indochina and Thailand, the vital interests of India, Japan, the United States, Indonesia, and Australia – specifically, Burma and the land route to the Indian subcontinent, control over the South China Sea, and control over the Straits of Malacca – would be in real and present danger. That is why Carter and Reagan each reaffirmed the applicability of our treaty commitments to Thailand and why ASEAN's major political thrust, overwhelmingly backed by North and South in the United Nations, is to effect the withdrawal of Vietnamese forces from Kampuchea and the line of the Mekong and to create an authentically independent Kampuchean government.

FOUR EFFORTS AT HEGEMONY

As Franklin Roosevelt suggested to the Japanese Ambassador in July 1941, a neutral Southeast Asia (of the kind ASEAN now proclaims) would satisfy the legitimate interests of all the powers, but Roosevelt could not accept Japanese control over the region. Roosevelt's policy has, in effect, been the policy of all his successors. And the fact is that for more than 40 years a succession of powers has sought hegemony in the region and met serious resistance. This sequence of efforts is reflected in the analysis thus far presented, but it may be useful to briefly specify when and the context in which each occurred.

First, of course, was the Japanese thrust of 1940-45. Its frustration required a homeric and bloody effort by the United States, Australia, New Zealand, Great Britain, China, and India.

Second came the systematic communist efforts to exploit by guerrilla warfare the postwar dishevelment of the region and the confusions and conflicts of the transition from colonialism to independence. Stalin organized this campaign impelled by (to him) the surprising likelihood that the communists would emerge victorious from the post-1945 civil war in China and by Truman's counterattack of Soviet aggression in Europe. The Truman Doctrine and Marshall Plan of 1947 clearly set a limit to the ample European empire Stalin acquired in the wake of the Second World War.

But with Mao evidently on his way to control over China in 1947, ambitious new communist objectives in Asia were enunciated by Zhdanov at the founding meeting of the Cominform in September. Open guerrilla warfare began in Indochina as early as Novmber 1946, in Burma in April 1948, in Malaya in June of that year, and in Indonesia and the Philippines in the autumn. The Indian and Japanese communist parties, with less scope for guerrilla action, nevertheless sharply increased their militancy in 1948. As final victory was won in China in November 1949, Mao's politico-military strategy was openly commended by the Cominform to the communist parties in those areas where guerrilla operations were under way. Stalin and Mao met early in 1950 and confirmed the ambitious Asian strategy, planning its climax in the form of the North Korean invasion of South Korea, which took place at the end of June 1950.

The American and UN response to the invasion of South Korea, the landings at Inchon, the March to the Yalu, the Chinese communist entrance into the war, and the successful UN defense against the massive Chinese assault of April-May 1951 at the 38th parallel brought this phase of military and quasi-military communist effort throughout Asia to a gradual end. Neither Moscow nor Beijing was willing to undertake all-out war or even accept the cost of a continued Korean offensive. And elsewhere the bright communist hopes of

1946-47 had dimmed. Nowhere in Asia was Mao's success repeated. Indonesia, Burma, and the Philippines largely overcame their guerrillas. At great cost to Britain, the Malayan guerrillas were contained and driven back. Only in Indochina, where French colonialism offered a seedbed as fruitful as postwar China, was there real communist momentum. The settlement at Geneva in 1954 permitted an interval of four years of relative quiet in Indochina.

Although there were latent tensions between Moscow and Beijing during this phase and some contest over control and influence of the various Asian communist parties, by and large the USSR and PRC conducted this second effort to achieve hegemony in Asia in concert.

The third effort emerged at a meeting in November 1957 in Moscow in the wake of the Soviet launching of Sputnik in October. The chiefs of all the communist governments assembled. They agreed the time was propitious for a concerted effort to expand Soviet power. As Mao said in Moscow:

> It is my opinion that the international situation has now reached a new turning point. There are two winds in the world today, the East wind and the West wind. There is a Chinese saying, 'Either the East wind prevails over the West wind or the West wind prevails over the East wind.' It is characteristic of the situation today, I believe, that the East wind is prevailing over the West wind. That is to say, the forces of socialism are overwhelmingly superior to the forces of imperialism . . . . The superiority of the anti-imperialist forces over the imperialist forces . . . has expressed itself in even more concentrated form and reached unprecedented heights with the Soviet Union's launching of the artificial satellites . . . . That is why we say that this is a new turning point in the international situation.[13]

Many enterprises followed from this assessment of "the new turning point": from Berlin to the Congo to the Caribbean. For our purposes, the most important was Soviet and Chinese agreement to permit Ho Chi Minh, under pressure from the communists in South Vietnam, to relaunch Hanoi's effort to take over Laos and South Vietnam by guerrilla warfare after four years of relative passivity.

The spirit at Moscow was relatively harmonious between Russia and China; but by early 1958 the split, long latent, became acute over the question of the degree of control Moscow would exercise over the nuclear weapons it promised to transfer to China.[14] From that time forward the competition for influence in Hanoi between Moscow and Beijing, long a major issue, became intense.

To 1965, by and large the Chinese influence was predominant. Hanoi's enterprise, notably its introduction of regular North Vietnamese units into South Vietnam in 1964, was orchestrated by the Chinese with the Indonesian confrontation with Malaysia. Sukarno left the United Nations and openly joined with the Chinese, North Vietnamese, Cambodians, and North Koreans in a new grouping of forces as Hanoi's efforts in South Vietnam moved forward toward apparent success. On 1 January 1965, Chinese Foreign Minister Chen Yi proclaimed, "Thailand is next." No leader in Asia, communist or noncommunist, doubted the potential reality of the domino theory in July 1965 when Johnson made his decision to introduce substantial US forces into the region. (This was the ominous setting Ambassador Beale evoked in his explanation of why Australia joined in the American effort [see note 9].)

The US move was followed by the joint communist effort, acquiesced in by Sukarno, to assassinate the Indonesian Chiefs of Staff and set up a communist government. It failed. And, for related but obscure reasons, Mao's Cultural Revolution began in China a few weeks later. The Russians took over the major role in Hanoi of arms supplier and economic supporter, a position they still occupy.

The fourth and current thrust for hegemony in Southeast Asia, to which we have already referred, was authored by Brezhnev. From the low point of their fortunes in 1965, the South Vietnamese moved forward slowly but consistently over the next two years in military, political, and economic terms. Then, in the face of their waning position, the North Vietnamese and the Viet Cong assembled their accumulated capital and threw it into a maximum effort at Tet 1968. The result was a major military and political victory for the South Vietnamese, but a concurrent major political victory for Hanoi in American public opinion.[15] With Nixon's decision for Vietnamization, Moscow proceeded to design and announce a new ambitious long-run policy based on a more confident position in Vietnam.

That policy was explained by Brezhnev to a group of communist leaders on 7 June 1969.[16] His plan was based explicitly on the "vacuum" left by the British withdrawal east of Suez, the expected US retraction in Asia reflected in Nixon's Guam Doctrine, and alleged Chinese efforts to expand into the resulting void. Implicitly, it drew its strength from the greatly expanded capabilities of the Soviet Navy generated during the 1960s and planned for the future. It also constituted a response to Nixon's interest in an opening to China.

The plan called for a new Collective Security System for Asia entailing a series of pacts with countries in Asia, the Middle East, and Africa, including Soviet bases in the periphery from the South China Sea to the western coasts of the Indian Ocean and the Persian Gulf. Over the next decade this policy, systematically pursued, included as major moves the setting up of Soviet bases in Indochina and support for the Vietnamese invasion of Kampuchea; the 1971 Soviet pact with India; the creation of new Soviet ties to Yemen and Ethiopia; and, indeed, the Soviet occupation of Afghanistan. The policy has been reflected further in the number of Soviet operational ship visits in the Indian Ocean. They rose from one in 1968 to an average of 120 a year from 1974 to 1976.[17]

The outcome of the Soviet-led Collective Security System for Asia, in the great arc from Vladivostok to Aden and Djibouti, is, evidently, still to be determined.

SOME REFLECTIONS

Before considering the future prospects of the region and US policy toward it, we might reflect a bit on the meaning of the analysis I have presented.

Perhaps the first thing to be said is that while Americans may still debate the importance of Southeast Asia to the balance of power in Asia as a whole, there is little ambiguity about the matter among the governments and peoples of Asia, including the Soviet Union.

As for us Americans, some may draw from the account I have sketched the simple conclusion that all nine of our Presidents since 1940 have been wrong – that is, that the United States has no serious legitimate interests in preventing the control of Southeast Asia by a major, potentially hostile power. In that case, they should advocate the abrogation of the network of commitments we have in the region and urge us to organize urgently to face all the profound military, diplomatic, and economic consequences that would flow from that decision.

If we assume that I have described more or less accurately the interests of all parties at stake in Southeast Asia, the sequence of events since 1940, and where the region now stands, there are a few reasonably objective observations to be made that provide perspective on our travail over Vietnam.

First, the nature of US interest in Southeast Asia is quite complex – more so in Vietnam itself; and even when US interests have been less complex, we have had difficulty acting on them in a forehanded way. When the chips were down in 1917 – with the German declaration of unrestricted submarine warfare in the Atlantic and the Zimmerman note promising the return of Texas to Mexico by a victorious Germany – it was not difficult for Wilson to gain congressional support for a declaration of war in a hitherto deeply divided country, and only five months after he was reelected on the slogans "He kept us out of war" and "Too proud to fight." But such critical circumstances were required to bring the country to act on the basis of a wide consensus. Similarly, it required Pearl Harbor to bring the United States into the Second World War after a long period dominated by an isolationism FDR couldn't break. And it took a straightforward invasion of South Korea to evoke a military response there. What Truman and Eisenhower, Kennedy and Johnson were trying to prevent in Southeast Asia was a circumstance so stark and dangerous that once again, late in the day, the American people would finally perceive that vital interests were in jeopardy and be plunged into major war.

Behind their efforts was a consciousness that there has been, historically, no stable consensus in our country on the nature of our vital interests in the world. We have oscillated between isolationism, indifference, wishful thinking, and complacency, on the one hand, and, on the other, the panic-stricken retrieval of situations already advanced in dangerous deterioration. We have operated systematically on the principle enunciated by Dr. Samuel Johnson: "Depend upon it, Sir, when a man knows he is to be hanged in a fortnight, it concentrates his mind wonderfully." Right or wrong, John Kennedy and Lyndon Johnson did not doubt that the American people and the Congress would react to support the use of force if communist forces were actually engulfing all of Southeast Asia; but they judged a typical, late, convulsive American reaction – a fortnight from the gallows – too dangerous in a nuclear age.[18]

Second, and quite specifically, they fought in Vietnam to prevent the situation we now confront and what may (but may not) follow from it, that is, large Vietnamese forces on the line of the Mekong backed by a major hostile power. Historians, as well as American citizens, will no doubt assess their judgment on this matter in different ways. What I am asserting here as a matter of fact is that US policy in the 1960s cannot be understood without grasping this dimension in the perspectives of Kennedy and Johnson.

A third objective observation is that within the American foreign policy establishment of the 1960s, including some in the Executive Branch, there was a kind of geological fault line between those who regarded the balance of power in Southeast Asia as important for the United States in itself and those who, holding what I have called an Atlanticist view, regarded the maintenance of our commitments there as significant only for the credibility of our commitments elsewhere – for example, in Europe and the Middle East.[19] The hypothesis of Gelb and Betts, stated at the beginning of this article, reflects the latter view. In the early 1970s, having gathered strength for some time, a version of that view became widespread, namely that the costs of holding the US position in Southeast Asia were excessive, even though our ground forces were withdrawn by 1972 and our air and naval forces in 1973. The view was not always expressed in the colorful terms quoted earlier from Galbraith and Eugene McCarthy, but it was there.

From the perspective of the 1980s, I would only observe that the view that Southeast Asia doesn't much matter may have diminished somewhat with the emergence of ASEAN and the remarkable expansion in the economies of its members, including sophisticated trade and financial relations with the United States. They may not have yet achieved the respectability of Japan in the eyes of Atlanticists, but they are clearly beyond the water buffalo state and on their way.

A fourth observation arises from the fixation in the quarter century after 1949 with China as the ultimate threat to Southeast Asia. I suspect, but cannot prove, that one element in the extraordinary performance of the American Congress toward Vietnam in the period 1973-75 may have been a belief that with Nixon's new opening to China the strategic threat to Southeast Asia had been once and for all lifted and, therefore, the aid promised by Nixon to Thieu could be ruthlessly reduced. The possibility of the Soviet Union replacing China as a threat to the region, not difficult to deduce from Brezhnev's collective security plan of 1969, appears not to have been envisaged by the Congress – and, perhaps, not by many in the Executive Branch.

So much for the complexities of interpreting the nature and extent of the countries of Southeast Asia.

Now, what about the future?

From one perspective, the Soviet position in the region – and Brezhnev's 1969 plan as a whole – does not, at the moment, appear on the verge of success. The movements of Soviet naval and air forces around the region constitute significant psychological pressure and political presence; but, for the time being, one would not expect a decisive Soviet thrust to dominate the region like that of Japan in 1941 and 1942. The Soviet Union confronts a considerable array of problems that render this an apparently unpropitious time for great adventures: the costly stalemate in Afghanistan; India's taking its distance from Moscow on Afghanistan, despite the 1971 treaty; the state of Poland and all its multiple implications for the Soviet security stucture; deep and degenerating problems within the Soviet economy. Similarly, the presence of Vietnamese forces on the Thai frontier are a source of great anxiety, indeed, to all the noncommunist governments of the region and China; but Hanoi appears to have quite enough trouble in South Vietnam, in Kampuchea itself, and in trying to achieve an economic revival at home, without plunging into a wider Southeast Asian war. Besides, it has been reminded forcefully that Chinese forces are on its northern frontier.

There are, no doubt, those who will say: Some but not all the dominoes have fallen; life goes on in most of Southeast Asia; what is there to worry about? But two facts should be remembered. First, the communists, unlike ourselves, are patient, persevering, and stubborn in pursuing their long-run strategies; and, second, there is no power capable of preventing the Soviet Union from dominating Southeast Asia – indeed, all of Asia – except the United States. Asia would promptly become a quite different place if the United States closed down Clark Field and Subic Bay, pulled the Pacific Fleet back to Hawaii, and announced that the guarantees to Thailand were no longer operative.

In short, despite the debacle of 1975, the possibility of an independent, neutral Southeast Asia – so important for so many, including the 300 million men, women, and children who live there – has not been lost. But that prospect requires a deep and steady understanding in the United States of the stakes involved – an understanding notably lacking in our nation in the intense domestic debate of the period 1965-75 and in the subsequent literature on the subject.

As a coda to this analysis, I would only add that beyond our time, in the next century, the peace of Asia is likely to depend on a solemn agreement between India and China that Southeast Asia should be supported by both in its desire for independence, thus creating a buffer that might avoid the two countries' repeating in Asia the tragedy of France and Germany in Europe. But that is a subject for quite another article.

NOTES

1. Leslie H. Gelb with Richard K. Betts, *The Irony of Vietnam: The System Worked* (Washington: Brookings, 1979), p. 25.
2. George C. Herring, *America's Longest War: The United States and Vietnam, 1950-1975* (New York: John Wiley, 1979), pp. 10-12. The heart of this passage is the following:

    The loss of an area so large and populous would tip the balance of power against the United States. Recent Communist triumphs had already aroused nervousness in Europe, and another major victory might tempt the Europeans to reach an accommodation with the Soviet Union.

The economic consequences could be equally profound. The United States and its European allies would be denied access to important markets. Southeast Asia was the world's largest producer of natural rubber and was an important source of oil, tin, tungsten, and other strategic commodities. Should control of these vital raw materials suddenly change hands, the Soviet bloc would be enormously strengthened at the expense of the West.

American policymakers also feared that the loss of Southeast Asia would irreparably damage the nation's strategic position in the Far East. Control of the offshore island chain extending from Japan to the Philippines, America's first line of defense in the Pacific, would be endangered. Air and sea routes between Australia and the Middle East and the United States and India could be cut, severely hampering military operations in the event of war. Japan, India, and Australia, those nations where the West retained predominant influence, would be cut off from each other and left vulnerable. The impact on Japan, America's major Far Eastern ally, could be disastrous. Denied access to the raw materials, rice, and markets upon which their economy depended, the Japanese might see no choice but to come to terms with the enemy.

American officials agreed that Indochina, and especially Vietnam, was the key to the defense of Southeast Asia.

3. Compiled by William G. Efros, *Quotations Vietnam: 1945-1970* (New York: Random House, 1970), p. 51.

4. *New York Times Book Review*, 4 August 1968, p. 24.

5. *The Memoirs of Cordell Hull* (New York: Macmillan, 1948), II, 1013-14.

6. In the Carter Administration those reaffirmations were made in May 1978 in Bangkok by Vice President Mondale; in Washington in February 1979 by President Carter; in July 1979 in Bali by Secretary Vance; and in June 1980 in Washington by Secretary Muskie.

7. The reference to the "bilateral clarification" is to the Rusk-Thanat communiqué of 6 March 1962, which stated that the United States's obligation in the event of aggression against Thailand "... does not depend on the prior agreement of all other Parties" to the Manila Pact.

8. India's policy toward Southeast Asia is traced to 1960 in Ton That Thien, *India and Southeast Asia, 1947-1960* (Geneva: Librarie Droz, 1963). India's concern was brought home starkly to me when I was sent to India and Pakistan by Kennedy and Rusk, 1-7 April 1963, to assess the likelihood of a settlement of the Kashmir question then under negotiation. At the insistence of the US Ambassador to India (J. K. Galbraith), I spent several hours at his residence with the Indian Army Chief of Staff General Chaudhuri. He underlined the critical importance to India and Pakistan of the continued independence of Burma, which depended, in turn, on the independence of Thailand. He described Burma as "India's Ardennes." Therefore, he wished me to know and to report in Washington India's concern for the continued independence of Laos and South Vietnam, which were buffers for Thailand and Burma. I later asked Nehru if this was a correct interpretation of India's views of its interests. He affirmed that it was. In Dacca I reported this view to Ayub who said that it was, of course, a view common to the military of both countries. Ayub went on to say it was one major reason for the urgency of settling the Kashmir issue. Such a settlement would permit joint staff talks and planning with respect to the subcontinent's northeast frontier, which he said would not be difficult since the officers on both sides had been trained together and shared a strategic view.

9. It is, I believe, worth pondering this passage from the memoir of Howard Beale, Australian Ambassador to Washington in the 1960s (*This Inch of Time* [Melbourne: Melbourne Univ. Press, 1977], pp. 168-69). Beale explains why Australia in 1965 joined in the effort to save South Vietnam:

It is now [1977] said that there is no foreseeable threat to the security of Australia within the next fifteen years. We have made friends with China; Russia and China are now rivals and not allies; the triumphant North Vietnamese – with an army which is the third largest, best equipped and most experienced military machine in the world and with an unrivalled experience in infiltration and subversion – will, we are told, stop within their own borders, and Thailand, Malaysia, Singapore and Indonesia can relax now that the imperialistic Americans have been defeated.

Perhaps one may be pardoned for being a little sceptical about some of this scenario; in any case the scene was not at all like that when Australia gave assistance [in 1965]. What seemed much more likely at the time was that, had there been no intervention, South Vietnam would have collapsed and so would Laos and Cambodia (as they have now done), and the whole of

Indo-China would have become communist; and, later still, Thailand, Malaysia and Singapore would also have been 'liberated.' There was no reason to suppose that communists would be content to stop in Indo-China for that was not what they had proclaimed or done elsewhere. This is what Lee Kuan Yew meant when he said, 'We may all go through the mincing machine.'

The most important problem for Australia was what might happen to Indonesia, 'the real prize' to quote George Ball . . . . Sukarno was already trying to perform a precarious balancing trick between the army and the P.K.I., and it seemed likely that, surrounded by regimes under communist control or influence, and with the United States no longer near at hand, the powerful P.K.I. would have prevailed and Indonesia would have become a communist state.

Success for the P.K.I. would have meant that Australia would have had as her nearest neighbour a communist regime of one hundred and twenty-five million people with (at that time) an uncertain border between Papua and West Irian, and the likelihood of endless disputes about boundaries, and about sea lanes and routes, overflight rights, and oil and mineral rights on or near the continental shelf in the Indonesia archipelago and the Timor Sea. Such a regime in Djakarta could have made Australia's life very uncomfortable indeed, with the strong possibility that, sooner or later, upon some issue or other, we would have had either to give way or fight.

Not all of this might have happened (although some of it has), but Australia went into Vietnam with the Americans so that it might be less likely to happen.

10. See Association of Southeast Asian Nations, *10 Years ASEAN*, compiled and edited by the ASEAN secretariat under the direction of Secretary-General Umarjadi Njotowijono, Djakarta, 1978, p. 14. The quotation is from the preamble to the founding Bangkok Declaration, signed 7 August 1967.

11. The confidence and strength built up in ASEAN between 1967 and 1975 by its continued high rate of economic and social progress, combined with the increased solidarity of the organization, contributed to an important result expressed in 1981 by the Malaysian Foreign Minister. (Keynote address by H. E. Tan Sri M. Ghazali Shafie, "ASEAN: Contributor to Stability and Development," at the conference on "ASEAN: Today and Tomorrow," Fletcher School of Law and Diplomacy, Boston, 11 November 1981, p. 15.)

In 1975 North Vietnamese tanks rolled past Da Nang, Cam Ranh Bay and Tan Son Nhut into Saigon. The United States withdrew their last soldiers from Vietnam, and the worst of ASEAN's fears, which underscored the Bangkok Declaration of 1967, came to pass. But ASEAN by then had seven solid years of living in neighbourly cooperation. Call it foresight, or what you will, the fact remains that with ASEAN solidarity there were no falling dominoes in Southeast Asia following the fall of Saigon to the Communists and the United States withdrawal from Southeast Asia.

12. W. W. Rostow, *The Diffusion of Power* (New York: Macmillan, 1972), pp. 265-72.

13. Quoted in John Gittings, *Survey of the Sino-Soviet Dispute, 1963-1967* (London: Oxford Univ. Press, 1968), p. 82.

14. For analysis of this critical turning point in modern history, see my *Diffusion of Power*, pp. 29-35.

15. For a detailed analysis of this episode, see my *Diffusion of Power*, pp. 438-503.

16. Brezhnev's speech and its strategic implications were well reported in a dispatch from Moscow in *The New York Times*, 13 June 1969, pp. 1, 5.

17. Richard B. Remnek, "Soviet Policy in the Horn of Africa: The Decision to Intervene," in Robert H. Donaldson, ed., *The Soviet Union in the Third World: Successes and Failures* (Boulder, Colo.: Westview Press, 1981), p. 130.

18. Here (from *Diffusion of Power*, p. 270) is Kennedy's articulation of his position late in 1961:

Before deciding American power and influence had to be used to save Southeast Asia, Kennedy asked himself, and put sharply to others, the question: What would happen if we let Southeast Asia go? Kennedy's working style was to probe and question a great many people while keeping his own counsel and making the specific decisions the day required. Only this one time do I recall his articulating the ultimate reasoning behind the positions at which he arrived. It was after the Taylor mission, shortly before I left the White House for the State Department.

He began with domestic political life. He said if we walked away from Southeast Asia, the communist takeover would produce a debate in the United States more acute than that over the loss of China. Unlike Truman with China or Eisenhower in 1954, he would be violating a treaty commitment to the area. The upshot would be a rise and convergence of left- and right-wing isolationism that would affect commitments in Europe as well as in Asia. Loss of confidence in the United States would be worldwide. Under these circumstances, Khrushchev and Mao could not refrain from acting to exploit the apparent shift in the balance of power. If Burma fell, Chinese power would be on the Indian frontier: the stability of all of Asia, not merely Southeast Asia, was involved. When the communist leaders had moved – after they were committed – the United States would then react. We would come plunging back to retrieve the situation. And a much more dangerous crisis would result, quite possibly a nuclear crisis.

Johnson stated a similar proposition in an address at San Antonio on 29 September 1967 (*Public Papers* [Washington: GPO, 1968], p. 488):

I cannot tell you tonight as your President – with certainty – that a Communist conquest of South Vietnam would be followed by a Communist conquest of Southeast Asia. But I do know there are North Vietnamese troops in Laos. I do know that there are North Vietnamese trained guerrillas tonight in northeast Thailand. I do know that there are Communist-supported guerrilla forces operating in Burma. And a Communist coup was barely averted in Indonesia, the fifth largest nation in the world.

So your American President cannot tell you – with certainty – that a Southeast Asia dominated by Communist power would bring a third world war much closer to terrible reality. One could hope that this would not be so.

But all that we have learned in this tragic century suggests to me that it would be so. As President of the United States, I am not prepared to gamble on the chance that it is not so.

And, retrospectively, in *The Vantage Point* (New York: Holt, Rinehart and Winston, 1971), pp. 152-53:

Knowing what I did of the policies and actions of Moscow and Peking, I was as sure as a man could be that if we did not live up to our commitment in Southeast Asia and elsewhere, they would move to exploit the disarray in the United States and in the alliances of the Free World. They might move independently or they might move together. But move they would – whether through nuclear blackmail, through subversion, with regular armed forces, or in some other manner. As nearly as one can be certain of anything, I knew they could not resist the opportunity to expand their control into the vacuum of power we would leave behind us.

Finally, as we faced the implications of what we had done as a nation, I was sure the United States would not then passively submit to the consequences. With Moscow and Peking and perhaps others moving forward, we would return to a world role to prevent their full takeover of Europe, Asia, and the Middle East – *after* they had committed themselves.

I was too young at the time to be aware of the change in American mood and policy between the election of Woodrow Wilson in November 1916 ('He kept us out of war') and our reaction to unrestricted German submarine warfare in the Atlantic in April 1917. But I knew the story well. My generation had lived through the change from American isolationism to collective security in 1940-1941. I had watched firsthand in Congress as we swerved in 1946-1947 from the unilateral dismantling of our armed forces to President Truman's effort to protect Western Europe. I could never forget the withdrawal of our forces from South Korea and then our immediate reaction to the Communist aggression of June 1950.

As I looked ahead, I could see us repeating the same sharp reversal once again in Asia, or elsewhere – but this time in a nuclear world with all the dangers and possible horrors that go with it. Above all else, I did not want to lead this nation and the world into nuclear war or even the risk of such a war.

This was the private estimate that brought me to the hard decision of July 1965.

19. For an analysis of this difference in perspective, see, for example, *The Diffusion of Power*, pp. 492-97.

This article appeared in the March 1983 issue of *Parameters*.

16

American-Vietnamese Relations

by DOUGLAS PIKE

The term ''normalization'' is a slippery one when used in international relations and is best avoided if possible. The United States has ''normal'' relations with the Soviet Union, Israel, Canada, South Africa, and Japan – but consider the enormous variety within each of these sets of associations. In truth there is no such thing as a ''normal'' relationship in world affairs today.[1]

What is meant by the term, properly used, is establishment of an official government-to-government connection at some specific level, which can range from the lowly interest section to the fully staffed embassy. As used here, establishment of normal relations would mean that the United States and the Socialist Republic of Vietnam exchange embassies and engage in at least a minimum level of diplomatic intercourse of the kind common among nations throughout the world.

''Normalizing'' relations would not mean a new ambiance between the two, or that either has changed its opinion of the other. It does not *necessarily* mean that US economic assistance would be provided Vietnam or that Hanoi would open its POW files to us.

A word should perhaps be said here in defense of diplomatic relations in general. As a working principle it is, I believe, better for a country to have a formal relationship with another than not to have it (even if an enemy), just as it is more valuable to talk and listen (again even to one's enemy or potential enemy) than not to do so. The problem, in those cases in which there is no recognition, always is the initial act of establishment, the getting from here to there. Once accomplished, most would agree that national interest is then better served.

However, diplomatic recognition is almost always regarded as a political statement. It can be argued logically that diplomatic relations are merely facilitative, that recognition is neither a gesture of approval nor an endorsement of past behavior. Despite this flawless logic, the fact remains that diplomatic recognition is almost universally seen as conferring legitimacy, if not honor. In the case of Vietnam, probably few Americans would argue that we should never under any circumstances have diplomatic relations with the present Hanoi government. Such a position in fact is irrational, since it reflexively precludes serving American national interest in the emergence of

205

circumstances in which it would be in our interest to have an embassy in Hanoi. Many Americans, possibly even the majority, are opposed to formal relations (based on public opinion polls of the late 1970s), but probably most of these would not object if they were already in place.

Parenthetically, I would at the outset dismiss out of hand various moral, ethical, and philosophic reasons for diplomatic recognition of Vietnam, first because diplomatic intercourse follows only from perceived national interest (on both sides) and not on abstraction or sentiment, and second because the United States owes Vietnam nothing, has no sins to atone for, nor has incurred any debt or obligation either as a result of its earlier presence in Vietnam or its conduct during the Vietnam War.[2]

A cautionary note should be sounded early in this article concerning the anticipated benefits that would accrue from establishing a formal relationship with Hanoi. There has been for several years a tendency among advocates to surround the act with unwarranted assumptions. In discussing normalization they list hoped-for developments – diminution of Soviet influence in Indochina, more benign behavior by the People's Army of Vietnam, economic investment opportunities for American business – and imply that these will come about more or less automatically once the American ambassador arrives in Hanoi. Those who hold this idea should be disabused of it as strongly as possible. Diplomatic recognition is no panacea for the problems between the two countries. This is not necessarily an argument against recognition, only counsel that representation is one thing and problem-solving another.

The experiences of various noncommunist countries dealing diplomatically with Vietnam in the postwar years validates this assertion. These also suggest some of the limits the United States might expect if it were to establish relations. About 85 countries now have formal relations with Hanoi. Much of this diplomatic association is nominal. In many instances the ambassador accredited to a nearby country – Thailand or China – is also accredited to Vietnam, an extra duty requiring the envoy to make periodic trips to Hanoi and tending to hold intercourse to a minimum.[3]

The cutoff of foreign aid by most noncommunist countries after Vietnam's invasion of Kampuchea of course chilled Hanoi's relations with these countries. Six European countries are now providing aid and seem to have fairly good working relations, particularly Sweden and France.[4] The Japanese and Indian missions are active, but the associations do not appear to be particularly deep. For most nations Hanoi is considered primarily as a listening post. Diplomats posted in Hanoi find their surroundings extremely trying and often regard their assignment as an exile.[5] Those who have worked in Hanoi counsel every arrival to do two things: first, to guard against high expectations; second, to remember that they are dealing not with people but with a system. This can be difficult, for appearances can deceive. Surrounded by generally helpful individuals, it is easy to believe that to succeed one need only to get to the right people. But in this sense there are no "right people"; there is only the system. To enter Vietnam some commercial visitors must fill out 14 separate application forms and supply 16 photographs for nine different Vietnam governmental agencies. It is the system which determines whether anything will come of an association. The system throws up the barricades and provides the inertia, victimizing Vietnamese and foreigner alike. It is the system that in the end doles out success or failure, resolves problems or makes them worse. This is not to say that the system cannot be dealt with, but it does mean that the chance for progress is diminished and that progress comes only at glacial speed.

Finally, by way of scene-setting, it is well to recount a bit of history. Vietnam had the opportunity to establish diplomatic relations with the United States shortly after the end of the Vietnam War but threw the chance away in a gesture that in retrospect was pure leadership blunder. This missed opportunity is worth examining briefly for the insight it offers on possible future relations.

The Carter Administration, soon after taking office, dispatched the Woodcock Mission (named after its chairman, Leonard Woodcock) to Hanoi to explore official thinking there. Hanoi leaders took a hard-line approach; they spoke of American economic obligations, mentioned the figure $3.25 billion,[6] and even made use of the term "war reparation" in the Hanoi press. The Americans explained the US foreign aid process, how it required congressional authorization and involved domestic politics that are part of the democratic process. They suggested that embassies be exchanged first, and that the newly arrived Vietnamese ambassador in Washington then begin soliciting economic assistance by making representations at the Department of State and lobbying on Capitol Hill, since that is the way it is done. The Hanoi Politburo, however, stood by its "precondition" – aid before recognition. The Americans demurred, and the misson ended inconclusively. There the matter stood for the next year or so, marked by occasional meetings at the United Nations level and deputy-assistant-level talks in Paris.[7] But this was a dynamic period. During 1977-78 Vietnam-PRC relations deteriorated, finally to the point where Hanoi officials were sufficiently fearful of the rising China threat to drop the precondition on establishing relations with the United States. Also during this period, however, US-PRC relations were solidifying. It was the time of the "opening to China," and the Carter Administration increasingly became convinced that the matter was coming down to a choice between Vietnam and China – for the United States, no hard choice to make.[8] The United States took no action on the new signals and overtures out of Hanoi. Then, at Christmastime 1978, the Vietnamese invaded Kampuchea, killing entirely the idea of establishing relations.[9] That is where the matter stands today. The point to note here is that Vietnam at the end of the year 1978 was denied what almost certainly it could have had at the beginning – and would have had, but for the poor judgment of its Politburo leadership.

POSITIONS

To provide a framework for examining this question of US-Vietnamese relations, it is necessary to set forth the positions of the various actors in the drama – principally, of course, the United States and Vietnam, but secondarily others in the region and around the world with a vested interest in any change in the US-Vietnamese relationship.

Vietnam. The Vietnamese position on relations with the United States is not entirely clear at the moment, despite what many outsiders tend to believe. Some observers assert that Hanoi is nearly desperate for recognition, but that contention does not hold up under scrutiny.

The surest guide or most reliable analytical approach here is to try to look at the idea in Politburo terms. The two general national-interest goals which the leaders obviously seek to serve are national security and economic development. These have been badly pursued in recent years by the leadership but still represent basic intent. The Politburo will evaluate the prospect of normal relations with the United States in these terms, asking: will relations enhance our security (or at least not decrease it), and will relations contribute to the nation-building task?

The answers to these questions at the moment appear to be in the affirmative, but not enthusiastically so. Vietnamese leaders from time to time say publicly that they want establishment of diplomatic relations, and when asked point-blank by visiting journalists, of course, are obliged to sound forthcoming. Hanoi media treatment of the subject is infrequent and then usually diffident or so densely ideological as to forestall sure conclusions. Were these editorials and theoretical articles pointedly negative, we could infer something from them, but being what might be called morally affirmative, they tell us very little.

From an analysis of Vietnam's national interest needs – security and nation building – one can reasonably assume that the Politburo is of the opinion that, all other things being equal, relations with the United States would serve these two interests, if only modestly. On that basis we can conclude that a firm proposal from Washington that embassies be exchanged (through strictly government-to-government channels, of course) would be accepted by Hanoi.

We cannot, however, be entirely sure that the decision would be based on national-interest considerations. As with other governments, domestic influences are at work in Vietnam. The political system operating at the Politburo level in Hanoi, as in the Sinic political system from which it is derived, is rooted in factionalism. The decision-making process within this system is characterized by – some would say cursed by – factional infighting, what the Vietnamese call *bung-di* or "faction-bashing." In the struggle for power among factions of the ruling group, the most common weapons are doctrinal arguments and policy issues. Thus a Politburo debate on whether or not to recognize the United States would in part be a factional struggle, carried on independent of the merits of the issue. One faction might oppose it simply because another faction favored it. That being the case, no outsider (nor even most Vietnamese insiders) can ever be sure of the outcome of a policy proposal.

Other internal Vietnamese factors also would be at work in such a decision, the key ones being the party's determination to maintain ideological purity, the various ongoing programs aimed at solving Vietnam's many economic problems, and internal security threats or the counterrevolution. Part of Hanoi's evaluation would be whether US presence would affect these. Probably the leadership would conclude that the arrival of the American ambassador and his staff would: (a) slightly compromise the party's ideological purity; (b) carry at least some promise of contributing to the improvement of the Vietnamese economy; and (c) have negligible meaning in terms of internal security.

United States. The Reagan Administration's enunciated position as of this writing is that the question of diplomatic relations with Vietnam is simply being held in abeyance and that this is a pragmatic position, not one born of dogma or punitiveness. Establishing diplomatic relations is treated chiefly as a matter of timing, when the correct conditions obtain. One of the correct conditions, perhaps the only one, is withdrawal of Vietnamese army troops from Kampuchea. The implication is that if this does not happen, there will be no change in present policy. Actually this is not so much a policy as a holding operation, or one might say a non-policy. In the longer run the US choice will come down to three policy options: roll-back of communism, presumably by funding and backing the resistance in Vietnam; determined containment of Vietnamese influence, which might be called the China recommendation; or minimal ''normal'' relations. The present holding operation, however, has not yet run its course and could last another few years.

Within the US government there is a somewhat broader spread of policy opinion than the official Regan Administration position. The hardest line taken appears to be in the State Department, principally because recognition is seen as damaging US-ASEAN and US-PRC relations, and the softest on Capitol Hill, where a few senators and representatives forthrightly advocate US recognition. This issue within the congressional scene is complicated by cross-purpose interests involving the resolution of Vietnam War casualties. The Pentagon, perhaps somewhat unexpectedly, seems to fall between State and the Hill. The rationale employed by those favoring recognition within the Pentagon is that it would offer opportunities to ameliorate to some extent Soviet presence in Indochina. However, as far as can be determined, these differing opinions do not approach anything like an internal policy split.

On the broader American scene – with respect to public opinion throughout the United States – a similar range of outlook exists as in the government, that is, spirited difference of opinion with no real fire in it. A few years ago passions ran higher, but these seem now to have cooled. Then there was more organized political pressure within the American system – both pro and con pressure – to act on the idea of diplomatic relations with Vietnam. To some extent this division was along traditional liberal-conservative lines, although there were numerous crossovers – conservatives who wanted recognition as a means of inducing Hanoi to account for American MIAs of the Vietnam War, and liberals who opposed it because they wanted to punish Hanoi for its postwar aggression. For a period in the late 1970s, elements of the business community, spearheaded by the US Chamber of Commerce in Hong Kong, pressed for US recognition of Hanoi. However, that pressure group dried up with the breach of relations between Hanoi and China when most of these businessmen, who were in the export-import business, were told by Beijing to choose, and sensibly most of them chose China. Anti-war activists, once monolithically dedicated to embracing Hanoi, split down the middle after the war over the human rights issue in Vietnam (reeducation camps, new economic zones) and over causes of the holocaust that developed in Kampuchea. In the past couple of years or so we have seen the rise of a new pressure group in the United States, the emigré Vietnamese. These number about 600,000, and while most of them remain apolitical, they are becoming increasingly organized; and most of their organizations are opposed to US recognition.

In sum, American public opinion remains divided, with only a minority favoring US relations with Vietnam, the remainder indifferent or opposed. Without the saliency of view that would seem to dictate policy in Washington, a decision to recognize Hanoi probably would draw no particularly strong or sustained reaction from the country.

Other Nations. A consideration for the United States, and presumably also for Vietnam, in contemplating diplomatic recognition is the effect it would have (or not have) on respective allies and adversaries.

China's position, it is generally assumed in the United States, is to stand against US recognition, even though China itself has an embassy in Hanoi. As far as can be determined, the United States has never formally put the matter to Beijing on the grounds that Beijing would reply it was none of China's business. Those familiar with Chinese attitudes say this is in fact the standard reply received in Beijing, although they put it down to evasiveness more than indifference and believe that China hopes the United States will not act until the Kampuchean question is settled.

Some ASEAN states – chiefly Thailand and Singapore – privately advise against a change of status in the US-Vietnamese relationship at present, meaning until there is a resolution in Kampuchea. The Philippines appears to concur but without strong feelings. Indonesia and Malaysia are somewhat equivocal as attitudes fluctuate; frequently there is disparity between what is said publicly and privately in Jakarta and Kuala Lumpur. All five ASEAN nations, however, appear to operate on the overriding principle that the issue should not be permitted to cause a division within ASEAN. In none of the five countries does the issue of US recognition of Hanoi seem to be considered a highly important one.

Japan takes something of the same attitude as the ASEAN states. There is mild interest and some concern that US recognition might become a disruptive factor in the region. Australian policies toward Vietnam in general appear at this writing to be undergoing reevaluation.

The Soviet Union may have firm opinions on the matter, but if so they are well hidden. Moscow officials tell Americans in avuncular fashion that the United States ought to recognize Hanoi, possibly hoping that the USSR will get credit for this in Vietnam. Some observers argue that Moscow is dissembling, that it would prefer continuation of the present isolation of Vietnam in the international arena, for this increases Vietnamese dependency and engenders fewer problems for Soviet diplomats in Hanoi. Clearly the USSR does regard the United States as a future competitor in Indochina, but probably does not regard arrival of a US mission in Hanoi as appreciably changing the geopolitical balance.

France and Sweden presumably would welcome US recognition, as would India. The rest of Europe (and the world) seems more or less indifferent to the matter.

ISSUES

A number of issues stand between the United States and Vietnam, some of them fairly important and others not. These, of course, exist independent of whether there are formal relations between the two countries. A few are germane to the question of recognition, but most represent conflicting interests and divergent views. Their existence is not an argument against formal relations – after all, the basic purpose of diplomacy is to resolve outstanding issues and, if this is not possible, to insure that the other side clearly understands the position being taken and why. In any event these issues will continue to exist and continue to plague the United States and the region, and presumably Vietnam, whether or not diplomatic relations exist.

Regional Unity. The fact of regionalism in Southeast Asia – both with respect to ASEAN and to the informally unified three Indochinese states – is central to much foreign policy thinking in both Washington and Hanoi. This is a major issue, not necessarily a contentious one, but one that does imply competing regional organizations.

If there is for the United States any single overarching principle that will guide foreign policy design in the region in the next decade or so, it will be expressed in an effort to move toward sociopolitical, economic, and military equilibrium within the framework of regional institutionalization. The institutions – ASEAN and the fledgling Federation of Indochina – are already in place, and to a large extent will be the forum in which both the struggle for power and ordinary day-to-day diplomatic activity will be conducted in the decade ahead.

Vietnam appears to have tacitly accepted this gauntlet of regional competition that has been thrown down. As a result, its major goal is to secure a cooperative, non-threatening Indochina peninsula – that is the main reason it is in Kampuchea today. It also seeks to prevent development of a regional anticommunist front, either a militant ASEAN, a revived SEATO (which China has implied is necessary), or any other regional group hostile to

Vietnam. In the same spirit, it seeks to limit superpower activity in the region, not only the United States and China but also (without appearing to do so) the USSR.

The struggle for power in Southeast Asia in the years ahead may vary in shape – triangular, quadrangular, or possibly polarized – but it will be conducted largely in the context of regionalism, between and among regional organizations. This will, of course, go on whether or not the United States and Vietnam have formal relations.

Kampuchea. The sad, bloodied little land of Kampuchea currently is the central issue in American-Vietnamese relations, as it is the touchstone of policy for all of the nations in the region. Kampuchea may not be the cause of all the instability in Southeast Asia, but it contributes to all; it is the eye of the storm. Nor will there be much progress toward any sort of regional stability until the Kampuchean issue is settled one way or another.

The Reagan Administration's position, as noted above, is that there can be no formal relationship with Vietnam until Vietnamese troops leave Kampuchea, which is not likely to happen in the foreseeable future. This is a comfortable position for the United States, for it minimizes the danger of getting into trouble in Indochina. And, it pushes ASEAN into taking more initiative and assuming more responsibility for war and peace in the area, long a US objective. Its chief drawback is that by definition it abrogates a US leadership role, since it says in effect that the United States will follow the ASEAN-China lead. As noted earlier, in actuality it is only a holding operation.

The most likely prospect for Kampuchea in the foreseeable future is simply more of the same. The struggle will go on with neither side being able to prevail, but neither so weak as to be in danger of collapse, and without any decisive developments or resolution. The second most likely prospect is Vietnamese success, that is, the Vietnamese army breaking the back of the resistance and more or less "pacifying" the country, or at least confining armed resistance to the more remote parts of the Cardamom mountains. The third or least likely prospect is a political settlement, the establishment of a new governing structure in Kampuchea that provides equitable representation for the major contending elements: the Coalition Government of Democratic Kampuchea (CGDK) (of three parts, the Khmer Rouge, the Sihanoukists, and the Son Sann and other "third force" elements) and the Hanoi-backed People's Republic of Kampuchea (PRK).[10] A united-front government composed of these elements would be only the first step toward a truly viable government, one that functions at the provincial, district, and village governmental levels and not simply at cabinet level in Phnom Penh. Few realize what a vastly difficult task creating a government in Kampuchea will be, under any circumstances.[11] The Vietnamese troops are not now in Kampuchea for altruistic reasons, but the Vietnamese military government there represents the only government there is. Its precipitous withdrawal without a new governing system ready to move into place would plunge the country into total anarchy in which the power struggle would devolve to the 13th-century warlord level, and suffering by the Kampuchean people would be worse than anything yet experienced.

Soviet Presence. The rather widespread presence of the USSR throughout Indochina represents an issue standing between the United States and Vietnam, although not to the extent that it is an issue between Vietnam and China.

Soviet geopolitical objectives in the region (and worldwide) are beyond the scope of this paper. However, passing mention is required of those Moscow objectives pursued regionally to which Vietnam contributes or plays a part. These appear to be: (a) a desire to dominate the region ideologically but to achieve this by measures short of Soviet involvement in war (in fact that theme – dominance without war – explains most Moscow moves in the region); (b) to intimidate Japan and curtail its efforts to move more deeply into the region; (c) to block resurgent US presence in Southeast Asia, or shut out the United States entirely if possible; (d) above all, to contain and neutralize China and isolate it from the region, militarily and psychologically; (e) to woo ASEAN states (and keep them non-military) with a view to increased Soviet influence; and (f) in principle, to increase Soviet air/naval/military presence in the region.

Some of these objectives do not directly involve Vietnam (and indeed some are counter to Vietnamese interests). The USSR's desire to increase its capacity to project force over long distances in Southeast Asia does involve and possibly even endangers Vietnam. Moscow's motives in this – whether benign and normal for a nation with regional interests, or something more ambitious and ominous – can only be surmised. In any case, Vietnam now cooperates fully. The USSR and Vietnam have a military alliance in all but name. They conduct combined defense planning and presumably are prepared for combined operations. Soviet navy ships and Soviet air force planes make full use of Vietnamese facilities and appear to be granted anything they want. Moscow has paid a rather high price for this, both economically and diplomatically, for its stock in Southeast Asia is the lowest in a decade, but apparently feels that it is getting its money's worth.

This Soviet-Vietnamese defense arrangement does constitute a strategic threat, but one essentially psychological and in conditions short of total war.[12] Most analysts believe that Moscow's military planners concluded early that Soviet bases in Vietnam would be excessively vulnerable in a war with the United States; therefore they have not incorporated their use in US war scenarios. Short of total war, however, the bases have greater utility. They help encircle China and would be useful in any limited war involving the USSR. They would be essential for Soviet intervention in the region, Afghan style. And the bases do intimidate Asia, not only by representing direct Soviet military action, but by associating Vietnam with Soviet military power and thus enhancing the threat offered by Hanoi.

I do not believe that the current Soviet-Vietnamese association is either as close or as durable as most observers contend. It is based on Soviet opportunism and Vietnamese dependency (for food and weapons), and will last at least as long as the USSR considers it useful and, on Hanoi's part, as long as Vietnam is unable to feed itself and the China threat continues. In any event, I do not believe that a nominal change of US-Vietnamese relations, as in the establishment of diplomatic relations, would have any effect, plus or minus, on the Soviet-Vietnamese alliance.

Vietnam Threat Potential. As is implicit in the discussion above, much of the military threat that Vietnam represents for Southeast Asia, which causes primary concern for the United States, derives from its association with the USSR. Vietnam by itself is not a credible threat to Southeast Asian countries, except Thailand, because it does not have the air and sea power to project force over long distances, to Indonesia for instance.

The People's Army of Vietnam, of course, is formidable – the third-largest armed force on earth. Vietnam today has under arms, including its paramilitary troops, at least three to four million persons, with the main force elements now topping one million. Vietnamese troops could invade and occupy Thailand in a matter of days, although there are many compelling reasons not to, not the least of which is that Vietnam probably would find its present Kampuchean impasse extended to all of the Indochina peninsula and greatly worsened. In terms of limited orthodox war, the Vietnamese army probably could hold its own against an invasion by China for a lengthy period, although not indefinitely.

Besides the orthodox military threat to parts of the region, Hanoi offers a second kind of threat, an indirect one, to the more distant reaches of Southeast Asia. It could fund and support insurgencies in any of the ASEAN countries. These might not in the end be successful, but with Vietnamese guidance and aid they could prove troublesome and costly to suppress.

Hanoi would like to see the countries of ASEAN move ever leftward until finally all become ''people's republics.'' Theoreticians writing in party journals in Hanoi assert this will happen whether or not there is any action by Vietnam. They hold the governments and societies of noncommunist Southeast Asia to be illegitimate and transitory, and soon to be swept ''into the dust bin of history,'' as the communist phrasemakers put it. The doctrinal problem for Vietnam is only a tactical one of how to push this process along: whether to organize and fund insurgencies and other left-wing challenges, to let history take its course, or by some other means.

For the moment at least, Hanoi has ruled out the insurgency approach. There is reason to believe that shortly after the end of the Vietnam War, Vietnamese generals took a long, hard look at the region's insurgents – concentrating on the Thai (actually there are three insurgent groups in Thailand) – and concluded that the guerrillas did not have the required qualities to be successful. Since then Vietnam has largely ignored insurgent appeals for assistance. This policy may change, of course, but clearly Hanoi must be convinced that an insurgent force has real prospect before it will back it with money and weapons.

There is a third threat that Hanoi could offer in that gray area between war and politics – what might be called a cold war or a psycho-political threat. The idea first surfaced in the late 1970s, when confidence was still high in Hanoi and the lure of expansionism still strong. Party theoreticians began developing a kind of economic security strategy for use in Southeast Asia. Its basic concept was that Vietnam should induce and pressure the ASEAN countries to cut their capitalist-multinationalist ties in exchange for guaranteed regional peace made possible by a cooperative, non-aggressive, non-expansionist Vietnam. The strategy was worked out in an elaborate rationale of doctrine, having to do with nationalism, collectivism, and non-alignment. After the time of troubles began in Vietnam, little was heard of the idea, but it is still there in the wings and we may not have heard the last of it.

We should be careful neither to understate nor exaggerate the threat potential Vietnam represents for Southeast Asia. The determinant – and it is here we should maintain our attention – is the USSR, which can either facilitate or inhibit military action by Hanoi. Moscow continually should be reminded by the nations of the region that they hold her accountable for the behavior of her surrogate.

Resolution of Casualties. In addition to the major issues standing between the United States and Vietnam, there are a number of lesser magnitude. There is an entire clutch of economic problems such as frozen assets, nationalized property, and demands for indemnification on both sides. There are humanitarian problems involving divided families and other difficulties that arose with the exodus of some 600,000 Indochinese to the United States.

And there is the knotty, most difficult, resolution-of-casualties issue, that is, the need for an accounting by Hanoi, to the extent it can, of the fate of some 2500 American servicemen listed as missing in action or as "fate unknown" in the aftermath of the Vietnam War. This is a singular issue, normally not one that appears in foreign affairs. Traditionally and logically, nations treat assuaging of bereavement as a humanitarian matter, not something to be bargained by diplomats. For complex reasons this issue – which now has a long and somewhat peculiar history – has become a more or less permanent impediment standing between the two countries, one that has at times assumed a disproportionate importance in terms of national interest. The issue cuts to the political bone in America, for it has taken on a deep psychological meaning. It affects the fundamental sense of responsibility in our highest officials, both in the executive and legislative branches. Professionals in foreign affairs commonly hold that most issues are negotiable, but not this one, and they become unsure how to deal with it. What should be done is clear. In the interests of both the United States and Vietnam, Hanoi should become convinced that the issue must be lifted from the foreign affairs level to the humanitarian level and dealt with independent of the foreign policy of either country. However, this would require a changed mind-set by the myopic, anachronistic men of the Hanoi Politburo, which is highly unlikely. Solving this problem may have to wait for a generational change in Vietnam.[13]

POLICY

I conclude with some thoughts about US policy and the implications of establishing formal US-SRV relations.

In US policy terms, Southeast Asia, of which Vietnam is part, does not have the importance of most other regions of the world, certainly less than North Asia, for example. It does not loom large in daily defense and foreign policy thinking at the highest levels in Washington; probably Vietnam has never been on the agenda of a Reagan cabinet meeting. The net meaning of this is that Washington and Hanoi have only minimal interest in the other – neither can be particularly useful to the other, nor offer much by way of credible threat. The chief US policy interest in Southeast Asia in general appears to be access to the region and the freedom to traverse it, which Vietnam could not prevent although it could destabilize the region if it chose to do so. Hence, it is a safe conclusion that the operational assumption in both Washington and Hanoi is that in the foreseeable future neither will become for the other a truly serious foreign policy or strategic problem.

Looking beyond the present policy of the holding operation, what can we expect eventually – what is feasible?

If (or when) diplomatic relations are established with Hanoi, it will later be recognized that the first step, the initial move, was the hardest. This is because of the danger that any change in US policy, even some limited overture, may be misread in Hanoi as confirmation that the SRV's hard-line policy is succeeding, bringing on an even harder Hanoi line with additional demands for concessions. The central problem in achieving any sort of forward progress is to get past this Politburo mind-set.

Once past this barrier, the exploratory process could proceed expeditiously, become easier, even mechanical. It would involve, on both sides, a series of confidence-building measures, to use a favorite Marxist term, exchanges, one by one, in sets of two, one at a time. Like a tennis match, the exchanges of bilateral gestures would continue.

What are these confidence-building measures? At first they would be the simple and trouble-free, gradually moving toward the more complex and significant. On the US side these could include an end to the US economic embargo, cultural exchange, academic/intellectual relations, joint health-medical research projects, technology transfer, and economic aid and investment. On Hanoi's part they could include resolution of casualties, orderly departure procedures, simplified entry and currency exchange, tourism, and cultural and academic relations.

Once this process is underway, and only then, can we address ourselves to the more finite US geopolitical objectives: regional stability, benign Hanoi behavior (with respect to our allies and friends, and even others in the region), an Indochinese political configuration (Vietnam, Laos, and Kampuchea) acceptable to all, less USSR intimacy in Indochina.

One cannot be sure that these goals will be advanced by establishment of more or less normal relations with Vietnam, and their pursuit should not be advertised or sold on the basis that they will. Still, the promise that our interests may be served is great enough to make it worthwhile to pursue this approach.

As the United States moves more deeply into the 1980s, therefore, it seems probable that it will, in part by design and in part as reaction to the rush of events, increasingly be guided in its Southeast Asia/Indochina policies by the principle of equilibrium within the framework of competing regional institutions. Creation and maintenance of this equilibrium will require an entire matrix of organizations, some large and some small, some of broad general purpose and some of narrow specific objective, some governmental, some private and multinational. It will be a vast organized arena in which the struggle for power will be conducted. In such a context, diplomatic intercourse of every country with every other country will become virtually mandatory. This means that establishment of US-SRV relations in the final analysis is not a question of whether, but of when, strictly a matter of timing.

NOTES

1. A major bibliographic source for this article is the Indochina Archive at the University of California, Berkeley, File 7-A, Vietnam Foreign Relations (US), approximately 15,000 pages of documentary material, of which about five percent deals directly with the subject of formal diplomatic relations; the remainder deals with issues between the two countries and a history of contacts since the end of the Vietnam War. Early material on the subject, circa 1976-77, was more voluminous but of less value in terms of today's policymaking. See Herman Kahn and Thomas Pepper, "United States Relations with Vietnam," Hudson Institute Report, December 1976, and by way of contrast, "Vietnam: 1976," a report to the Senate Foreign Relations Committee by Senator George McGovern, March 1976. The best single source of material on this subject probably is the US Congress, "U.S. Aid to North Vietnam," House Subcommittee on Asian and Pacific Affairs, 19 July 1977, a Committee on International Relations Print. "Claims Against Vietnam," a House of Representatives report dated 30 April 1980, outlines the legal issues involved with US nationals' losses incurred through nationalization in Vietnam and also contains information on Hanoi assets frozen in the United States. "Indochina," a report released by the Senate Foreign Relations Subcommittee on East Asia and Pacific Affairs, 21 August 1978, contains a 150-page study by the author entitled "Vietnam's Future Foreign Relations," which includes a chapter on US-Vietnamese relations. "Adjudication of Claims Against Vietnam," by the House Subcommittee on Asian and Pacific Affairs, 27 July and 25 October 1979, contains background material on losses by US individuals and companies through nationalization of property in Vietnam and on Hanoi assets frozen in the United States. See also "Relations with the United States," a Congressional Research Service Vietnam Study, April 1982, pp. 63-69. For representative arguments on immediate recognition of Hanoi, see "For Normalizing Relations With Hanoi," by Richard Walden and Gary Larsen, in *The New York Times*, 29 April 1982; also "Diplomatic Relations With Vietnam Should Be Restored," by Rank Price, *National Vietnam Veterans Review*, March 1982.

2. In strict interpretation of diplomatic protocol, Hanoi owes the United States at least an

apology for violating the agreements signed with the United States in February and March 1973. The Paris Agreements, whatever else was their meaning (for instance the extraordinary concession of allowing Hanoi to keep 40,000 troops in someone else's country, legally), clearly stipulated no force augmentation, yet virtually the entire North Vietnamese army was in South Vietnam near the end of the war (April 1975). This represented a total breach of our agreement.

3. In some instances this relation is only nominal; one envoy with such an arrangement appeared twice in Hanoi in three years, on arrival to present his credentials and for his farewell call upon departure.

4. The other four are Belgium, the Netherlands, Denmark, and Finland. In some instances these countries have picked up economic aid projects dropped after Vietnam invaded Kampuchea. In some cases assistance appears to be only token, for the purposes of quieting domestic criticism.

5. See the author's "Experience of Various Countries in Dealing with Vietnam," a study prepared for the US Congress, House of Representatives, Subcommittee on Asian and Pacific Affairs, January 1979. For a hilarious account of diplomatic life in Hanoi, see "Waiting for the Fruits of Victory," by Siegfried Kogelfranz in *Der Spiegel*, 3 and 13 February 1978.

6. In mid-1973, as part of the Paris Agreements arrangements, representatives from the United States (Agency for International Development) and the DRV held a series of technical-level meetings in Paris. The two sides discussed US economic assistance to Vietnam to which the United States had agreed as part of the "binding up the wounds of war" effort in the Paris Agreements. Among the documents coming out of these meetings was a Hanoi-supplied list of desired US-assisted reconstruction aid. The price tag on the list totaled about $3.25 billion. Another document was a White House memorandum (that may or may not bear Richard Nixon's signature, the matter being in doubt) in which the United States acknowledged this level of economic need, and implied that the United States would make such money available. However, at these meetings and in various other ways (including Kissinger press conferences), the United States stressed two points: that the executive branch representatives in Paris did not have the authority to commit the United States to granting $3.25 billion since this was a power reserved for the Congress, and that the United States considered any economic assistance for North Vietnam dependent on Hanoi's military restraint in the South. In any event, because of these conditional qualifications, there never was a clear and legal US debt obligation.

7. The United States during this period also acquiesced (by refraining from veto) in UN membership for Vietnam; it also pledged to end trade restrictions and other embargo measures once diplomatic relations were established.

8. Some critics have argued that the United States is to be blamed for the Vietnamese invasion of Kampuchea on the grounds that recognition would have restrained Hanoi. An examination of Hanoi's motives and purposes in attacking Kampuchea suggests that US recognition was an irrelevant matter. Actually the United States can count itself fortunate – it escaped the embarrassment of a Vietnamese act of war at about the time the new US ambassador would have been arriving in Hanoi to open formal relations.

9. Other factors also had contributed to the slowdown of movement toward establishing relations. These include the refugee exodus, Hanoi's decisions to join CEMA and sign a Treaty of Friendship and Cooperation with the USSR, and the rise of influence of a small but powerful group of congressmen who, in the name of the resolution-of-casualties issue, signaled the White House that it faced a heavy political battle on Capitol Hill centering around the MIA question.

10. The concern here must be with institutions, not individuals. Almost certainly there is no place in the future governing structure of Kampuchea, whatever it becomes, for either Pol Pot or Heng Samrin personally. Both are total anathema to almost all Khmer. Probably other top figures on both sides will also have to go.

11. The British Hanoi watcher, Denis Duncanson, has done some calculations on this and concludes that even with the best political settlement in Kampuchea, it will remain almost a mathematical impossibility for the society to produce in less than a generation sufficient leaders, technicians, and bureaucrats, so completely decimated is its middle class. See "Who Will Govern Cambodia," in *The World Today* (London), June 1982.

12. Not all agree on this. A common view in influential circles in the United States and Europe is that Soviet moves in the Pacific in the last decade are the result of a natural concern for a region

that increasingly affects Soviet interests and that its actions there are normal and not aggressive. Some contend that the United States and the USSR actually have little to quarrel over in Southeast Asia, unlike other regions of the world.

13. See the author's "Policy Dimension on the Indochina POW-MIA Issue," a policy-planning position paper dated August 1979 (copy in the Indochina Archive, University of California, Berkeley). See also the SRV White Paper, "On the Question of Americans Missing in the Vietnam War," Hanoi, Ministry of Foreign Affairs, 1980.

This article appeared in the autumn 1984 issue of *Parameters*.

17

Vietnam and the Six Criteria for the Use of Military Force

by DAVID T. TWINING

On 28 November 1984, Secretary of Defense Caspar W. Weinberger delivered a speech that deserves attention both within and beyond the military forces and government of the United States. This historic document was personally written by Mr. Weinberger, endorsed by the National Security Council, and discussed with and approved by the President.[1] It represents a maturation and sophistication of our strategic judgment; more importantly, it adapts and clarifies defense policies of a different time and slower world to the exigencies of the present and the challenges of the future.

Questions concerning the role and use of armed force by a democratic state within a turbulent, pluralistic world are central, vital, and absolutely fundamental as never before. War has always been the ultimate political act, but threats to our sovereignty have now become increasingly gray, obscuring clear lines of war and peace by means of terrorism, uncertain alliances, and hidden intentions. It is the irony of the present era that assassinations, bombings, and technology theft are facilitated by the very freedoms totalitarian forces seek to destroy.

While strategic nuclear war remains a real concern, this is the least likely security contingency we face. Instead, most challenges to US sovereignty and interests lie at the lower end of the conflict spectrum, the significance of which democratic nation-states have traditionally been unwilling or unable adequately to grasp. Added to the ambiguity of the ever-changing strategic environment is the fourth dimension of military affairs, space. In the days ahead, the all-enveloping nature of security challenges facing the West will increasingly intrude upon our lives, making us less rather than more secure.

The Weinberger policy statement represents an operational guide for a future in which purposefully cumbersome democratic states must coexist with totalitarian states unencumbered by public opinion and individual freedoms. As Mr. Weinberger has observed, the responsible use of military force is a moral issue, and military power is but one tool among many. For democracies, however, it is most appropriately fhe final political tool when all else fails.

In his speech, Mr. Weinberger enunciated six criteria to be met before the use of military power is considered appropriate. The quintessential significance of these standards is their role as a catharsis of past debates, doubts, and national trauma. Because of this thoughtful and far-reaching analysis, these six tests provide positive guidance and direction for meeting future challenges to our security and national interests. The uneasy legacy of Vietnam, more than any single factor or event in this century, has demanded this reappraisal.

THE SIX TESTS

I. "*The United States should not commit forces to combat overseas unless the particular engagement or occasion is deemed vital to our national interest or that of our allies.*"[2]

According to Mr. Weinberger, national interest – ours or our allies' – will determine if the application of force is indeed appropriate. US troops and national will are not to be substituted for those of our allies, nor will the United States become the world's policeman. Allies will be supported with economic and military aid to help in their self-defense, but national interest will be the measure by which this decision is made. Nor will the United States announce in advance, as with Korea in 1950, that particular regions are beyond our strategic perimeter.

From the beginning of the Vietnam War, there was no agreement on what was at stake and which US national interests, if any, were involved. The 1964 Gulf of Tonkin Resolution explicitly stated that the peace and security of Southeast Asia were "vital" to US national interests. Many similar references to US "interests" and "objectives" led to a "verbal extravagance" which confused both American policymakers and the public at large as to the issues at stake and their priority.[3]

By being clear about whether a possible interest is vital – that is, a goal or purpose of such significance to justify the use of national power for its defense or attainment – the term provides a useful measure with which to evaluate critically the justification for and results of actions taken on its behalf.[4] To those who led the nation in the early years of the Vietnam War, the conflict was viewed as essential to our security, to our allies, and to South Vietnam. Yet only the President can truly define and defend that determination. In the end, the case was neither defined nor defended well.

By making it imperative that a national security problem be analyzed to determine if it indeed represents a vital national interest, Mr. Weinberger has made explicit a consideration which was never clear during the Vietnam era. This very important factor, seen over the litany of Vietnam pathos, is the first of the six criteria which validate the use of force in the current era.

II. "*If we decide it is necessary to put combat troops into a given situation, we should do so wholeheartedly, and with the clear intention of winning. If we are unwilling to commit the forces or resources necessary to achieve our objectives, we should not commit them at all.*"

If a vital national interest requires committing US troops to combat, the force so committed must be of sufficient size and strength to assure victory. Once this decision has been made, there can be no question of our resolve to win. Military force will not be incrementally drawn into combat, a strategy "which almost always means the use of insufficient force."

In many respects, the conduct of the Vietnam War represented the antithesis of this policy. The United States won every major tactical engagement, yet lost the war. Because of a fear of direct Chinese and Soviet involvement, US objectives were cast in negative terms of preventing the fall of South Vietnam rather than in positive terms of defeating the source of the insurgency, North Vietnam. This produced what has been called an "unimaginative strategy of attrition and cautious escalation which yielded unsatisfactory results in the long term."[5]

By restricting the military means in pursuit of limited objectives, the United States fought a war of attrition which corresponded to the enemy's strategic doctrine, first published in 1947 and reissued by Hanoi in 1962. This doctrine sought a protracted war. According to Truong Chinh, the preeminent North Vietnamese theoretician, "The guiding principle of the strategy of our whole resistance must be to prolong the war." This would lower enemy morale, unite the North Vietnamese people, increase outside support, and encourage the antiwar movement to tie the enemy's hands. "To achieve all these results, the war must be prolonged, and we must have time. Time works for us."[6] This strategy worked against the French and, with time, it would be effective against the Americans.

Colonel Harry G. Summers, Jr., author of the profound analysis of the Vietnam War *On Strategy*, has asserted that the United States failed to concentrate its efforts on the source of the conflict – Hanoi – and mistakenly pursued the symptom of the war – the guerrilla. Because of the failure of our strategic military doctrine, "It was four North Vietnamese Army corps, not 'dialectical materialism,' that ultimately conquered South Vietnam." While guerrilla forces distracted US forces in a tactic of trading space for time, time ran out for an army committed to using restricted means to achieve limited, negative objectives. This permitted regular North Vietnamese forces to achieve a decisive victory following the US withdrawal.[7]

The failure of US military professionals to understand the dynamics of the Vietnam War, Summers observed, has led to continuing confusion over tactics and strategy. By failing to achieve decisive victory over the source of the war, "North Vietnam's tactical failures did not prevent their strategic success, and in strategic terms people's war *was* a success." The victorious strategy in this, as in all wars, has not changed. "Carrying the war to the enemy and the destruction of his armed forces and his will to fight through the strategic offensive is the classic way wars are fought and won."[8]

III. "*If we do decide to commit forces to combat overseas, we should have clearly defined*

*political and military objectives. And we should know precisely how our forces can
accomplish those clearly defined objectives. And we should have, and send, the forces needed
to do just that.''*

The failure to pursue victory – destroying the enemy's forces and will to fight
in order to achieve the political objective for which victory is sought – has been
termed the essence of our strategic failure in Vietnam.[9] Because the
Clausewitzian political aim of war is the quintessential goal and war is its
means, political and military objectives contributing to that end may never be
considered in isolation of one another.[10] Yet this was done in Vietnam in much
the same way as it was during previous conflicts in which American forces were
employed. In reviewing the mixed results victory had brought the United
States following World War II, former Secretary of Defense James Forrestal
declared, ''The great mistakes were made during the war because of American
failure to realize that military and political action had to go hand in hand.''[11]

The essential unity of political and military objectives in pursuit of the
ultimate political object of war was not readily apparent during the Vietnam
era. The tendency of Americans to view military and political operations as
separate, compartmented functions eventually proved fatal against an enemy
with a clear understanding of its objectives and their contribution to the war's
ultimate political aim. Hanoi, which saw its military struggle in the South as
the intermediate stage of broader regional political ambitions, had little to fear
from those who saw only the limited military struggle as threatening.[12]

Since US military and political objectives were never clear – largely because
victory in the classical sense was not sought and the war's relevance to the
national interest was clouded at best – the enemy retained the initiative. Until
1969, when the sanctuaries were first invaded, bombing became more
aggressive, Vietnamization was emphasized, and pacification began to show
real progress, the war was in ''a state of perpetual motion. It could have gone
on forever.'' As S. L. A. Marshall observed, ''Once the commitment was made,
the war need not have been muddled through to indecisive and nationally
convulsive conclusions in a manner wholly unworthy of a great power.''[13]

Because political and military objectives were not clearly enunciated, the
United States was placed in a position of reacting to North Vietnamese political
and military actions. This led to widespread confusion in Vietnam, among US
allies, and among the American people. Even 20 years following the
introduction of American troops at Da Nang, the misunderstanding and
confusion over US objectives persist.

While Hanoi ''skillfully combined political and military means in pursuit of
clearly defined political objectives to exploit the problems of a democracy in
conducting a distant war,'' things were less satisfactory for Washington. After
the war, former Vice President Hubert Humphrey wrote, ''We seem to have
gotten things in reverse order. We all know that knowledge is power, but in
Vietnam we acted as though power gave us knowledge. Therein, possibly, lay

our greatest mistake.''[14] Because the United States failed to define and adopt consistent and clear strategic objectives leading to the political end for which the war was fought, we were condemned to tactical rather than strategic success.[15]

The failure to translate US tactical success, accomplished with such valor and sacrifice, to strategic success is our most enduring failure of the war. Because we did not adequately define our objectives or comprehend the role of battlefield success in contributing to larger strategic goals, the aims for which the Vietnam War was fought were never within our grasp.

IV. *"The relationship between our objectives and the forces we have committed – their size, composition, and disposition – must be continually reassessed and adjusted if necessary."*

The conditions and objectives of a conflict inevitably change, and this requires that combat requirements be adjusted accordingly. National leaders must conduct a continuous assessment to determine whether the conflict is indeed in the national interest and if military force is appropriate for its resolution. If the assessment concludes this is the case, victory must then be sought. If not, as Mr. Weinberger states, ''we should not be in combat.''

One of the major lessons of Vietnam is the necessity to conduct a continuous and honest review of the premises underlying a particular national policy. This implies a willingness to accept responsibility in the case of policy failure, when it becomes apparent that the price for a specific policy has become unacceptable. In Vietnam, the driving premise of containing communist expansion led successive Presidents to accept a growing commitment to South Vietnam without fully determining if US vital interests were involved or, if so, had changed. Once the United States became heavily involved, the need to preserve national prestige overrode any intrinsic importance of South Vietnam itself.[16]

A continuous assessment of objectives and requisite military forces requires a receptivity to a spectrum of possible ideas and views, particularly by the President. According to Townsend Hoopes, President Lyndon Johnson primarily relied on a small circle of advisors among whom the premises of US involvement were seen as a choice between appeasement or military resolve. Hoopes has said that no one saw the need to redefine US interests or to question the basic requirement to counter communism forcefully. ''To the President's men in early 1965,'' Hoopes said, ''there seemed no logical stopping point between isolationism and globalism.''[17]

This prevailing atmosphere led to the suppression of dissenting views, an attitude that originated not in the bureaucracies but with the President and his key advisors. According to Richard Holbrooke, ''They knew what they wanted to hear, and they took steps which squeezed other points of view out of the reporting system.'' This prevented the bureaucracies from carrying out their role of promoting continuity in policy and noting the risks particular decisions hold for larger policy positions. Because broad strategic issues were not adequately debated, the President's ultimate vulnerability before history was vastly increased.[18]

When reflecting on the entire Vietnam experience, one must agree with David M. Abshire, who noted, "The foremost lesson is that wise decisions on foreign intervention require a constant accommodation of means to ends and of strategy to objectives."[19] This constant assessment process, the adjustment of means to ends, forces to objectives, is culminated by a single act of courage and supreme statesmanship: admitting, when judged to be appropriate by the most senior authorities, that "we should not be in combat."[20]

V. *"Before the United States commits combat forces abroad, there must be some reasonable assurance we will have the support of the American people and their elected representatives in Congress. This support cannot be achieved unless we are candid in making clear the threats we face; the support cannot be sustained without continuing and close consultation."*

No war – whether the tragedy of Vietnam or the quick victory in Grenada – can receive a guarantee of public support in advance of military action. What is desired, however, is the reasonable expectation that the American people and their elected representatives will understand the necessity for action when the case for it has been clearly made. This requires effective, decisive action by a chief executive who acts in what he believes to be the national interest. This also requires a frank dialogue between the executive and legislative branches over the nature of the threat prompting the military intervention. The American people have always supported a President who acts in a timely manner to serve or protect what are perceived to be vital national interests.

The Vietnam War proved, if anything, the validity of this basic principle: that the domestic environment must be considered when troops are to be committed to combat in a foreign land and, once committed, that close, continuous, and candid consultation with the American people and with Congress must be maintained.[21] If Grenada has shown the merits of the effective, responsible use of military power, Vietnam, according to Secretary of State George Shultz, "shows that public support can be frittered away if we do not act wisely and effectively."[22]

In prosecuting the Vietnam War, President Johnson made the deliberate decision not to mobilize the national will of the American people by seeking a declaration of war from Congress. As a result, maintaining public support for the war and its rising costs became increasingly difficult – a strategic lesson that was lost on neither Hanoi nor many in Washington. In a 14 October 1966 top secret memorandum to Secretary of Defense McNamara, General Earle G. Wheeler noted that "communist leaders in both North and South Vietnam expect to win this war in Washington, just as they won the war with France in Paris. In this regard, the Joint Chiefs of Staff consider that there is reason for such expectations on the part of the communist leadership."[23] As General

Lewis M. Walt later wrote, "American opinion has been as much a target in this war as an enemy soldier in the sights of a rifle."[24]

While a reprehensible attack such as Pearl Harbor or some other clear act of war that inflames public sentiment makes the issue of public support less problematic, few national leaders expect future tests of the national will to be this clear-cut. Instead, there are many less-distinct contingencies in which a President must act, where a *reasonable* assurance of support is sought. As Mr. Weinberger has observed, future challenges will be mostly gray, precisely the most troublesome national security problems with which democracies must deal. This uncertainty does not preclude a decisive response; it only makes it more difficult.

The burden of decision is never easy for a democracy, particularly a world power which is judged by both its action and its inaction.[25] History is replete with acts of courage, and the future will call for more. While the Vietnam era may not have been our proudest moment, it has inextricably linked the requirement of public support to the commitment of US troops for foreign combat.

VI. "*The commitment of US forces to combat should be a last resort.*"

The resort to military force by a democracy, particularly its American variant, is not just a deliberate, rational decision, but a moral one as well. This stems not from the purpose for which a war is conducted, but from its nature. As Clausewitz has succinctly stated, "The character of battle, like its name, is slaughter, and its price is blood."[26]

General John A. Wickham, Jr., former US Army Chief of Staff, has said that in a future war soldiers must know that the conflict in which they are engaged is important to their country. Because the commitment of troops to combat is inevitably a moral decision, the nation has a moral responsibility to its troops. According to General Wickham, "Once we commit force, we must be prepared to back it up and win as opposed to just sending soldiers into operations for limited goals."[27]

Until man's inherent propensity toward violence is more fully restrained, governments will continue to consider armed conflict an option of state policy. However, the maintenance of standing armies and their use in the course of relations with other nations is a necessity democratic governments would prefer to avoid. To state explicitly that US forces will be deployed in combat as a last resort is to acknowledge John Keegan's assertion that the essence of armies lies not in what they "are," but in what they "do": the "infliction of human suffering through violence," of "combat *corps à corps*."[28]

In this view, no responsible person starts a war without clearly knowing what is to be achieved – its political purpose – and how it is to be conducted – its operational objective. These, in turn, establish the "scale of means and effort" required to attain the ultimate political objective.[29] In Vietnam, the ultimate objective was never clear, its operational corollary was obscure, and the scale of effort was imprecisely defined.

This failure of strategic analysis during the Vietnam War produced a confusion of ends and means, of scale and utility. In an effort to limit US and South Vietnamese casualties, firepower was substituted for manpower. Over eight million tons of munitions – three times that dropped on both Europe and Japan during the Second World War – were expended in the Vietnam War.[30] In one extreme example, as many as 1000 sorties and the loss of 95 aircraft were required before laser-guided bombs downed North Vietnam's Thanh Hoa bridge on 13 May 1972, after more than seven years of effort.[31] During the 1967-68 siege at Khe Sanh, more than 75,000 tons of ordnance were dropped from B-52 aircraft over a nine-week period – the most explosives dumped on a tactical target in history.[32]

The war cost the United States $165 billion, representing only direct costs of the war rather than the total expense of US military programs and indirect costs to the American government and society. Another $24 billion was expended on aid to the South Vietnamese government between 1955 and 1975.[33] Robert Komer has estimated that the United States spent more on intelligence than North Vietnam spent on the entire war.[34] Soviet support to Hanoi is believed to have cost no more than one-thirtieth the sum the United States expended annually; for Moscow, it was a low-cost, low-risk strategy.[35]

No statistics are more sensitive to a democracy than combat casualties. To those affected by the deaths of over 58,000 Americans, the trauma of nearly 2500 missing in action, and the pain of 300,000 wounded, the cost will always be too high.[36] The scars of this war 8000 miles from the American mainland persist, yet it is the loss of its own to which each country, parent, spouse, and child is drawn. The number of North Vietnamese and Viet Cong dead is far higher, some 925,000,[37] but the difference in societal values and the manner in which the popular will is translated into national deeds of armed combat make Western nations particularly sensitive to casualties, especially their own. For democratic nations, it is this human cost and sense of individual worth it represents – more than any other factor – that makes the commitment of US forces to combat truly a last resort.

CONCLUSION: DEMOCRACIES AND LIMITED WAR

Implicit in most analyses of the Vietnam War is that democracies lack the will and the means required to maintain a protracted struggle under contemporary conditions. The usefulness of the six major tests enunciated by Mr. Weinberger is that they acknowledge that the spectrum of threat now faced by the United States has complicated but not negated the possibility of an appropriate, measured response. This is consistent with the Clausewitzian principles of war, which recognize that every period has its own unique form of conflict, with particular constraints and preconceptions. This requires that threats which give rise to hostile acts must be analyzed and, in the current era, accommodated by defense policy.[38]

The contemporary spectrum of conflict with which we are confronted has as its source what Harlan Cleveland terms "the disintegration of national governance."[39] The limited ability of many national governments to cope with social resentment and frustrated expectations has created new opportunities for those seeking radical change through widespread disorder and state-sponsored terrorism. The record of such change since World War II reflects a declining number of democratic states amidst a growing number of centrally controlled, single-party, authoritarian and totalitarian states with disenfranchised, mobilized populations. To adapt to this new reality requires a forward-looking defense policy capable of recognizing military objectives within the larger political milieu and decisively responding to them.

Clausewitz taught that war is the continuation of politics and that armed force is but a means of state policy contributing to the ultimate political objective. It is this political purpose which determines the nature of the military instrument selected as well as its use. A vigorous and ambitious policy requires a more absolute and active military effort; a subtle policy requires a more precise military means. Policy will determine the character of the war but not its operational details; "the posting of guards or the employment of patrols" is best left to those responsible for securing the military objective.[40] The tailoring of military means to meet political aims is the challenge of contemporary defense policy. It was the strategic failure of policymakers and strategists of the Vietnam era that this was not appropriately done.

It is the political objective of our potential adversaries that lies at the heart of the current defense challenge facing the United States. Military weapons such as the 441 Soviet SS-20s and their vast destructive power mask the larger political challenge they represent. The uniquely pragmatic prism through which Americans view the world and interpret its events has obscured the more enduring, and perhaps more sophisticated, political aims of those intent upon our destruction. George Kennan has decried the "almost exclusive militarization of thinking" by which US officials view the Soviet challenge. At the same time, Norman Podhoretz has spoken of the "politically pampered American experience" as responsible for our strategic naiveté.[41]

Did the United States understand the political nature of the Vietnam War? Robert Komer has acknowledged that "Hanoi was far wiser than we in seeing the struggles as essentially a seamless web, a political, military, economic, ideological, and psychological conflict."[42] General Vo Nguyen Giap, in reviewing the Tet Offensive after the war, indicated much the same: "For us, you know, there is no such thing as a single strategy. Ours is always a synthesis, simultaneously military, political, and diplomatic – which is why, quite clearly, the Tet offensive had multiple objectives."[43] The failure to comprehend and counter Hanoi's political objectives, from which its subordinate goals flowed, led the United States to concentrate on the military challenge to the detriment of the larger political war.

The legacy of this failure has been the incremental expansion of a harsh mechanism of oligarchic rule supported by Soviet military power. To focus exclusively on that military power, however, will overlook Moscow's political objectives in theWestern Hemisphere and in the larger world. The success of the USSR's low-cost, low-risk strategy during the Vietnam War and the subsequent consolidation of ties with Hanoi have undoubtedly convinced the Soviet leadership to pursue similar efforts elsewhere, in Africa, Asia, and Latin America. According to Jean-François Revel, this is an unprecedented period in which communist inefficiency does not prevent the expansion of a centrally directed and controlled system of power.[44]

The political utility of the expanded Soviet military presence has given client states the confidence to act with relative impunity. In Central America, this had led Nicaragua to evacuate peasants from rural areas to create free-fire zones and strategic hamlets, and to conduct search-and-destroy operations against opposition forces with interior lines of communication and external sanctuaries.[45] Those who see this situation as "another Vietnam" would do better to identify whether Nicaragua is akin to Vietnam's North or South. To those who believe poverty and political oppression created the conditions leading to the political crisis in Grenada before the US intervention, a review of documents captured there should dispel the myth of revolutionary spontaneity.[46]

Mr. Weinberger's reasoned and thought-provoking criteria for the use of military force acknowledge the growing political utility of Soviet military power in all its permutations. By placing the role of armed force in its proper strategic perspective, Mr. Weinberger addresses the larger political threat to our way of life posed by Soviet and proxy military power. He also acknowledges a future in which a proliferation of external unrest and the reality of Soviet global ambitions pose grave risks to our way of life at all levels of the conflict spectrum.

Mr. Weinberger's six criteria for the use of military force will not endanger American democracy but will foster it at home and abroad. The criteria recognize that US military strategy must have a political aim and that this larger aim, for ourselves and for our potential adversaries, determines security or threat, friend or foe. As long as our basic freedoms remain intact, these guidelines will permit thoroughly democratic means to be mobilized properly and appropriately against those seeking anti-democratic ends. The will and the power for this purpose are thereby strengthened.

There have been in the 20th century two kinds of revolution: the totalitarian revolution and the democratic revolution. The first one has been an abysmal failure, the second a reasonable success – but only the people who live under totalitarianism know this.[47]

NOTES

1. Richard Halloran, "U.S. Will Not Drift Into Combat Role, Weinberger Says," *The New York*

Times, 29 November 1984, p. 1.

2. Caspar W. Weinberger, "The Use of Force and the National Will," *Baltimore Sun*, 3 December 1984, p. 11. All six tests and their detailed descriptions are from this source.

3. BDM Corporation, *A Study of Strategic Lessons Learned in Vietnam*, Vol. 3: *U.S. Foreign Policy and Vietnam, 1945-1975*; 8 vols. (Mclean, Va.: BDM Corporation, 1980), p. 142.

4. Ibid., pp. 1-1 to 4-3.

5. W. Scott Thompson and Donaldson D. Frizzell, eds., *The Lessons of Vietnam* (New York: Crane, Russak, 1977), p. 15. Representative John McCain paid an emotional visit to Hanoi in early 1985, where he had spent 5 1/2 years as a US prisoner of war. In discussing the major result of the trip, he described it in terms of the loss of close friends with whom he had served. "My thinking about them again reinforces my opinion that the United States should not send its young men to fight and die in a conflict unless the goal is victory." "Inside Vietnam: What a Former POW Found," *U.S. News and World Report*, 11 March 1985, p. 34.

6. Truong Chinh, *Primer for Revolt: The Communist Takeover in Viet-Nam* (New York: Praeger, 1963), pp. 111-12. Truong Chinh at one time was the Secretary-General of the Vietnamese Communist Party and Vice Premier of North Vietnam.

7. Harry G. Summers, Jr., *On Strategy: A Critical Analysis of the Vietnam War* (New York: Dell, 1984), p. 123; also pp. 114-28.

8. Ibid., pp. 130-31; p. 249.

9. Ibid., p. 46. See also Sir Robert Thompson in *Lessons of Vietnam*, pp. 98-99.

10. Carl von Clausewitz, *On War*, ed. and trans. Michael Howard and Peter Paret (Princeton: Princeton Univ. Press., 1976), p. 87.

11. Anne Armstrong, "Shortsighted and Destructive," in *The Roosevelt Diplomacy and World War II*, ed. Robert Dallek (New York: Holt, Rinehart, and Winston, 1970), p. 95.

12. Edward Lansdale, "Contradictions in Military Culture," in *Lessons of Vietnam*, pp. 42-43.

13. Robert Thompson in *Lessons of Vietnam*, p. 100; S. L. A. Marshall, "Thoughts on Vietnam," in ibid., p. 55.

14. David M. Abshire, "Lessons of Vietnam: Proportionality and Credibility," in *The Vietnam Legacy: The War, American Society and the Future of American Foreign Policy*, ed. Anthony Lake (New York: New York Univ. Press, 1976), p. 396; Hubert Humphrey, "Building on the Past: Lessons for a Future Foreign Policy," in ibid., p. 364.

15. Summers, p. 152.

16. BDM Corporation, *Strategic Lessons*, Vol. 3: *U.S. Foreign Policy and Vietnam, 1945-1975*, p. EX-6; pp. 3-56 to 3-57. Admiral Elmo R. Zumwalt has written that Vietnam in the early 1960s was not vital to our national interests, but it later became so "because we had linked our sacred national honor to it." Elmo R. Zumwalt, "Costing the Vietnamese War," in *Lessons of Vietnam*, pp. 201-02.

17. Townsend Hoopes, *The Limits of Intervention* (New York: Longman, 1978), pp. 7-16.

18. Richard Holbrooke, "Presidents, Bureaucrats, and Something In-Between," in *Vietnam Legacy*, pp. 162-63. Holbrooke noted that the JCS probably raised strategic issues more than anyone, but that their rigid stance caused their positions to be discounted in advance. Ibid., p. 163.

19. Abshire, "Lessons of Vietnam," in *Vietnam Legacy*, pp. 392-93.

20. Weinberger, p. 11.

21. BDM Corporation, *Strategic Lessons*, Vol. 4: *U.S. Domestic Factors Influencing Vietnam War Policy Making*, p. EX-9.

22. George Shultz, "The Ethics of Power," address at Yeshiva University, 9 December 1984, US Department of State, *Current Policy*, No. 642 (Washington: GPO, 1984), p. 3.

23. US Joint Chiefs of Staff, "Actions Recommended for Vietnam," Memorandum for the Secretary of Defense, JSCM-672-66, 14 October 1966, p. 2.

24. Lewis M. Walt, *Strange War, Strange Strategy: A General's Report on Vietnam* (New York: Funk & Wagnalls, 1970), p. 200. Former President Nixon has written, "In the end, Vietnam was lost on the political front in the United States, not on the battlefront in Southeast Asia." Richard Nixon, *No More Vietnams* (New York: Arbor House, 1985), p. 15.

25. Shultz, p. 3.

26. Clausewitz, p. 259.

27. George C. Wilson, "War's Lessons Struck Home," *The Washington Post*, 16 April 1985, p. A9.

28. John Keegan, *The Face of Battle* (Middlesex, England: Penguin Books, 1978), p. 28. One

former battalion commander in Vietnam said, "Remember, we're watchdogs you unchain to eat up the burglar. Don't ask us to be mayors or sociologists worrying about hearts and minds. Let us eat up the burglar our own way and then put us back on the chain." Wilson, p. A9.

29. Clausewitz, p. 579.
30. Robert Komer in *Lessons of Vietnam*, p. 96.
31. Robert Thompson in *Lessons of Vietnam*, p. 104.
32. Stanley Karnow, *Vietnam: A History* (New York: Penguin Books, 1984), p. 540.
33. Charles Mohr, "History and Hindsight: Lessons from Vietnam," *The New York Times*, 30 April 1985, p. A6, citing *The Vietnam Experience*, Vol. 1 (Boston: Boston Publishing Co., 1981, and US Defense Department).
34. Komer in *Lessons of Vietnam*, p. 270.
35. William Zimmerman, "The Korean and Vietnam Wars," in Stephen S. Kaplan, *Diplomacy of Power: Soviet Armed Forces as a Political Instrument* (Washington: Brookings Institution, 1981), p. 355.
36. Tom Morganthau, et al., "We're Still Prisoners of War," *Newsweek*, 15 April 1985, p. 35; "Hanoi-U.S. Relations Still Icy," *U.S. News and World Report*, 26 August 1985, p. 27. See also, Jeffrey Record, "Casualties," *Baltimore Sun*, 26 February 1985, p. 13.
37. Richard Butwell, "Vietnam War," *Encyclopedia Americana*, 1984 international ed., Vol. 28, p. 112b.
38. Clausewitz, p. 593.
39. Harlan Cleveland, "Defining Security: A Sober 'Threat Analysis,'" *The Inter Dependent*, (November-December 1983), p. 3.
40. Clausewitz, pp. 605-06.
41. Steven J. Dryden, "U.S. Says Soviets Adding SS20s Despite Freeze," *The Washington Post*, 18 September 1985, p. A23; Ronald Steel, "The Statesman of Survival," *Esquire* (January 1985), p. 72; Norman Podhoretz, "The Present Danger," *Commentary*, 79 (March 1980), 39.
42. Robert Komer, "Was There Another Way?" in *Lessons of Vietnam*, p. 211. Bernard Brodie, reflecting on the Vietnam War in 1972, wrote much the same: "Our failures there have been at least 95 percent due to our incomprehension and inability to cope with the political dimensions of the problem." Bernard Brodie, "Why Were We So (Strategically) Wrong?" *Military Review*, 52 (June 1972), 44.
43. Karnow, p. 535.
44. Jean-François Revel, *How Democracies Perish*, trans. William Byron (Garden City, N.Y.: Doubleday, 1983), pp. 353-55.
45. "Sandinistas Forcing Thousands Out of War Zone," *The New York Times*, 19 March 1985, p. A11.
46. Paul Seabury and Walter A. McDougall, eds. *The Grenada Papers* (San Francisco: Institute for Contemporary Studies, 1984).
47. Jean-François Revel in "Letters from Readers," *Commentary*, 78 (October 1984), 22.

This article appeared in the winter 1985 issue of *Parameters*.

18

Low-Intensity Conflict Doctrine: Who Needs It?

by ROD PASCHALL

The US Army is revising its doctrine for low-intensity conflict . . . or counter insurgency . . . or stability operations. This facet of operational-level doctrine has had many names. Additionally, a new and more encompassing definition of low-intensity conflict is being created. The Army's last experience in this field was not a happy one, and unless a careful review of past errors and lessons is made, future endeavors are not likely to be any more glorious than the recent unpleasantness in Southeast Asia.

The new definition is apt to include terrorism counteraction, as well as peacekeeping and rescue operations. Low-intensity conflict is therefore rapidly becoming a catchall. Before peripheral activities begin to obscure the essentials, a word on the additions is in order. Published principles and standard procedures for both rescue and peacekeeping operations are probably long overdue for the US Army, but these subjects can hardly be characterized as proper war-fighting doctrine at the operational level. Terrorism counteraction may be considered at the operational level of doctrine, but the terrorist must be placed in perspective. Despite his capability to be a nuisance, to conduct spectacular media events, and to provoke resource-consuming counter-measures, the terrorist has yet to overthrow a government, threaten a vital interest of the United States, create a popular mass-based army, or cause a sizable deployment of the US armed forces. The insurgent, however, is a wholly different matter. Insurgents have toppled governments. For this reason alone, the focus of our future low-intensity conflict doctrine should be centered on methods to defeat the insurgent.

The writers of low-intensity conflict doctrine must answer several vital questions before they set about their task: Should our doctrine be founded on some sort of hypothetical threat or on practical experience? Should the US armed forces fight the insurgent or should US efforts be directed to providing advice and assistance to allies who are fighting insurgents? And if we do not fight the insurgents ourselves, what military measures should we take against those nations that sponsor insurgency?

The proposal here is to look to empirical evidence as opposed to a dimly perceived future threat. The evidence selected is that of the Asian insurgent, not because his methods are directly transferrable to other regions of the world, but because he has been the most successful, the one who is more apt to be emulated, and because his methods pose the most difficult obstacles for the counterinsurgent. To write our future doctrine without considering the Asian insurgent is to hope our adversaries will be lesser breeds. The best way to depict such a threat is to look first at the doctrine of the Asian Marxist insurgent and then examine how he applied that doctrine. By tracing the evolution of our own doctrine it is possible to learn from our own experience. A careful examination of the past leads to rational, experience-based conclusions: our new doctrine should not be based on US forces fighting insurgents unless a US military government exists; we should continue a doctrine based on US assistance and advice to allies beset with the insurgent; and our range of options against insurgency should include mid-intensity, not low-intensity, offensive ground operations against those nations that sponsor insurgency.

ASIAN MARXIST INSURGENCY DOCTRINE

The doctrine of the Asian insurgent is easy to understand and remained relatively unchanged from the 1930s until the 1970s. The prime oracles have been Mao Tse-tung, Truong Chin, and Vo Nguyen Giap. They were successful practitioners of the craft of insurgency and recorded their doctrinal precepts. Although Mao had written earlier tracts, the clearest explanation of his thought came in 1939, after considerable experience against both the Chinese Nationalist and Japanese armies. Truong Chin's concepts were first printed during 1946 and 1947. Giap's best doctrinal work was produced after he defeated the French in the 1950s. The experience of all three included warfare against their own countrymen as well as war against the forces of an industrialized nation. Each of the authors wrote not only for his own followers but for an international audience as well. They all addressed a central theme: how a peasant army could defeat the army of a modern industrialized state. With one exception, their prime tenets were identical.

Mao's *On Protracted War* included the three familiar stages: guerrilla warfare, mobile warfare, and positional warfare. He described mobile warfare as battle using regular forces so as to annihilate the enemy. Mao's concept of positional warfare sought to engage the adversary in a war of attrition. Guerrilla warfare preceded both of these stages and was envisioned to subject the enemy to both attrition and annihilation. Although Mao advocated the creation of mobile, regular forces from local guerrilla units, he said that these guerrillas were to be replaced as they moved on. In Mao's doctrine, guerrilla warfare is a continuous activity — even into the final stages of war. The guerrilla would exist at the start of the conflict and would play an important part at the end.[1]

Truong Chin adopted Mao's three stages but described them in a different way. His concept has been translated as an initial phase of contention or low-level combat followed by an equilibrium stage in which mobile combat is featured on both sides. He saw the final stage as a counteroffensive by the insurgent forces that have by then created regular combat units. Truong Chin's terminology has been translated in other portions of his works using Mao's guerrilla, mobile, and positional phases.[2] He too stated that the need for guerrillas was continuous, and claimed that their prime task was to keep the enemy dispersed, allowing his defeat in detail.[3] Truong Chin largely parroted Mao, but the essential difference is the use of the general uprising, a well-timed, carefully managed insurrection: a peasant coup d'état. This technique had been briefly successful for the Vietnamese communists in 1945 against the Japanese. Truong Chin attributed the lack of complete success for the 1945 general uprising to a lack of revolutionary fervor in South Vietnam.[4]

Vo Nguyen Giap described the first two stages of insurgent warfare in the same manner as Mao: the guerrilla and mobile warfare phases. Giap's last stage has been translated as entrenched camp warfare, possibly due to the specific nature of his success at Dien Bien Phu. There seems little point in arguing the difference between Mao and Truong Chin's positional and Giap's entrenched camp phase.[5] Up to this point, the Vietnamese appear to be reading Mao. The difference between Mao and the two Vietnamese is that the Vietnamese have added the concept of a general insurrection to Mao's doctrine. The Vietnamese doctrine writers believed in a comprehensive clandestine organization that would have the capability to overthrow the target government in a single blow. Like Truong Chin, Giap selected the Vietminh uprising in 1945 against the Japanese as his practical example.[6] While the Vietnamese concept of a general uprising can be seen as an important distinction, all three are in agreement on the concept of continuous guerrilla warfare. The Vietnamese leaders stress the essential need for guerrilla troops to be maintained and their activities to continue throughout each phase of the war. In Giap's eyes, a prime value of guerrilla actions is to cause the enemy to defend everywhere, making him vulnerable to defeat in detail.[7]

The endgame for the Asian insurgent is to place his adversary in a position where he must not only face regular troops in stand-up battles, but face the guerrilla as well. If one were to define low-intensity conflict as a form of warfare where irregulars fight regular armed forces, then the Asian insurgent's first phase could be described as low-intensity conflict. If one defines mid-intensity conflict as battle between regulars, the last two phases of the Asian insurgent model would be mid-intensity conflict. But it is essential to note that the irregular is still on the battlefield, still contributing. Thus, the last two stages are a combination of both low- *and* mid-intensity conflict. Not only does the counterinsurgent have to defend everywhere, he must fight in two types of conflict.

This early doctrine of the 1930s, 1940s, and 1950s may be viewed as being applicable only to unique, communist experience against two overextended and vulnerable foes, the Japanese and French. However, Vietnamese devotion to the doctrine extended beyond the 1950s. In 1967, Vo Nguyen Giap, as the North Vietnamese Defense Minister, reaffirmed his faith in the doctrine and perhaps gave the clearest rationale for why it should be retained. He stated that guerrilla warfare in South Vietnam had forced American troops to be employed in pacification tasks, a role that prevented their total concentration against Viet Cong and North Vietnamese main forces. He claimed that continued adherence to the established doctrine would ensure that the large numbers of American, allied, and South Vietnamese forces would be dissipated. They would have to defend everywhere. Giap also stated that following the doctrine would render useless the American mobility advantage. The Americans would be reactive and always one step behind.[8]

The Asian insurgents had thus devised a doctrine of warfare to counter and defeat an industrialized state's advantage in mechanized mobility. The doctrine had also compensated for their opponent's ability to field large numbers of troops. Success for the Asian insurgent was predicated on the ability to protract the war, to coordinate the efforts of local and regular troops and guerrillas, and to offset their enemies' mobility and numerical advantage by maintaining great depth to the battlefield. The enemy must be continuously presented with local guerrilla actions as well as large-unit, stand-up battles. It is for this reason that in the midst of knockdown, drag-out battles against regulars, Americans in Vietnam found themselves referring to ''The Other War,'' the counterguerrilla campaign.

APPLICATION OF ASIAN INSURGENT DOCTRINE

The application of this insurgent doctrine within Indochina can be divided into the various Indochina wars. The First Indochina War, 1946-54, resulted in a victory for the Vietminh over the French and their Vietnamese allies. The Second Indochina War involved the United States, its allies, and the Republic of Vietnam pitted against the combination of the South Vietnamese Viet Cong and the North Vietnamese army. This second war can be dated from 1960 and logically terminated with the negotiated cease-fire of January 1973. The Second Indochina War began with a northern-supported insurgency in the South, but by the time US combat forces entered, North Vietnamese regulars were being employed in South Vietnam in battalion-sized strengths. US ground forces thus began a conflict in which both guerrilla and main force units were being employed throughout the country. In 1973, at the negotiated close of this second conflict, the same situation prevailed. The Second Indochina War was therefore inconclusive. The Republic of Vietnam still existed; the communists had not won, but they had not lost. Since there was no definite outcome of this war, the applied doctrine of one side or the other cannot clearly be judged as either successful or unsuccessful.

The Third Indochina War, from January 1973 until April 1975, can be analyzed in the light of conclusive results. Like the First Indochina War, it resulted in a communist victory. There is little doubt as to how the Republic of Vietnam fell. Excellent accounts are available from both South Vietnamese and American officials who were involved witnesses of the defeat. We also have the story of the other side. The North Vietnamese general who led the final phase of the campaign has written his account, and we now have the record of Colonel General Tran Van Tra, the military commander of COSVN, the Central Office of South Vietnam. Tra's account is particularly important, since it is highly probable that he was the actual initiator of the plan for the final 55-day campaign that concluded the war. He was probably the most experienced soldier on either side.

A native of the Saigon region, Tran Van Tra began his insurgent career in the general uprising of 1945. Tra was caught and imprisoned by the French, but on gaining his freedom he resumed his efforts, walking all the way to North Vietnam in order to meet Ho Chi Minh. At this 1948 meeting, Tra received a mandate for the "liberation" of South Vietnam. His exact position, authority, and status are unclear for the 1950s, but he claims to have commanded all Viet Cong elements in South Vietnam in 1963 and probably became the theater commander of the B2 Front in 1967. This theater of war contained two-thirds of the Republic of Vietnam's population and most of its industry and food crops. It stretched from Darlac Province in the highlands to the tip of the Cau Mau Peninsula, fully half of South Vietnam. Tra directed Viet Cong and North Vietnamese army (NVA) forces in this region against US, allied, and South Vietnamese forces during most of the Second Indochina War. At the 1973 cease-fire, Tra was appointed by Hanoi's leadership to represent the People's Revolutionary Government delegation in Saigon.[9]

As soon as it became apparent that the Saigon talks would be of little importance in the eventual outcome of the conflict, Tra returned to his command of B2 and began planning for the 1973-74 Dry Season Campaign. Tra's efforts reflected the same objectives as those of his early campaigns: using his main force elements to thrust and parry with Army of the Republic of Vietnam (ARVN) divisional units while his guerrilla and local force units expanded their control of population and resource areas. For the B2 Front, this meant using old line divisions, the 7th and 9th, to keep the ARVN 5th, 25th, and 18th divisions occupied and reactive in the Government of Vietnam's (GVN) III Corps area. Tra sent his remaining divisional unit, the 5th, further south into the upper Mekong Delta of the GVN IV Corps area against the ARVN 7th, 9th, and 21st divisions. The "big-unit war" had a number of purposes, but an important one for Tra was to provoke the large ARVN units to stay concentrated. This would prevent their use in rooting out the VC infrastructure and guerrillas with small-unit actions in populated regions. Tra's major objective was to increase his control of the Mekong Delta's resources.[10]

The results of Tra's 1973-74 offensive were rapidly felt by the South Vietnamese and duly observed by the few Americans left in Saigon. ARVN had claimed victory over Tra's rice control efforts in early 1973, but as the campaign began to develop more fully, their control of the Delta's resources began to slip. The IV Corps area became the most intense area of combat in June 1973, and that year saw the highest incident rate of the entire war.[11] As GVN control of the Delta began to fade, a rise in guerrilla forces was also noticed. One of the most serious effects of Tra's Delta Campaign was that disappearing GVN control diminished Saigon's ability to recruit for its own army. The senior GVN military officer, General Cao Van Vien, noted that South Vietnamese citizens were being enlisted into enemy ranks before they reached an eligible age for service to the Republic of Vietnam. The South Vietnamese army failed to meet its strength level while enemy guerrilla strength was expanding. At the beginning of 1973, overall enemy guerrilla strength in South Vietnam was rated by ARVN at only about 41,000. Of this, 13,000 or about 30 percent were in the Delta. This was the base upon which Tra was building.[12] In order to equip his growing forces, Tra persuaded his superiors in Hanoi to dip into his future supply allocations so that COSVN could receive earlier shipments of weapons.[13]

By the end of 1973, widespread battles against guerrilla and local force elements throughout the Republic of Vietnam began to tell on the South Vietnamese army. In Hau Nghia Province, just north of Saigon, the Rice Harvest Campaign had caused more ARVN casualties than the NVA main force offensive of Easter 1972.[14] Further north, in I Corps, VC units had begun their recovery, interrupting the rice harvest, interdicting roads, and disrupting GVN programs.[15] In mid-1974, the leadership of COSVN had enough confidence in their growing capabilities against deteriorating ARVN strength to sense a final end to the long war. In June, and unknown to Hanoi, COSVN was predicting the possibility of triumph in 1975 or 1976. By September, a plan was available that took into account the lessons learned from the disastrous 1968 Tet Campaign. Tra estimated that forces available to him in the south would not be enough to win rapidly. He believed that with three additional divisions from the north, the balance would be so tipped that a quick victory in 1975 was entirely possible.[16]

When Tra was ordered back to Hanoi in October 1974 for a planning conference, he found that his optimism was not shared by the northern military leadership. The Hanoi conference continued into late January 1975 and was marked by acrimony. Tra's representation was to the Military Commission of the Central Party Committee. His opposition within that body was General Van Tien Dung, a respected northerner who had never been to "Nam Bo," the southern half of South Vietnam.[17] Dung, probably remembering the failed 1968 Tet Campaign, the high casualties suffered during Lam Son 719 fighting in Laos in 1971, and the bloody Easter Offensive of 1972, was evidently not ready to put his faith in Tra's hopes. He instructed Tra to wait until 1976.[18]

The northern leadership had not provided COSVN with a proportionate share of manpower resources since 1968. For example, despite the fact that COSVN was responsible for half of the south, Hanoi had apportioned COSVN only 25 percent of the replacements shipped south.[19] Perhaps another factor in Dung's thinking was that the Delta was now increasingly inaccessible. Not only had the Khmer Republic denied ports that had been used in the late 1960s, the Khmer Rouge, Hanoi's supposed allies, were skirmishing with VC and NVA forces.[20] Additionally, Dung considered that Tra's guerrilla pressure in the Delta was not enough to prevent the three ARVN divisions there from reinforcing the three divisions of III Corps for the defense of Saigon.[21] Using any rule of thumb ratio for the attacker, the communists would have to assemble sizable numbers of large divisions just for the battle of Saigon if ARVN's Delta divisions joined the ARVN III Corps divisions.

As the conference wore on, Tra's credibility was bolstered by a victory in the south and evidently by his persistence. Tra was able to report that by December 1974, 500 of the 3300 GVN outposts had fallen to his forces in the Delta and that for the first time in the long war, an entire GVN province, Phuoc Long, had been conquered.[22] Despite this impressive demonstration of clout in the Delta and success in the lower highlands, Tra finally had to go over the head of the military commission to sell his plan. In December, Tra requested and received an audience with Le Duan of the Central Party Committee to state his case.[23] Tra was convincing. On 9 January 1975, Le Duc Tho announced to the central military commission that 1975 was to be the year for the final offensive.[24] After Tra convinced the northerners that Ban Me Thuot and not Duc Lap should be the opening target, he again headed south to direct his forces in their final campaign.[25]

Although it was unknown to Tra and Hanoi's leadership, one of their worst fears was realized soon after their offensive began at Ban Me Thuot in March. President Thieu decided to cut his losses and consolidate. Thieu outlined a plan to his senior military officer, General Cao Van Vien. The plan was to withdraw from the north and hold about half the country.[26] Both Tra and the northerners had dreaded what they termed the "Gavin Plan," the establishment of a defensible enclave in southern South Vietnam.[27] Unfortunately, Thieu and his military leaders could not execute a withdrawal that would save most of their northern ARVN units. The only significant fighting elements that Thieu managed to save were parts of the Airborne Division, the Marine Division, and the 22nd Division. With the advice of General Frederick C. Weyand, sent from Washington by President Ford, President Thieu then established a second enclave. The new defensive perimeter protected Saigon with a line that extended from the Cambodian border through Cu Chi, Bien Hoa, and Xuan Loc to the coast.

President Thieu's decision was predictable. Thieu knew that the strength of the South rested in the Delta and the III Corps area. He had indicated his reluctance to pay any large price in the northern reaches of South Vietnam when he overruled General Abrams's objections and refused to reinforce his forces in Laos during the 1971 Lam Son 719 operation.[28] The fear of the northern Marxist hierarchy regarding a southern enclave was based on the possibility of the eventual commitment of US ground forces if ARVN was able to establish a defensible position. During the Hanoi planning conference, Pham Van Dong had said that possibly only US air and naval action could be expected during the final offensive, but that would not be powerful enough to deter success.[29] After the first successful blow at Ban Me Thuot, the communists imagined that they faced a formidable problem. It would be some time before the armor columns of the northerners could reach the south. Thieu could not be allowed to consolidate all of his available forces in a solid defense perimeter north of Saigon. If Thieu could portray a valiant defense and bog down the communist attack, it was entirely possible that the new American President would eventually honor President Nixon's promise and assist in the defense.

Dung, Tra's opponent in the planning process, had been appointed to lead the northern forces in the highlands. Despite his initial success, he faced serious problems. Even if he were successful in defeating or displacing the South Vietnamese forces in the II Corps area, he was not assured of being able to secure his ever-lengthening line of communications as he plunged southward. Unless his rear could be secured for him, his forces would rapidly be absorbed in a version of Napoleon's 1812 Russian Campaign. Napoleon had experienced "strategic consumption," the need to establish garrisons along the route of march. Dung's problems became even greater when consideration was given to his need for supplies. As his lines of communication lengthened, the more he needed to transport, the greater his need for logistical units, and the greater his requirements for rear security garrisons. Both of these able commanders, Tra and Dung, thus had to contend with classic military problems that have always had the potential of sapping an operational-level offensive of its power. There is no doubt as to the competence, daring and determination of the communist Indochinese military forces in the 1960s and 1970s, but they were not immune to the cruel realities and fundamental requirements of war.

In less than 60 days, Dung and Tra had triumphed. They had overcome the toughest of age-old military problems in what superficially appeared to be a rapid blitzkrieg offensive that had been conducted with apparent ease. How had they solved their problems? First, consider Dung's difficulties. His logistical problem had been largely reduced with Tra's planning and aid. Several months before Dung had crossed the South Vietnamese border, Tra had ordered his guerrilla and local force elements to begin prestocking clandestine forward depots for the impending battle of Saigon. It was a massive task involving the movement and hiding of some 33,000 tons of food, fuel, ammunition, and other supplies.[30] Dung's second problem, securing his rear, was also substantially reduced by guerrilla and local force elements in the first and second corps regions of the northern half of South Vietnam. Their task was a crucial one. There is no indication that significant numbers of the hundreds of thousands of South Vietnamese Regional and Popular Force troops in this area withdrew with the retreating ARVN main force units. Thus, Dung would have a sizable and potentially dangerous enemy in his rear. However, communist guerrilla and local forces not only countered this threat but, in fact, seized a number of important objectives such as Qui Nhon and the Phuoc Ly and Phuoc Hai peninsulas. These forces also assisted the northern main force invaders in securing Hue and Da Nang. As guerrilla and local force elements were left in the wake of southbound North Vietnamese divisions, they provided invaluable services to Dung in repairing roads and organizing for the protection of his rear.[31]

Perhaps the greatest service that the communist forces in the south performed for the northern invasion was accomplished in the Delta. Tra had previously sent a main force division to that region in order to contest the three Delta ARVN divisions. There were a number of regimental-sized main force communist units in the Delta. Additionally, the Delta had the largest numbers of regional and local communist guerrilla troops of the four corps regions. No one knows the percentage of northerners in these Delta forces. In 1972, General Cao Van Vien estimated that northern troops made up 60 to 80 percent of the communist local units throughout the country.[32] It is highly probable that a far higher percentage of the Delta's local units were of southern origin. With access through Cambodia increasingly contested and the decrease in the numbers of northern replacements going into the Delta, the southerners probably predominated by 1975.

When the victorious Dung arrived to take command of the Saigon Campaign in April, he reported on the rapid growth of guerrilla units that would be supporting his forces.[33] The performance of these forces was to be vital to the success of the last phase of the overall campaign. If the three ARVN divisions in the Delta could have reinforced the defensive perimeter being established by the three divisions above Saigon, the invasion might have been brought to a halt. However, Thieu's three Delta division commanders rapidly found themselves in a major contest for control of their region. All during the months of March and April, fighting raged in the Delta and was so intense that Thieu had to reinforce the area even in the face of a northern armor assault plunging southward toward Saigon. Initially, in March, a brigade of marines was ordered south of Saigon to fight enemy guerrilla and local forces.[34] By April, the only ARVN division to escape from the north relatively intact, the 22nd Division, was also deployed south of Saigon and not in the line of defense that was being established north of the capital. Communist guerrilla and local forces in the south had performed well, precisely as Tra had planned.[35]

Not only did the communist guerrilla and local forces greatly assist in seizing many objectives to assist the northern invaders, they had secured the main force rear, prestocked supplies for the North Vietnamese armor columns, kept lines of communications operable, and prevented the establishment of a viable South Vietnamese defense of III Corps and IV Corps regions. In the end, ARVN had to defend everywhere, fulfilling the doctrine of Mao, Truong Chin, and Giap.

But what of the general uprising, the facet of Vietnamese insurgent doctrine that differed from Mao? When the final campaign finally unfurled, it appeared that the northern victory was not accompanied by the same phenomenon that had occurred in 1945 and 1968. According to Tra, the general uprising was ordered and executed, but in a very special fashion. Having been the theater commander of B2 during the Tet attack of 1968, Tra believed that his severe losses and failure were due to the inability of his guerrilla and local force elements independently to attack and hold ground against enemy regular forces. He had based his plan of 1975 on the lessons of the Tet Offensive and understood well the protests of guerrilla and local force representatives who conferred with him prior to the 1975 offensive. Tra's ultimate decision was to refuse to set a specific date and time for the general uprising until the very last moment, when main force elements were deep in the south, close to the ARVN combat units. During the extended planning session in Hanoi, Dung had been against a general uprising. The Vietnamese communist military leadership was therefore badly divided over Truong Chin's doctrinal dictum of the general uprising.[36]

The communist political leadership, however, had little doubt of the need to follow Truong Chin's doctrine. On 31 March 1975, as Dung was moving south, he received a message from the Political Bureau which stated that in the forthcoming month, the time would be ripe for a general uprising. Shortly after Dung arrived at Loc Ninh and took command of all military forces for the Saigon Campaign, he received yet another Political Bureau message. This one stated that a general uprising was to be executed. If that were not enough, Hanoi dispatched a political overseer in the form of Le Duc Tho to Loc Ninh. Among the messages and guidance he brought, one had to do with the power of the underground in Saigon and the need to use it during the campaign.[37] Hanoi was determined to offer the southern infrastructure, guerrillas, and local forces a stake in the victory. Their support would be needed later in the control of the south.

Tra had been made a deputy to Dung for the Saigon Campaign, and in the end his views seemed to prevail. Tra's plan was to use the general uprising not to attack ARVN regulars, but to seize vital facilities in densely populated areas, to prevent sabotage and destruction by withdrawing or trapped South Vietnamese forces, and to make the transfer of power as trouble-free as possible. Although the general uprising would affect every area of contested control, it was primarily aimed at Saigon, a city that was jammed with over three million people, many of whom were armed but dispirited. Dung and Tra obeyed their orders from Hanoi but waited until the last minute, 29 April, to call for the general uprising. They coordinated it with the actual attack of

Saigon's crumbling defenses by main force elements. It is quite possible that there would have been no need for the general uprising, since any sort of GVN discipline or organized resistance was rapidly vanishing. However, Dung's troops were often greeted in Saigon by working public services, utilities, and facilities that had already been taken over by an in-place communist infrastructure, a move that was greatly aided by the evacuation of much of Saigon's leadership.[38] The general uprising was an anticlimax and was never designed to duplicate the disaster of 1968, but it was nevertheless executed. Dung and Tra had faithfully followed the prime tenets of their established doctrine.

Beginning in the 1930s, Asian insurgent leaders had developed a highly successful doctrine of warfare. The answer to Mao, Truong Chin, and Giap even at this date is not to be found in "minor warfare," "counterguerrilla operations," "operations against irregulars," "stability operations," or even "internal defense and development." The Asian leaders never intended to win by using only guerrillas, irregulars, or the creation of internal instability. At the heart of their doctrine lay a far greater, more encompassing concept. From its inception, it entailed the fielding, employment, and triumph of a regular armed force supported by guerrilla and local forces. Their adversaries may have had to begin the conflict against the irregular, but they would finish it in stand-up battles against regulars at the same time they were fending off the guerrilla.

Looking back at the Third Indochina War and the actions of Tran Van Tra, it is clear that he knew he could not win with guerrilla and local forces alone, hence his request for three fresh divisions to augment his own main force units for the final campaign. It is also unlikely that North Vietnamese regulars could have defeated the South Vietnamese without the support and preparation provided by guerrilla and local force units in the south. Without these elements, they would have faced many more ARVN divisions to counter the northern armor columns. NVA logistical problems would have multiplied, and large numbers of armed GVN forces would have been unchecked in the northerners' rear. It is highly probable that the Vietnamese communists never even considered a campaign that was to be wholly conducted by guerrillas or one that was to be conducted solely by regulars. Their doctrine was clear — both were to be used, and used in concert.

US LOW-INTENSITY CONFLICT DOCTRINE

The US doctrine to counter the insurgent predates the Asian insurgent doctrine but has a more checkered career. In the early years of this century, the US Army regarded guerrilla warfare as a somewhat trivial matter which posed certain legal questions. In 1905, the Army Field Service Regulations stipulated that before imposing the death penalty on a captured guerrilla, the commander should convene a board of three officers, but if that was not possible, one would do. Authority for summary execution vanished with Senate ratification of the Hague Conventions of 1907, and by 1911 doctrine for what was termed "minor warfare" appeared. "Irregulars" were pictured as a battlefield irritant, because "they assemble, roam about and disperse at will." The specified remedy was aggressive small-unit activity.[40] It is not surprising that Army officers of this era would treat guerrilla warfare in such a cavalier fashion. Many field grade officers had a successful background in both the Indian Wars and the Philippine Insurrection. It was a military activity that the US Army excelled in, one that would only be lightly touched upon as a lesser, included problem of conventional warfare.

While Army doctrine dealing with guerrilla warfare all during the first half of the century was superficial and usually covered in four to five pages, the Marine Corps took a more thoughtful, detailed approach to the subject in 1940. In the USMC *Small Wars Manual* of that year, Corps writers who were obviously experienced devoted over 380 pages to methods designed to defeat the guerrilla.[41] The Marine authors drew attention to the fact that the time-honored Clausewitzian dictum of destruction of the enemy armed force often would not be the prime objective. They said that a more likely mission would be to establish satisfactory conditions for negotiations or the achievement of a stable government. They also remarked on the utility of employing native troops.[42] Although this appears to represent excellent doctrine for a US intervention and subsequent counterguerrilla operations, it was not predicated on answering Mao's concept, and, more important, its basis rested on substantial US control of the political processes of the country undergoing insurgency, the host nation.

Army doctrine in 1941, 1944, and 1949 took little note of the more substantial Marine doctrine of 1940. The Army afforded the other side of the coin, offensive guerrilla warfare, equal space with counterguerrilla warfare. The writers went so far as to drop the pejorative term "guerrilla" in favor of the word "partisan." Army counterguerrilla doctrine in this era remained at less than one percent of the Field Service Regulations.[43] The first substantial body of counterguerrilla doctrine produced by the Army was published in draft by the Infantry School one month prior to the invasion of South Korea by the North Korean army. Based on a study of Soviet and Allied World War II experience, the draft matched the earlier USMC effort of a decade before in detail and analysis. The doctrine specified three prime objectives in the defeat of the guerrilla: isolation from the civil populace, denial of external support, and destruction of the guerrilla movement. The manual did not take Mao or Truong Chin's concepts into account, assumed the existence of a US military government in the conflict area, was predicated on US forces executing the operations, and appeared to be pointed at a European scenario. The draft drew attention to the probable utility of helicopters but treated the use of indigenous troops lightly. It was published with little change in February 1951.[44]

A sudden, high-level focus on counterguerrilla doctrine came with the

Kennedy Administration in 1961. As one of his first actions, the President expressed his displeasure over the apparent lack of emphasis by the armed forces on the subject.[45] As a result, Army doctrine highlighted counterguerrilla operations by expanding its treatment in the keystone operational manual, *FM 100-5*. Whereas unconventional warfare usually had occupied about one or two percent of the manual before the expressed presidential interest, operations against irregulars, guerrilla warfare, and "situations short of war" absorbed about 20 percent of the revised edition. However, there was little substantive change in concept. Basic counterguerrilla doctrine in the early 1960s envisioned US troops carrying the burden of fighting guerrillas, albeit with increased reliance on host-country troops. The doctrine writers also added to the three tenets of isolation, blocking external support, and destruction; they additionally stressed the need for intelligence at the inception of operations and the provision of economic assistance to the host state in order to undercut the popular appeal of the guerrilla. The possibility of external support for the guerrilla was discussed, but the writers evidently believed that measures such as internal border control would suffice to stymie such activity. In sum, the Kennedy "counterinsurgency era" did not produce a revolution in Army doctrine.[46]

In 1967, in the midst of the Vietnam War, a noticeable and substantive change began to occur in Army counterinsurgency doctrine. In 1964, the doctrine writers had characterized the Army's role in counterinsurgency as "the major military role." Three years later and after considerable practical experience in Southeast Asia, this was changed to read "a major role." Increasing emphasis was placed on indigenous troops fighting the guerrilla. Texts for this form of warfare began to read like a US government directory as the doctrine writers spelled out what such organizations as the Agency for International Development, the Department of State, and others were supposed to do in a counterinsurgency war. Army writers continued in this vein, reversing the role for US ground forces as host-nation troops were pictured as conducting the actual fight against the guerrilla. The recommended counterinsurgent role for the US Army was increasingly envisioned as advisory in nature.[47]

One of the first acts of the 1969 Nixon Administration was to announce the "Guam Doctrine" or "Nixon Doctrine," stating that the host government bore the primary responsibility for providing manpower for its own defense during an insurgency. This policy was clearly identified, with the President's name affixed, in an Army manual in 1972. The book went on to state that US military involvement would be so minimized as to "remain in the background." While previous manuals had understandably had more to say about the Army's role and functions, the 1972 and successor 1974 manuals provided more coverage of the roles and functions of other US government agencies.[48]

If the Nixon Administration had inherited a satisfactory situation in

Vietnam, it would have had no need to proclaim the Guam Doctrine. There would also have been no need for the changes in Army doctrine had the initial body of literature proved successful. The Army entered the counterinsurgency era with flawed doctrine and changed it during the course of the Vietnam War. The prime error was that previous counterguerrilla warfare doctrine was based on an underlying assumption that the United States would have substantial control of the governmental processes of the host nation. Growing doctrinal references during the war to the roles and functions of other US governmental agencies in counterinsurgency were little more than a hope that these agencies would correct the ills of the host government, garner the trust of the people, and undercut the appeal of the guerrilla. The simple fact was that the United States harbored no ambitions to revive colonialism and would not resort to a US military government. Such an act probably would have proved to be counterproductive, creating more guerrillas than were killed or won over. Counterguerrilla warfare is highly political in nature. The ability to win is based on both military and political actions of the beleaguered host government. The United States was not willing to provide a surrogate government for the Republic of Vietnam, nor would it have been wise to do so. And, at this date, the United States is still unlikely to do so in a Third World state. The Guam Doctrine merely stated a fundamental American policy, one that already had been recognized, even if belatedly, by Army doctrine.

A PERSPECTIVE ON LOW-INTENSITY CONFLICT DOCTRINE

Asian insurgent doctrine emerged from a now-distant era. Except in the Soviet bloc, colonialism is no longer operative, and it is quite possible that the West will never again see itself pitted against the type of forces it faced in the 1950s and 1960s. Certainly, the North Vietnamese did not use this doctrine in Laos or against Pol Pot's Kampuchea. However, success is often copied. If Asian insurgent doctrine appears again, it would be an error to label the American counterdoctrine as "low-intensity conflict." The Asian insurgent or one who faithfully duplicates his methods fully intends to create a battlefield that features both low- and mid-intensity conflict.

Our future doctrine must not continue to ignore essential, effective operations against those nations that sponsor insurgency. The United States has subjected its soldiers to two wars since World War II wherein the enemy was afforded contiguous sanctuary, free from offensive US ground operations. The payment for this policy has been a lack of US military success; protracted, indeterminate combat; erosion of American public support for US aims; and, most important, increased US casualties. We should have learned by now that a policy of independent air and naval action against an enemy sanctuary does not deter aggression. It may, in fact, strengthen the hand of the aggressor government. This policy was as indecisive in Vietnam as it had been in Korea.

As noted above, the North Vietnamese leadership was quite willing to risk US air and naval action against their homeland in 1975. Affording sanctuary for the insurgent is particularly damaging to the cause of the counterinsurgent, since experience clearly indicates that the absence of a sanctuary has often been coincident with the defeat of insurgent movements.

In the specific case of the Asian insurgent, or one following his example, offensive ground operations within the contiguous sanctuary are particularly vital to the counterinsurgent. The regular and regional forces that this breed of insurgent must create will be harbored, nurtured, and poised in the sanctuary awaiting the opportune moment. For the counterinsurgent to win, these forces must be defeated. For the counterinsurgent to survive, these forces must, as a minimum, be engaged. The counterinsurgent must therefore go beyond the bounds of low-intensity conflict and into a realm of mid-intensity conflict. These operations may be wholly conducted by the nation beset with a foreign-sponsored insurgency, by US armed forces, or both.

The last time the Army revised its insurgency counterdoctrine was in 1981. On beginning their task, the writers were directed to use the term "low-intensity conflict." They were also informed that the manual would supersede all other doctrine in the field. Thus, several supporting manuals dealing with such subjects as counterguerrilla operations, advisory duties, base defense, border control, and intelligence went out of print.

The resulting and current manual has a number of acknowledged weaknesses. By definition, the writers could not delve into mid-intensity conflict and were therefore precluded from detailing the obvious counter to Asian insurgent doctrine: offensive ground operations against the sponsoring nation. A doctrinal subset for counterterrorism was also missing from the 1981 version despite a number of sensational PLO activities in the 1970s. However, it was known at the time that most US allies were creating their own counterterrorist units and that it would be unlikely that any nation would seek to have the US Army enforce its public laws. Additionally, within the United States, the FBI was organizing a Hostage Rescue Team for use in domestic terrorist incidents. The absence of counterterrorist doctrine may be a shortcoming, but it is not a major deficiency. The prime deficiencies of the 1981 manual stem from a highly restrictive definition and the absence of subordinate and supporting doctrinal literature.

Our current doctrine, however, does have some strengths. The thrust is directed at the host nation solving its own insurgency problems with aggressive ground operations, population control, economic development, and political action. The aim is to encourage Third World states to offer their citizens a stake in their own governments, an essential action that is unlikely to be effected by the United States. The manual is therefore in accord with the Guam Doctrine, a policy that the United States has rarely referred to but has closely followed for the last 16 years. The manual has also captured as many of the hard-won lessons of the Vietnam War as space would permit. Finally, it has been translated into Spanish and has been used at the School of the Americas by Latin American allies of the United States.

The Army has thus provided its friends with its own experience. If it is useful to the allies of the United States, that should be reason enough for continuation. However, revision is inevitable and probably needed. The new doctrine writers should not be constrained by a restrictive definition, particularly one that precludes advocacy of offensive, mid-intensity ground operations on the soil of those nations that sponsor insurgency. But as the first order of business, the writers should give much study and thought to whether or not the United States should fight insurgents. If our new doctrine is based on the use of US forces against the insurgent, let us hope we face lesser breeds and that Asian insurgent doctrine is somehow forgotten or is beyond the reach of our adversaries. To keep an Asian-style insurgent within the bounds of low-intensity conflict is to attempt the impossible. Second, if the writers envision the use of US troops in fighting the insurgent, serious consideration must be given to the imperative of the US military government. To attempt to fight the insurgent without the levers of political power is to risk a repeat performance of our Southeast Asian experience. We would simply be pitted against the guerrilla, once again without the ability to undercut his appeal or control his movements. If the writers study the past, they will conclude that the United States Army does not need counterinsurgent doctrine for its own use but that the Army should continue providing such doctrine for US allies and the Americans who assist them. In the end, it will be these soldiers who need that doctrine.

NOTES

1. Mao Tse-tung, *On Protracted War* (Peking: Foreign Languages Press, 1967), pp. 85-86, 89.
2. Truong Chin, *Primer For Revolt*, ed. Bernard Fall (New York: Praeger, 1963), pp. 146-83. Originally published as a series of newspaper articles in 1946-47. Truong Chin's actual name is believed to have been Dang Xuan Khu.
3. Ibid., p. 193.
4. Ibid., p. 36.
5. Vo Nguyen Giap, *People's War, People's Army* (Washington: GPO, 1962), pp. 103-08.
6. Ibid., pp. 83, 87.
7. Ibid., p. 108.
8. Vo Nguyen Giap, *Big Victory, Great Task* (New York: Praeger, 1968), pp. 32-33, 55-57, 87.
9. Tran Van Tra, *Vietnam: History of the Bulwark B2 Theater, Vol. 5: Concluding the 30-Year War* (Ho Chi Minh City: 1982), pp. 7, 118, 127, 209, 219.
10. Ibid., pp. 32, 56, 59-64.
11. William E. Le Gro, *Vietnam from Cease Fire to Capitulation* (Washington: US Army Center of Military History, 1981), pp. 51, 62-63, 73.
12. Ibid., p. 51; and Cao Van Vien, *The Final Collapse* (Washington: US Army Center of Military History, 1983), pp. 31-35, 45, 162.
13. Tra, p. 61.
14. Stuart Herrington, *Peace With Honor?: An American Reports on Vietnam 1973-1975* (Novato, Calif.: Presidio Press, 1983), pp. 37-39.
15. Le Gro, pp. 62-63.
16. Tra, pp. 92-94.
17. Ibid., p. 160.
18. Ibid., pp. 114, 132.
19. Le Gro, p. 39.

20. Author's diary, Phnom Penh, Khmer Republic, December 1974.
21. Van Tien Dung, *Our Great Spring Victory: An Account of the Liberation of South Vietnam,* trans. John Sprangens (London: Review Press, 1977), p. 20.
22. Tra, p. 117.
23. Ibid., pp. 114-19.
24. Dung, p. 27.
25. Tra, pp. 121, 139.
26. Vien, p. 78.
27. Tra, pp. 95-96. Tra's written analysis of the Gavin Plan was confirmed as being accurate by LTG Gavin in an interview with the author on 17 May 1985.
28. Bruce Palmer, Jr., *The 25-Year War: America's Military Role in Vietnam* (Lexington: Univ. Press of Kentucky, 1984), pp. 113-14.
29. Tra, p. 125.
30. Ibid., p. 91.
31. Dung, pp. 103-05, 113-15, 122, 138.
32. Vien, p. 19.
33. Dung, p. 151.
34. Le Gro, p. 167; Vien, p. 140.
35. Tra, p. 123.
36. Ibid., pp. 35, 88-94, 132, 139.
37. Dung, pp. 132, 155-56, 159.
38. Tra, 196-202.
39. US Army, *Field Service Regulations* (Washington: GPO, 1905), pp. 207-08.
40. US Army, *Infantry Drill Regulations* (Washington: GPO, 1911), pp. 139-40.
41. US Marine Corps, *Small Wars Manual* (Washington: GPO, 1950), p. 9.
42. Ibid., p. 2-2.
43. US Army, *FM 100-5 Field Service Regulations* (Washington: GPO, 1941, 1944, and 1949).
44. US Army Infantry School, *Operations Against Guerrilla Forces* (Ft. Benning, Ga., May 1950). Also see US Army, *FM 31-30 Operations Against Guerrilla Forces* (Washington: GPO, 1951). The lack of attention to Mao or Truong Chin extends beyond this period. In 1953, a bibliography compiled for the Department of Army on unconventional warfare contained over 220 references, some of them Asian, but no references to Mao or Truong Chin. See US Army, ACSI "Bibliography on Unconventional Warfare," 404th Strategic Intelligence Detachment, 13 July 1953 (US Army Military History Institute Document Archives).
45. Lloyd Norman and John B. Spore, "Big Push in Guerrilla Warfare," *Army*, March 1962, pp. 28-36.
46. US Army, *FM 31-15 Operations Against Irregular Forces*, May 1961; *FM 100-5 Field Service Regulations: Operations*, February 1962; *FM 31-16 Counterguerrilla Operations*, February 1963.
47. US Army *FM 100-20 Field Service Regulations: Counterinsurgency*, April 1964; *FM 31-16 Counterguerrilla Operations*, March 1967; and *FM 100-20 Field Service Regulations: Internal Defense and Development*, May 1967.
48. US Army, *FM 100-20 Field Service Regulations: Internal Defense and Development*, November 1974.

This article appeared in the autumn 1985 issue of *Parameters*.

About the Editors and Contributors

GENERAL BRUCE PALMER, JR., USA RETIRED, is a consultant on military affairs. A combat veteran of three wars, he served two tours in Vietnam, the latter including service as commander of Field Force II and deputy commander of US Army Forces. Later he was vice chief of staff of the Army. General Palmer is the author of *The 25-Year War: America's Military Role in Vietnam* (1984).

COLONEL LLOYD J. MATTHEWS, USA RETIRED, is editor of *Parameters: Journal of the U.S. Army War College*. He holds a Ph.D. from the University of Virginia, an M.A. from Harvard, and a B.S. from the US Military Academy. Colonel Matthews served as an infantry officer in Vietnam during the period 1964–65 and was subsequently a professor and associate dean at the Military Academy.

CAPTAIN DALE E. BROWN, USA, is assistant editor of *Parameters: Journal of the US Army War College*. He earned an M.A. in history from Ohio State University. Captain Brown is an air defense artillery officer and has served in a variety of air defense assignments in the United States and Europe.

DR. JEFFREY CLARKE, LTC, USAR, is a historian at the US Army Center of Military History. He has taught history at Rutgers University and the University of Maryland and is currently adjunct associate professor of history at the University of Maryland-Baltimore County. Dr. Clarke holds a Ph.D. in history from Duke University and commanded a military history detachment in Vietnam, 1969–70. His volume in the official Vietnam War series, *Advice and Support: The Final Years, 1965–73*, is forthcoming, and he is currently preparing a combat volume in the same series.

DR. ALEXANDER S. COCHRAN, JR., LTC, USAR, is a historian at the US Army Center of Military History. A graduate of Yale University, he has received M.A. and Ph.D. degrees in history from the University of Kansas. He served on active duty as a Regular Army officer from 1961 through 1976, including two tours in Vietnam. Dr. Cochran has taught military history at the University of Notre Dame and the University of Kansas.

MAJOR MICHAEL W. DAVIDSON, USAR, is president of the Wind

River Energy Corporation. He is a graduate of the University of Louisville, where he also earned M.S. and J.D. degrees. Major Davidson's active-duty assignments were with the 7th Special Forces Group at Fort Bragg, North Carolina, and with the Ranger Company of the First Air Cavalry Division in Vietnam.

DR. JOE P. DUNN is an associate professor of history at Converse College. He is a graduate of Southeast Missouri State University and earned his M.A. and Ph. D. in American history from the University of Missouri. He served in the US Army in Vietnam in 1969–70. His "On Legacies and Lessons" is the opening chapter of a collection of essays titled *The American War in Vietnam*, which will be published by Greenwood Press in 1987.

DR. JOHN M. GATES is a professor of history at the College of Wooster, where he teaches military, American, and Latin American history. He received his B.A. and M.A. from Stanford and his Ph.D. from Duke. Dr. Gates is the author of *Schoolbooks and Krags: The United States Army in the Philippines, 1898–1902* (1973). His article, "The Alleged Isolation of US Army Officers in the Late 19th Century," received the Harold L. Peterson Award for exemplary work in American military history.

DR. RICHARD A. HUNT is currently writing the official history of the pacification program in Vietnam for the US Army Center of Military History. He holds a Ph.D. from the University of Pennsylvania. A former Army captain, Dr. Hunt served in 1970–71 as a historian in the Office of the Military Assistance Command Vietnam. He is co-editor of *Lessons from an Unconventional War* (1981) and author of "The Challenge of Counter-insurgency" in *Second Indochina War Symposium*, ed. John Schlight (1986).

DR. PAUL M. KATTENBURG is a retired US Foreign Service Officer and a professor of political science and international studies at the University of South Carolina. He was educated at the University of North Carolina (B.S.), George Washington University (M.A.), and Yale University (Ph.D.). His works include *The Vietnam Trauma in American Foreign Policy, 1945–75* (1980).

DR. GUENTER LEWY is Professor Emeritus of Political Science at the University of Massachusetts. He has also taught at Columbia and Smith College. After serving in the British army from 1942 to 1946, he took his baccalaureate degree at City College of New York and subsequently earned M.A. and Ph.D. degrees at Columbia University. Professor Lewy authored the widely acclaimed *America in Vietnam* (1978).

MR. HUNG P. NGUYEN is a Ph.D. candidate in Soviet studies at the Johns Hopkins University School of Advanced International Studies, where he earned his M.A. degree in the same field. A native of South Vietnam, he received his undergraduate degree in economics from Lebanon Valley College.

COLONEL ROD PASCHALL is currently the director of the US Army Military History Institute, Carlisle Barracks, Pennsylvania and has served in low-intensity conflict situations in Laos, Vietnam, Cambodia, and as the commander of DELTA. His military assistance includes service in Egypt,

Thailand, and Honduras. Colonel Paschall holds an M.A. from Duke University and an M.S. from George Washington University; he is a 1978 graduate of the US Army War College. His staff experience includes service in the Office of the Joint Chiefs of Staff.

MAJOR DAVID H. PETRAEUS, USA, is an assistant professor in the Department of Social Sciences, US Military Academy. He is a graduate of the Military Academy and the US Army Command and General Staff College and holds an M.P.A. and Ph.D. from Princeton University's Woodrow Wilson School of Public and International Affairs. Major Petraeus has served with the 509th Infantry in Vicenza, Italy, and with the 24th Infantry Division at Fort Stewart, Georgia. This article draws on research for his doctoral dissertation on military thinking about the use of force in the post-Vietnam era.

DOUGLAS PIKE is director of the Indochina Studies Project at the University of California at Berkeley. Mr. Pike is a retired US Foreign Service Officer whose specialty is Southeast Asia. He is the author of five books dealing with Vietnam, the latest being *PAVN: People's Army of Vietnam* (1986).

COLONEL JOSEPH H. PISTORIUS, USAR RETIRED, was a strategic research analyst and Army Reserve advisor at the Army War College when he co-authored an extensive study on Reserve mobilization from which this article was extracted. Colonel Pistorius holds a master's degree from Wayne State University. His military education includes the Industrial College of the Armed Forces and Air War College, as well as the Army War College.

DR. JÁNOS RADVÁNYI is a professor of history at Mississippi State University. From 1948 to 1967 he was a member of the Hungarian Diplomatic Service. He rose to the position of Chief of Mission in the United States and in that capacity was personally involved in the wartime negotiations between the United States and North Vietnam, particularly in 1965–66. Professor Radványi was granted political asylum in the United States in 1967. He is the author of *Hungary and the Super Powers* (1972) and *Delusion and Reality: Gambits, Hoaxes and Diplomatic One-Upmanship in Vietnam* (1978).

DR. W. W. ROSTOW received his B.A. and Ph.D. degrees from Yale University and attended Balliol College, Oxford, from 1936 to 1938 as a Rhodes Scholar. He has taught history and economics at Columbia, Oxford, Cambridge, and MIT, and is currently professor of economics and history at the University of Texas. His career has included service in the US State Department and as special assistant to Presidents Kennedy and Johnson. His latest book is *The United States and the Regional Organization of Asia and the Pacific, 1965–1985* (1986).

BRIGADIER GENERAL JOHN D. STUCKEY, ANG, was a strategic research analyst and Army National Guard advisor at the Strategic Studies Institute, US Army War College, when he co-authored a study from which this article was taken. General Stuckey received a Ph.D. from the University of Oregon and is a graduate of the US Army War College.

COLONEL HARRY G. SUMMERS, USA RETIRED, is military affairs

commentator for the *Los Angeles Times* and a contributing editor with *U.S. News & World Report*. Prior to retirement from the Army, he held the General Douglas MacArthur Chair of Military Research at the Army War College. A combat infantry veteran of the Korean and Vietnam Wars, Colonel Summers is the author of *On Strategy* (1982), regarded as a classic work on the Vietnam War. His most recent book, *Vietnam War Almanac*, was voted one of the outstanding source books of 1985 by the American Library Association.

COLONEL DAVID T. TWINING, USA, is director of Soviet and East European Studies in the Department of National Security and Strategy, US Army War College, where he holds the George C. Marshall Chair of Military Studies. Colonel Twining graduated from Michigan State University and earned an M.P.A. from Syracuse University and an M.A. in Russian Area Studies from Georgetown University. He served in intelligence assignments during two Vietnam tours.